Mapping Cities in the MENA Region

Visualising the Untold Narratives of Heritage

Kulturelle und technische Werte historischer Bauten
Hg. von Klaus Rheidt und Werner Lorenz

Band 9

Zeido Zeido, Suna Çağaptay (eds.)

Mapping Cities in the MENA Region

Visualising the Untold Narratives of Heritage

Birkhäuser · Basel

This publication is funded by the German Research Foundation (DFG) in the framework of the Research Training Group 1913 «Cultural and Technological Significance of Historic Buildings», Brandenburg University of Technology Cottbus–Senftenberg; Leibniz Institute for Research on Society and Space, Erkner; Department of Archaeology at Humboldt University of Berlin and Faculty 6, Architecture, Civil Engineering and Urban Planning at Brandenburg University of Technology Cottbus-Senftenberg. The first editor's research was made possible by the generous funding of the Gerda Henkel Foundation.

Concept: Zeido Zeido, Suna Çağaptay
Project coordination: Albrecht Wiesener, Sophia Hörmannsdorfer
Copyediting: William Hatherell
Layout, typesetting and editing: Sophia Hörmannsdorfer
Cover design: Jörg Denkinger
Printing and binding: Beltz Grafische Betriebe GmbH, Bad Langensalza
Cover illustration: The MENA region and the seven cities discussed in this volume highlighted on the world map (Z. Zeido 2023).

Library of Congress Control Number: 2025935544

Bibliographic information published by the German National Library
The German National Library lists this publication in the Deutsche Nationalbibliografie; detailed bibliographic data is available on the Internet at http://dnb.dnb.de.

The book is also available as an ebook (ISBN PDF 978-3-0356-2567-7).

ISBN 978-3-0356-2566-0

Im Westfeld 8, 4055 Basel, Switzerland
Part of Walter de Gruyter GmbH, Berlin/Boston

Questions about General Product Safety Regulation:
productsafety@degruyterbrill.com

9 8 7 6 5 4 3 2 1

www.birkhauser.com

Contents

Preface

Zeido Zeido

This edited volume started as a passion project immediately after I finished my doctoral work researching Aleppo's urban history and urban heritage. Suna Çağaptay, my co-editor, was there from the early stages of my academic journey since I took a class of hers during my Master studies.[1] Since then, she has become a mentor and a dear companion in my academic quest.

While working on Aleppo, I maintained that to understand the city, one needed to look at the full picture as anything other than a holistic city-scale approach would not be sufficient.[2] I have sat in different conferences and expert meetings during my research period listening to suggestions and solutions based on the experience of other cities, especially, since I was working in a German institution, in post-World War II Europe. These perspectives were highly interesting and educational, but to an Aleppine, many experts seemed to miss crucial points about the city.

Most notably, many professionals who talked about a city, talked only about one part of that city. In the case of Aleppo, this was the old city (the World Heritage Site to be exact).[3] Discussions for the most part looked only at that site and ignored the rest of the city, as if the World Heritage Site stood alone as an island rather than forming only a portion of the big city. Similarly, some reports of international organisations that crossed my path seemed to miss (if not ignore) basic known facts about the political, social, and economic factors that shape the city.

The issue of ignoring parts of the city, or looking at it from a unilateral lens, is one of the themes of this edited volume. In response to this tendency, the initial idea was to create studies to cover the whole of the cities under consideration. Another issue that formed another theme was to narrate what is often being overlooked or missed in the story of the city. This means, in part, addressing all the key factors that are shaping or have shaped these cities.

During the period of working on my doctoral dissertation, I became an associate member of the DFG Research Training Group 1913 that was established in Brandenburg University of Technology. In addition to the lectures and excursions that I joined, I had the opportunity to apply for my own volume project in the book series «Kulturelle und technische Werte historischer Bauten». The series, which explores the cultural and technological significance of historic structures, offers insights into architectural history, conservation, and urban development. This volume was selected as the 9th book of this series as it covers various topics in that regard, specifically, the urban development of seven selected cities. It examines the various structural and urban forms in each one of them, including the technical, cultural, and historic dimensions that shaped the urban and architectural forms in those places.

The seven cities chosen for this volume are spread over the MENA (Middle East and North Africa) region. Going from east to west, each of the following chapters narrates a story about Dubai in the United Arab Emirates, Shiraz in Iran, Aleppo in Syria, Cairo and Alexandria in Egypt, Casablanca in Morocco, and Nouakchott in Mauritania. This edited volume highlights those cities across the

MENA region. Although there are many commonalities and intersected histories, individual cities also have many unique features, geographies, and political and social contexts.

Acknowledgments

I sincerely thank the Gerda Henkel Foundation for its generous funding. Without their support, my research on Aleppo – and the resulting edited volume – would not have been possible. I would like to acknowledge the input of the external reviewers of the chapters, and to voice my appreciation for the work that they have done voluntarily.

I extend my gratitude to Albrecht Wiesener, the coordinator of the DFG Research Training Group 1913, as well as the exceptional and thoughtful contributions of William Hatherell, our copy-editor, and Sophia Hörmannsdorfer, the series's layout designer and typesetter.

I am grateful for the support of my friends and colleagues who advised and encouraged me along this journey. Last, but not least, I sincerely thank all of the authors, my co-editor, and the other academics who were involved in this project for putting up with me and my vision for this edited volume and persevering through the rigorous editing process that we had. I was privileged to work with each and everyone of them.

Cottbus, March 2025
Zeido Zeido

Mapping Cities in the MENA Region
An Introduction

Zeido Zeido, Suna Çağaptay

This edited volume examines seven cities scattered across the MENA (Middle East and North Africa) region, from Dubai in the east to Nouakchott in the west. Each chapter follows the urban evolution and expansion story of one of these cities since the late 19th or early 20th centuries up until the present day in order to narrate how a small city at that time came to be what it is today. This time span marks the transformation and expansion of what is typically now perceived as the old quarter, to the vastly spread city of today.

The chosen time span also highlights the repercussions of the shared yet distinguished cross-influences that these cities witnessed, particularly from the Ottoman Empire and European colonial powers. The different controlling periods and manners in which these powers ruled meant that these cities experienced different circumstances and were on different trajectories. This led to the production of different urban outcomes that are still visible today.

Pre-Independence: Different Trajectories

In the late 19th century, on the one hand, the Ottoman empire ruled Aleppo directly, but ruled Cairo and Alexandria only nominally, and had no significant control over them. Although it looked to expand, and its rule spread in the areas surrounding it, the Ottoman Empire could not reach Dubai.[4] On the other hand, Shiraz[5] and Casablanca were always out of the empire's reach, as was the land on which Nouakchott would be created around three decades after World War I and the fall of the Ottoman Empire.

Colonial powers ruled different regions in different styles and periods. Between 1912 and 1956, France ruled over the protectorate of Morocco earlier, longer, and arguably much more harshly[6] and directly than it ruled the mandate of Syria and Lebanon between 1920 and 1946.[7] French rule created a segregated city for Europeans only in Casablanca,[8] where a new European architectural style was introduced. However, Aleppo, an important Ottoman city, had already shifted from its traditional architecture to a more European-like style half a decade before France came to rule it. In the case of Mauritania, the country's borders were carved out from the colonies of French West Africa, and Nouakchott was practically created from scratch three years before the country's independence.[9]

Between 1882 and 1914, Egypt was a de facto British protectorate, governed through a complex, multi-layered system of governance: a government within a government within yet another government, all ultimately under British control from London. Great Britain effectively controlled the country from behind the façade of the Khedive Royal family,[10] which itself functioned semi-autonomously but was still nominally part of the Ottoman Empire. This arrangement evolved in 1914 when Britain officially declared Egypt a protectorate during World War I. However, public outrage following the end of the war, evident most notably in the 1919 Revolution, forced Britain to issue a unilateral declaration of Egypt's independence in 1922. Even so, the true sovereignty of Egypt remained elusive until the full British withdrawal after the Suez Crisis in 1956.[11]

During this extended period of British influence, Egypt witnessed major transformations in its urban planning, particularly in its two largest cities, Cairo and Alexandria. These changes have left enduring imprints that remain visible to this day. In contrast to the situation in Egypt, the British colonial power was not interested in Dubai itself. Rather, its interest was mostly limited to securing its maritime routes to protect British ships from piracy. In 1820, the British established a protectorate in what is today the UAE, northern Oman and Bahrain after defeating local tribes, and later set up the Trucial System in 1835.[12] In 1836, the Sheikhdom of Dubai passed to Maktoum bin Butti, and the Maktoum family has ruled Dubai ever since. The lack of British interest in Dubai itself and the limited area and wealth of pre-oil Dubai probably explain why colonialism had almost no mentionable effect on Dubai's architecture. On the other hand, Cairo and Alexandria saw noticeable attempts at a grand European-like style of architecture and planning before the arrival of the British, arguably a mark of European influence.[13] Furthermore, British interests, especially their industrial and shipping interests in Alexandria, left visible marks and reshaped the planning and industrial heritage of the city.

Methods: Visualisation and a City-Scale Overlook

In addition to the focus period of each chapter, which covers the city in question from the late 19th or early 20th century up until today, the geographical focus of each chapter is city-scale. Each chapter narrates a story that is not often discussed, aided by visuals such as maps, sketches, timelines, or explanatory models. Additionally, each chapter discusses the historical, political, social, and economic aspects, and how each one of these aspects influences how the city evolved and expanded and how these combined aspects leave their mark on the city. In other words, each chapter moves beyond a one-sided story, such as that city plans or buildings are merely the creations of urban planners or architects.

The illustrations created by the different authors attempt to visualise for readers the untold story behind each city. The chapter devoted to Dubai uses an explanatory model to show the intricate relationship between Dubai Municipality, holding companies, companies, and freezones to explain who, where, and how several mega projects were constructed. An accompanying map that highlights different parts of Dubai complements the explanatory model and shows how Dubai's municipality relinquished its authority over chunks of the city's lands to several mega financial entities that self-regulate what they construct. Another map shows the social fraction using a similar method.

In the case of Shiraz, colourful cityscape sketches show how rapid urban growth has diminished the gardens that have dominated the city's skyline during most of its long history and pushed these gardens out to the cliffs of the mountains that entrap the city.[14] The reimagined cityscape paintings of each period are accompanied by a map that utilises GIS to further clarify the expansion of the city and the location of the landmarks dominating the landscapes. Furthermore, the sketches track how historic landmarks disappeared from the cityscape when they were covered by large modern structures.

In the case of Aleppo, a ‹mental map›, an idea that has proved influential since it was introduced by the urban theorist Kevin Lynch[15], is used to show the architectural diversity of the city. Each part of the city that possesses a distinctive architectural style is highlighted on the mental map. A timeline graph shows when each of these different urban spaces and architecture styles of Aleppo emerged and was discontinued, as well as some of the specific historical events that contributed to the creation of Aleppo's architectural styles and their going out of fashion.

To explain how al-Sisi's New Administrative Capital[16], which is still under construction near Cairo, is nothing new, a hand-sketched map of each administrative, and arguably politically driven, expansion of Cairo since the 19th century is presented for readers. One map of the entire city today shows how Cairo is a mosaic consisting mostly of the collection of these administrative areas built by each new ruler of Egypt since then. The Nouakchott chapter offers different maps, each one loaded with different layers expressed in different colors. Laying out the axes of the city and its expansion over the years on one map, or laying out where the sand dunes move or where the floods hit the city on a second map, allows the reader to comprehend the complexities of the city. Another map in this chapter shows the urban patterns spread over Nouakchott. Furthermore, the chapter breaks down these urban patterns to their different types of dwelling units and provides several computer-generated and hand-drawn sketches for them.

Pinned sites, highlighted locations and coloured railways on several maps of Alexandria guide the reader through the urban growth story of the city, which is often presented as a one-sided narrative. The story of Alexandria's growth often focuses on the east, where the tramlines ran, and where the beautiful neighbourhoods and palaces of the elites were established in the late 19th century. These maps help in telling a story beyond a unilateral lens that overlooked the industrial heritage on Alexandria's western side.

For Casablanca, two maps are utilised. In the first map, different areas of the city are highlighted in different colours, with the dates indicated so the reader can follow the development and story of the city. The second map utilises GPS to visualise the relocation of the residents of the marginalised working-class ghettos. A number of arrows tracking the movement of these groups clearly show how the residents of these ghettos are again pushed to the outskirts today.

A City Story: Untold Narratives

The first chapter titled *Dubai's Urban Transformation: Unveiling the Interplay of Heritage and Futuristic Development* delves into the urban evolution of Dubai, the second largest and most populous emirate of the United Arab Emirates (UAE). Sami Ibrahim, an urban planner and a specialist in governance and transnational urbanism, narrates the historical context of the city and outlines its development in three distinct phases: the heritage of the past, from its foundation to the discovery of oil; the post-oil era, dominated by postmodern architecture; and the current era, characterised as the heritage of the future and marked by government-led megadevelopments since the beginning of the 21st century.

The chapter tells the story of Dubai from the time when it was a small town at the end of the 19th century up until today's world city. Despite the establishment of the first master plan in 1960[18], Dubai primarily expanded into vacant lands. These expansions were not planned by the municipality, nor were they the result of unplanned settlements, but rather uniquely designed by giant economic entities. The story of Dubai's pursuit of global prominence, especially since the beginning of this century through large-scale projects, and some of its results, such as fragmented social cohesion, is fairly well-known. However, the legal framework that led to a fragmented city authority, fragmented urban regulations, and in turn a fragmented city is less familiar.

In this chapter, Ibrahim draws an explanatory model to clarify the intricate connections between government entities, free-zone authorities, free zones, corporations, holding companies, and construction companies and their projects in Dubai. Parallel to the explanatory model, he shows on a map where these authorities are located physically, and how they fragment Dubai.

Having several independent authorities responsible for different patches of Dubai has led to a fragmented urban fabric, creating an imbalance between progress on the one hand and heritage preservation and social cohesion on the other. Furthermore, while the city showcases its historic architecture for tourism, it selectively preserves visually appealing forms from the late 19th and early 20th centuries. However, some neighbourhoods from later periods were demolished because they do not reflect Dubai's aspiration to a modern and futuristic image. Thus, this chapter sheds light on the urban development trajectory and the complex interplay between heritage, ambition, and economic realities in shaping the city's identity.

The second chapter about Shiraz titled *The Historic Urban Landscapes of Shiraz: Visualising the City's Skyline Evolution* discusses how the skyline of this historic city in southern Iran has evolved dramatically over fourteen centuries. The chapter follows the urban landscape of the city and how it changed in each century. A special focus is put on the last century and its rapid urban growth. Farnaz Mohseni, an urban planner and heritage specialist, visualises the city's skylines and the landmarks that defined it in each of these periods. Mohseni paints Shiraz's silhouette across twelve historical periods, from the 7th century to the 21st century, in watercolour. These sketches showing the urban evolution of Shiraz are accompanied by a map and description of the urban changes of each period. The reader can follow not only the expansion of the city on the maps and sketches, but also the emergence and disappearance of major landmarks over time.

The chapter uses quantitative methods, and the skyline illustrations are created through a structured approach that goes beyond free-style sketches to offer realistic depictions of urban scenes. Utilising a GPS-based programme, the landmarks shown on each sketch are positioned on a parallel map that belongs to the same period.

Mohseni highlights how Shiraz was always remarkable in being entangled with its gardens, and how urban sprawl reduced these gardens and pushed them towards the mountains that surround the city.[17] The skyline illustrations bring to light how the green spaces of Shiraz are expanding and retreating over time. Accordingly, the visuals animate the story and details of the urban growth, landscape development, and green gardens of Shiraz.

The chapter also discusses the importance of preserving green spaces and suggests balanced development through effective urban regulations. Mohseni underlines the need for a comprehensive approach to urban planning that respects both historic preservation and modern society's contemporary demands.

The third chapter titled *A ‹Mental Map› of Aleppo: The City's Urban Evolution and its Architectural Styles* aims to provide a simplified yet clear understanding of the urban spaces of the city. The chapter uses the work of Kevin Lynch[19] (1918–1984), an urban theorist who suggested that residents of the same city share a certain image of their city and how it looks like. One of Lynch's key ideas was the concept of ‹districts›. Unlike municipal districts drawn randomly by virtual lines, Lynch's districts are areas in the city that share distinguished common characters.

With the help of other Aleppines, Zeido Zeido, an architect and researcher focused on urban heritage, presents a map that translates how the different spaces of Aleppo are viewed by – at least a group of – its dwellers. The chapter lays down a map that splits Aleppo into different areas or ‹districts› that share common dominant architectural characteristics.

The chapter then discusses the history and architecture of each of these areas. It discusses when and how its architectural forms developed as well as some of the political or social factors that played a role in the creation or shaping the architectural characters of these ‹districts›. The created mental map is highlighted with six colours to represent these six ‹districts›.

Additionally, this chapter visualises the passage of time in the city so the reader can follow when each of the discussed districts and architectural style appeared, or when these districts stopped expanding and their architectural forms were discontinued as well as the historic events that corresponded with their manifestation.

Subsequently, by using this map and a timeline of selected events, interviews, and secondary resources, the chapter discusses different relevant aspects regarding Aleppo's built heritage and architectural evolution. Some of these discussions include heritage protection regulations[20] and the «value» grasp of locals for each architectural style. The chapter also briefly discusses the division of Aleppo[21] during the recent conflict. By laying the mental maps with the highlighted districts next to the war-division map, the reader easily realises that the city was already physically polarised and that the west–east division of the city was not random at all.

The fourth chapter titled *Cairo: A Mosaic of New Capitals* narrates how each ruler of Egypt since the early 19th century founded and favoured a new section within present-day Cairo, resulting in a disproportionate allocation of capital and urban development. This chapter explores and maps each one of these new sections that were supposed to take over the role of an administrative district at some point. Omar Abolnaga, a specialist in urbanism and urban governance, discusses the political motives behind these shifts and the achievements of each regime in establishing an administrative district. He also assesses the effectiveness of each reallocation of capital and how these districts function today.

Retrospectively, these capitals are the urban legacies of the former rulers of Egypt, namely Mehmed Ali, Abbas I, Ismail, Tewfiq, Nasser, Mubarak, and nowadays al-Sisi, whose new capital[22] has been the subject of media attention for some time. These districts, initially conceived as independent or semi-independent capital cities boasting concentrated wealth and power, are at present largely integrated into Cairo. However, when examined closely and pieced together, they reveal Cairo's formal landscape as an incomplete mosaic marked by gaps and forgotten narratives.

Through the synthesis of archival records, maps, and urban literature, this chapter unearths fragmented historical narratives surrounding Cairo's former capital cities while raising crucial questions about the ongoing project of the New Administrative Capital of al-Sisi.

The fifth chapter titled *Tracing the Omitted Physical Transformations: Re-Narrating the Urban Development of Alexandria between the Mid-19th and Early 20th Centuries* is set in Alexandria, when Egypt witnessed the onset of the so-called modern industries. It was during this phase that many Egyptian cities witnessed rapid urban developments to host the population influx stimulated by economic, commercial, and industrial investments.[23] The port city of Alexandria was one of those Egyptian cities that undertook a predominant role during Egypt's modern development at the time. A significant amount of literature has studied the historical urban development of Alexandria during this phase. Nevertheless, these studies predominantly focused on the socio-economic and commercial aspects that were condensed on the east side of the city's urban development, omitting the imperative role of modern industries condensed on the city's west shore in powering the city's modern urban development and as a key factor that reshaped the city.

With the help of archival records, historical maps, and secondary literature, Mirhan Damir, an educator and industrial heritage specialist, traces and analyses these physical changes that were drivers for the city's development between the mid-19th century and the early 20th century. In this chapter, she presents a complementary narrative to the city's historical urban development, highlighting the underemphasised but inextricable role of modern industries. As an extension, she explains the ripple effect of the positioning of industrial heritage on the west shore on steering the location of workers' housing, relocation of older industries, and possibly the positioning of suburban development and upper-class establishments away from these industries.

By mapping this omitted narrative, Damir's study contributes to illuminating the still undervalued physical attributes of the city's industrial heritage, which should be considered in future conservation and city development policies. This is particularly relevant today, when many of the physical traces of Egypt's industrial heritage are rapidly being demolished.

The sixth chapter titled *Redoing the Peripheries: Displacement, Segregation, and Urban Sprawl in Casablanca* goes back to the colonial urban planning that has irrevocably shaped Casablanca's urban development, similar to many other North African cities. While colonial patterns of socio-spatial segregation, namely the creation of a new Europeans-only part of town,[24] has visibly marked the city's morphology, a broader legacy of colonial planning continues to prevail.

In this chapter, Raffael Beier, a scholar of migration, urban displacement, and inequality, and Torben Dedring, a geomatics specialist, narrate these colonial continuities by highlighting three common threads: urban re-imagination, resettlement, and land speculation. Using cartography, Beier and Dedring narrate the post-millennial story of Casablanca and how its desire to be a world-class metropolis[25] has been a driver for remaking socio-spatial segregation at the metropolitan level. Casablanca's image-driven transformation pushes long-term stigmatised, politically undesired, and socially marginalised population groups to remake their districts.[26] Thus, these groups are pushed away from their old central working-class districts – the «old peripheries» – towards distant resettlement site – the «new peripheries».

Through megaprojects, urban renewal, resettlement of marginalised urban dwellers, and a construction boom led by land speculation, Casablanca aspires to change its image. The working class, which was seen as an unpleasant necessity during colonial times, was pushed to the periphery. Today, seen again as a burden to the city's international economic ambitions and its aspirational image, these people are expected to reside outside the perimeter of the imagined world-class city, symbolised by the growth of urban megaprojects. Thus, Beier and Dedring argue in their narrative that current urban planning since the 2000s addresses urban deficiencies by producing «new peripheries» in a way that resembles the creation of the «old peripheries» known as Bidonville under colonial rule. While the core city is renewed and upgraded, the construction of new peripheries is driven by land speculation and population resettlement, lacking integrated urban planning at the metropolitan level.

Finally, the seventh chapter titled *Urbanising the Desert: The Case of Nouakchott* tells the story of how an unassuming fishing village was chosen to be the new capital of Mauritania in 1957,[27] just three years before the independence of the country. Supposed to represent national unity, the site of Nouakchott aimed, at least nominally, to bridge the cultures of the Moors and the Black Africans. The droughts of the 1970s drove thousands of previously nomadic people to settle on the outskirts of a city designed only for 15,000 people,[28] leading to an urban sprawl that the governing bodies could not or did not care to deal with. Today Nouakchott is home to almost two million people.

The city's location and hostile natural environment, trapped between encroaching sand dunes and the rising level of the Atlantic Ocean, only exacerbates the challenges of urban sprawl. With few historic buildings, the heritage of Nouakchott is instead brought to life through the relationships between its people, the environment, and the spaces they form.[29]

The ethnic groups represented in Nouakchott today have strong ties to the areas of origin, and tensions between various groups are evident in the formation and occupation of the city. The neo-urban society in the city has to contend with profound changes in identity, not least with a dramatic shift in understanding of land ownership.

While land speculation is a fundamental component of urbanisation in Nouakchott, class, wealth, language, and ethnicity are all intermingled issues that lead to different forms of architecture, urban patterns, and different population densities in one of the least dense capitals in the world. Social issues and components uniquely define the relationship between settlers, land, and landscape in Nouakchott.

Three scholars, Zuzanna Krzyżanowska, a conservation architect specialising in regeneration and development, and Elizabeth Ryall and Chloe Loader, specialists in development and emergency practice, demonstrate that behind the apparent chaos and informality dominating Nouakchott, there is an underlying organisation, ways of functioning, and unspoken prospects like land grab, understood by residents of the city.

In summary, as a result of their intersected histories and cultures, the cities in the MENA region share many common features, yet every city has its own unique character and set of issues. These urban hubs have expanded far beyond their charming old towns. As each chapter demonstrates, it is often a futile attempt to resolve an issue of one part of the city without considering the rest of it. Furthermore, the different issues of any place are usually entangled with one another. Therefore, understanding the city as one unit, its development history and culture is important. This consideration is especially crucial for international bodies that get involved to protect historic old towns, or in some cases private entities from abroad that get contracted to design a general plan or «improve» the city.

1 Zeido 2015.
2 Zeido 2020.
3 UNESCO 2012.
4 Alaydrus 1998, 170–175.
5 Mohseni 2023.
6 Abu-Lughod 1980.
7 Khoury 1987.
8 Abu-Lughod 1980.
9 Pazzanita 2008; Pitte 1977.
10 Hunter 1998, 180–195.
11 Abu-Lughod 1971.
12 Ramos 2009, 4.
13 Sami 1928.
14 Mohseni et al. 2020b; Mohseni et al. 2020a.
15 Lynch 1960.
16 Al-Sharq al-Awsat 2022.
17 Mohseni 2023.
18 Ramos 2009, 13.
19 Lynch 1960.
20 Zeido 2023.
21 Zeido/Ibold 2019.
22 Al-Sharq al-Awsat 2022.
23 Crouchley 1938.
24 Abu-Lughod 1980.
25 Beier 2019b.
26 Beier 2019a.
27 Pazzanita 2008.
28 Vium 2016, 345.
29 Pitte 1977.

Abu-Lughod 1971
J. Abu-Lughod: Cairo: 1001 Years of the City Victorious (Princeton 1971).

Abu-Lughod 1980
J.L. Abu-Lughod: Rabat: Urban Apartheid in Morocco (Princeton, NJ 1980).

Alaydrus 2014
محمد حسن العيدروس: تاريخ الخليج العربي الحديث والمعاصر.
M. Alaydrus: Modern and Contemporary History of the Arabian Gulf (Kuwait 2014).

Al-Sharq al-Awsat 2022
السيسي متمسك ببناء العاصمة الإدارية رغم الصعوبات و الانتقادات. الشرق الاوسط.
Al-Sisi Sticks to Building the New Administrative Capital Despite the Difficulties and Criticisms. 6 July 2022, https://aawsat.com/node/3743991 (6 August 2022).

Beier 2019a
R. Beier: From the City to the Desert: Analysing Shantytown Resettlement in Casablanca, Morocco, from Residents' Perspectives. UA Ruhr Studies on Development and Global Governance, vol. 72 (Berlin 2019).

Beier 2019b
R. Beier: Worlding Cities in the Middle East and North Africa. Arguments for a Conceptual Turn. Middle East – Topics & Arguments 12, 2019, 28–32.

Crouchley 1938
A. E. Crouchley: The Economic Development of Modern Egypt (London 1938).

Hunter 1998
F. R. Hunter: Egypt under the Successors of Muhammad 'Ali, in: M. W. Daly (ed.): The Cambridge History of Egypt, Volume Two, Modern Egypt from 1517 to the End of the Twentieth Century (Cambridge 1998) 180–197.

Khoury 1987
P. S. Khoury: Syria and the French Mandate: The Politics of Arab Nationalism, 1920–1945 (London 1987).

Lynch 1960
K. Lynch: The Image of the City (Cambridge, MA 1960).

Mohseni et al. 2020a
F. Mohseni / S. Lotfi / M. Shole: Proposing an adapted visibility analysis methodology for the building height codes of the Shiraz development plan. Sustainable Cities and Society 61, 2020, https://doi.org/10.1016/j.scs.2020.102347.

Mohseni et al. 2020b
F. Mohseni / S. Weidner / M. Kloos: A historical analysis and the identification of driving forces behind the evolution of the urban macro skyline of Shiraz, Iran. Journal of Cultural Heritage Management and Sustainable Development 10, no. 4, 2020, 413–427, https://doi.org/10.1108/JCHMSD-09-2019-0110.

Mohseni 2023
Safeguarding the Visual Integrity of the Historic Urban Landscape (HUL) through Contextualised Instrument Development: The Case Study of Shiraz (Doctoral Thesis). Brandenburg University of Technology (Cottbus 2023).

Pazzanita 2008
A. G. Pazzanita: Historical Dictionary of Mauritania, 3rd ed. (Lanham MD 2008).

Pitte 1977
J.-R. Pitte: Nouakchott, capitale de la Mauritanie (Paris 1977).

Rabinow 1992
P. Rabinow: France in Morocco: Technocosmopolitanism and Middling Modernism. Assemblage 17, 1992, 52–57.

Ramos 2009
S. Ramos: The blueprint: a history of Dubai's spatial development through oil discovery. Harvard Kennedy School, Harvard [online, 2009], https://www.belfercenter.org/publication/blueprint-history-dubais-spatial-development-through-oil-discovery (27 February 2025).

Sami 1928
امين سامي: تقويم النيل. الجزء الثاني.
A. Sami: The Nile Calendar, vol. 2 (Cairo 1928).

UNESCO 2012
UNESCO: Ancient City of Aleppo. [Online 2012], UNESCO World Heritage List: http://whc.unesco.org/en/list/21/multiple=1&unique_number=24 (5 February 2018).

Vium 2016
C. Vium: Enacting immanent potentialities: Tcheb-tchib strategies at the centre of the urban fringe in Nouakchott, Mauritania. Singapore Journal of Tropical Geography 37, no. 3, 2016, 343–362, https://doi.org/10.1111/sjtg.12158.

Zeido 2015
Z. Zeido: Re-establishing the architectural codes of Aleppo city after war (Master Thesis). Bahçeşehir University (Istanbul 2015).

Zeido 2020
Z. Zeido: Reclaiming the Architectural Heritage of Aleppo after the Syrian War (Doctoral Thesis). Brandenburg University of Technology (Cottbus 2020).

Zeido 2023
Z. Zeido: Attempting to document and rehabilitate Aleppo between 1994 and 2011: the ramifications of pre-conflict built heritage mismanagement and the effects of the scarcity of documentation on options available for post-conflict conservation. Built Heritage 7, no. 3, 2023, https://doi.org/10.1186/s43238-023-00084-2.

Zeido / Ibold 2019
Z. Zeido / N. Ibold: The Division of Aleppo City: Heritage and Urban Space, in S. Frank / M. Ristic (eds.): Urban Heritage in Divided Cities: Contested Pasts (London 2019).

Dubai's Urban Transformation
Unveiling the Interplay of Heritage and Futuristic Development

Sami Ibrahim

In this chapter, I decrypt the facts underpinning the urban transformation of the emirate of Dubai, the second largest and the most populated emirate of the United Arab Emirates (UAE), by shedding light on the historical context in which the city developed and highlighting the city's distinct phases of development. The urban growth history of Dubai can be divided into three main phases. What I will call «the heritage of the past» comprises the first phase, from Dubai's foundation circa 1833 until 1966 when oil was discovered. During this phase, urbanisation was confined to the city's current historical neighbourhoods: Deira, Al-Shindagha, and Bur Dubai (see fig. 1 later). The second phase occurred between 1966 and the late 1990s, when Dubai witnessed repeated attempts to channel its growth and was mostly dominated by a postmodern architectural style. The third phase, «the heritage of the future», runs from the beginning of the 21st century up until the present day, and has witnessed the establishment of government-owned megadevelopers in charge of building the current skyline of the city.

Since the development of the first master plan for Dubai in 1960, the city has been mainly built on abundantly available vacant lands, and therefore there was no reason to redevelop or demolish existing areas, with a few exceptions. Throughout this chapter, I will be giving particular attention to two neighbourhoods that exemplify the destruction of historical and postmodernist areas: Al-Bastakiya in Bur Dubai as an example of the destruction of a pre-1960s neighbourhood, and Al-Satwa as an example of the destruction of a postmodernist neighbourhood.

By examining these cases, I argue that the intersection between built heritage, a futuristic vision, and an ambitious economic model has led to Dubai's geographically, socially, and administratively fragmented urban fabric. By tracing the city's evolution from its humble beginnings to its current state, this chapter offers valuable insights into the intricate dynamics of Dubai's urban growth, revealing the interplay between its rich heritage, aspirations for the future, and economic realities.

The Port of Lengeh and the Changing Fate of Dubai

To understand the modern history of Dubai, one must go back to 1833, when the original settlement was founded by some 800 members of the Al-Bu-Falasa group, a subgroup of the Bani Yas tribe who left Abu Dhabi to settle at a point south of Sharjah, under the leadership of Maktoum bin Butti (the ruler of Dubai between 1836 and 1852) and Ubaid bin Said Al-Falasi. By the beginning of the 1830s, the period seen by historians such as Christopher M. Davidson and Graeme Wilson as the founding date of Dubai, the British political resident reported that Dubai Creek had around 1,200 inhabitants, with newcomers almost doubling the settlement's original population.[1] Al-Falasi died shortly after 1836, thus consolidating the reign of the Maktoum family, the ruling family in Dubai ever since.

The European powers, starting with the Venetians, followed by the Portuguese, the Dutch, and finally the British, were interested in the Gulf region primarily to secure their trade routes to and from the Indian subcontinent to the east.[2] This meant that from the 15th century until the end of the 19th century, as long as trade convoys could move unobstructed within the Gulf region, the European powers would not have to get involved in the affairs of the Gulf colonies. Neither were European merchants keen to trade with the region, believing that the efforts required to do so were more than the rewards given the climate and the local economies.[3]

The second half of the 19th century proved to be more prosperous for the Lower Gulf region, especially for fishing and the pearl trade. In January 1820 the British marked the defeat of the local tribes, who had carried out pirate attacks on their trade ships, with the signing of the General Treaty of Peace with the regional sheikhs of Bahrain and what was then northern Oman (including the present-day United Arab Emirates). This treaty included an agreement to end the pirate attacks and would commit Britain to maintain and enforce this peace, mostly in the interests of their trade pursuits. Thus an official British Protectorate was established in 1820, and the Trucial System was set in place in 1835, with the region coming to be known as the Trucial Coast.[4]

The new system provided a calmer environment for the pearl economy. Between the 1870s and the late 1890s, the export of pearls from Dubai increased tenfold,[5] attracting regional attention and spurring immigration into Dubai, especially from Persians, Banyans, and Indian-British Hindu merchants.[6] Dubai merchants were well integrated into the distribution networks of the Lower Gulf, and operated mainly through the Persian port of Lengeh, a central point for British trade between India, Persia, and Europe. Nonetheless, researchers such as Mohamed Hasan Alaydrus have pointed out that the protectorate deepened the political divisions in the region and boxed in the role of local merchants to agents and distributers of goods monopolised by European companies, leading to the collapse of local crafts.[7]

While pearl expeditions managed to intensify trade in Dubai during the latter part of the 19th century, the Persian port of Lengeh, across the Persian Gulf from Dubai, remained the main distribution centre in and for the region. This central position of Lengeh was established in the 18th century and continued throughout the 19th century, attracting many Indian merchants to settle in Lengeh and mix with the local trading community. Over time, Dubai merchants intermingled with this group, and from 1877 until 1902 they controlled the distribution trade from Lengeh to the Trucial Coast.[8] By the turn of the century, Lengeh's fate suffered drastically due to Tehran's imposition of imperial tariffs and controls on re-exported goods, reaching as high as 400% on some products, especially on goods traded by Arab merchants.[9]

In 1904, in what would mark a changing point in the history of Dubai, its ruler, Maktoum bin Hashar (r. 1894–1906), cancelled the 5% customs fees to declare that trade through the port of Dubai would be exempt from tax and control, immediately attracting Lengeh's re-export business across the Persian Gulf to the port of Dubai.[10] Soon all trade between Britain and India would pass through Dubai, so that by 1905 some 34 steamboats regularly docked in the port of Dubai, increasing the annual volume of cargo to 70,000 tons. The British India Steam Navigation Company also moved its distribution centre, making Dubai its strategic warehouse for British trade routes. As a result, Dubai merchants profited greatly from the increased flow of goods, and a large Persian and Indian trading community from Lengeh emigrated to Dubai.

It should be noted that, while the treaties offered internal stability to the different states of the Trucial coast to prosper, Britain was wary of the Ottomans spreading their dominance to the gulf region in the late 19th century, especially after the Ottomans succeeded in taking over Kuwait and Qatar. However, Ottoman control did not reach or surpass Abu Dhabi despite the conflict that broke

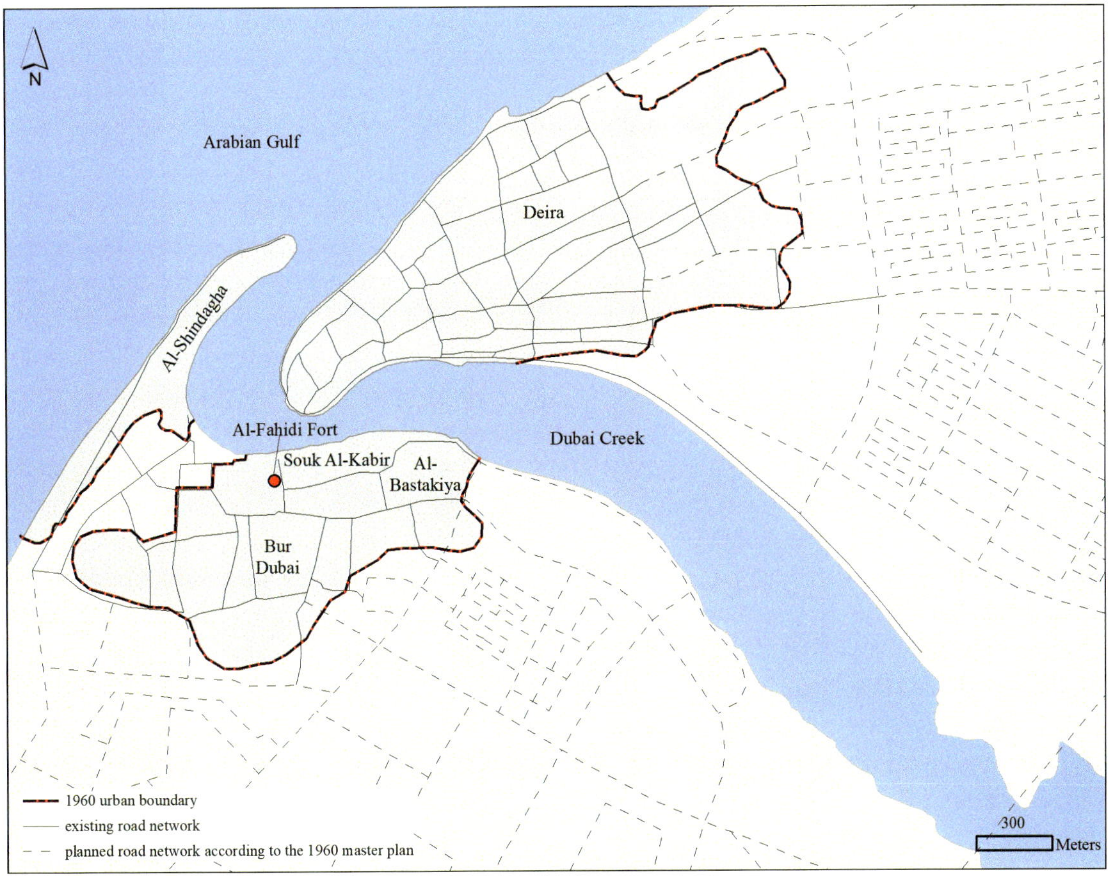

1 Boundaries of Dubai's three main neighbourhoods in 1960.

out in 1887 over the region between Qatar and Abu Dhabi, which moved hands between the two until World War I.[11]

The Heritage of the Past

Economic growth has greatly affected Dubai's traditional society, translating into a more established lifestyle and an appreciation for modern amenities. The growing wealth of the local population has opened new and broader prospects and a more sophisticated way of life for the city's residents. The newly acquired status of the merchants was reflected, not only in their way of life, but also in the architecture of the city. While the first houses were constructed from palm branches, prominent merchants erected new houses built of clay. Merchants arriving from India and Persia in the early 20th century also brought with them their way of life as well as their architecture. They invested their wealth in building coral stone houses decorated with wind towers (see fig. 4 later)[12] in the Al-Bastakiya and Al-Shindagha neighbourhoods (fig. 1), adding a distinctly cosmopolitan flavour to the city.[13]

Maktoum Bin Hashar's announcement in 1904 of the elimination of customs fees was no coincidence, as the city council was made up of leading merchants. Fatma Alsayegh, a scholar who focuses on the history and society of Gulf cities, explores the relationship between Dubai's merchant class and its Ruler throughout the 20th century, underlining this delicate but important relationship throughout the emirate's development process. Alsayegh describes this relationship between the Ruler and the merchant class at the beginning of the 20th century:

> Since the Ruler's income was not as high as that of the pearl merchants, and which could fluctuate at times with the market, the Ruler often looked to these merchants for financial assistance, increasing his dependence on them, leading to a unique situation where merchants were often able to dictate their wishes. The Ruler, fully aware of this fact, appointed them in his Majlis in exchange of their financial contributions.[14]

The Majlis served as a sort of pre-municipal grouping, headed by the Ruler, where the financial power of the merchants gave them considerable influence in the decision-making process. They supported certain community initiatives through philanthropic projects to build several schools and a hospital, thus giving particular attention to providing basic social infrastructure, but at the same time creating a blur between the public and private spheres within the ruling elite.[15]

As a settlement, Dubai developed around its creek, which reaches into the desert and forms a natural port. Bur Dubai, stretching west of the creek towards Abu Dhabi, was the main area accommodating urban development in the early years of the 20th century, reflecting the economic prosperity generated by fishing and the pearl trade. The first commercial quarters, including the Souk Al-Kabir (or the Meena Bazar[16]), as well as Al-Bastakiya, were built by Arab, Persian, and Indian merchants arriving from the other side of the Persian Gulf. On the other side of the creek, the neighbourhood of Deira had already been established in the 19th century (see fig. 1), but it was only with major infrastructure projects undertaken in the 1960s that Deira began to gain more attention as an urban centre,[17] especially when oil was discovered in 1966. Significantly, on 16 January 1968, the British government declared its intention to terminate the treaty with the Trucial States, following the announcement of Harold Wilson, Britain's then prime minister, that all British troops were to be withdrawn from east of Suez, including Singapore, Malaysia, and the Persian Gulf, by the end of 1971.[18] For around four years, the rulers of these states engaged in discussions and negotiations to finally agree on the political and constitutional structure to be adopted once the British withdrew.[19] Hence, on 2 December 1971, the United Arab Emirates (UAE) was officially formed.[20]

Along with the 800 Al-Bu-Falasa members who arrived in 1833, Dubai has witnessed two main immigration waves.[21] The first, arriving at the beginning of the 20th century, was mainly made up of Arabs from the Iranian coast attracted by the opportunities and economic freedom that Dubai offered. Coming from the Bastak region of southern Iran, they settled in Al-Bastakiya, a newly formed neighbourhood. The second wave arrived at the end of the 1960s, mainly consisting of a low-skilled workforce mix from India, Pakistan, and Iran, and a relatively small number of skilled workers arriving from Europe and the United States. This flow reflected the fact that British companies, to which Dubai had granted contracts for the construction of major infrastructure projects (such as the airport, the port, roads, and hotels), were drawing a cheap labour force from these countries.[22] In general, UAE citizenship was granted only to those who could prove that their ancestry in the country dated prior to 1925.[23]

Despite these accelerated events, Dubai's population grew slowly, rising from 1,500 inhabitants in 1833 to 10,000 in 1900, reaching only 59,000 inhabitants by 1968.[24] This first period of slow growth resulted in a limited physical expansion of the urban fabric. Between 1900 and 1955, Dubai's 10,000 inhabitants were concentrated in the three neighbourhoods forming one single core around the creek: Deira, with 350 stores and 1,600 houses inhabited by Arabs, Persians, and Baloch, the latter making up the majority of the inhabitants; Al-Shindagha, serving as the residence of the ruling family with 250 houses inhabited only by Arabs; and Bur Dubai, the smallest of these neighbourhoods with 200 houses and 50 shops, dominated by a population of Persian and Indian merchants.[25] Until 1955, Dubai covered an area of only 3.2 square kilometres.[26]

The Failing Attempts of Channelling Dubai's Growth

Dubai's historic relationship with the British government, as well as with British banking institutions and consultancy firms, was integral to the emirate's modernisation project. While commercial oil was discovered in Abu Dhabi in 1958 and later in Dubai in 1966, early oil exploration in what is the UAE today (mainly Abu Dhabi) started in the 1930s.[27] With the resumption of oil exploration after World War II, various British institutions settled in Dubai to establish their presence in a growing city. In 1947 a British political resident moved to the city, a year after the British Imperial Bank of Iran had signed an agreement with the emirate to set up its office in Dubai. In 1952 the bank changed its name to the British Bank of the Middle East (BBME). It would enjoy a banking monopoly until 1963.[28]

Since the late 1930s, the dredging and widening of the creek was considered the most imperative infrastructure project in Dubai to increase the flow of goods and to ensure the arrival of heavier equipment needed for oil exploration. In 1954, and with the help of his political connections to the British Raj and the BBME to secure funding for the project, Prince Rashid Al-Maktoum (the Ruler from 1958 until his death in 1990) called on Neville Allen, an engineer in the British company of Sir William Halcrow, to carry out the hydrographic work necessary for the development of the creek. The dredging and widening of the creek were completed in the late 1950s, allowing steamboats up to a capacity of 800 tonnes to embark.[29]

Beyond the widening of the creek, and through the same political networks to secure funding in the pre-oil period, Dubai also called on the London-based architect John Harris to develop the first master plan for the city in 1960 to manage its expansion as well as its new infrastructure projects. With the growth of economic activity and the development of the creek, Sheikh Rashid foresaw, or was convinced, that this urban expansion needed to be guided by appropriate development.[30] Promoting continuity to the existing urban fabric, the plan suggested the extension of the already built neighbourhoods of Bur Dubai and Deira.[31] The suggestions of this first plan were implemented faithfully by developing the road infrastructure and zoning the city into residential, commercial, and industrial districts. To guide the city's expansion, Harris designed a grid overlaying roads and residential areas extending into the desert east of Deira district and east and south of Bur Dubai.[32] Likewise, the Dubai municipality was officially established in 1957 and given responsibility for implementing Harris's plan.[33]

The widening of the creek and the port, as well as the implementation of the first master plan, happened at the same time as Sheikh Rashid's enactment of the law on land ownership in 1960. The new law, modelled on the Sudanese land ownership law drafted after the independence of Sudan from Britain in 1956, was an essential tool used to capitalise on the land owned by the Sheikh for wealth accumulation. Later the law would be used, as part of a broader strategy, to invest in Dubai through major infrastructure projects and to take advantage of the value-add once those major projects were completed.[34] Under the law, any land that had been occupied by a property for a long period of time belonged to its occupant. Elsewhere, ownership went to the Sheikh. Thus, in areas where permanent houses were already built as early as 1960, the right to dispose of the plots belonged to their residents. In areas not yet urbanised at the time, the Sheikh could sell the land, lease it, assign it to certain uses for a certain period, or assign it to the municipality for the development of public amenities. And if the land

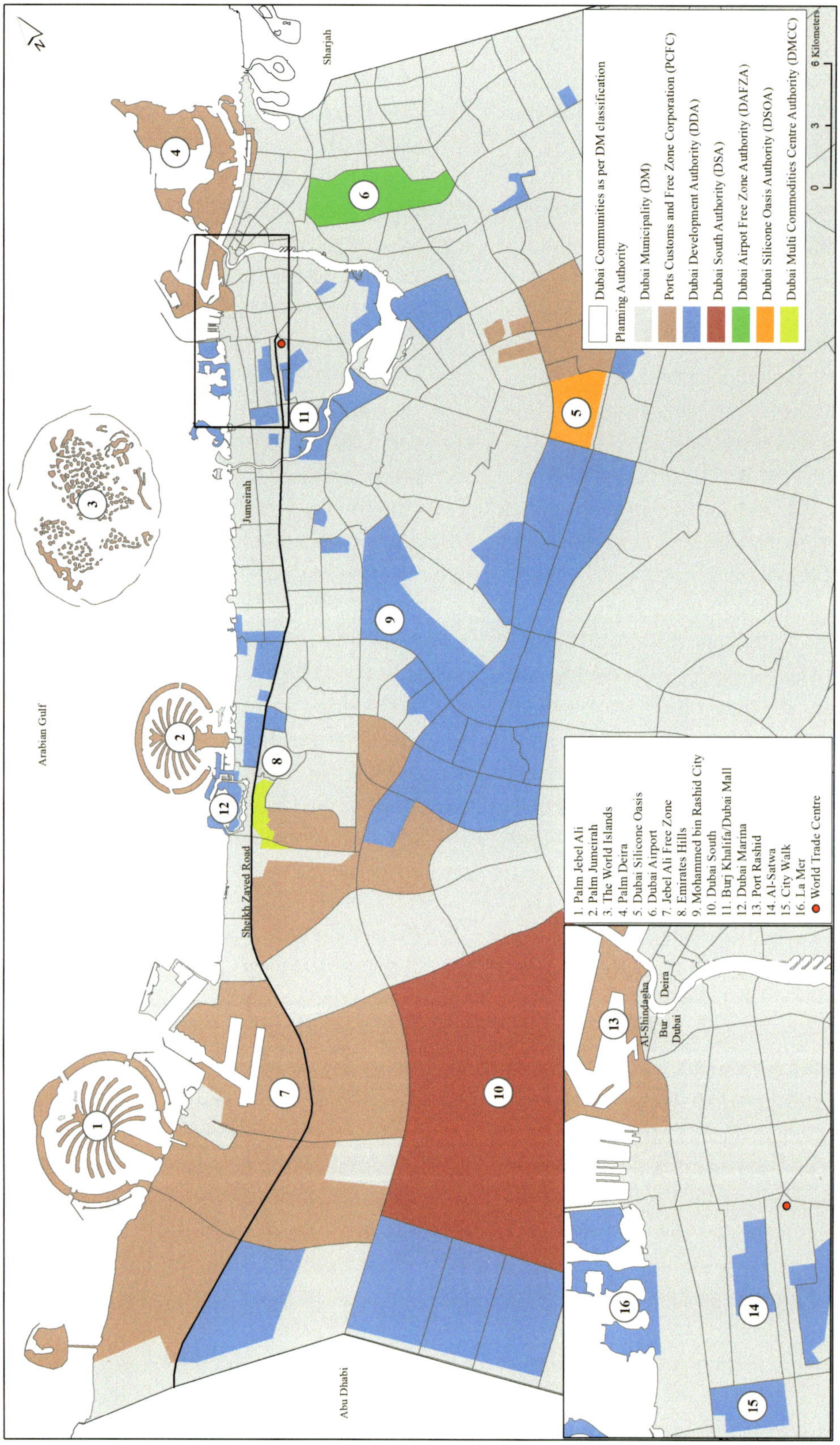

2 Fragmentation of regulatory bodies in Dubai today.

was provided free of charge, the Sheikh reserved the right to recover it in the future. Thus, the fact that the Sheikh could freely dispose of land outside of the urban area of the 1960s allowed him considerable control over urbanisation.[35]

With Dubai's urban expansion beyond the creek and its economic development accelerated since 1969 due to oil exports from the first deep-water field discovered in 1966, Harris was forced to revise his plan in 1971. The updated plan called for a concentric urban development around the creek, strengthening this area as a structuring axis of the city. Without access to the original 1960 and 1971 plans and further information, it is difficult to speculate if parts of the urban fabric were demolished for the sake of expanding the creek. However, I would argue that both plans respected the existing urban areas, as up until 1971 the city was still growing from its centre and both the 1960 and 1971 plans extended the existing urban area. The discontinuity with the existing urban area began in 1979 with the inauguration of the World Trade Centre, built beyond the city's urban boundary on the main axis leading from Dubai to Abu Dhabi, and to Jebel Ali port, which was also inaugurated in 1979 some 30 kilometres south of the city centre.[36] As a result, the city began to stretch along Sheikh Zayed Road, an axis perpendicular to the creek in the direction of Abu Dhabi with new low density residential areas lining the coast that would later be known as Jumeirah (fig. 2).

Between 1985 and 1988, Doxiadis Associates, a Greek architecture and urban planning consultancy, was commissioned by Dubai municipality in coordination with the United Nations Urban Development Project to develop a new urban plan for Dubai. The suggested development plan was prepared with a twenty-year perspective extending up to 2005 and was a first attempt to reflect on the future development of the entire emirate of Dubai, unlike the previous plans that focused only on the creek and its surroundings.

In 1993 Dubai municipality restarted working on a new master plan, focusing this time on the urban area and its extensions only – a plan that was mainly based on the city's economic and urban growth as an engine for its future development. However, most of the new plan's strategic development objectives did not see the light of day, particularly those concerned with the city's compactness, the establishment of green corridors structuring urban sprawl, and the provision of a certain social mix between the local and expatriate populations in residential areas.

The objective of the 1993 plan was to guide the development of Dubai until 2013. However, Dubai municipality was not able to cope with, nor to foresee, the massive growth of the population (see table 1 later) and the real estate sector due to the emergence of the megadevelopers and the establishment of regulatory authorities for the free zones towards the end of the 20th century, taking control of a considerable part of the city's urban development. Thus, the municipality was forced to review its spatial plan in 2003 to incorporate the challenges resulting from these rapid changes, especially regarding the city's expansion and its governance.

The Heritage of the Future

In fact, in the early 1990s, Sheikh Mohammed bin Rashid Al-Maktoum (r. since 2006) was only the Crown Prince of Dubai. Even though he was not the effective ruler, his older brother Sheikh Maktoum bin Rashid Al-Maktoum (r. 1991–2006) heavily relied on him in designing Dubai's future as a modern commercial and business centre.[37] Building on his father's efforts, Sheikh Mohammed bin Rashid Al-Maktoum has announced that Dubai's diversified economic activities aim at reducing the emirate's dependence on oil as the sole source of income.[38]

Following the logic of this strategy, free zones were established under civil law, which strongly encouraged foreign companies to settle in Dubai. Free zones were geographically demarcated

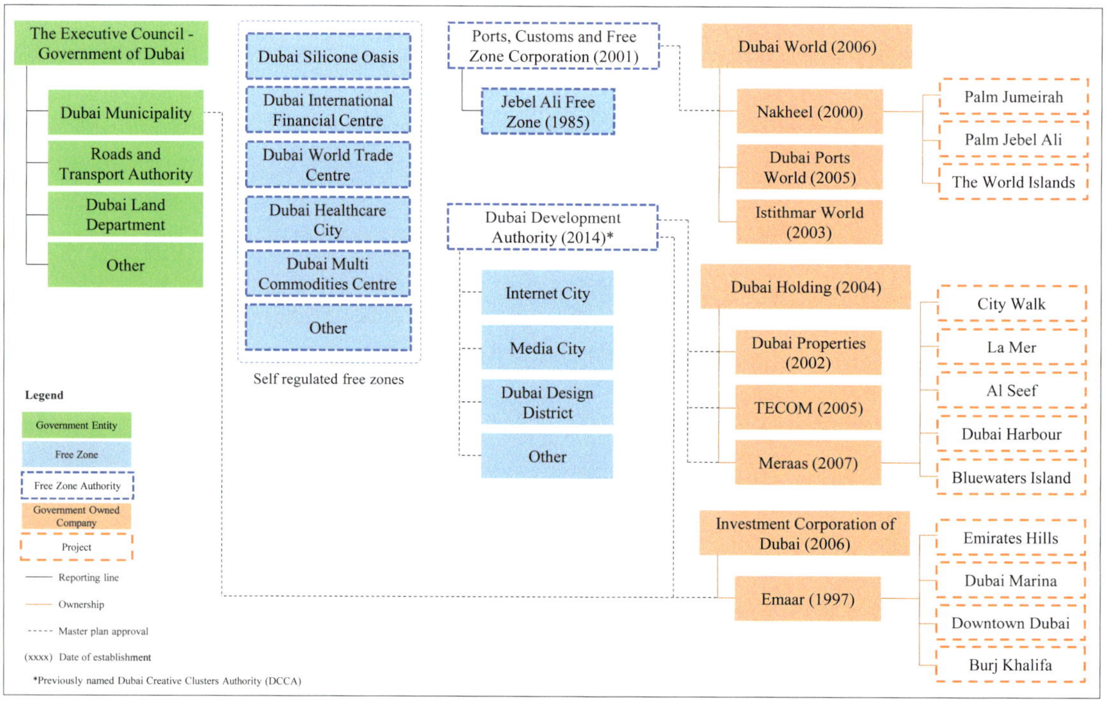

3 Non-exhaustive organisational chart drawing the relationship between the free zones, their authorities, the different government-owned holdings and their subsidiaries.

from the mainland and a space where companies enjoyed a 100% tax exemption for 50 years, and 100% ownership compared to 49% on Dubai's mainland – since at the time, the Gulf Cooperation Council (GCC) prohibited non-GCC nationals from land ownership – as well as flexible labour laws.[39] Thus, these free zones did not need to comply with Dubai's local legislative framework, including its employment, visa, and nationalisation of the labour market laws. As a result, multinational companies based in these free zones enjoyed full ownership and repatriation of profits, as opposed to strict laws on profit and sharing property ownership with the local population outside of the zones.[40] Jebel Ali Free Zone was the first free zone to be established in 1985 with nineteen companies, along with its own regulatory authority, the Jebel Ali Free Zone Authority (JAFZA) (fig. 3).[41]

As free zones attracted foreign investments into Dubai, several government-owned companies were created to support the growth of the economy. In 1997, Emaar was established by Mohammed Al-Abbar under the guidance of Sheikh Mohammed. In March 2000, the company made a public offering and received a grant of land on which it launched its first megaprojects: Emirates Hills and Dubai Marina.[42] Today, the Investment Corporation of Dubai (ICD) is the main shareholder of Emaar with around 30% of the shares listed in the Dubai financial market.

Despite its beautiful beaches and a hot to warm climate all year round, Dubai was limited by its size with a coastline only 70 km long. Believing that Dubai should not be limited by its small size, Sheikh Mohammed formed a team responsible for studying the possibility of expanding the city's coastline and decided to carry out several land reclamations projects to build artificial islands off the emirate.[43] Thus, Nakheel, another government-owned real estate development company was established by Sheikh Mohammed in 2000, and in 2001 began to develop the Palm Jumeirah, the first of their ambitious projects. Between 2003 and 2009, Nakheel added several similar projects: another palm-shaped island, the Palm Jebel Ali, and the World, an archipelago of 300 islands designed to imitate the continents of the world.[44]

In 2002, Dubai Properties, the third government-owned real estate company was established and is today a member of Dubai Holding, the global investment company managing Sheikh Mohammed's corporate portfolio. In 2006 Sheikh Mohammed established Dubai World (see fig. 3), a holding company that managed and led a portfolio of businesses and projects for the government of Dubai aiming to make Dubai a hub for global commerce and tourism.[45] In addition to the Jebel Ali Free Zone, the largest companies within Dubai World, which included Nakheel, Dubai Ports (the main port operators), and Istithmar World (the asset management arm), were managed like private corporations. Although all of these entities were government-owned, this management style was the vision and directive of Sheikh Mohammed as expressed through official decrees.[46]

To summarise, in the mid-2000s and in addition to Emaar, the Emirate of Dubai had founded two more real estate development levers, Nakheel and Dubai Properties, respectively under the two government-owned holding companies, Dubai World and Dubai Holding (see fig. 3). The trio that Nakheel and Dubai Properties formed with Emaar operated in a hybrid, half-private, half-public mode that became characteristic of the emirate.[47] The Ruler financed these corporations while allowing them great decision-making autonomy and stimulating competition between them. In just a few years, this corporate structure enabled the establishment of numerous free zones (Media City, Healthcare City, Internet City, etc.), luxurious hotel complexes, office towers, malls, and urban enclaves (Emirates Hills, Jumeirah Islands, Arabian Ranches, etc.).

In 2007 Sheikh Mohammed established Meraas as another real estate developer with the objective of building several signature projects in real estate, retail, and hospitality such as City Walk and La Mer. In 2020, following the directives of Sheikh Mohammed, Meraas became a subsidiary of Dubai Holding (see fig. 3).

In November 2009, following the 2008 global financial crisis, Dubai World announced that it was defaulting on its debt payment schedule, causing Dubai's real estate bubble to explode. As a result, Dubai municipality announced in 2011 a new spatial plan up to the year 2020. Covering the entire territory of the emirate of Dubai, the plan considered the impacts of the 2008 financial crisis, especially in terms of the projection of demographic and economic growth, and tried to optimise the use of land in response to growing environmental issues and to the city's changing socio-economic conditions. Although the Dubai Structural Plan 2020 was approved by the Executive Council of Dubai (the local government of Dubai), it was not executed due to the municipality's weak political position and limited influence on the Ruler compared to the powerful megadevelopers who saw in the plan a weakening of their power. In particular, the 2020 plan suggested the implementation of a new urban governance system for Dubai through the establishment of a Supreme Urban Planning Council, in charge of Dubai's strategic spatial planning and the coordination of development activities among the various actors, as well as the promulgation of an urban planning law that would eventually limit the megadevelopers' freedom of action. Finally, in early 2021 Dubai announced its latest urban plan, the Dubai 2040 Urban Master Plan. However, its content remains undisclosed to the public.

By the time Sheikh Mohammed took power in January 2006, he was already widely known as the «CEO of Dubai». When American journalist Steve Kroft, as part of a CBS 60 Minutes[48] special called «Dubai Inc.», asked Sheikh Mohammed if he should be called the CEO of Dubai, he replied: «I think so, yes. I changed the way government works (...) to make it work like a big business.»

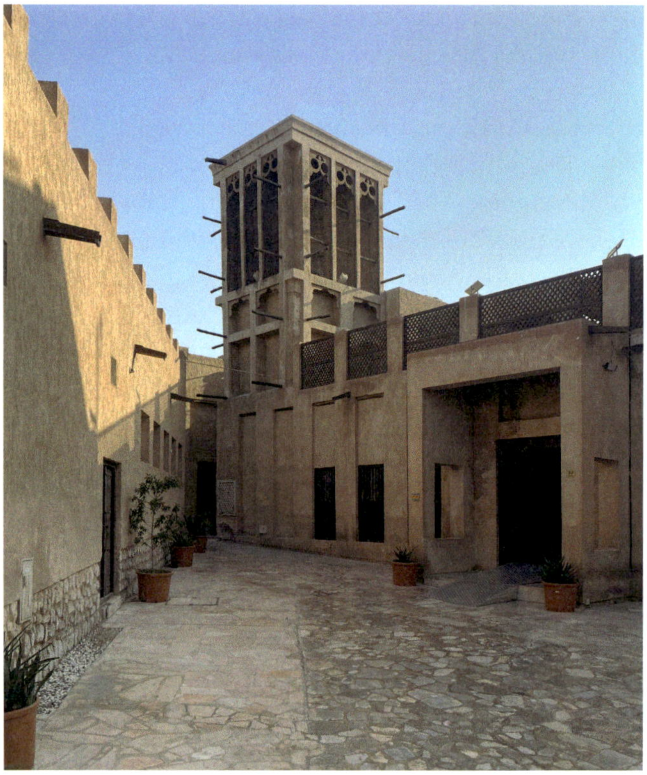

4 Coral stone palace decorated with a wind tower in Al-Bastakiya neighbourhood.

And when Kroft asked him what motivates him to build Dubai, he replied: «I want Dubai to be number one. Not in the region, but in the world (...). Number one in everything: higher education, health, housing (...). Just making my people the highest way of living».[49]

I argue that by envisioning Dubai's transition from an oil economy, real estate development played a major role in implementing Sheikh Mohammed's vision to build one of the world's best destinations for tourism, particularly by seeking to captivate the emirate's investors and visitors with a series of megaprojects where government practically merges with private enterprise. As such, Dubai arguably sets an example of what could be termed a fragmentation of power over spatial and regulatory jurisdictions. This system flourished with the rapid expansion of free zones and megadevelopments at the beginning of the 20th century. It was mainly a consequence of the absence of a unified urban planning regulation that clearly sets out the procedures for granting building permits, land use allocation, and approval of urban master plans. These free zones and government-owned megadevelopers were explicitly created to implement the Ruler's economic vision through a business-friendly approach to planning and development. The overlap between these power-linked developers within a single holding company and their corresponding regulatory authorities did not allow for adequate separation of powers, a condition that the legal system in most countries would require (see fig. 3).

Zooming into the Transformation of the Built Heritage

Delving deeper into Dubai's urban evolution, the following sections of this chapter bring our focus to specific areas, providing a closer examination of the recent transformation that shaped Dubai's built heritage of the pre-1990s period. By scrutinising two distinct periods, I aim to illuminate the changes that occurred within Dubai's built environment landscape. The first section delves into Al-Bastakiya, an iconic neighbourhood renowned for its wind towers and traditional architecture (fig. 4), offering a glimpse into the pre-1966 era. The second section turns our attention to Al-Satwa, a vibrant enclave that emerged during the late 1970s and 1980s, embodying the spirit of postmodernist architecture. Through these case studies, I uncover the intricate interplay of history and urban development, ultimately contributing to a comprehensive understanding of Dubai's current fragmented urban fabric and the forces that have shaped it.

Transforming the Pre-1966 Architecture

As described earlier, Al-Bastakiya neighbourhood, known mainly for its Persian community, had reached its maximum size of approximately 4 hectares in the 1960s. With the introduction of urban design guidelines in 1968 following the city's first master plan, developed by the London-based architect John Harris in 1960, Al-Bastakiya benefited from a prohibition on demolition or alterations other than for minor maintenance.[50] However, the neighbourhood witnessed a period of decline in the 1970s when its local residents left their homes for newly developed suburbs, leaving the historic buildings to deteriorate and become residences for squatters and low-income labourers.[51] In addition, the extension of the nearby Ruler's office in 1984 resulted in the demolition of a large part of Al-Bastakiya.[52] Some sources indicate that Dubai municipality had already demolished half of the neighbourhood by 1988 for modern redevelopment purposes,[53] hence requiring the intervention of Prince Charles, visiting Dubai in 1989, to argue for its preservation after receiving a letter from Rayner Otter, a British architect, who renovated the house he was living in and sought the prince's support to protect the architectural heritage of the neighbourhood.[54] Nevertheless, despite the decision to protect Al-Bastakiya, Dubai municipality started buying the houses and evicting their inhabitants to eventually renovate them and reconstruct the demolished ones towards the end of the 1990s and replace them with government offices, high-end art galleries, restaurants, and coffee shops.[55] However, at some time between 2012 and 2013, Al-Bastakiya neighbourhood was renamed Al-Fahidi Historic District, taking the name of the city's historic fort located near the neighbourhood. Furthermore, news of the renaming was absent from local newspapers and barely traceable in a few blog posts interested in Dubai's built heritage.[56]

Transforming the Post-Modernist Architecture (1966 to 1990s)

Through his extensive work on Dubai's urban transformation over the past two decades, Khalid Alawadi, a scholar who focuses on sustainable urbanism, reveals that the city's post-2008 planning purposely destroyed many traditional neighbourhoods to expand its culture of excess and superlative architecture. Among the different case studies he explores, the destruction of Al-Satwa neighbourhood perfectly represents this approach to Dubai's urban development. Al-Satwa sits on Sheikh Zayed Road, an urban highway corridor and a few hundred metres away from Dubai's new downtown area, one of Emaar's major developments, housing the Burj Khalifa and Dubai Mall. According to Alawadi, Al-Satwa neighbourhood was originally planned in the late 1960s to provide subsidised housing for local Emirati families who were housed in the area until the early 1990s.[57] However, with the massive growth of the city's urban development, the size of the working class has increased dramatically, leading to a substantive socio-cultural transformation of Dubai's central area (comprised of Dubai's historical centre and its surrounding neighbourhoods), including Al-Satwa. As a result, the migration of local families to newer subsidised suburban residential areas enabled the working class to take control of the neighbourhood in the mid-1990s, accommodating since then labourers and low-income workers, mostly from India, Pakistan, Bangladesh, and the Philippines.[58]

In 2007 Al-Satwa neighbourhood was allocated to Meraas in order to transform it into a luxury district called Jumeirah Garden City, comprising high-end hotels and skyscrapers.[59] As the occupants of houses in Al-Satwa did not own them, they were relocated to other neighbourhoods in the city, and the original owners, who had left the neighbourhood long before, were compensated by the government. However, just after starting the demolition process of the existing buildings, the project was halted in 2008 due to the significant impact of the global financial crisis on Dubai.[60] It seems that today Meraas has resumed the execution of a new but less ambitious redevelopment plan for the neighbourhood as shown on its website:

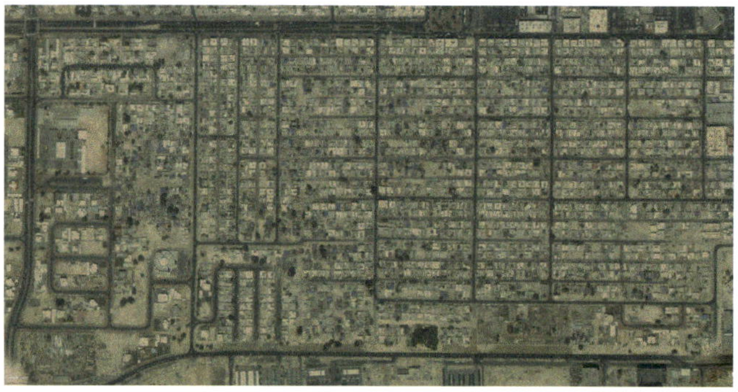
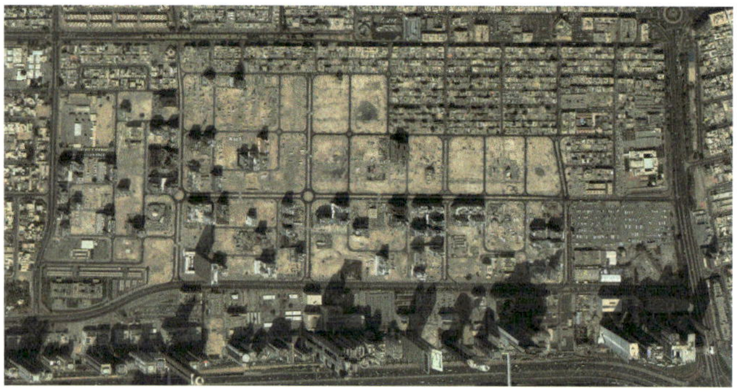
5 Satellite images showing Al-Satwa neighbourhood in 2007 and 2021.

> In line with Meraas' plans to revitalise Dubai's bustling Al-Satwa area, much of the area has undergone redevelopment. Following its comprehensive facelift, Jumeirah Garden City is set to emerge as a medium density, mixed-use neighbourhood that features residential apartments, retail spaces, public facilities, hotels and parks.[61]

Consequently, what has been described in 2008 as the «marvellous Manhattan of Dubai»,[62] has been reduced to a land subdivision project offering freehold ownership[63] of plots, and allowing a building height of G+8 following the Dubai Development Authority (DDA) planning rules and regulations and not those of Dubai municipality.

To further illustrate the magnitude and rapidity of the demolition in Al-Satwa, two satellite images (fig. 5) vividly depict the transformation that took place in the neighbourhood between 2007 and 2021. These images serve as visual evidence of the level of change and highlight the rapidly evolving urban landscape of Dubai (figs. 6 and 7).

6 Al-Satwa's traditional urban fabric in the foreground. The newer mid-rise buildings appear on the right side of the background.

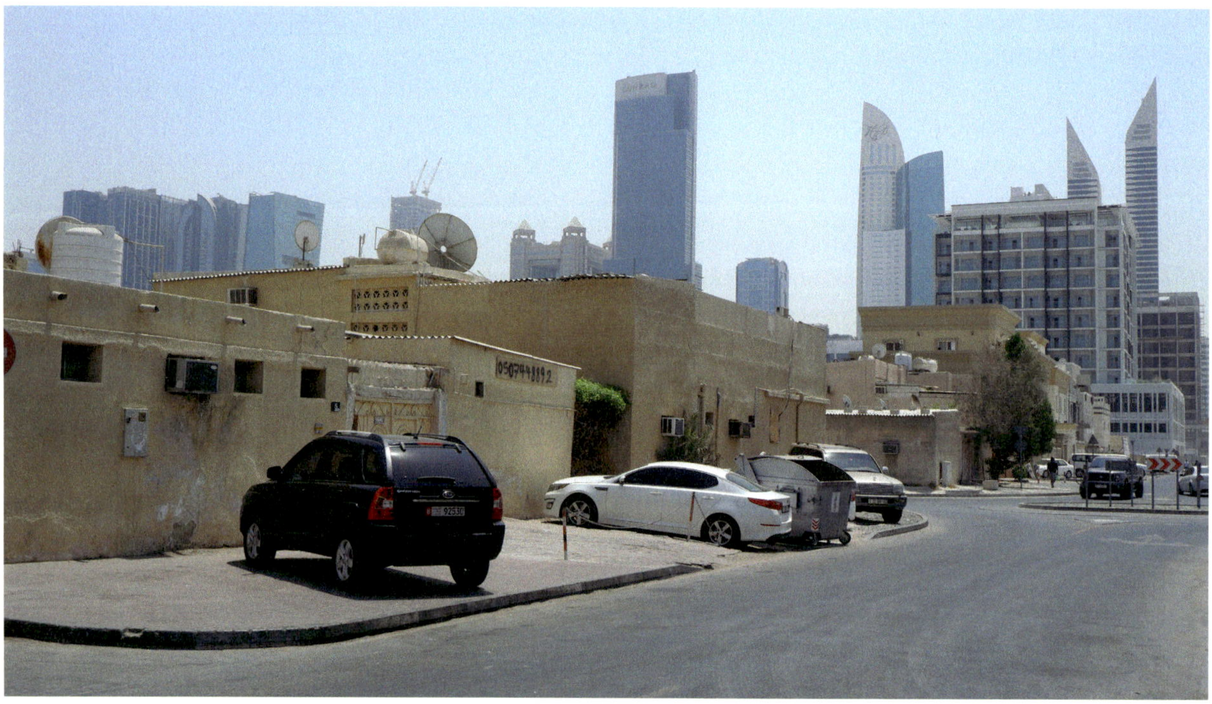

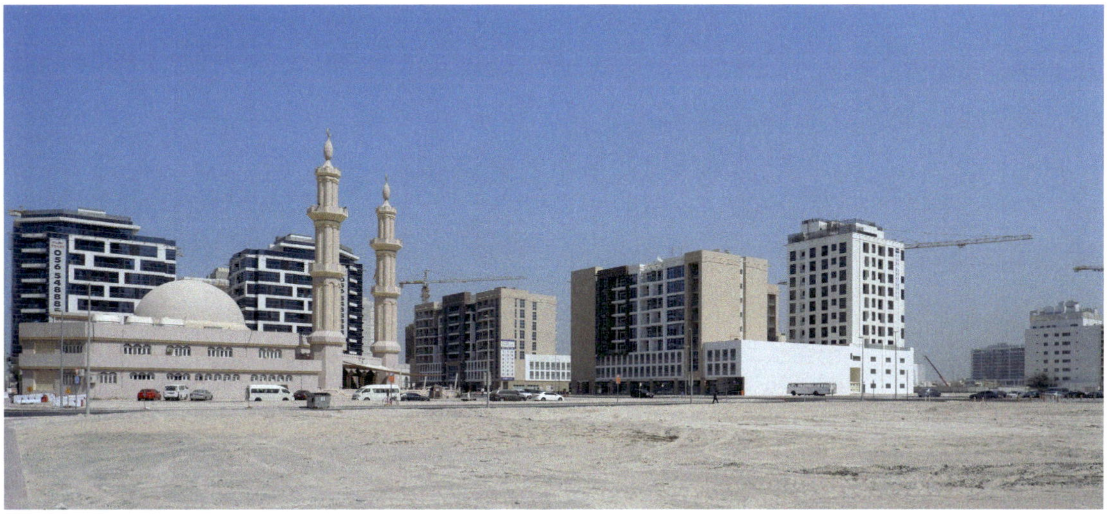

7 New buildings in Al-Satwa neighbourhood as per Meraas's updated redevelopment master plan.

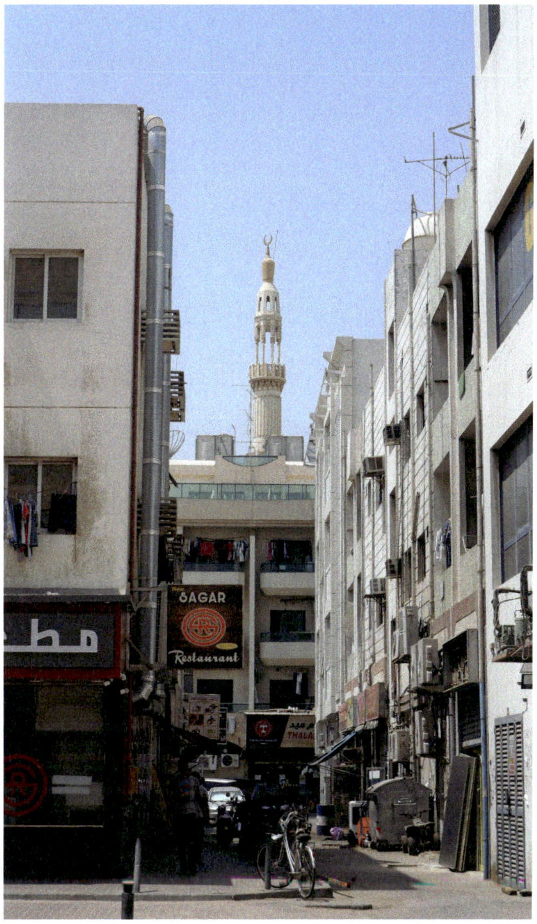

8 Al-Satwa urban fabric with its network of alleyways and narrow grid of low-rise buildings.

Despite the fact that some have seen in the destruction of Al-Bastakiya and Al-Satwa a way of transitioning to modernity by getting rid of an insalubrious neighbourhood, Al-Satwa is arguably one of the best performing neighbourhoods at the urban level. Its urban fabric characteristics offer a rich network of alleyways (locally called *sikkas*) and a narrow grid of low-rise buildings, which together provide high walking permeability and passive shading (fig. 8), thus promoting social interaction and economic activity on the street level.[64] These features of walkability are seldom seen in post-1990s urban planning, which prioritised highways, cars, and massive towers and parking spaces. In addition to these urban features, I argue that there is a unique architectural quality to the postmodern buildings built between the 1960s and 1970s (fig. 9) as well as the few remaining examples of the Arab or traditional houses with central courtyards (see fig. 6). Postmodernist and traditional houses showcase elements that were created by and for the local context of the city, which I would argue Dubai must protect, learn from, and integrate into its modern development projects.

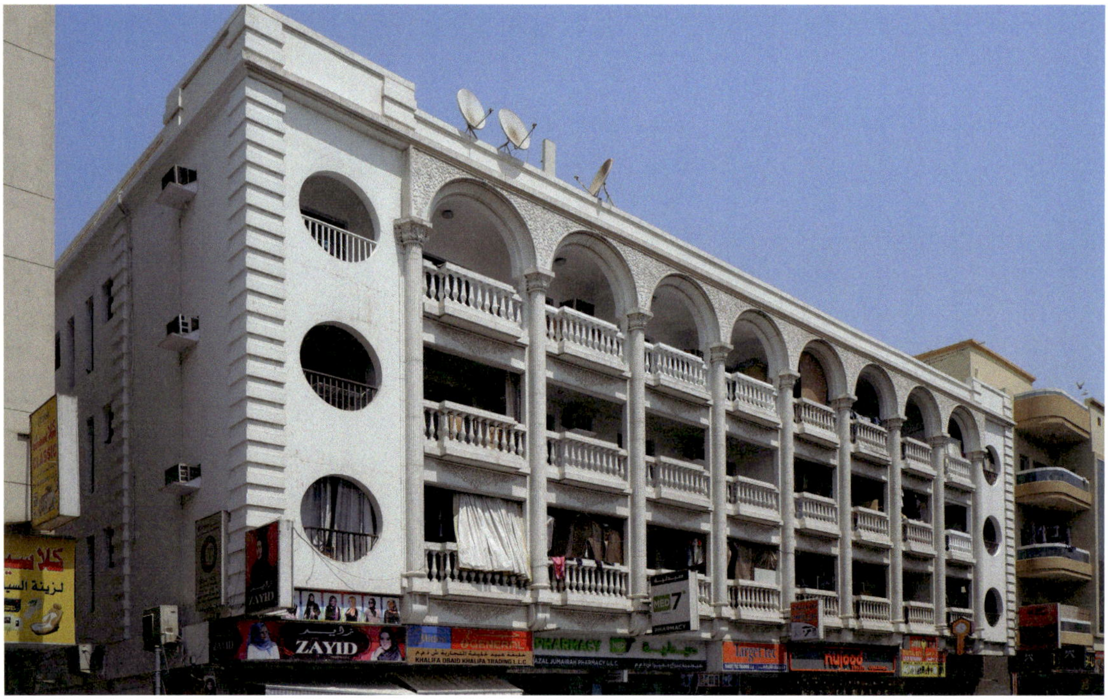

9 Example of a postmodernist building in Al-Satwa.

A Global City in the Making

The examination of the cases of Al-Bastakiya and Al-Satwa neighbourhoods reveals a significant imbalance between preservation and progress in Dubai's urban transformation as Al-Bastakiya faced demolition after its decline, while Al-Satwa witnessed a substantive socio-cultural transformation. These examples illustrate the intentional destruction of traditional neighbourhoods to make way for extravagant architecture and luxury developments, symbolising Dubai's culture of excess. As a result, I argue that for Dubai, the city of today is to be considered the heritage of tomorrow.

As I have demonstrated, Dubai has embarked on an ambitious journey to construct its envisioned future architectural and urban heritage since the beginning of the 21st century. Under the vision of its current Ruler, Dubai has presented a very specific image of the global city.[65] Extreme but not unique, the understanding of the so-called «Dubai model» offers us the opportunity to tell the story of a city in the making. Described as a living laboratory and the largest construction site in the world after Shanghai,[66] Dubai's urban development is characterised by an array of megaprojects, including the iconic palm-shaped islands and the towering Burj Khalifa. These megaprojects have propelled Dubai beyond its traditional image as an oil-based economy, aiming to compete with the world. Yet, even though Dubai has been equipped with a series of spatial urban plans since the early 1960s, the real dynamic behind the city's development remains the mega urban development projects. The city's growth has been spearheaded by the government-owned megadevelopers who leveraged the administrative flexibility of free zones, establishing their own authorities to regulate business licensing, infrastructure and urban planning, and the granting of building permits, circumventing the authority of

Dubai municipality. As a result, Nakheel's projects fall under the authority of the Ports, Customs and Free Zones Corporation (PCFC) established in 2001. Dubai Properties and Meraas projects are under the authority of the Dubai Creative Clusters Authority (DCCA), created in 2014 to manage all real estate projects under Dubai Holding and renamed the Dubai Development Authority (DDA) in 2018 (see fig. 3). As for Emaar, its projects are either under DDA if the development is in a free zone, or under Dubai municipality when the project takes place in Dubai's mainland.

As a result, and in the absence of an urban planning law, all spatial plans developed by the municipality were not legally binding, nor did Dubai municipality have the political power to enforce their implementation on these players, who were in fact representing the Ruler's economic and investment strategy itself. These new agents were committed to intensifying a new economic and urban development model, declaring Dubai a global city under construction. Moreover, the Ruler's tendency to make Dubai a unique model to follow has been reflected in his strong desire to invest in different economic sectors through the establishment of a multitude of government-owned holdings: a governance model often referred to as neoliberal, but really a form of state-monopoly capitalism fuelled by a growing appetite to invest through large state-owned firms.

Thus, I argue that this land of freedom for star-architects and urban development professionals, coupled with the abundance of financial resources of its ruling elite, facilitates the spectacularising of real estate megaprojects, which have become artificial symbols giving the illusion of a coherent urban policy. This is a phenomenon specific to Dubai, where questions such as the preservation of the existing historic urban fabric or the protection of the city's architectural heritage that highlights its modern urban history are not considered. Furthermore, planning is characterised by a vague and fragmented regulatory framework and the absence of laws[67] relating to the protection of the built heritage. This situation has naturally pushed Dubai's megadevelopers to make the least complex choices, either by developing empty land, the main reason behind Dubai's endless urban sprawl towards the desert, or by demolishing existing neighbourhoods that they feel have lost their shine and no longer reflect Dubai's brand to replace them with new projects, often involving the displacement of the low-income migrant population without facing objection or raising public debate, as I have shown in the case of Al-Satwa.

A Fragilised Global City

As I have argued in the previous section, Dubai's ruling elite has invested in an entrepreneurial strategy to promote the city since the end of the 20th century, representing its ultra-capitalist economic vision, debatably making Dubai a spectacular city, a land of freedom for architects and urban planning professionals, but at the same time producing a rather fragile and complex urban environment to manage. In fact, for Yasser Elsheshtawy, a scholar focusing on urbanisation in developing societies, especially in Middle Eastern cities:

> This vision looks at the city as a provider of real estate. A few state-owned developers – that is, the ruling family – divide available urban land and sell it to high-worth individuals. The result is a fragmented urban fabric geared toward exclusivity, where liveability and urbanity – in short, a sustainable urban environment – are issues that are dealt with, if at all, after the fact.[68]

For Khaled Alawadi, a specialist in Sustainable Urbanism, urban spaces in Dubai are produced for the fulfilment of the political interests, economic aspirations, and housing necessities of Emirati nationals. As a result, the private real estate developers control around 45 % of Dubai's urban land, with much of this land labelled as free economic zones in which non-nationals are allowed to own up to 100 % of the property or businesses and where land-use regulation can be redefined and adjusted by each free-zone authority.[69] Davide

Ponzini, a scholar focusing on urban and cultural policy, argues along with Alawadi that while bigness has emerged as a successful branding strategy for attracting international attention and capital to Dubai, the urban design derived from it has failed to create an integrated city fabric. Instead, it has generated a fragmented landscape made of disconnected patches, urban fabric broken up by large transportation infrastructure, and large swathes of vacant lands.[70]

In fact, in its aspiration to become a global city, Dubai has become since the beginning of the 1960s one of the most important destinations for massive flows of labour and migrants. As a result, Dubai continues to build its economy and reputation by importing knowledge and expertise in addition to attracting a vast unskilled labour force. In 2022, Dubai's migrant population represented 92 % of the 3.5 million people forming its total population (table 1). It is also a predominantly male population, comprised of 69 % men and only 31 % women (fig. 10),[71] mainly due to the large number of construction workers forming 26.5 % of Dubai's total workforce.[72] Similarly, in 2020, non-Emiratis represented 61 % out of the 92,206 employees working in Dubai's government entities.[73]

An increasingly fragmented workforce structure made up of a transnational, highly qualified elite and a «vast army of low-skilled workers»[74] contributes to the formation of this multicultural society,[75] continuously transforming the structure of the urban territory. Most of the mega-developers' projects were and are still designed to target the medium-high and high-income population, mainly investors seeking financial profitability from their real estate investments, western expatriates, and some socio-professional categories from Arab countries, resulting in a clear form of city-wide socio-spatial segregation. While the medium-to-high income population choose their places of residence according to their income and preferences, and while the national Emirati population live in exclusive subsidised neighbourhoods, low and middle-low-income workers, mainly from Southeast Asia, find themselves squeezed into either the historic districts of Deira and Bur Dubai, or into neighbourhoods developed in the 1970s and 80s such as Al-Satwa, originally designed for the middle-income expatriate population (fig. 11). In both cases, housing units in those areas are in poor condition and modern amenities and urban infrastructure are not properly provided.

Consequently, I argue that the urban development of the city, overtaken by its economic development, has led to a strong socio-spatial polarisation between its different social groups and, inevitably, to its fragmentation, making Dubai a series of cities within the city, through fragmentation of jurisdiction over urban development and land management among different authorities on one side, and socio-spatial polarisation between social groups on the other side. That is an additional specificity of urban planning in Dubai where geographical separation by class, profession, and function with its own distinct format of rights and

Table 1 Dubai population from 1881 until 2022.

1881	1902	1939	1953	1968	1971	1975	1985
12,000	15,000	20,000	50,000	59,000	95,880	183,187	370,778

1993	2000	2005	2010	2015	2020	2022
610,926	862,387	1,321,453	1,905,476	2,446,675	3,411,200	3,549,000

10 Dubai population pyramid in 2020.

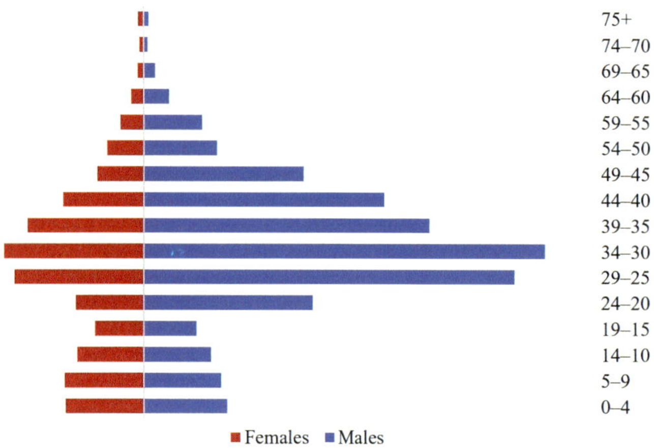

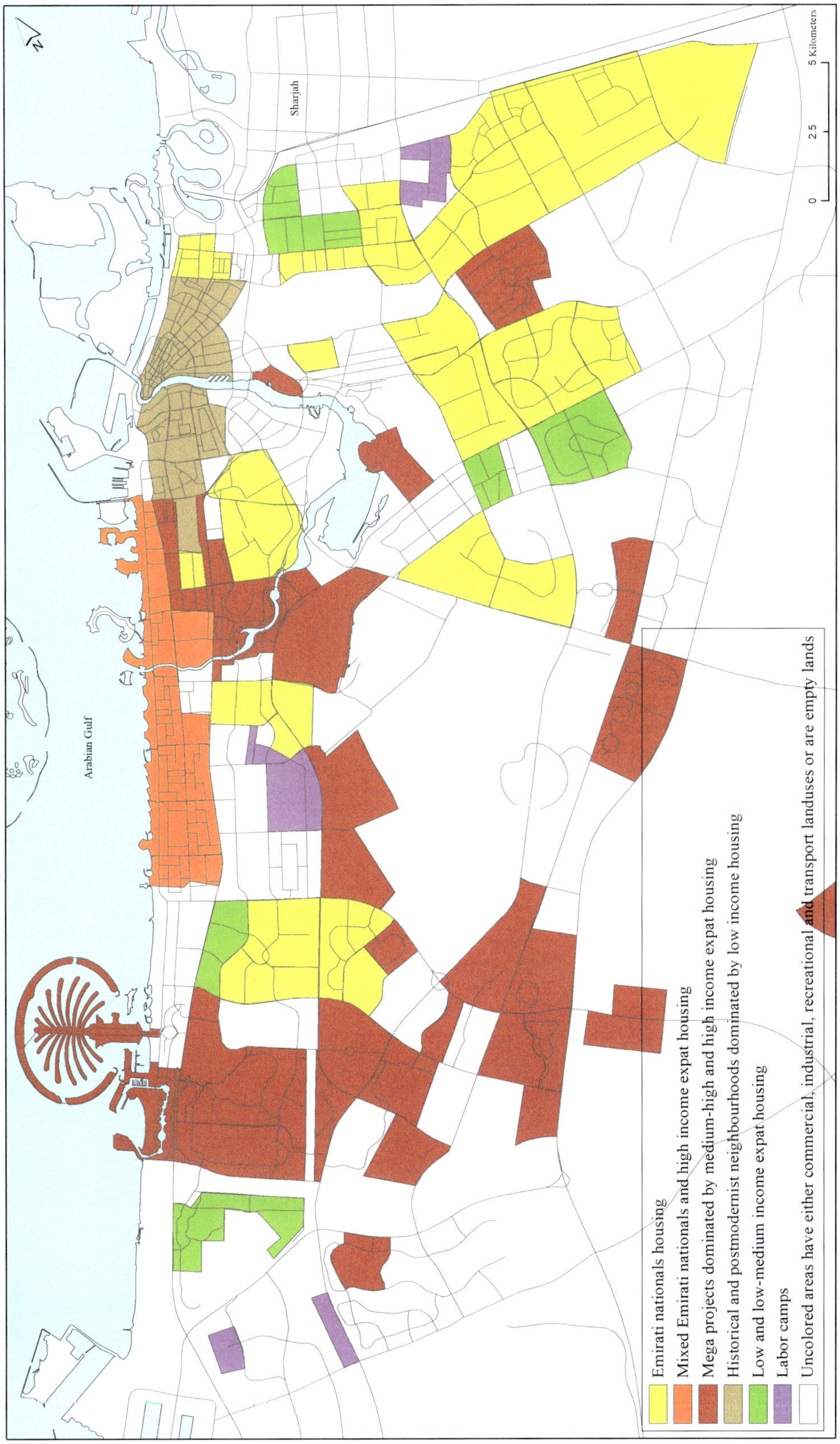

11 Socio-spatial segregation in Dubai.

privileges, takes place. Therefore, Dubai expands, elaborates, and makes formal separations as to who can be where and what is allowed in given spaces. When crafting inclusions or exclusions, authorities do not need to satisfy a voting public, political parties, or a civil society.[76]

Dubai: A Unique Model or the Result of an Incomplete Transformation Process?

Even though Middle Eastern cities offer an extremely rich historical accumulation, Davide Ponzini argues that mega-development projects in Gulf cities, especially Dubai and Abu Dhabi in the UAE, and Doha, the capital city of Qatar, are perceived and managed within a fundamentally weak planning system and, in terms of land use, aloof from the existing urban fabric.[77] For Steffen Hertog, a scholar who focuses on the political economy of the developing world, these large-scale real estate projects can be described as tools of economic diversification, vehicles of self-enrichment for the ruling elites, attempts to deepen strategic alliances with the world's economic powers, or simply princely follies driven by surpluses too large for a government to manage.[78] In fact, within the historically weak local expertise in urban planning, development actors in the region have always been dependent on an intense importation of foreign know-how.[79] With its abundant financial resources coming mainly from the oil business, Dubai offers an unprecedented opportunity to these international players. And given that land in Dubai is controlled by its Ruler, the highly centralised process of decision-making, limited political participation, and sufficient budgetary resources, the city faces few obstacles in implementing the vision of its leadership as architects and international design offices become readily available.

In that sense, Laura Lieto, a scholar focusing on urban informality and trans-national urbanism, argues that Dubai embodies its own characteristics since urban development professionals working in this city, along with other Gulf cities, do not really face the same constraints they have to deal with elsewhere, as issues such as environmental protection, for example, are not seen as a barrier to urban growth. Likewise, on the social level, since what is considered elsewhere as a claim to the right to the city does not pose obstacles to development, as a cultural right groups do not possess the power to insist much on protecting the vestiges of tangible memory. Consequently, questions such as revitalisation and gentrification have little impact. As a result, Dubai offers the galvanising idea of a «land of freedom» far from strict development guidelines and other normative constraints from a western professional elite point of view.[80] The city responds to the local ruling elite aspiration of a «world-class urban planning» where everything is brand new, unique, and emblematic.[81]

All of this leads to an unplanned approach in producing the city, where laws do not really matter, but rather the ruling elite presents itself as flexible and unique. In fact, throughout the history of Dubai's urban development, this principle of flexibility has been taken too far, perhaps in order not to restrict the megadevelopers, which are mainly owned by the Ruler. At the same time, the succession of Dubai's urban master plans did not offer enough tools to control the city's development. If this recurring quality in the political discourse of the ruling elite and the urban development professionals means a certain level of agility to adapt to constantly changing circumstances, it would also signify informality and the absence of a precise form of a decision-making process. Thus, this quality gives the ruling elite enough leeway to organise the city according to their vision, or rather their own interests and those of the market. As a result, I argue that Dubai's development process did not ensure the synergy between the role of best practices and the specificities of the city itself, as it continues to import new experiences deemed successful elsewhere because, for its ruling elite, there is no time for trial and error. Hence the city runs the risk of easily losing its attractiveness when financial and spatial resources are no longer available for Dubai to reinvent itself.

Conclusion

In an attempt to position their cities globally and strengthen their competitive abilities, political leaders and ruling elites are undertaking major investments in the form of large-scale urban development projects. These megaprojects come as a response to the restructuring of global capitalism, in which large cities have become «key nodes of accumulation».[82] In that perspective, the role of transnational models and their links to megaprojects and mega-events appear as an important aspect in how these megaprojects emerge and are articulated in the development objectives of these cities.[83] Although the concept of megaprojects is not recent, it is currently resurging in both the Global North and Global South. But if in most of the northern cities, mayors and local political leaders envision megaprojects as a response to meet the needs of a growing population, with deteriorating facilities or access to technology, water, and energy,[84] megaprojects in emerging countries may have other ideological objectives insofar as they denote the possibility of policy innovation that may go beyond economic motivations,[85] at the same time fuelling real estate speculation, urban sprawl, displacement of population, and an increase in environmental risks.[86] To conclude, I summarise the major findings discussed in this chapter that are specific to the urban transformation of Dubai in regard to the city's pursuit of global positioning through large-scale projects.

Firstly, the urban transformation of Dubai encapsulates the pursuit of global positioning and competitive advantage through large-scale urban development projects. These megaprojects, influenced by transnational models and ideologies of urban growth, have shaped the norms and aspirations of what constitutes a global city. However, as I have shown, the consequences of these projects in Dubai are complex and multifaceted. The fragmented nature of Dubai is evident in its geography, architecture, social fabric, and administrative structure, highlighting the challenges related to a sense of community and cohesion. Consequently, Dubai became a mosaic of real estate megaprojects housing a group or groups of expatriates that the ruling elite does not see the need to transform into a real society. Thus, this transient population, with its highly paid expatriates and low-income workers, has no rights outside of the labour law. As a result, Dubai's cities within the city do not pose any societal issue, as the concern to ensure their cohesion around the same system of values does not exist.

Secondly, the city's approach to historic architecture reveals a selective emphasis on attractive and visually appealing forms rather than a comprehensive commitment to preservation. These observations highlight the intricate dynamics between Dubai's aspiration for global recognition and the complexities it faces in balancing progress, heritage, and social cohesion. As I have shown, throughout its history Dubai has embraced various urban styles and periods to fit its global vision. The city has simultaneously embellished, destroyed, and created urban spaces from the pre-1966 period of urbanisation within historic neighbourhoods, to the post-oil era of 1966–1990 dominated by postmodern architecture, and finally the present-day focus on megadevelopments. This process underscores the significance of discussing these three distinct periods and urban styles, as they have contributed to shaping the city's identity and character.

Thirdly and finally, while Dubai is showcasing its pre-1966 architecture for tourism and economic purposes as I have shown in the case of Al-Bastakiya, it is evident that the city is less concerned about preserving all kinds of built heritage forms and more focused on avoiding plain or unattractive urban spaces as shown in the case of Al-Satwa. This approach aligns with the overall objective of projecting a modern, vibrant, and futuristic image to the international community.

1 Davidson 2008, 12–13; Wilson 2006, 29. A political resident was a diplomatic position that included consular and liaison duties in the British Empire.
2 Ramos 2009, 1.
3 Owen 2008, as cited in Ramos 2009, 1.
4 Ramos 2009, 4. According to historians, the Gulf was part of Britain's informal empire to protect the British India trade and communication routes. However, academia usually refers to the mainstream narrative around the British presence in the Gulf and overlooks theories about the nature of the British imperialism in the region. If for the British, the attacks on their ships carried out by the local tribes were considered piracy, for the tribes it was their response to the refusal of the British to pay the tolls levied by local tribes on all shipping in and out of the Gulf. Thus, the defeated local tribes ended up signing an anti-piracy treaty, which is nothing but the General Treaty of Peace of 1820, that the British imposed on them. Subsequently, the rulers of the Trucial States signed the Perpetual Maritime Truce in 1835 followed by exclusive agreements with the British, not only to give up their rights to wage war by sea in return for British protection against maritime aggression, but bounding them into exclusive political relations with, and ceded control of their external affairs to, the British Government. This arrangement cast Britain in the roles of protector, mediator, arbiter, and guarantor of settlements, until leaving the Gulf in 1971 (Onley 2005).
5 Davidson 2008, 22–23; Gabriel 1987, 139; Lorimer 1970.
6 Onley 2007.
7 Alaydrus 1998, 204.
8 According to Alsayegh, Dubai claimed the greatest number of men working in fishing and pearl trading in the region with 6,936 workers and 335 ships, thus becoming the economic and commercial centre of the Trucial States towards the end of the 19th century (Alsayegh 1998, 89).
9 Alsayegh 1998, 89.
10 Gabriel 1987, 71.
11 Alaydrus 1998, 170–175.
12 A traditional Persian architectural element used to create natural ventilation in buildings. This wind tower works due to the low-pressure difference between the base and the top of the column. Thus, each time the wind blows through the top of the column, the pressure difference helps in lifting warm air up the top and bringing cool air down the column. It is usually constructed with adobe: a mixture of clay, straw, and water, a natural material that has strong heat storage and emission capacities which facilitate the extraction of hot air (Dehghan Kamaragi 2014).
13 Alsayegh 1998, 93.
14 Alsayegh 1998, 90.
15 Ramos 2009, 8.
16 Arabic for the port bazaar.
17 Mathew 2014, 54.
18 French 1990, 220.
19 Alabed 2001, 121.
20 Mayo et al. 2010, 3.
21 Pacione 2005, 256.
22 Pacione 2005, 258.
23 An Emirati national with full citizenship is any Arab who was settled in any of the seven member emirates of the UAE during or before 1925, and who has maintained his residency there until the enforcement of Federal Law number 17 of 1972 on Nationality and Passports. The 1925 date was chosen because oil had not yet been discovered then, and thus the Emirati population at that moment would not include those who immigrated later, attracted by the promises of wealth associated with oil extraction. However, Emirati nationals who cannot prove their ancestry in the UAE prior to 1925 are considered second-class citizens: they own a passport issued by one of the seven emirates, but cannot enjoy the same range of benefits as full citizens such as low or no taxation, subsidised water and electricity, free public education and healthcare, land and subsidised loans to build homes. Another category of Emirati natives are the «bedoon» or stateless. Most of these people belong to Bedouin and nomad groups who used to move within the borders of the UAE and its neighbouring countries. They were not issued citizenship documents or passports as the British administration during the 1950s found the process difficult and tedious. Once the UAE federation was established and gained independence in 1971, they could not demonstrate their citizenship. In 2008, the government gave them a passport from the Comoro Islands instead of offering them citizenship. The stateless are also unable to enjoy any citizen rights. Jamal 2015, 621–622.
24 Pacione 2005, 257.
25 Pacione 2005, 259.
26 Pacione 2005, 259.
27 Ramos 2009, 17.
28 Ramos 2009, 12.
29 Ramos 2009, 13.
30 Ramos 2009, 13.
31 Reisz 2021, 115–117.
32 Pacione 2005, 260.
33 Ramos 2009, 14.
34 Balfour-Paul 1991; Hamza 1968, as cited in Ramos 2009, 14.
35 Ramos 2009, 14.
36 Pacione 2005, 260.
37 Davidson 2008, 145.
38 Mayo et al. 2010, 447–448.
39 Mayo et al. 2010, 7.
40 Kanna 2011, 142.
41 Jebel Ali Free Zone Authority n.d.
42 Kazerouni 2017. A public offering means putting the company's shares on the stock market.
43 Moody 2008.
44 Mayo et al. 2010, 8.
45 Ellis 2007.
46 Mayo et al. 2010, 8.

47 Barthe 2017.
48 «60 Minutes» is a television news magazine broadcast on CBS, an American commercial broadcast television and radio network.
49 Sheikh Mohammed bin Rashid Al Maktoum, interviewed by Steve Croft on CBS «60 Minutes: Dubai Inc.», originally broadcast on October 2007.
50 Anne Coles and Peter Jackson (2007), as cited in Elsheshtawy 2010, 78.
51 Elsheshtawy 2010, 78–79.
52 Elsheshtawy 2010, 79.
53 Dhal 2009.
54 Sabith 2022.
55 Reuters 2008.
56 Dubai FAQs 2014.
57 Alawadi 2014, 358.
58 Alawadi 2014, 362.
59 Hope 2009.
60 Alawadi 2014, 364.
61 Meraas n.d.
62 Flashy Dubai 2008.
63 Freehold ownership grants the owner an absolute ownership of the property and the land on which it is built with no time restrictions. Properties referred to as freehold in Dubai are those located in designated areas in which non-nationals can enjoy absolute ownership of the property.
64 Elsheshtawy 2010, 225; Alawadi 2018.
65 According to Saskia Sassen, a global city is characterised by its role as a strategic site for the coordination and control of global economic activities. It serves as a hub for advanced business services, finance, and specialised functions that facilitate the operations of transnational corporations and global networks. Global cities are distinguished by their capacity to attract and concentrate high-skilled professionals, global capital, and cultural diversity, creating an environment conducive to innovation, knowledge exchange, and economic competitiveness on a global scale (Sassen 2001).
66 Davis 2007, 8.
67 To the knowledge of the author at the time of writing this chapter, Dubai lacks any legislative text (law or decree) that regulates the classification and protection of antiquities, archaeological sites, and historical buildings.
68 Elsheshtawy 2019, 235.
69 Alawadi et al. 2018, 118.
70 Ponzini/Alawadi 2021, 6.
71 Dubai Statistics Center 2020a.
72 Dubai Statistics Center 2019.
73 Dubai Statistics Center 2020b.
74 John Friedmann (1986), as cited in Lieto 2019, 130.
75 Lieto 2019, 130.
76 Molotch/Pozini 2019, 306-307.
77 Ponzini 2019, 91.
78 Hertog 2019, 276.
79 Aoun/Teller 2016.
80 Rob Imrie and Emma Street (2011), as cited in Lieto 2019, 136.
81 Lieto 2019, 135-136.
82 Harvey 1989; Neil Brenner (1998, 2004), as cited in Kennedy 2015, 163.
83 Kennedy 2015, 166.
84 Olds 2001.
85 Healey 1986.
86 Paul Gellert and Barbara Lynch (2003), as cited in Kennedy 2015, 164.

Alabed 2001
I. Alabed: The historical background and constitutional basis to the federation, in: I. Alabed / P. Hellyer (eds.): United Arab Emirates: a new perspective (London 2001) 121–144.

Alawadi 2014
K. Alawadi: Urban redevelopment trauma: The story of a Dubai neighbourhood. Built Environment 40, no. 3, 2014, 357–375.

Alawadi 2018
K. Alawadi: Lifescapes Beyond Bigness (London 2018).

Alawadi et al. 2018
K. Alawadi / A. Khanal / A. Almulla: Land, urban form and politics: A study on Dubai's housing landscape and rental affordability. Cities 81, 2018, 115–130.

Alaydrus 1998
محمد حسن العيدروس: تاريخ الخليج العربي الحديث والمعاصر.
M. Alaydrus: Modern and Contemporary History of the Arabian Gulf (Kuwait 1998).

Alsayegh 1998
F. Alsayegh: Merchants' role in a changing society: The case of Dubai, 1900–90. Middle Eastern Studies 34, no. 1, 1998, 87–102.

Aoun / Teller 2016
O. Aoun / J. Teller: Planning urban megaprojects in the Gulf: The international consultancy firms in urban planning between global and contingent. Frontiers of Architectural Research 5, 2016, 254–264.

Balfour-Paul 1991
G. Balfour-Paul: The end of empire in the Middle East. Britain's relinquishment of power in her last three Arab dependencies (Cambridge 1991).

Barthe 2017
B. Barthe: Dubaïland, vertigineuse folie d'un magicien de l'immobilier. Le Monde, 7 August 2017.

Davidson 2008
C. Davidson: Dubai: The Vulnerability of Success (New York 2008).

Davis 2007
M. Davis: Le stade Dubaï du capitalisme (Paris 2007).

Dehghan Kamaragi 2014
G. Dehghan Kamaragi: Les systèmes de ventilation et refroidissement dans l'architecture traditionnelle du golfe persique, histoire des dispositifs, modélisation, évaluation des performances. Ph.D. thesis, Université Paris-Est [online, 2014], https://theses.hal.science/tel-03435253.

Dhal 2009
S. Dhal: Expressions in time: A slice of history. Gulf News, 5 November 2009 [online, 2009], https://gulfnews.com/general/expressions-in-time-a-slice-of-history-1.523634.

Dubai FAQs 2014
Dubai FAQs: Bastakiya - Al Fahidi Historical Neighbourhood, Dubai. Dubai FAQs, 11 September 2014 [online, 2014], https://www.dubaifaqs.com/bastakiya.php.

Dubai Statistics Center 2019
Dubai Statistics Center: Percentage Distribution of Employed Persons by Main Economic Activity and Gender [online, 2019], https://www.dsc.gov.ae/Report/DSC_SYB_2019_03%20_%2002.pdf (21 March 2021).

Dubai Statistics Center 2020a
Dubai Statistics Center: Population by Gender [online, 2020], https://www.dsc.gov.ae/Report/DSC_SYB_2020_01_01.pdf (21 March 2021).

Dubai Statistics Center 2020b
Dubai Statistics Center: Distribution of Employed Persons by Nationality [online, 2020], https://www.dsc.gov.ae/Report/DSC_SYB_2020_03_05.pdf (21 March 2021).

Dubai Statistics Center 2020c
Dubai Statistics Center: Population by Gender and Age Groups [online, 2020], https://www.dsc.gov.ae/Report/DSC_SYB_2020_01_05.pdf (21 March 2021).

Ellis 2007
D. Ellis: Meteoric rise of Dubai drydocks. Lloyd's List, 14 June 2007.

Elsheshtawy 2010
Y. Elsheshtawy: Dubai: behind an urban spectacle (London 2010).

Elsheshtawy 2019
Y. Elsheshtawy: Real estate speculation and transnational development in Dubai, in: H. Molotch / D. Ponzini (eds.): The New Arab Urban (New York 2019) 235–255.

Flashy Dubai 2008
Flashy Dubai: Jumeirah Garden City: Marvelous Manhattan of Dubai. Flashy Dubai, 2 December 2008 [online, 2008], https://flashydubai.com/jumeirah-garden-city-marvelous-manhattan-of-dubai/.

French 1990
D. French: The British Way in Warfare, 1688–2000 (London 1990).

Gabriel 1987
E. Gabriel: The Dubai Handbook (Ahrensburg 1987).

Hamza 1968
K. Hamza: Dubai: The pearl of the coast. Al Massaref Magazine (Beirut 1968).

Healey 1986
P. Healey: Diffusion of the new town idea in the developing world, in: I. Masser et al. (eds.): Learning from other countries: the cross-national dimension in urban policy-making (Norwich 1986) 125–137.

Hertog 2019
S. Hertog: A quest for significance, in: Molotch / Ponzini 2019, 276–299.

Hope 2009
B. Hope: Meraas cuts back Jumeira Gardens. The National News, 4 March 2009 [online, 2009], https://www.thenationalnews.com/business/property/meraas-cuts-back-jumeira-gardens-1.491588/.

Jamal 2015
M. Jamal: The «tiering» of citizenship and residency and the «hierarchization» of migrant communities: The United Arab Emirates in historical context. The International Migration Review 49, no. 3, 2015, 601–632.

Jebel Ali Free Zone Authority n.d.
Jebel Ali Free Zone Authority: About us [online, n.d.], http://jafza.ae/about-us/.

Kanna 2011
A. Kanna: Dubai, the city as corporation (Minneapolis 2011).

Kazerouni 2017
A. Kazerouni: Le miroir des Cheikhs (Paris 2017).

Kennedy 2015
L. Kennedy: The politics and changing paradigm of megaproject development in metropolitan cities. Habitat International 45, 2015, 163–168.

Lieto 2019
L. Lieto: Planning for the hybrid gulf city, in: Molotch / Ponzini 2019, 130–146.

Lorimer 1970
J. Lorimer: Gazetteer of the Persian Gulf, Oman, and Central Arabia (London 1970).

Mathew 2014
N. Mathew: Understanding Space, Politics and History in the Making of Dubai, a Global City. Ph.D. Thesis, University of the Witwatersrand [online, 2014], https://core.ac.uk/download/pdf/39675585.pdf.

Mayo et al. 2010
A. Mayo et al.: Sheikh Mohammed and the making of Dubai, Inc. Harvard Business School Case 410-063, Harvard, 2010.

Meraas n.d.
Meraas: Lands and Plots [online, n.d.], https://www.meraas.com/en/real-estate/lands-and-plots/al-satwa.

Molotch / Ponzini 2019
H. Molotch / D. Ponzini: The New Arab Urban (New York 2019).

Moody 2008
A. Moody: The universe up for sale? The Observer, 15 June 2008.

Olds 2011
K. Olds: Globalization and urban change: capital, culture, and Pacific Rim mega-projects (Oxford 2001).

Onley 2005
J. Onley: Britain's informal empire in the Gulf, 1820–1971. Journal of Social Affairs 22, no. 87, 2005, 29–45.

Onley 2007
J. Onley: The Arabian frontier of the British Raj: merchants, rulers, and the British in the nineteenth century Gulf (Oxford 2007).

Owen 2008
R. Owen: Cities of the Persian Gulf: past, present and future. Lecture delivered at the University of Nicosia, Nicosia, 14 October 2008.

Pacione 2005
M. Pacione: City Profile Dubai. Cities 22, no. 3, 2005, 255–265.

Ponzini 2019
D. Ponzini: Mobilities of urban spectacle, in: Molotch / Ponzini 2019, 79–96.

Ponzini / Alawadi 2021
D. Ponzini / K. Alawadi: Transnational mobilities of the tallest building: origins, mobilization and urban effects of Dubai's Burj Khalifa. European Planning Studies 30, no. 1, 141–159 [online, 2021], https://doi.org/10.1080/09654313.2021.1908233.

Ramos 2009
S. Ramos: The blueprint: a history of Dubai's spatial development through oil discovery. Harvard Kennedy School, Harvard [online, 2009], https://www.belfercenter.org/publication/blueprint-history-dubais-spatial-development-through-oil-discovery (27 February 2025).

Reisz 2021
T. Reisz: Showpiece city: How architecture made Dubai (Stanford 2021).

Reuters 2008
Reuters: Old Dubai clings to life as new city rises. Reuters, 28 May 2008 [online, 2008], https://www.reuters.com/article/us-emirates-dubai-bastakiya-idUSL1442874320080528/.

Sabith 2022
S. Sabith: Historical Al Fahidi neighbourhood to be revitalised announces Dubai Crown Prince. Middle East Architect, 10 January 2022 [online, 2022], https://www.middleeastarchitect.com/insight/al-fahidi-rennovation-announced.

Sassen 2001
S. Sassen: The global city: New York, London, Tokyo, 2nd ed. (Princeton 2001).

Wilson 2006
G. Wilson: Rashid's legacy: The genesis of the Maktoum family and the history of Dubai (Dubai 2006).

Image Sources

1, 2, 11 S. Ibrahim 2023. All three maps were drawn based on publicly available information, personal observations, and field visits conducted by the author between 2017 and 2022. Therefore, information shown in the maps might not be fully accurate as it partially reflects the author's observations.

3 S. Ibrahim, 2021. Information gathered from a number of the listed sources in the bibliography.

4 Photo by S. Ibrahim, 2023.

5 Google Earth.

6–9 Photos by S. Ibrahim, 2021.

Table 1 Dubai Statistics Centre 2020a.

10 Dubai Statistics Centre 2020c.

The Historic Urban Landscapes of Shiraz
Visualising the City's Skyline Evolution

Farnaz Mohseni

The city of Shiraz in the south of Iran, with a history of more than fourteen centuries as an urban settlement, has long been admired because of its remarkable skyline. During a period of almost a millennium and a half, the overall landscape of the city has changed frequently. Significant landmarks, such as gardens, mosques, and bazaars, were built, demolished, or renovated, while the city's borders were subject to massive alterations.[1] Although dynamic throughout its history, Shiraz's urban landscape has developed at a rapidly increasing pace over the past century.[2] As a result of rapid urban growth, the preservation of the historic landscape of Shiraz is a matter of concern.[3]

Given this background, it is of premium importance to understand the evolutionary process of Shiraz's macro[4] landscape development over time and especially in the modern era. Based on the author's previous quantitative study of the different driving forces shaping Shiraz's urban landscape over time,[5] this chapter presents the results of that study in a more accessible way in order to reach a wider audience. As a result, this chapter researches the evolution of Shiraz's skyline over the city's history, and particularly during the past century, relying on scientific and systematic visualisation techniques.

The sensory, particularly visual, dimension of the landscape plays an integral role in perceiving the environment.[6] Mapping and visualising the landscape is defined as a tool to narrate, comprehend, and illuminate the spatial–visual characteristics of the scene.[7] Therefore, visualisation techniques are commonly applied in planning and landscape design as a decision-making tool to facilitate communication between lay people and experts.[8] Another application of landscape visualisation is to reconstruct the process of landscape change over the course of time through qualitative and quantitative methods of historical analysis.[9] A wide range of techniques for landscape mapping and visualisation are currently available, including hand drawings, computer-based 3D modelling, compartment analysis, grid cell analysis, and virtual reality.[10]

Both 3D visualisation methods of sketching and computer-based technologies have advantages and disadvantages. While objective digitalised visualisations and hyper-real renders can capture the precise details of the landscape, they can be time-consuming, complicated, and expensive. By contrast, analogue drawings can be made quickly and have the advantage of demonstrating an artistic taste that supports speculation through a less detailed representation of the landscape with openness for gaps in the illustrations. However, sketches can be regarded as a subjective method.[11] All in all, the most suitable visualisation technique depends on the task and must be tailored for the purpose of the research or project.[12]

This study uses hand-made visualisations and sketches to investigate the process of urban landscape formation in Shiraz. A list of landmarks constructed in each period and their location was extracted by relying on historical documents. Thirteen maps of Shiraz landmarks belonging to thirteen spans of the city were produced. Subsequently, twelve hand-drawn sketches were made based on the maps and the list of monuments. Finally, a qualitative analysis of the evolution of the Shiraz landscape was conducted based on the drawings.

Methodology

Shiraz, located in the Fars Province in the south of Iran, has a long and eventful history dating back to the 7th century. The city was known for its eye-catching urban macro landscape, reported and depicted by many historians and travellers centuries ago. The view of Shiraz from the Quran Gate in the northeast of the city, in particular, is repeatedly mentioned in historical sources as an outstanding and welcoming scene.[13] Since the Quran Gate at the Allaho Akbar Valley, the city's main entrance, is located on an elevation on the north-eastern hillside, the observer is provided with an expansive view over Shiraz with all its gardens and blue domes. However, rapid urban growth during the past century has negatively affected Shiraz's remarkable macro landscape by destroying historic structures or blocking the view of the city's monuments.[14]

Consequently, this chapter aims to investigate the evolution of Shiraz's landscape over time and the effects of contemporary developments. Shiraz's skyline in twelve historical periods, from the 7th century up until the 21st century, is evaluated in the form of twelve precise watercolour sketches of the city's landscape at the macro level. The major landmarks in each span were allocated accurately in the paintings by adopting a systematic approach. These twelve hand-drawn illustrations go beyond the pure free-style sketches often used in brainstorming in urban design. In order to paint the urban scenes close to reality, four systematic and structured steps were conducted as follows:

Step 1

A comprehensive investigation of the history of gardening, architecture, and urban planning in Shiraz was undertaken based on primary and secondary sources.[15] A comprehensive list of landmarks built in each period was produced (table 1).

	The landmarks	Pre-Islamic	Early Islamic / Saffarid / Abbasid	Daylamite / Shabankara Rulers	Seljuks	Atabaks	Ilkhanate / Injuid / Muzaffarid	Timurid / Kara Koyunlu/Ak Koyunlu	Safavid	Hotak / Safavid II / Afsharid	Zand	Qajar	Pahlavi	Islamic Republic
1	Delgosha Garden	x				x			x	x		x	x	x
2	Mortaz Ali T.	x							x			x	!	!
3	Bandar Fortress	x		x		x	x	x						
4	Abu Nasr Castle	x												
5	Atiq Mosque		x	x		x	x	x	x			x	!	!
6	Saadi (Eastern) Bridge		x	x	x	x	x	x	x	x	x	x		
7	Ali bin Hamzeh Bridge		x	x	x	x	x	x	x	x	x	x	!	!
8	Ali bin Hamzeh T.			x		x		x	x	x	x	x	x	x
9	Baba Kouhi T.			x		x	x		x			x	x	x
10	Haji Bazaar			x		x	x						!	!
11	Gahvareh Did (Div)			x					x			x	x	x
12	Quran Gate			x					x		x	x	x	x
13	Sheikh Kabir T.			x		x	x	x	x	x				
14	Adudi Dome			x	x	x								
15	Kard-i Fannā Khusraw and Suq al-Amir			x										
16	Shiraz defensive wall			x	x	x	x	x			x	x		
17	Adudi Palace and G.			x										
18	East Sabouh abaad G.			x					x					
19	Eram Garden				x				x		x	x	x	x
20	Saadi Khanqah / T.				x	x	x	x	x		x	x	x	x
21	Qaracheh School and G. (later Takht G.)				x	x		x	x			x		
22	Zahedeh School				x	x								
23	* Taji School				x	x								
24	Mankoubras School				x	x								
25	Shah Cheragh T.					x	x	x	x	x	x	x	x	x
26	Mohammad bin Musa T.					x		x	x	x	x	x	x	x
27	Sunquri G. (later Khold-e Barin Park)					x						x		x
28	Atabak G. (Nov Mosque)					x		x	x		x	x	x	
29	Qatlaq G. (Seyyed Alaoddin Hossein T.)					x			x	x	x	x	x	x
30	Sunquri Mosque					x	x							
31	Sunquri Bazaar					x								
32	Square Atabaki Bazaar and Suq Kabir					x								
33	Sar-e Hoz-e Aqa Bazaar					x			x					
34	North Sabouh abaad G.					x								
35	Bibi Dokhtaroon T.						x	x	x		x	x	!	!
36	Jahan nama G.						x		x		x	x	x	x
37	Takht-e Zarrabi						x		x			x	!	!
38	Sheikh Hasan Kia T. and Sheikh Abubakr Allaf T.						x	x	x					
39	Mahmud Shah T.						x							
40	Majd-e Roumi Ribbat						x		x					
41	Abish Khatoon T.						x		x	x	x	x		
42	Jaafar abaad Castle						x		x					
43	Shah abu Ishaq Castle						x							
44	Haji Rokn od-Din Razgou T.						x							
45	Toqa G.						x							
46	Majd-e Roumi G.						x							
47	* Eghbal abaad G.						x							
48	Hafez T.							x	x	x	x	x	x	x
49	Golshan G. (later Afif abaad G.)							x	x			x	x	x
50	Qasr od-Dasht village and Gardens							x	x			x	x	x
51	Davood Khan (later Mesgar ha) Bazaar								x			x	!	!
52	The Nov (Isfahan Gate) Bazaar								x			x		
53	Seyyed Tajoddin Qarib T.								x				x	x
54	Jenazeh (later Vakil) Mosque								x		x	x	x	!
55	Chehel tan G.								x		x	x	x	x

The landmarks	Pre-Islamic	Early Islamic / Saffarid / Abbasid	Daylamite / Shabankara Rulers	Seljuks	Atabaks	Ilkhanate / Injuid / Muzaffarid	Timurid / Kara Koyunlu/Ak Koyunlu	Safavid	Hotak / Safavid II / Afsharid	Zand	Qajar	Pahlavi	Islamic Republic
56 Haft tan G.								x		x	x	x	x
57 The original Nazar G.								x		x	x	x	x
58 Nari G.								x				x	x
59 Imamzadeh Abdollah T.								x				!	!
60 Dar al-Salam Cemetery								x		x	x	x	x
61 Khan School								x			x	x	!
62 Imam Qoli Castle								x					
63 Hafez Chahar bagh								x					
64 Baghshah Chahar bagh								x			x		
65 The Nov G.								x		x	x		
66 Padeshah-e Kachal G.								x					
67 Khold-e Barin G.								x					
68 Qavam abaad G.								x				x	x
69 Salari G.								x	x		x		
70 Kalantari G.								x	x		x	x	
71 Aqa baba Khani G.								x		x	x		
72 Derki G.								x					
73 Baghshah								x					
74 * Fath abaad G.								x					
75 * Eish abaad G.								x					
76 * Hosein abaad G.								x					
77 * Golab kadeh G.								x					
78 * Hasan beigi G.								x					
79 * Sharaf G.								x					
80 * Saad abaad Khargahi G.								x					
81 * Barekat G.								x					
82 * Mahmoud abaad G.								x					
83 * Kholjan G.								x					
84 Vakil Bazaar										x	x	x	!
85 Karim Khan Citadel										x	x	x	!
86 Aqa baba Khan Mosque										x	x	!	!
87 Aqa baba Khan (Vakil) School										x	x	!	!
88 Mir Hamzeh Carvanserai										x	x		
89 Naqqarakhaneh Building										x	x		
90 Abu al-Fath Khani G.										x		x	
91 Ilkhani G.											x	x	!
92 Jannat G.											x	x	x
93 Narenjestan G.											x	x	!
94 Navabi G.											x	x	x
95 Imamzadeh Ibrahim											x	!	!
96 Balivaz G.											x		
97 Behjat abaad G.											x		
98 Poodonak G.											x		
99 Habib abaad G.											x		
100 Khandaq G.											x		
101 Rashk Behesht G.											x		
102 Zaaferani G.											x		
103 Zaki Khan G.											x		
104 Keshmiri G.											x		
105 Keifi G.											x		
106 Mirza Mohammad Reza G.											x		
107 Neshat (Mirza Naeim) G.											x		
108 Nov Moshiri G.											x		
109 Shahzadeh Beigum G.											x		
110 Rahmat abaad G.											x		
111 Sheikh G.											x		
112 Saheb Ekhtiar G.											x		
113 Safa G.											x		
114 Samad Aqa G.											x		
115 Ata al-Dawla G.											x		
116 Fath abaad G. (II)											x		
117 Golkhaneh G.											x		
118 Monshi bashi G.											x		
119 Mansour abaad G.											x		
120 Nasrieh G.											x		
121 Farhad abaad G.											x		
122 Hosein abaad Citadel											x		
123 Musalla Vault											x		
124 Baghcheh Bank (later Pars Restaurant)											x	x	
125 Shiraz University (main campus)												x	x
126 Shiraz University (later University of Technology)												x	x
127 Shiraz University (later Shiraz Technical and Engineering College)												x	x
128 Ministry of Justice												x	!
129 Melli G.												x	x
130 Azadi Park												x	x
131 Bahar Park												x	x
132 Morvarid Park												x	x
133 Luna Park and Rabbani Complex												x	x
134 Valiahd (later Valiasr) Park												x	x
135 Dehqan G.												x	x
136 Kafshgar G. (Namazi Hospital)												x	x
137 Khalili G.												x	x
138 Minou G.												x	x
139 Hafezieh Stadium												x	x
140 Khwaju Kermani T.												x	x
141 Shiraz Silo												x	x
142 Fars Cement Factory												x	x
143 The International Airport of Shiraz												x	x
144 Doran Air force District												x	x
145 Zerehi (armored) Training Center												x	x
146 Airborne District												x	x
147 Polo Field (later the Imam Hosein Garrison)												x	x
148 Dar al-Rahmeh Cemetery												x	x
149 Minouye Salar G.												x	
150 Old Airport of Shiraz												x	
151 Valiasr Bridge													x
152 The National Library													x
153 Shams Hotel													x
154 Aseman Hotel													x
155 Shiraz Grand Hotel													x
156 Chamran Hotel													x
157 Parseh Stadium													x
158 Baba Kouhi Park													x
159 Koohpayeh Park													x
160 Koohestan Park													x
161 Olive fields (Bash G.)													x
162 Chamran Greenway													x
163 Quran Gate public space design													x
164 Bein al-Haramain													x
165 Persian Gulf Complex													x

Table 1 List of landmarks in Shiraz. The x shows the period in which the landmark was visible. An asterisk is placed before the landmarks with an unknown location. The exclamation mark signifies the existence but non-visibility of a landmark in modern times.

A landmark at the macro level is defined as any human-made or natural structure visible from the mountains surrounding Shiraz, where the observer can have an overview of the city's skyline. This definition does not imply any judgement or approval in terms of the architectural beauty of the contemporary buildings or their compatibility with the context. For example, although the Aseman Hotel, built in the 21st century, has become controversial in relation to efforts to safeguard Shiraz's historic urban landscape,[16] it is still listed as a landmark in this research.

A challenge in extracting the landmarks is that in the majority of historical periods there was no visual record, such as old paintings or photos of Shiraz's silhouette, which would have helped with the purpose of this research. However, a useful index for recognising the urban monuments is that most Shiraz lay buildings prior to the 19th century had a maximum height of two storeys.[17] Consequently, any construction taller than a moderate-size two-storey building was treated as a landmark. This would include all the gardens, most mosques, schools, tombs, and castles with evidence of domes, minarets, and tall portals. Moreover, any construction outside the city wall was labelled as a monument.

Nevertheless, information on the presence of a previously built landmark in later periods can be significantly blurred in historical documents. Consequently, the chart, and in turn the illustrations, have only presented the landmarks with concrete evidence of their existence. Historical records for the landscape of Shiraz are not much more comprehensive in earlier historical periods, especially before the Dylamites. Also, visual documents about Shiraz were mainly produced by western travellers who visited Shiraz only after the 17th century. This limitation in historical sources reduces the accuracy of visualisations. Of course, this gap would be minimised in the context of cities with more comprehensive historical sources.

Considering the definition of a landmark as a monument visible on the skyline, one can notice an essential point in table 1, especially in the columns related to modern times. Some monuments, such as the Ali bin Hamzeh bridge, are not marked as a landmark in table 1 under the columns of the Pahlavi and the Islamic Republic periods, although the bridge exists in good physical shape today. This is because the bridge's identification would be barely possible in the macro landscape, and it has been literally lost in the mass of high-rise buildings constructed over the past century. In consequence, even though still-standing monuments such as the Mesgar ha bazaar or the Vakil mosque are important cultural heritage assets, they are marked with an exclamation mark in the last two columns of table 1, indicating they are no longer visible on the macro skyline.

Step 2

Relying on the information from table 1, maps of Shiraz belonging to thirteen historical periods of the city were produced. While the position of the majority of monuments could be found in historical sources, only an approximate location of some landmarks is available. The buildings with relatively more precise positions are included in the investigation because they would have a minor effect on the sketches' accuracy at the macro scale. However, a small number of monuments with no record of their location were excluded from the maps and the paintings. These landmarks are only mentioned in the maps' legends with an asterisk (see for instance fig. 12). Moreover, the existing landmarks are presented in red. The monuments that no longer exist are shown in blue.

Step 3

In order to undertake a comparative analysis between twelve visualisations of Shiraz in different political periods, it is of crucial importance that all the views share the same visualisation technique, viewpoint, and viewing angle. Considering the gaps in historical information about Shiraz, a hand-drawn style was selected as the most suitable option. Being imperfect does not constrain the usefulness of these visualisations.[18] Moreover, our perception of the environment is not pure realism either. It has been argued that less-detailed representations are only interpreted as slightly less complete. In this context, loose realism and hand-drawn sketches can better support the opportunity of openness for perception and viewers' speculation of scenarios with gaps in details.[19]

The author chose to paint all the sketches in panoramic pictures with a similar size and frame in a way that would cover the most visible landmarks of Shiraz across all periods. Moreover, in choosing a viewing place, three main goals are considered. The viewing place must be a location that overlooks the most landmarks of Shiraz in all periods and that is well known for its particular view of the city in the historical sources. Moreover, the common view should depict the urban development process of the city in a clear-cut way. Shiraz's panoramic landscapes were photographed in 2019 from thirteen viewpoints on the hillside of the city's mountains. Although many viewpoints oversee a considerable number of monuments of Shiraz, it is primarily the Quran Gate area that bears a historical significance in the sources. Consequently, the elevated view of Gahvareh Did (Div), the historic watchtower next to the Quran Gate, was selected as the main viewing point. This view was not only chosen as a sketching point in old depictions of Shiraz's skyline[20] (fig. 1) but has also overseen a remarkable number of landmarks over time, making it an ideal viewpoint for representing the city's urban development process.

Step 4

In order to sketch and paint twelve illustrations of Shiraz, the panoramic photo of Shiraz from the Gahvareh Did (Div), next to the Quran Gate, which was taken during the survey, was first projected on paper. Relying on table 1 and maps from step 2, the location of each landmark, as well as the area of the city in each period, was marked on twelve paper sheets. It is essential to consider that some of the landmarks may exist in table 1 and the maps. Still, they are not found in the visualisation because they are either not visible in the view frame of the Quran Gate viewpoint or are too far from the Gahvareh Did watchtower. The twelve watercolour drawings were originally painted on paper sheets with the same size of 50 by 10 cm. Allocating the landmarks precisely on the sheets of paper, the rest of the sketch was drawn with a fountain pen. Finally, colour was added to the black and white illustration with watercolour, following the perspective rules applied to the colour tone (fig. 2). The outcome of this visualisation

1 The Voyages of Jean Chardin is one of the most valuable sources in studying the history of Shiraz during the Safavid period. Chardin's travel book includes exciting and informative illustrations of Shiraz, among which the macro landscape of the city viewed from the Gahvareh Did (Div) could be mentioned.

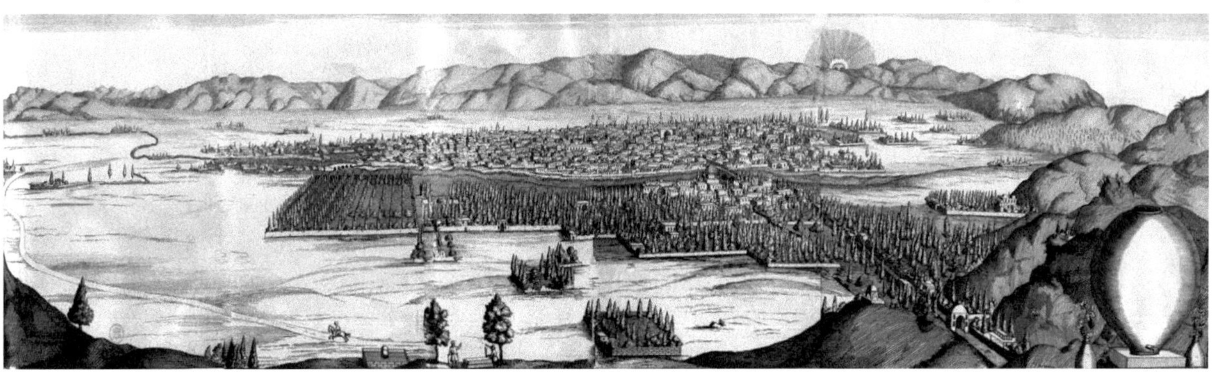

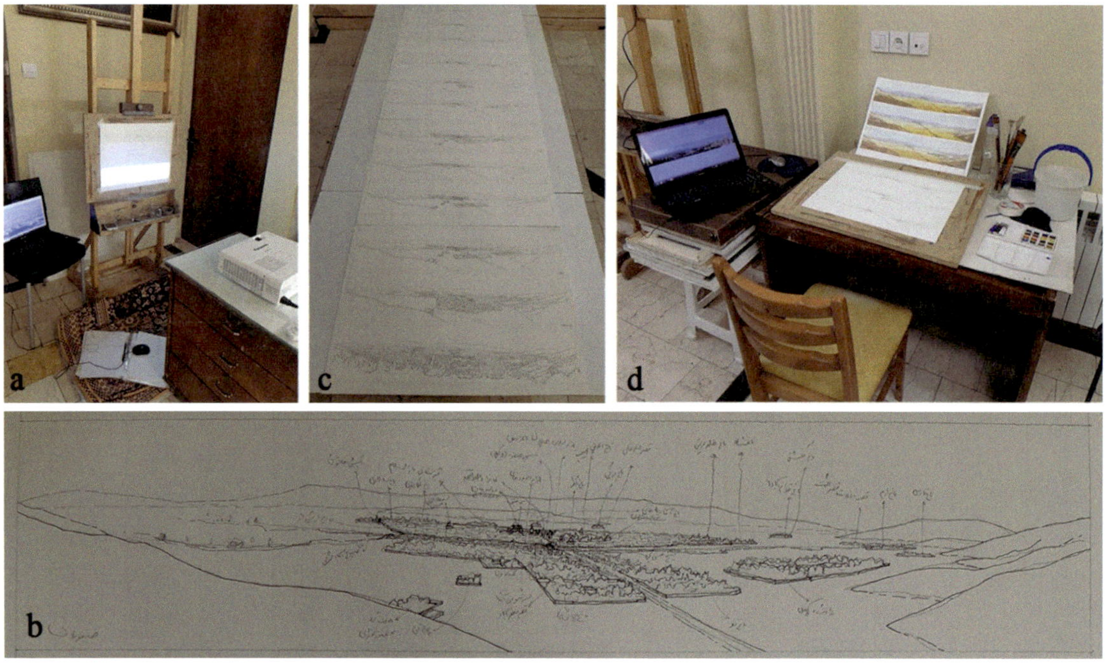

2 The panoramic photo is projected on paper, and the landmarks are allocated (a). Next, the sketch of Shiraz is drawn with a fountain pen (b shows this step for the Safavid period). After erasing the pencil marks on all twelve drawings (c), the colour was added with the watercolour (d).

3 Shiraz during Pre-Islamic eras.

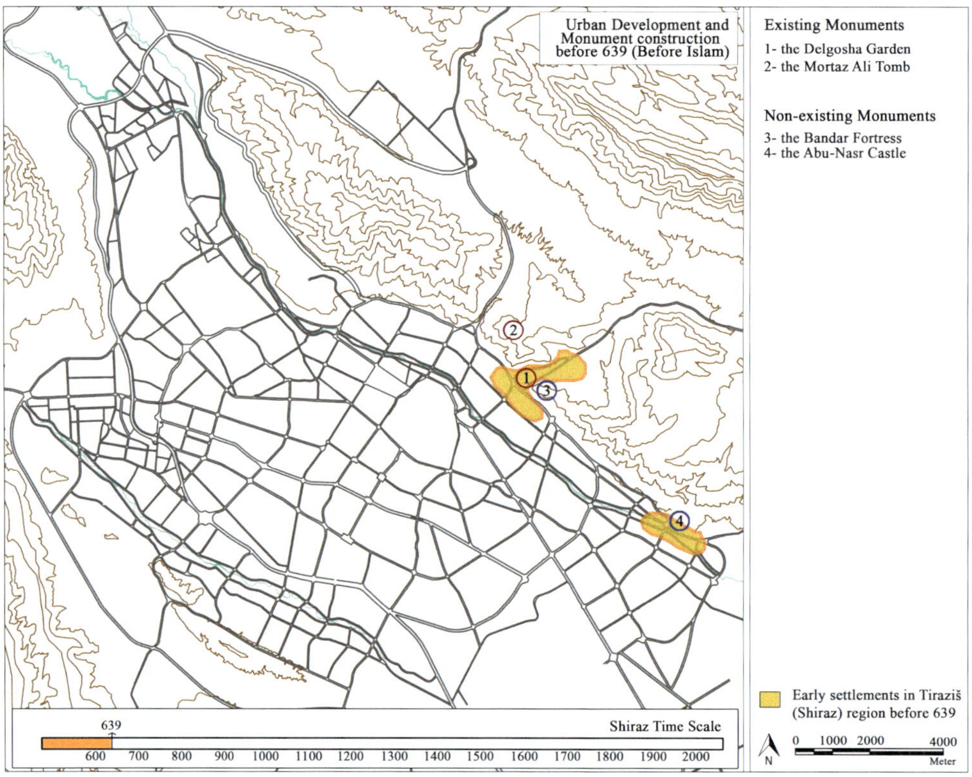

method is presented in the next section. At the same time, the illustrations are used to analyse the development process of the macro landscape of Shiraz over fourteen centuries.

The Evolution of the Macro Landscape of Shiraz

Although the macro landscape and landmarks of the pre-Islamic era were investigated during steps 1 and 2, the author decided to produce visualisations of Shiraz only after its establishment as a city in the 7th century. Nevertheless, a short description of pre-Islamic Shiraz (fig. 3) is provided in the following section.

From 639 AD to 934 AD: Early Islamic Era, Saffarid and Abbasid Periods

Many historical records and archaeological findings support the theory that the Shiraz Plain was occupied by scattered settlements centuries before the Islamic conquest.[21] Many landmarks, such as the Bandar Fortress, the Abu Nasr Palace, and the Mortaz Ali tomb dating back to the Achaemenid Empire (550 BC–330 BC), the Parthian Empire (247 BC–224 AD), or the Sasanian Empire (224 AD–651 AD), prove the existence of early settlements in the east and south-east of present-day Shiraz.[22] However, the current Shiraz historic core dates back to the 7th century, built on a circular plan as the military camp used by the Muslims in their fight with the indigenous Persian residents based at the Bandar Fortress (fig. 4). Of course, as a camp for Muslims, it must have contained a mosque. As a circular planned town[23] developed from the initial camp in the early Islamic centuries, it is logical that Shiraz would have had a Jame Mosque,[24] a bazaar, and a Dar al-Khalifa.[25] Nevertheless, there is no concrete evidence of those buildings' architectural details or location. In other cities in the same region, the mosques were architecturally simple during the early Islamic era.[26]

The lack of historical documents from 639 AD to 934 AD is unfortunate for the study of Shiraz's macro landscape. However, there is evidence that a bridge close to the later-named Saadi Gate in the northeast of Shiraz must have existed on the Dry River or the Khorramdareh River, according to two arguments. First, there are many records of conflicts between Indigenous residents accommodated in the Bandar Fortress on one side of the seasonal river and the Muslims living in the camp on the other side. Moreover, prior to the 16th century, the Saadi Valley next to the Bandar Fortress was the main entrance to the Shiraz Plain. Consequently, it is only logical to assume that there must have been an eastern bridge over the river connecting the Shiraz Plain to the Saadi Valley. Additionally, a second bridge would have been visible. Although the Quran Gate was probably not constructed before 934, military activities during early Islamic times and the geographical accessibility of the Allaho Akbar Valley outside the Shiraz Plain support the idea of the construction of a bridge at the location of the later Ali bin Hamazeh bridge.[27] Finally, the Atiq Mosque was constructed during the reign of the Saffarids and was possibly built at the location of the initial Jame Mosque.[28] This mosque would most probably have been visible on the skyline of Shiraz before 934. It is known from the sources that Shiraz town did not have a defensive wall until the 10th century (fig. 5).

From 934 AD to 1066/1067 AD: Daylamite and Shabankara Period

Country, political capital, and governmental independence are fluid concepts in Shiraz's history. However, this chapter does not attempt to explain the levels of centralisation of the state at various times, but rather assumes that Shiraz was the political capital of the Daylamites. Being the political centre would have brought wealth to the city, which would naturally lead to urban development and shifts in the city's skyline (figs. 6 and 7). The Adudi Palace and gardens were built as the royal

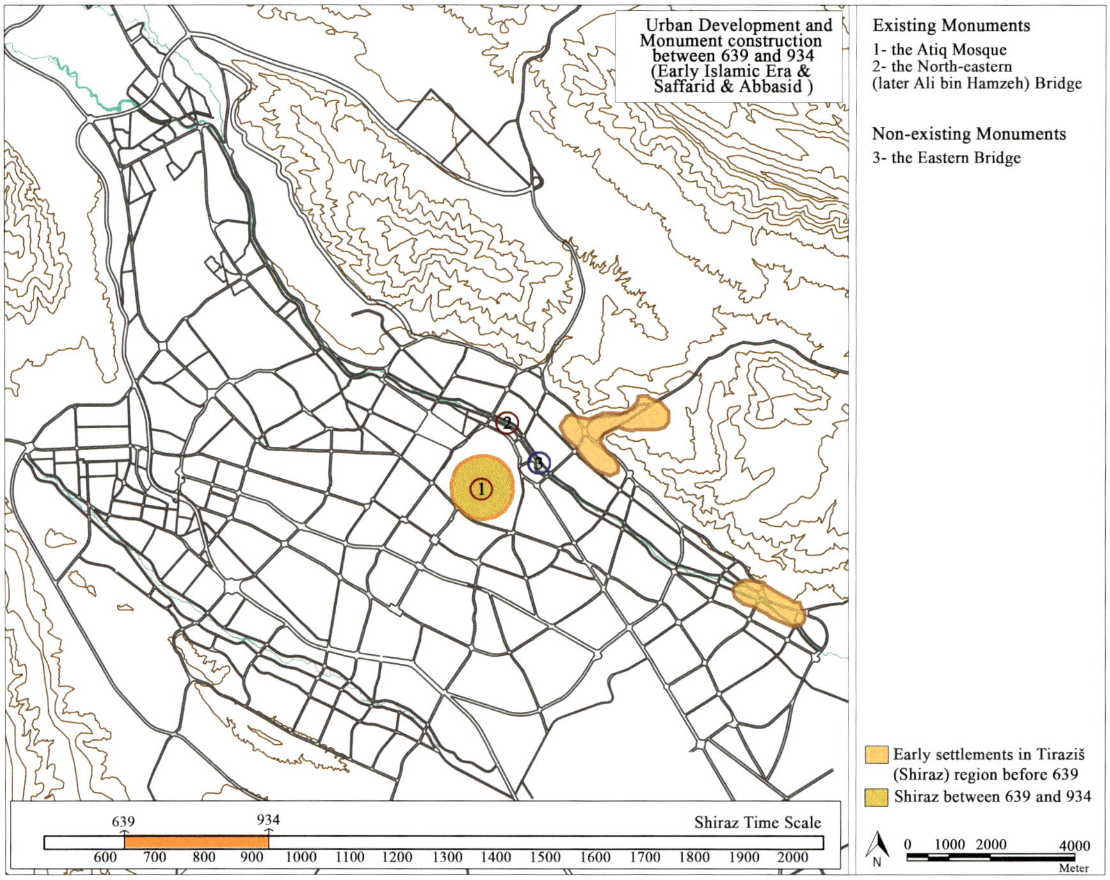

4 Shiraz in Early-Islamic, Saffarids, and Abbasid eras.

5 Shiraz's macro landscape depicted from the Gahvareh Did (Div) close to the Quran Gate shows the city's overall view from the Early-Islamic era to the Abbasid era.

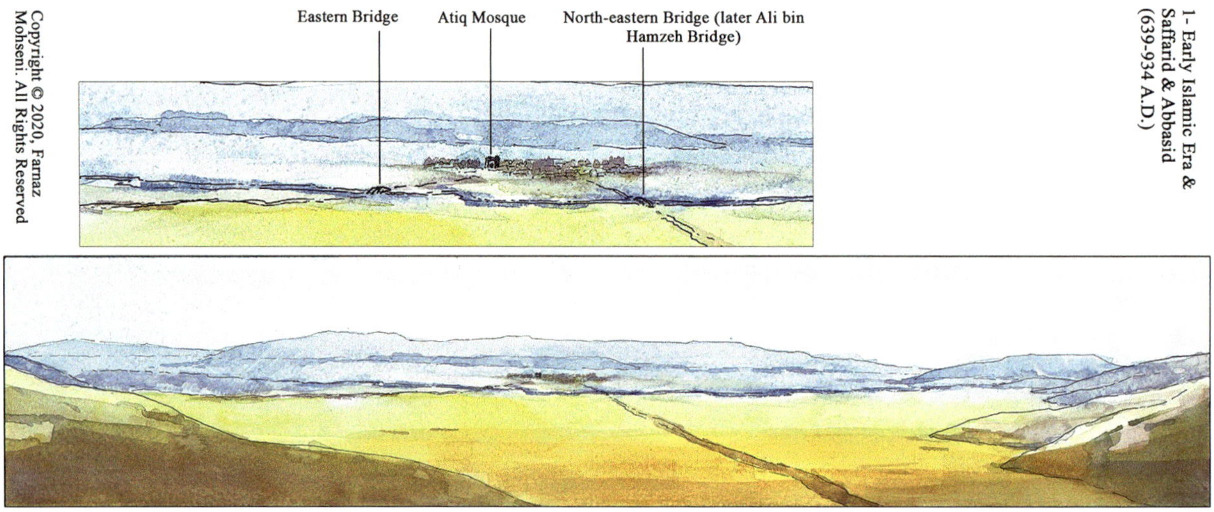

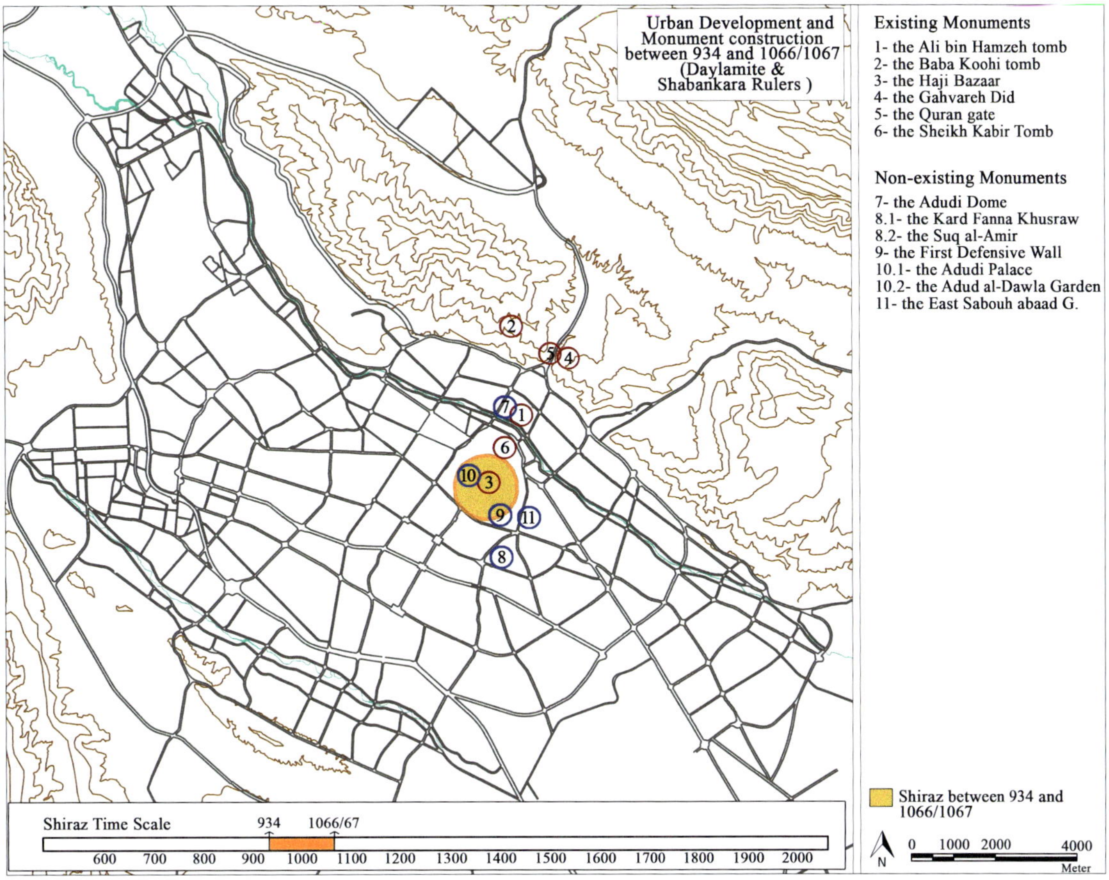

6 Shiraz during Daylamite and Shabankara rulers.

7 Shiraz's macro landscape depicted from the Gahvareh Did (Div) close to the Quran Gate shows the city's overall view from the Daylamite era to the Shabankara era.

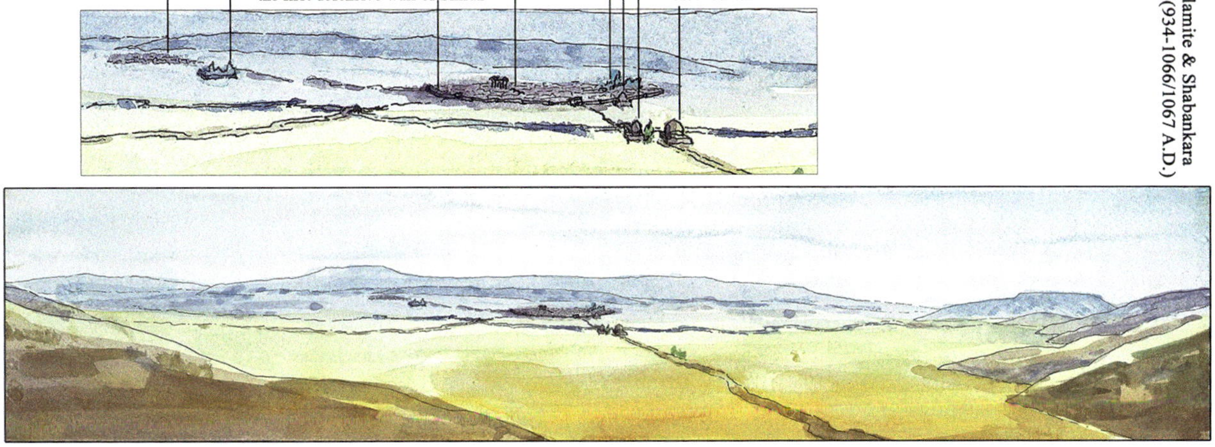

2- Daylamite & Shabankara Rulers (934-1066/1067 A.D.)

house of the ruler. The Haji bazaar, now the oldest bazaar in Shiraz, was constructed, as well as the Al-Amir suq.[29]

At the same time, military activities played an integral role in shaping the macro landscape of Shiraz. The city's first defensive wall was constructed,[30] as well as the Adudi Dome, which was a place for keeping the king's elephants, used during wars. Kard-i Fannā Khusraw, the first satellite town of Shiraz, was built to help with the army's accommodation. Not visible in the view illustrated in figure 7 is the Gahvareh Did (Div), the watchtower constructed on top of the mountain to oversee the Allaho Akbar Valley, one of the city's main entrances. Also not visible in the view is the Bandar Fortress, which had been destroyed for centuries, and was rebuilt to watch over the Saadi Valley, the most crucial entrance to the Shiraz Plain.[31]

The religious tolerance of the Daylamite kings influenced the skyline of Shiraz. The tomb of Sheikh Kabir, the Sunni figure, as well as the Ali bin Hamzeh Dome, the Shia figure, would both have been seen in silhouette. At the same time, traditional pre-Islamic Persian events, such as Nowruz, would be celebrated in public places such as bazaars as well as in the Kard-i Fannā Khusraw, while the city was one of the most important centres for Sufism. Not visible in figure 7 are the Khanqah and tomb of the Sufi, Baba Kouhi, in present-day Shiraz, which date back to the Daylamites.[32] Nonetheless, many of these landmarks could not have been constructed if the water sources were not provided. Environmental factor have, directly and indirectly, influenced the city's general form. The network of *qanats* (underground water channels), the underground water infrastructure, and water reservoirs dug during Daylamites, such as the Rokni, and Guyim qanats, shaped the city's main structure, the direction of development, and the gardens' location.[33] After the Daylamites, Shiraz experienced a period of wars and attacks from the Shabankara rulers and the Seljuks, during which the city and its landmarks were damaged.

From 1066/1067 AD to 1148 AD: Seljuk Period

The Seljuk sultans had a strict belief in Hanafi Islam, which may have led to the establishment of many madrasas in Shiraz (fig. 8). It is crucial to point out that a madrasa is a religious college for Islam, though Islamic topics may not be the only subject studied. A number of schools built in Shiraz during the reign of the Seljuks have records of tall structures like minarets or domes, including the Zahedeh, Taji, and Mankoubras schools. These schools show the effect of the sultans' religious views on the skyline of the city.[34] Other than schools, the establishment of gardens such as the Qaracheh School and Garden, later the Takht Garden, and the Eram Garden are other Seljuk contributions to Shiraz's landscape.[35] Finally, Saadi, the great poet of Shiraz, lived and thought Sufism in his Khanqah[36] and garden. He was later buried in his own Khanqah, which is not in the frame of figure 9 but is nowadays one of Shiraz's main tourist destinations.

From 1148 AD to 1264 AD: Atabak Period

Shiraz's selection as the capital of the Salghurid Atabaks brought wealth and power back to the city, resulting in the blooming of the macro landscape and the development of city landmarks. The construction of the Sunquri bazaar, the Atabaki Square bazaar and the Kabir suq, as well as the Sar-e Hoz-e Aqa bazaar, shows the city's economic growth. During the Atabak period, Shiraz survived Mongol invasions by showing flexibility and paying tribute to Mongol rulers. Avoiding war in this way saved Shiraz's landmarks and architectural significance. The city was also expanded in area compared to previous times (figs. 10 and 11).[37]

The tombs of some Shia religious sacred figures were discovered during the Atabak period, and shrines were constructed upon their graves, such as Shah Cheragh, Mohammad bin Musa, and Seyyed Alaoddin Hossein at the Qatlaq Garden.[38] As for other influences of religion on Shiraz's macro landscape, the Sunquri Mosque was constructed, and the Nov Mosque (the new mosque) was built in the royal gardens of Atabak.[39] Finally, following

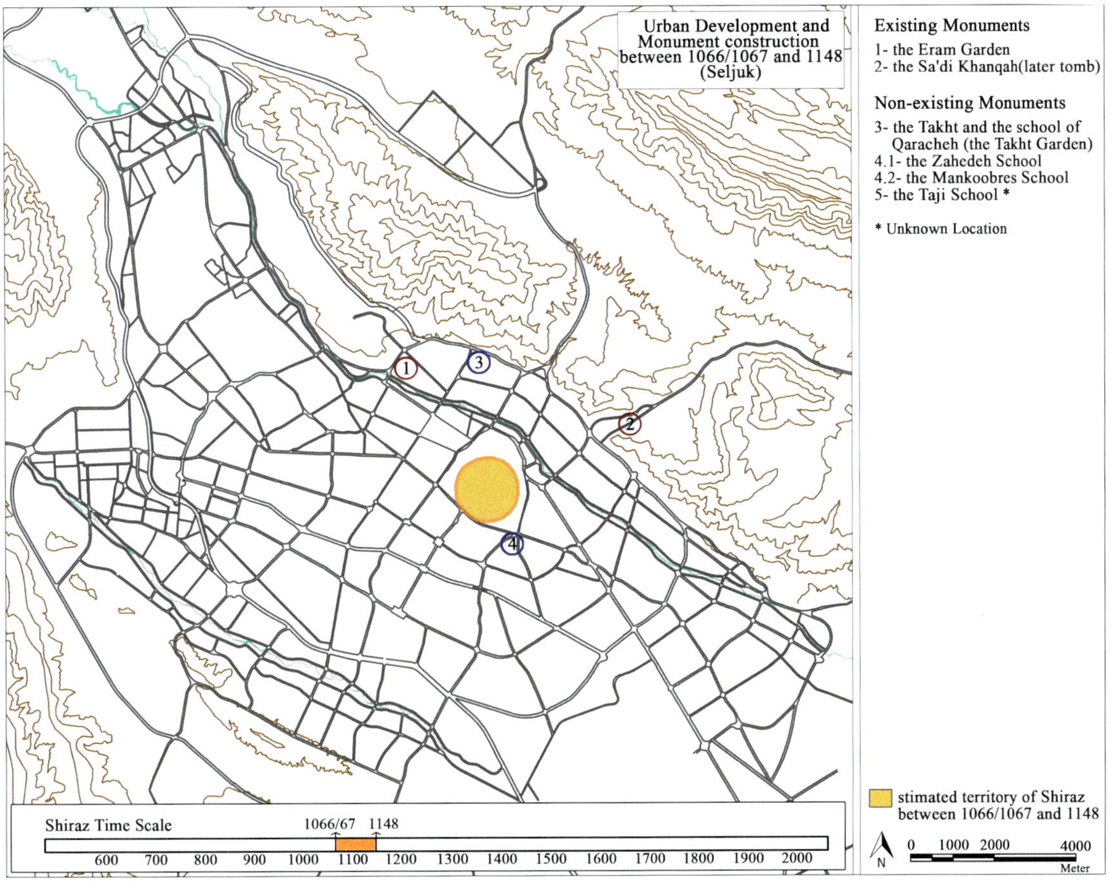

8 Shiraz during the Seljuks.

9 Shiraz's macro landscape depicted from the Gahvareh Did (Div) in the Seljuk period.

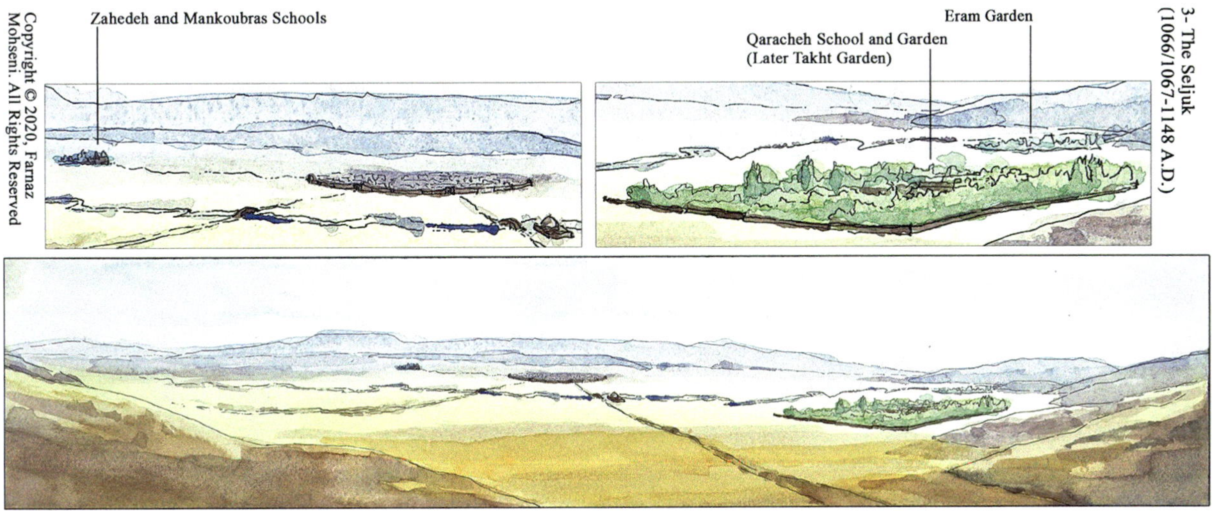

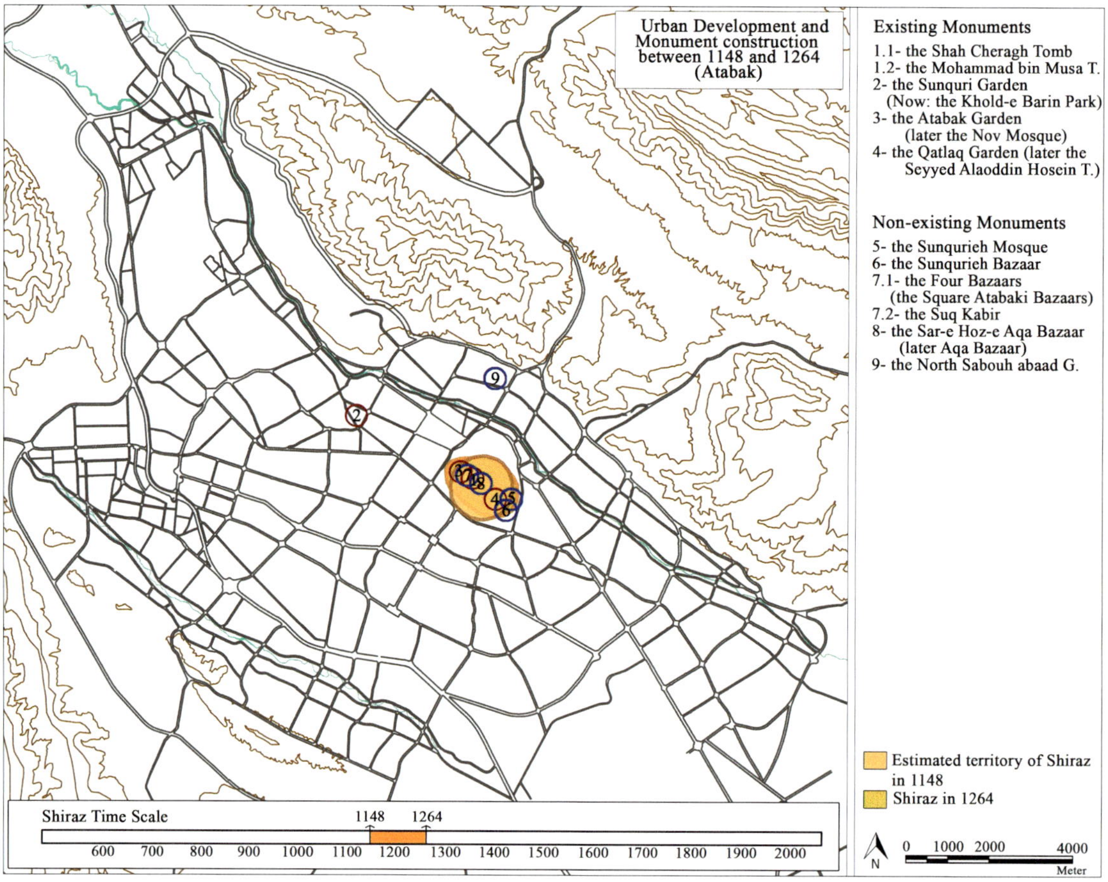

10 Shiraz during the Atabaks.

11 Shiraz's macro landscape depicted from the Gahvareh Did (Div) view in the Atabak period.

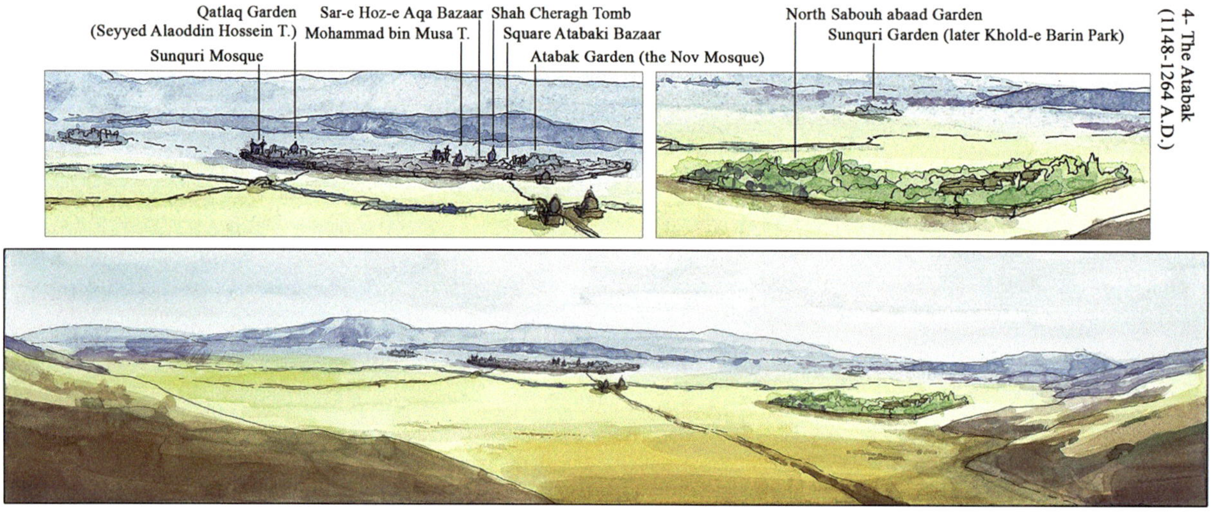

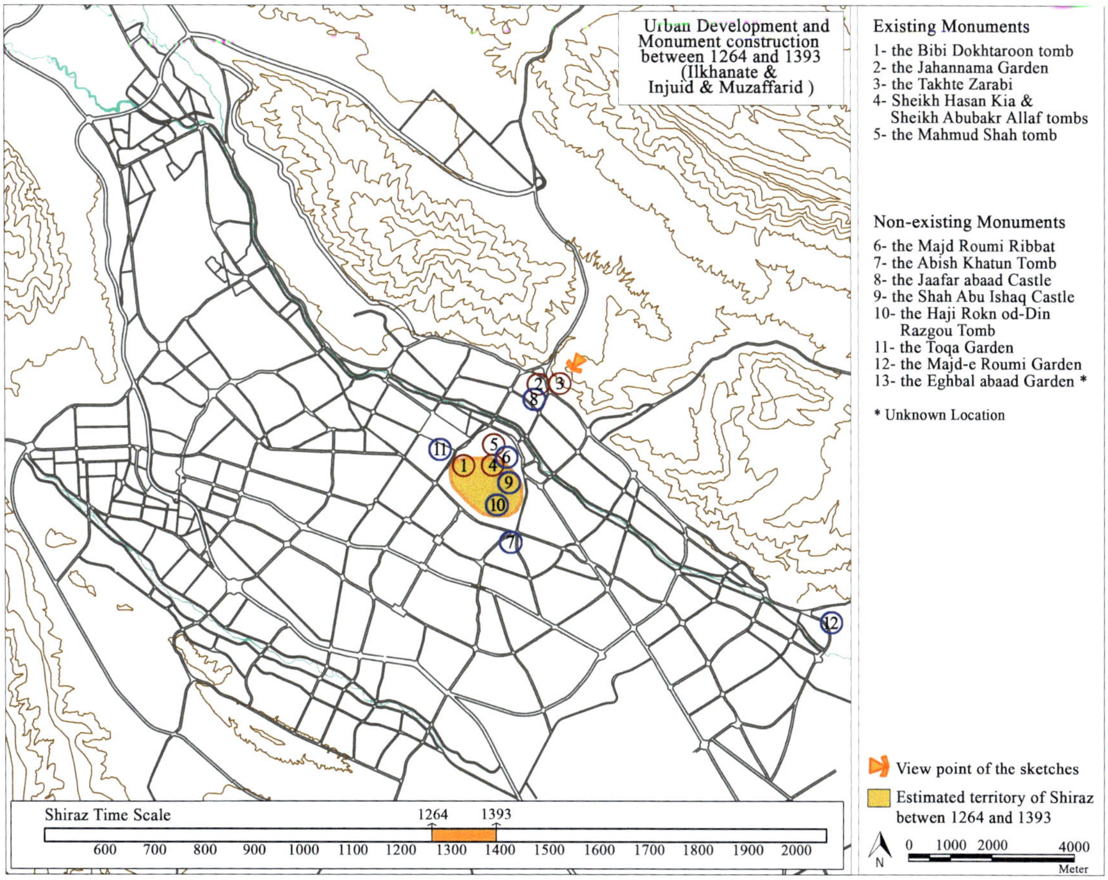

12 Shiraz during Ilkhanate, Injuid, and Muzaffarid periods.

13 Shiraz's macro landscape from the Gahvareh Did (Div) view is shown from the Ilkhanates to the Muzaffarids.

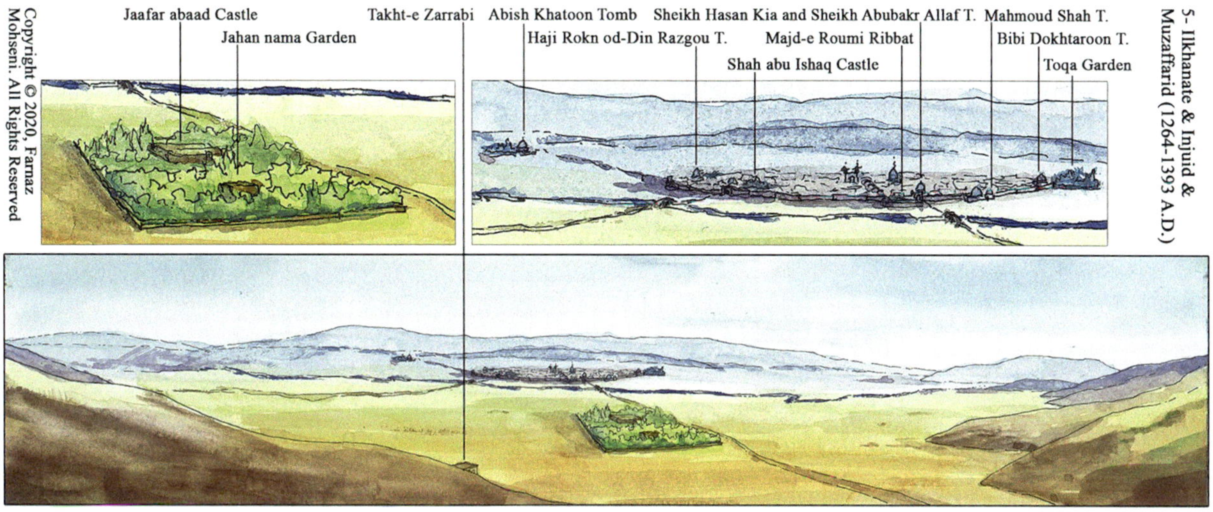

the long tradition of creating gardens in Shiraz, many green structures were added to the city's silhouette such as the gardens of Sunquri, North Sabouh abaad, Qatlaq, and Atabak.[40] There are records of green areas in the Musalla and Jaafar abaad plains on the north and northeast sides of Shiraz and in the foreground of figure 11, by virtue of Zangi Qanat's construction. Nevertheless, since there is no information about the location, name or number of specific gardens, they are not included in the visualisations. Also, qanats provided water for the lands around the Bandar Fortress in the Saadi Valley and for the Delgosha Garden during the time of the Atabaks.[41]

From 1264 AD to 1393 AD: Ilkhanate, Injuid, and Muzaffarid Periods

By the time of the death of the last Atabak, Shiraz had been under the direct control of Ilkhanate or Mongols for 71 years. Some landmarks were built from time to time, depending on the stability of the state, such as the Majd-e Roumi Ribat[42] and the Majd-e Roumi Garden.[43] From 1335 to 1393, Shiraz was ruled by the Injuid and Muzaffarid dynasties while being chosen as the political centre. As a consequence of Shiraz's political prominence, the Jaafar abaad Castle[44] and the Shah abu Ishaq Castle[45] were built as two of the most important landmarks on the skyline (fig. 12). Nevertheless, the author believes that the politically central role of Shiraz for such a short period was insufficient to establish a concrete base for urban development compared to the Atabak period. Military activities, lack of political stability, and the constant changing of the state did not lead to remarkable landscape development. Consequently, the significant development of the macro landscape from the Seljuks to the Atabaks is not visible from the end of Atabak times until 1393 (see figs. 9, 11 and 13).

Ibn Battuta, who travelled to Shiraz in the 14th century, describes Shirazi people, and women in particular, as religious folk who participated in many religious activities.[46] It seems that this spiritual trend played an integral role in forming some landmarks in the city's skyline. Landmarks of religious figures such as the Bibi Dokhtaroon, the Sheikh Hasan Kia and the Sheikh Abubakr Allaf, and the Haji Rokn od-Din Razgou tombs appeared on the silhouette. The tombs of former kings and Atabaks like Mahmud Shah and Abish Khatoon were other monuments in the macro landscape.[47] Takht-e Zarrabi, initially a water reservoir, was built by the Grand Cadi, the grand judge, in the northeast of Shiraz.[48] The Jahan nama, Toqa, and Eghbal abaad gardens were also green spaces prominent on the skyline, showing the importance of environmental factors and gardening traditions in the history of Shiraz.[49] Especially, Ibn Battuta describes Shiraz as a city surrounded by gardens.[50] However, since the names and locations of these green spaces are unknown, at least as far as the author is aware, they were excluded from the drawings.

From 1393 AD to 1503 AD: Timurid, Kara Koyunlu, and Ak Koyunlu Periods

The records of macro landmarks in Shiraz from 1393 to 1503 are limited to the tomb of Hafez, the famous poet of Shiraz, the Dar al-Safa School, which later became the Golshan Garden, and the Qasr od-Dasht village and gardens in the northwest of Shiraz (figs. 14 and 15). The Qasr od-Dasht gardens are nowadays the largest green space in Shiraz; around 1,000 hectares of these historic gardens still exist in present-day Shiraz and they form the most crucial environmental asset to the city. Although this is the first reference to the Qasr od-Dasht in the literature,[51] the author believes that the Qasr od-Dasht gardens had existed long before at the same location but with different names or sizes over time. The existence of the required infrastructure, such as qanats, to transfer water from northwest hillsides and the Guyim region[52] makes a solid basis for this argument. Nevertheless, given the lack of specific evidence, the author did not introduce the Qasr od-Dasht gardens to the skyline sketches of previous periods.

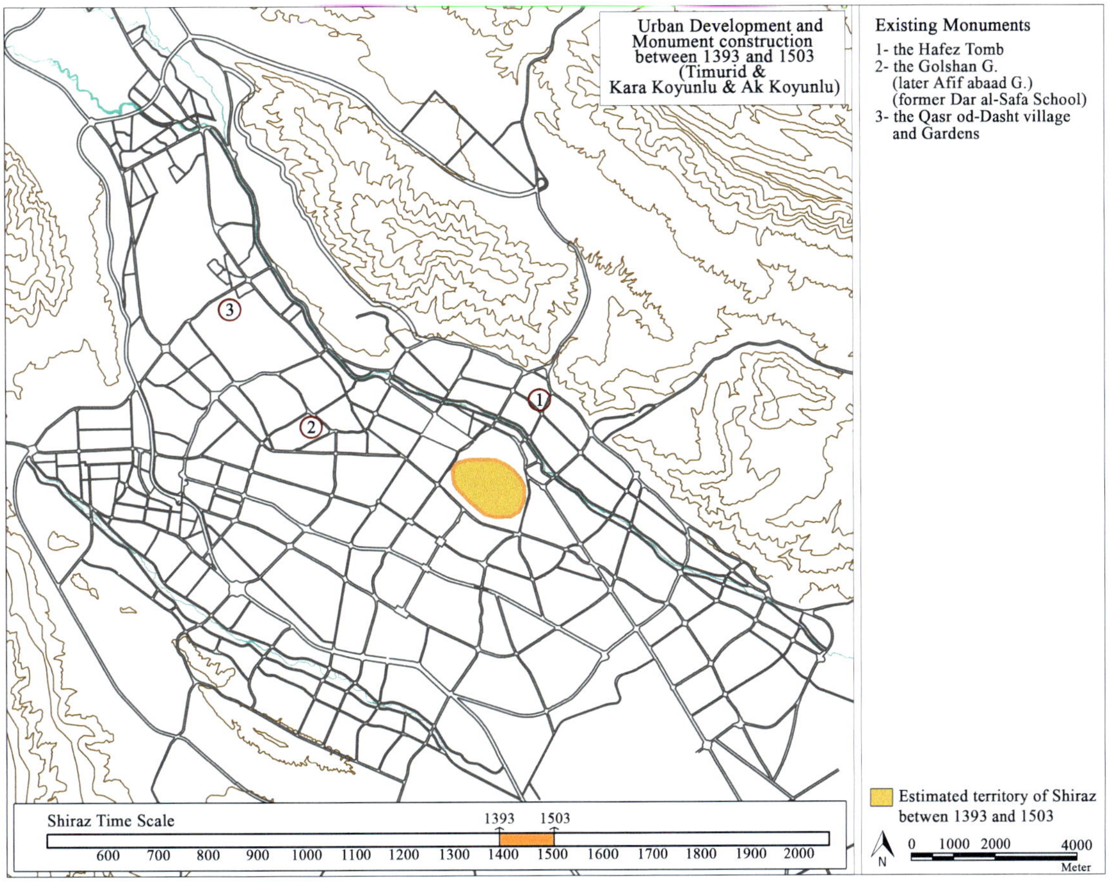

14 Shiraz during Timurid, Kara Koyunlu, and Ak Koyunlu periods.

15 Shiraz's macro landscape from the Gahvareh Did (Div) view is shown from the Timurids to the Ak Koyunlos.

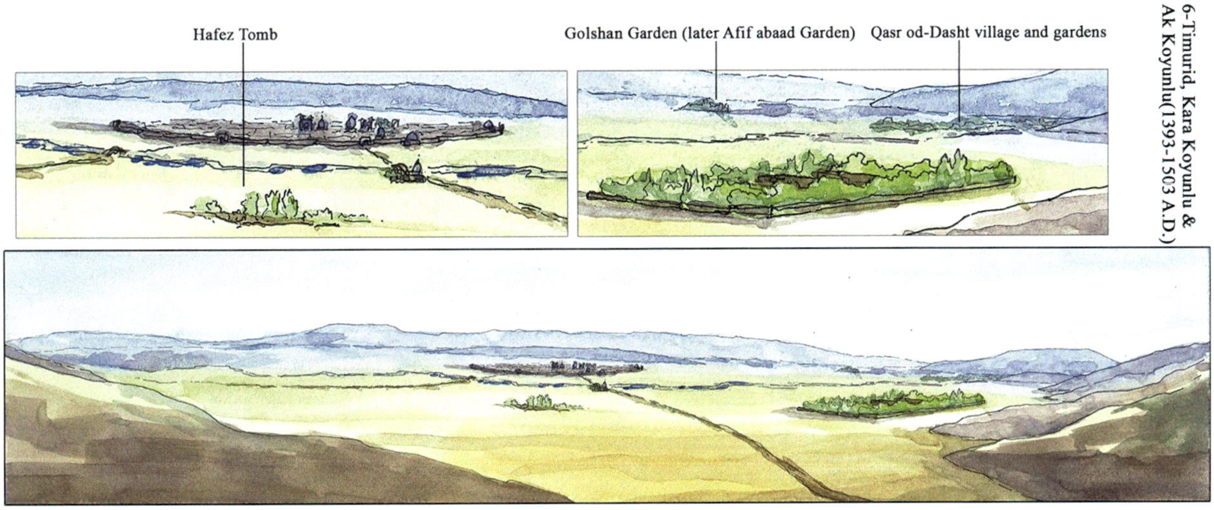

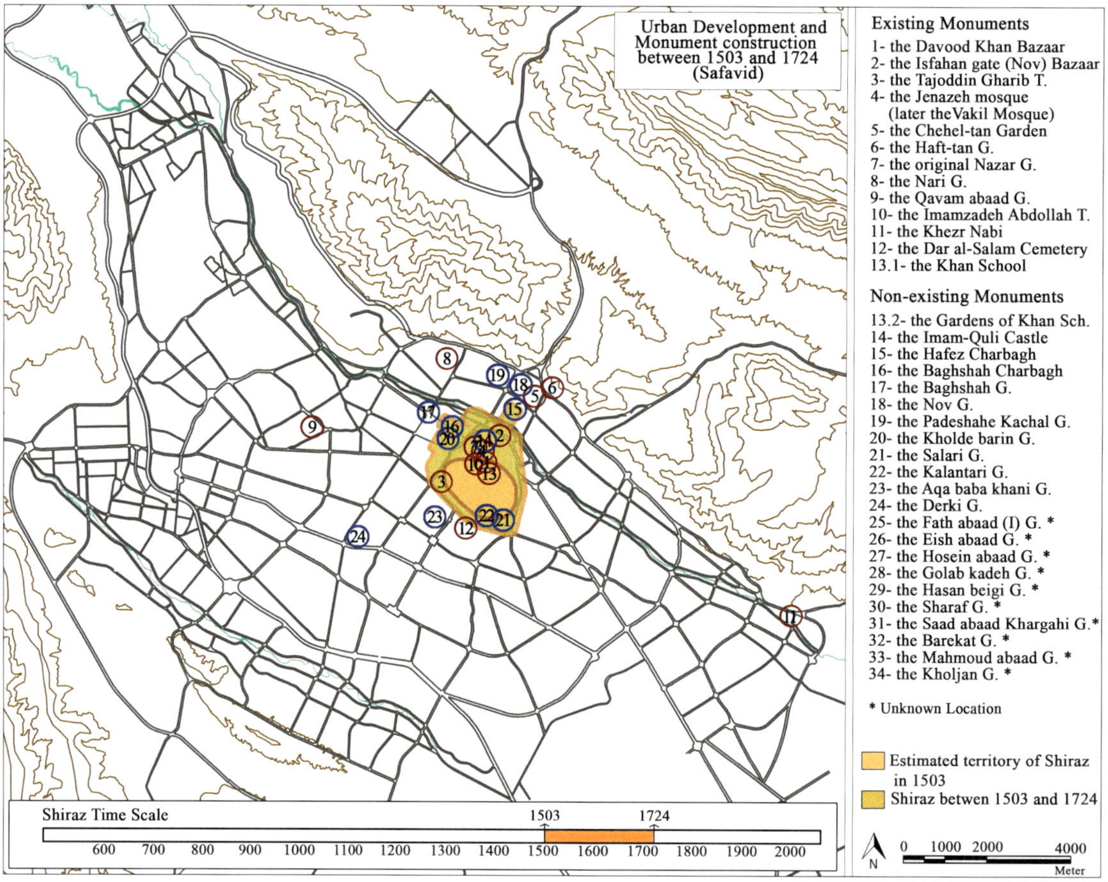

16 Shiraz during the Safavid empire.

From 1503 AD to 1724 AD: Safavid Period

For more than 220 years, Shiraz and Fars Province were under the empire of the Safavid Kings. Although the city was not the country's capital, it was the political centre of Fars Province. Even though the central government neglected Shiraz and Fars Province after 1629, the city experienced marvellous days during the reign of Shah Abbas I (1588–1629). Allahverdi Khan and later his son Imam Quli Khan, two loyal and trusted generals and statesmen of Fars Province, played an integral role in Shiraz's blooming times in terms of political and military stability, as well as through economic boom and urban development (figs. 16 and 17). Being the provincial city of these statesmen, Shiraz became the home of the Imam Quli Castle. Also, the silk trades of Shah Abbas brought many caravans[53] to Shiraz, and the economic growth led to the construction of the Davood Khan (later Mesgar ha) and Nov (Isfahan Gate) bazaars as well as many caravanserais[54] adjacent to the bazaars.[55] Lastly, Fars was the only province where wine was produced and exported as it was forbidden in the rest of the country. Because of the close relationship between the king and the Fars statesmen, the king considered an exemption for wine production, despite his religious perspective against wine. As the natural consequence of this flexibility and the financial benefits of the wine trade, there are records of vineyards around Shiraz.[56]

Moreover, the Safavid kings were known for their strong position favouring Shia Islam. Consequently, the tomb domes of Shia religious figures started to appear in silhouette, such as those of Seyyed Tajoddin Qarib and Imamzadeh Abdollah. However, other respected Sunni tombs were either neglected or saved by changing their religious background from Sunni to Shia.[57] Other religious buildings, such as the Jenazeh (later Vakil) Mosque and the Khan School, were built and shaped the city's macro landscape. The Dar al-Salam cemetery is the oldest in Shiraz, with some graves dating back to early Islamic times.[58] Based on sketches by Jean Chardin and Cornelis de Bruyn in the 18th century, the cemetery's appearance on the skyline appears to date from the Safavid period.[59] Some trees are visible at the approximate location of the cemetery in these old drawings.

Transport considerations also shaped the macro landscape. Imam Quli Khan demolished a part of the hillside of the Allaho Akbar Valley

17 The blossoming of Shiraz's macro landscape from the Gahvareh Did (Div) view is evident during the Safavid Empire.

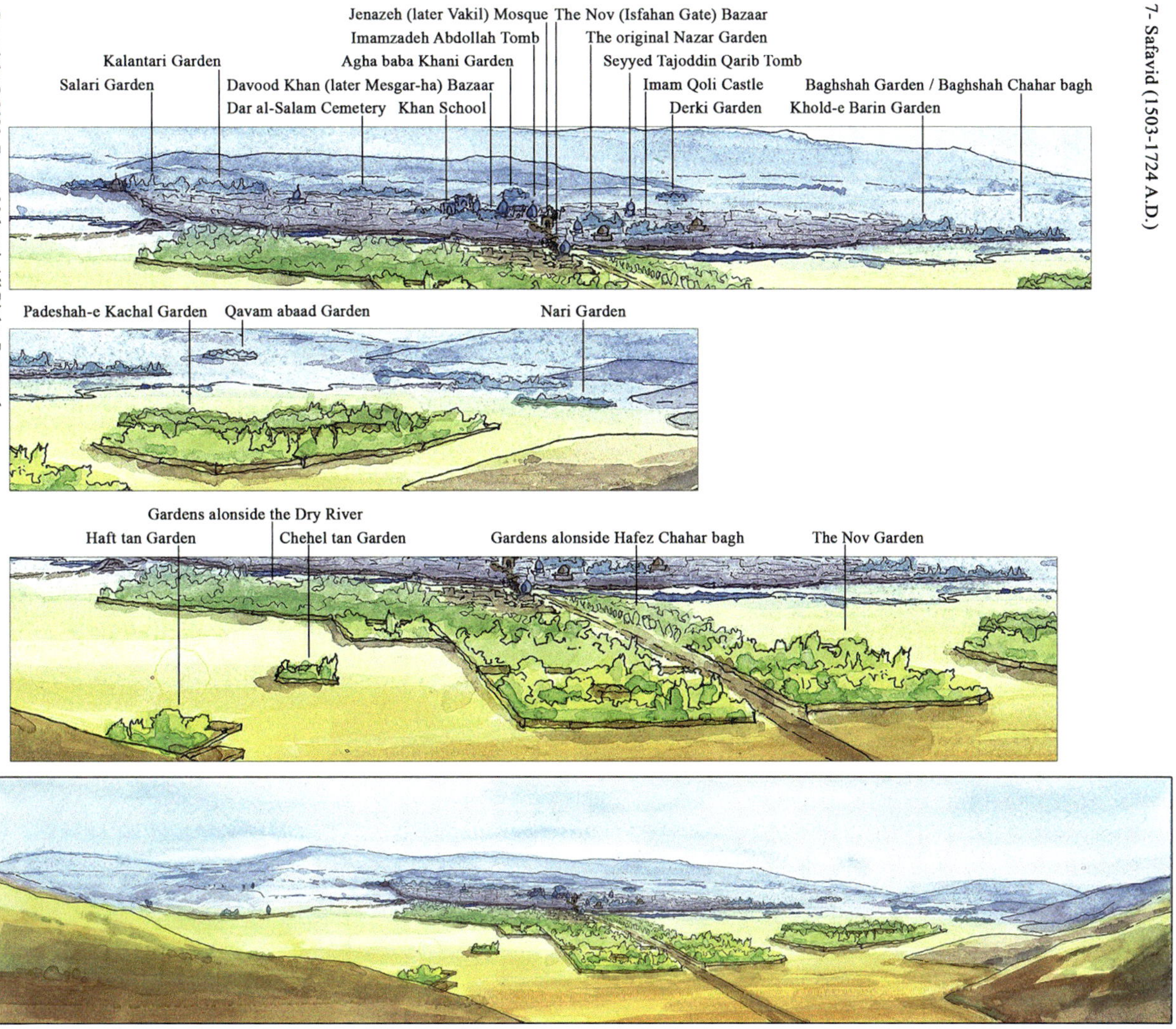

at the Quran Gate. By broadening the valley, the Quran Gate pathway became the main entrance of Shiraz instead of the Saadi Valley and the distance between Shiraz and Isfahan, the capital, became shorter.[60]

Finally, the Safavids adapted a unique urban planning and design approach based on gardening. The recurring feature of Safavid urban planning in some Iranian cities, including Shiraz, was the «*Chahar bagh*». *Chahar baghs* are historical boulevards with gardens and rows of trees alongside them. The Hafez Chahar bagh and the Baghshah Chahar bagh were clearly visible in Shiraz's macro landscape in the 17th and 18th centuries.[61] Moreover, a considerable number of gardens were created, or perhaps renovated, including the original Nazar Garden, the Nov Garden, the gardens of Nari, Chehel tan, Haft tan, Padeshah-e Kachal, Khold-e Barin, Qavam abaad, Salari, Kalantari, Aqa baba Khani, Derki and Baghshah. The list continues with more gardens, the location of which could not be found by the author, such as the gardens of Fath abaad, Eish abaad, Hosein abaad, Golab kadeh, Hasan beigi, Sharaf, Saad abaad Khargahi, Barekat, Mahmoud abaad, and Kholjan.[62] The author holds the view that it is highly possible that a number of these gardens already existed before the Safavids since the infrastructure, including the qanats, had already existed for centuries. Moreover, there were records of green spaces around the city with no clear names or locations during previous periods. Consequently, the author believes that some of these gardens had existed prior to the Safavid era. As mentioned in the methodology section, the author did not add these gardens to her sketches of previous periods as there was no clear-cut evidence of their existence.

From 1724 AD to 1754 AD: Hotak, Safavid II and the Afsharid Period

After Shiraz's glory days during most of the Safavid Empire, the city went downhill in terms of urban development and macro landscape (figs. 18 and 19). First, the flood of 1668 caused extreme damage to the urban fabric and landmarks. One third of the buildings were destroyed, and many inhabitants emigrated from Shiraz to other cities after the flood.[63] Within 30 years, the Safavid Empire fell to the Hotaks,[64] and later on, Nader, the Safavids general, defeated the Hotaks. He claimed the throne himself and established the Afsharid Kingdom. The many wars and conflicts in such a brief period were destructive for Shiraz's landscape and urban planning, and most importantly, many gardens around the city were destroyed. The wood from the trees was used to warm up the soldiers while Shiraz was under siege.

From 1724 to 1730, famine, heavy snow, and the cold breeze, as well as cholera, resulted in the death of many people in Shiraz. Although the ruler of Fars ordered the planting of trees in the city in 1730 and minor renovations were undertaken by the order of Nader Shah, Shiraz never returned to the marvellous days of the 16th and 17th centuries. Moreover, to fund his military conquests, Nader Shah imposed burdensome taxes. Laypeople were so impoverished that they fled to other countries, and many settlements were left deserted.[65] Consequently, Shiraz never had the opportunity to recover from the previous disastrous events until the Zand period.

From 1754 AD to 1791 AD: Zand Period

In less than 90 years, Shiraz was diminished in size following a train of disastrous events. Consequently, when Karim Khan, the first king of the Zand Dynasty, took over power and selected Shiraz as his capital, many renovations to the city were on his list. It is crucial to clarify that many landmarks in Shiraz, known as Karim Khan's contributions, are actually massive renovations of older landmarks such as the Chehel Tan Garden. That is why the list of built landmarks (fig. 20) during the Zand Dynasty appears surprisingly short. Karim Khan reduced the number of neighbourhoods and the city's area. He built a massive defensive wall around the shrunken area of Shiraz. For protection against the many challenges and rebellions

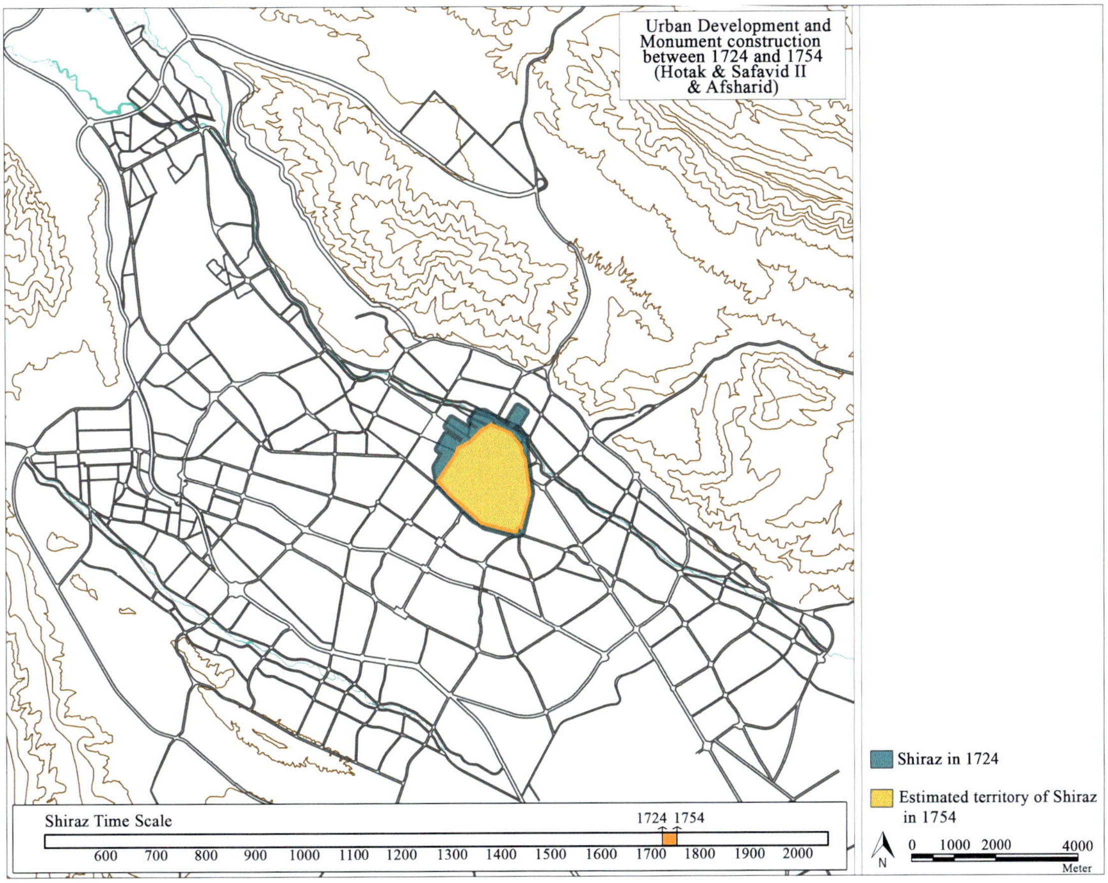

18 Shiraz during Hotak, Safavid II, and Afsharid periods.

19 Shiraz's macro landscape from the Gahvareh Did (Div) view from Hotaks to Afsharids.

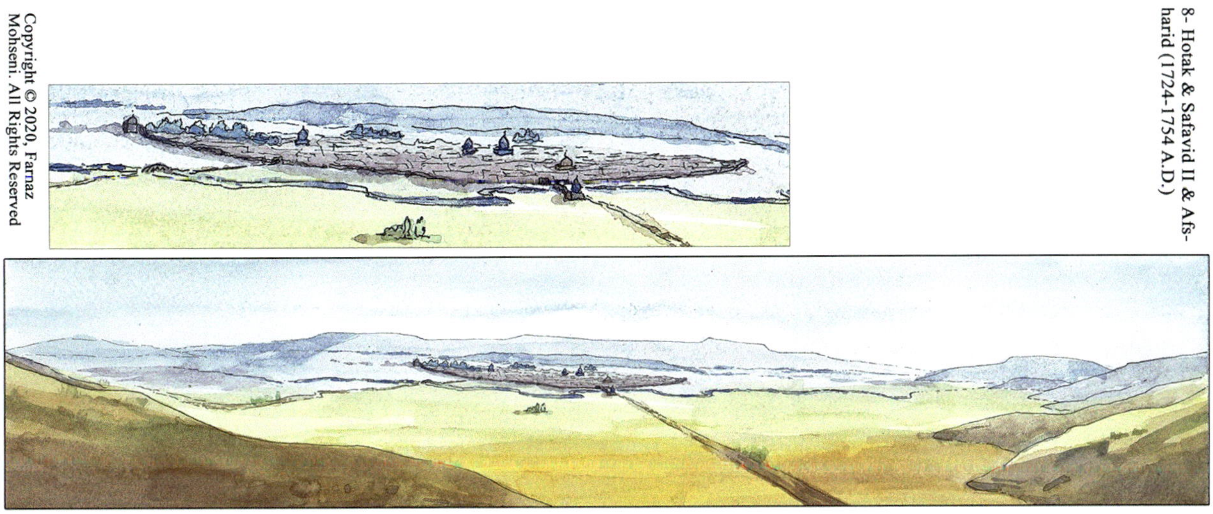

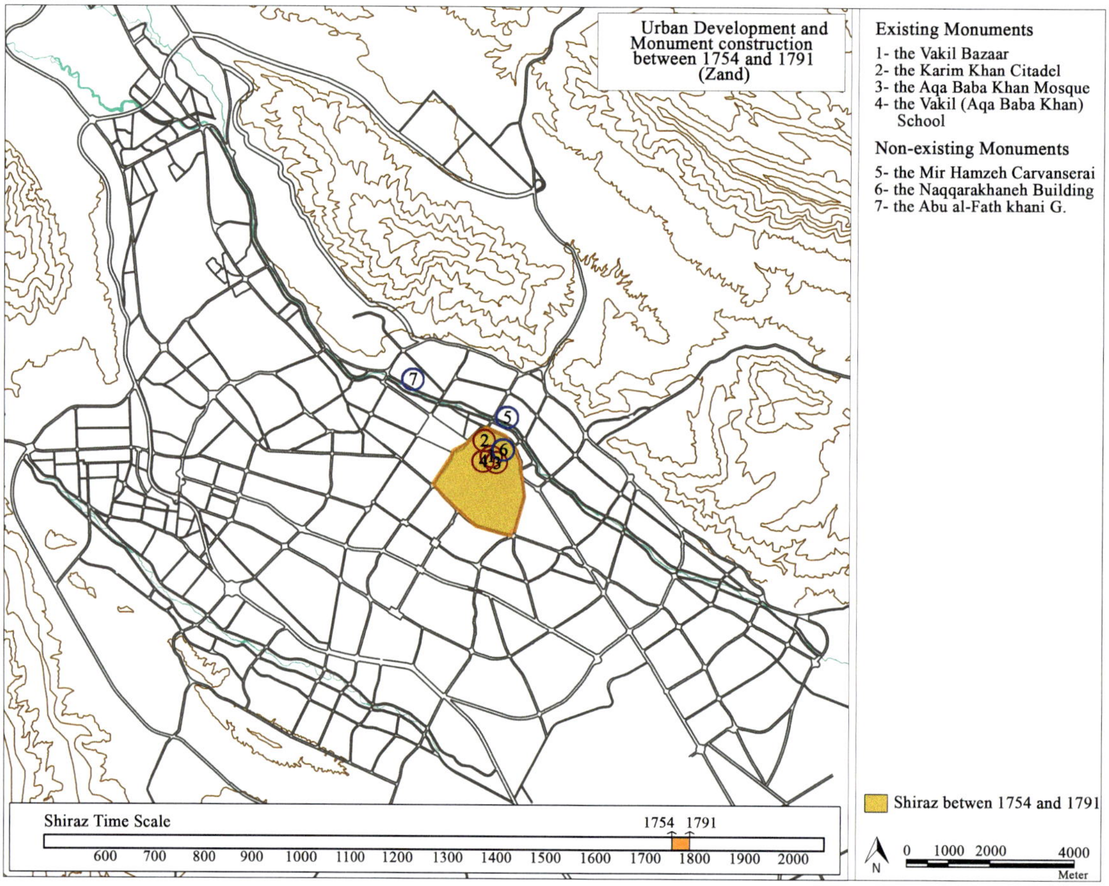

20 Shiraz during the Zand period.

21 Shiraz's macro landscape from the Gahvareh Did (Div) view during the Zand period.

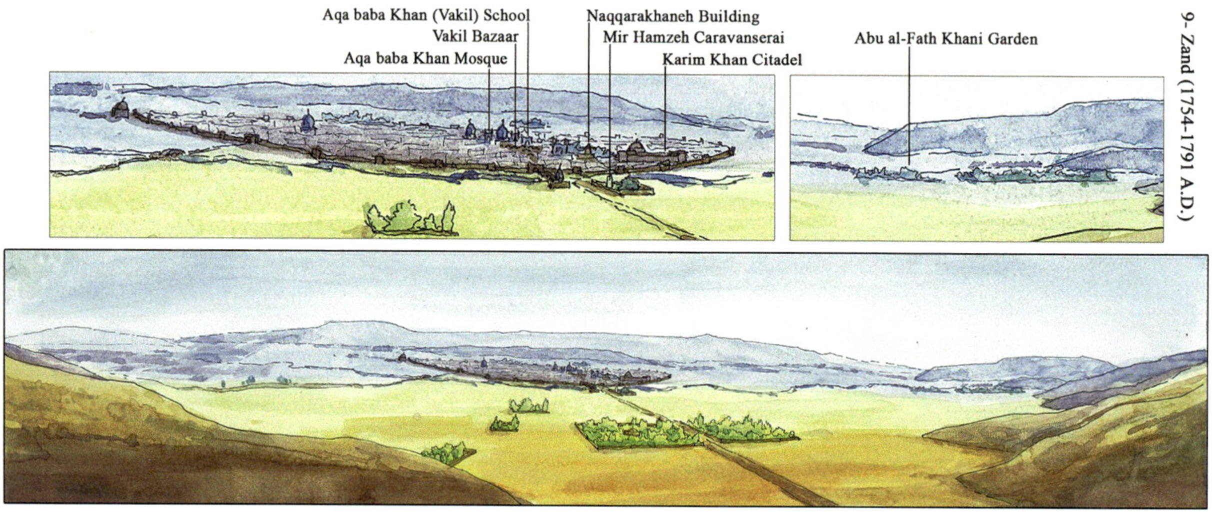

against him, he constructed a citadel within the city walls. Even today, the Karim Khan Citadel is one of the city's main tourist attractions. It was located as a part of the Zand complex, consisting of several monuments and two main urban squares next to the citadel, the Mashq and Naqqarakhaneh squares. As for other parts of the complex, there was also the court called the Divankhaneh, as well as the Naqqarakhaneh building, a place where kettledrums were played. The economic flourishing of Shiraz was expressed in the skyline through the construction of new bazaars. The Vakil bazaar, nowadays one of the most famous bazaars in Iran, was built as a part of the Zand complex.[66] Moreover, the Mir Hamzeh caravanserai was constructed during the Zand period.[67] Showing Karim Khan's environmental concerns, pieces of water infrastructure such as qanats and water reservoirs were built or repaired. This provided the concrete foundation for many other landmarks, including the gardens. Many gardens were renovated, such as the Jahan nama, Chehel tan, Haft tan and Nov gardens, while the Abu al-Fath Khani garden was built during the Zand period (fig. 21). Alireza Aryanpour argues that the Nazar Garden, a part of the Zand complex and the King's Harem, was most probably completed before the Zands. However, it was rearranged perfectly, and its pavilion was constructed by Karim Khan.[68] Chardin's sketch of Shiraz's landscape during the Safavids may seem a bit blurry, but, it shows what appears to be a garden at the approximate location of the Nazar Garden during the reign of the Safavids.[69]

The same argument can be made for the Vakil Mosque, another component of the Zand complex. An inscription in the Vakil Mosque, as well as Chardin's descriptions, establish that the mosque was probably at the location of an older mosque called the Jenazeh Mosque, which dated back to the Safavids. Moreover, the Aqa baba Khan School and Mosque were constructed during Zands, shaping the city's skyline. Being in favour of cultural figures, Karim Khan also ordered the renovation of the Saadi and Hafez tombs.[70]

From 1791 AD to 1925 AD: Qajar Period

In 1791, after the fall of the Zands, the country's capital shifted to Tehran. Shiraz was now only the provincial city of the Fars State. Agha Mohammad Khan Qajar destroyed Shiraz's massive wall and filled in the moat.[71] The city did not have a defensive wall again until Fath-Ali Shah's coronation in 1797, when one of the Qajar princes rebelled against the king and built a clay wall around Shiraz. Also, as another military and security impact on the macro landscape, Farmanfarma, the ruler of Fars, ordered the construction of the Hosein abaad Citadel, which was actually a wall separating the administrative buildings from the rest of the city (fig. 22).[72]

At the same time, not being the political capital meant that Shiraz's economic growth was at risk during the Qajar dynasty. In fact, in the 1890s, a trade path was developed by the Lynch English Company along the Karoon River in the southwest of Iran, which connected the port directly to Isfahan. Previously, goods had passed through Shiraz in order to reach Isfahan and later Tehran, the capital. Lord Curzon claims that Shirazi merchants were anxious about the possible impact of the Karoon trade path on their business.[73] The economic situation became even more complicated when a significant amount of the capital had to be spent on the repair of damage caused by several earthquakes.

A massive earthquake in Shiraz in June 1824 led to the demolition of many buildings. Only two months later, in August 1824, another earthquake, even more destructive than the first, caused the destruction of a vast number of monuments that had survived the first earthquake. The domes of Shah Cheragh, Seyyed Alaoddin Hossein, Ali bin Hamzeh, and Mohammad bin Musa, as well as the clay wall, were destroyed. Only a couple of vaults of the Vakil bazaar remained. Almost three decades later, in May 1853, another earthquake occurred in Shiraz. Thousands of people died, and several mosques and schools were damaged.[74] While the damage to the human-made macro

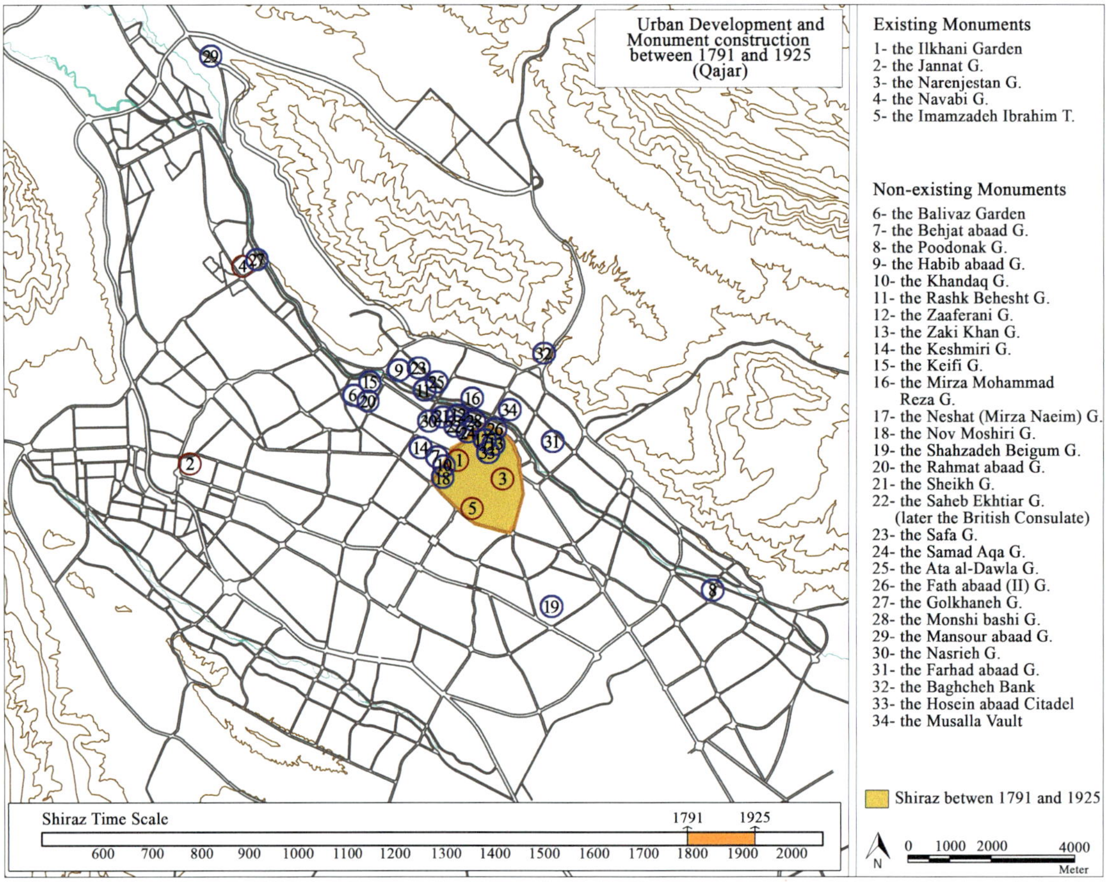

22 Shiraz during the Qajar period.

landmarks was significant, the green infrastructure and gardens were more likely to survive the earthquakes. Consequently, it is not surprising to see vast green areas in Shiraz's macro landscape during the Qajar period (fig. 23).

The adverse effects of economic difficulties and earthquakes on constructing new landmarks and demolishing old monuments are undeniable. However, the city's political status was relatively stable for 134 years. As a result of less destructive conflicts, the gardens were flourishing in the silhouette of Shiraz in the 19th century. It could be concluded that gardening is deeply rooted in Shiraz's culture as well as the collective memory of its residents. Consequently, green spaces survived the most challenging economic crises and grew back after many disasters. It can also be concluded that it was only through infrastructure such as the qanats, constructed during times of stability, that the urban system recovered itself, and the gardens flourished in Shiraz's macro landscape. A clear-cut example was in 1847, when Saheb Ekhtiar, the ruler of Fars, brought water from the Shesh Pir river through canals into Shiraz. He also ordered the elites of the city to build themselves gardens outside the Baghshah Gate. The street that Saheb Ekhtiar suggested was a replica of the old Safavid Baghshah Charbagh at the same location. A brief view of figure 23 shows a corridor of green spaces northwest of Shiraz.

Relying on the research of Aryanpour and other scholars, the long list of gardens created during the Qajar period includes the gardens of Ilkhani, Jannat, Narenjestan, Navabi, Balivaz, Behjat abaad, Poodonak, Habib abaad, Khandaq, Rashk Behesht, Zaaferani, Zaki Khan, Keshmiri, Keifi, Mirza Mohammad Reza, Neshat, Nov Moshiri, Shahzadeh Beigum, Rahmat abaad, Sheikh, Saheb Ekhtiar, Safa, Samad Aqa, Ata al-Dawla, Fath abaad (II), Golkhaneh, Monshi bashi, Mansour abaad, Nasrieh, and Farhad abaad.[75] However, the author must state that most of these gardens probably existed long before the Qajars. As the underground water network had already existed for centuries, landmarks, especially the green spaces, would have been shaped alongside the qanats and canals. Sometimes they might have disappeared and reappeared later with a different name, size, or plan, and indeed the historical sources on landmarks are more comprehensive in recent centuries. This

23 The view from the Gahvareh Did (Div) view during the Qajar period shows the significant role of green spaces in shaping Shiraz's macro landscape.

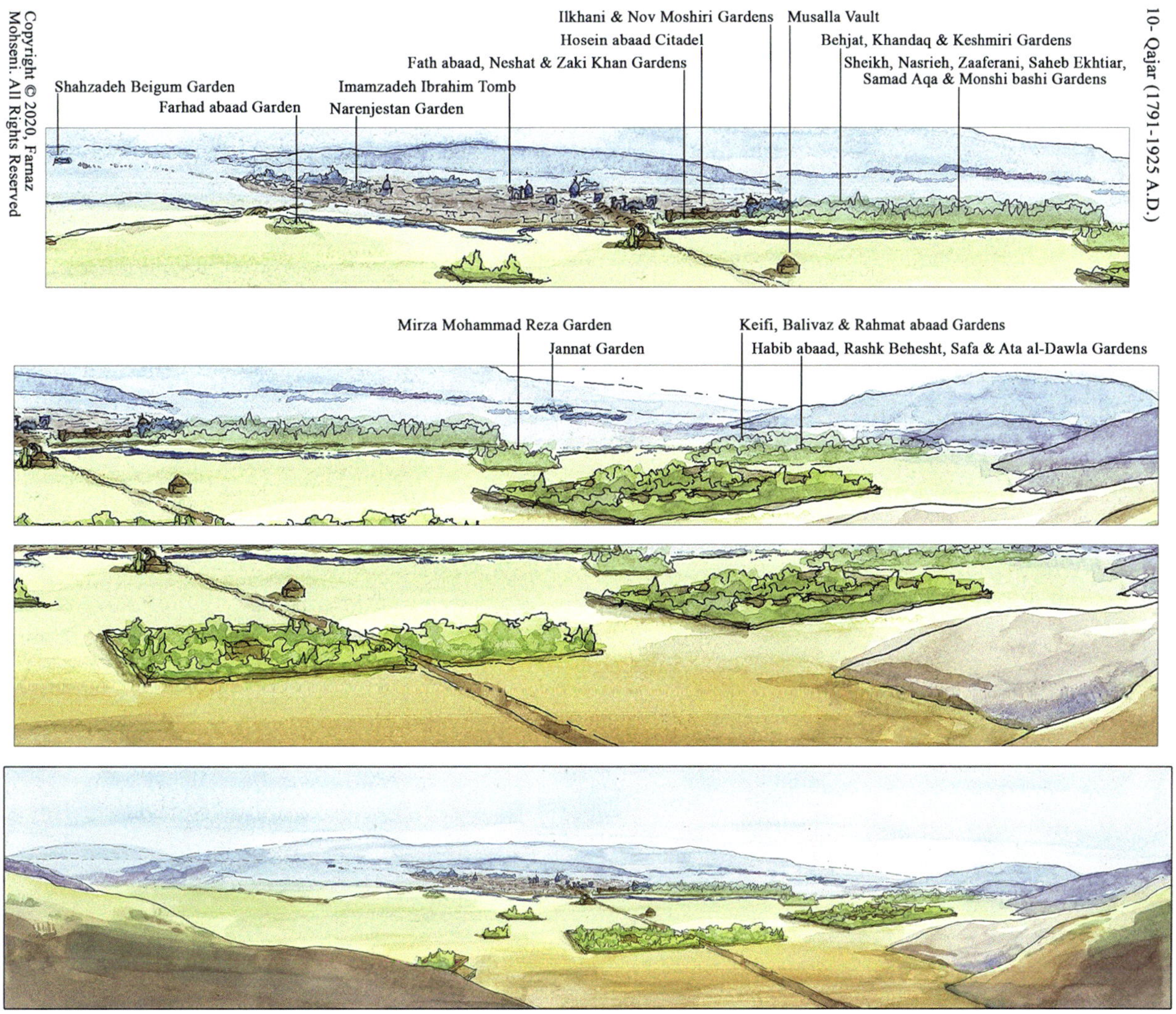

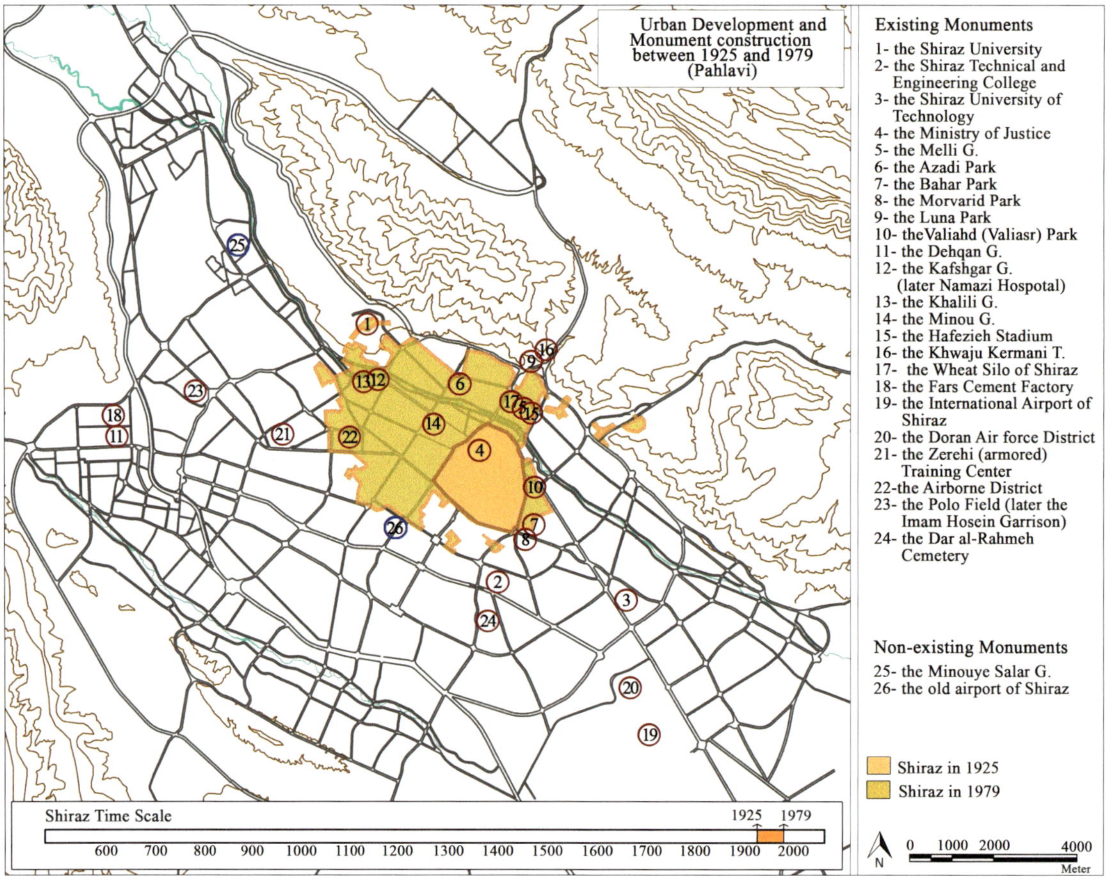

24 Shiraz during the Pahlavi period.

argument especially applies to the vast Qasr od-Dasht gardens northwest of Shiraz. Nevertheless, the fact that Shiraz's green landscape was dominant during the 19th century is still apparent, even based on the limited historical sources.

Finally, the Musalla vault and the Imamzadeh Ibrahim tomb are two landmarks with sacred and religious use, built during the Qajar period. Moreover, Mahmoudieh House, or Baghcheh Bank, was another landmark constructed on the western hillside of the Allaho Akbar Valley.

From 1925 AD to 1979 AD: Pahlavi Period

The 1930s is known as the beginning of modernisation in many Iranian cities, including Shiraz. The new construction technologies and the increasing utilisation of motor vehicles led to rapid urban development and wide streets and boulevards, within and outside the historic fabric. Within half a century, Shiraz grew significantly in area, and the height of new buildings increased.[76] Over 50 years, Shiraz's size expanded around five times, and many old landmarks that existed physically, like the Khan School or the Haji bazaar, were lost visually in the mass of new neighbourhoods. The city mostly grew towards the north and northwest (fig. 24).

What makes the Pahlavi period different in shaping the city's macro landscape is the variety of driving forces compared to previous times. First of all, the traditional juridical and administrative system was replaced with modern governmental and legal establishments. This is reflected in the silhouette through the construction of buildings such as the Ministry of Justice.[77] The Iranian Railway project that connected the Persian Gulf in the south to the Caspian Sea in the north did not pass through Shiraz. Afterwards, Shiraz was no longer the traditional storage place of goods and a connector of southern ports to the rest of the country.

Nevertheless, between 1966 and 1975, a significant rise in the oil price resulted in increased capital in cities, which in turn led to migration from rural areas to peripheral urban districts. In addition, the Shah's White Revolution in 1963[78] sped up rural-to-urban migration. Because of the new land reform laws, one of the principal articles of the white revolution, the government bought land from the Khans, the feudal nobles in Iran, and sold it to peasants for a price below the market value. Later on, many farmers sold their lands and migrated to cities.[79] Shiraz's population boom was so significant that the city demanded a more expanded cemetery, the Dar al-Rahmeh cemetery (fig. 25).

Meanwhile, the religious factor still played a role in shaping the skyline. For instance, the Ali bin Hamzeh Dome was rebuilt with a different physical appearance during Pahlavi, using a steel structure. Also, the Aqa bazaar (the Sar-e Hoz-e Aqa bazaar) was demolished during the project of merging the courtyards of the Shah Cheragh and Mohammad bin Musa tombs. Additionally, after destroying the original Quran Gate to widen the city's main entrance, a new gate was designed and constructed in 1949, a couple of metres away from its original location.[80] Another factor in the landscape shift was the establishment of many military camps around the city in different directions,[81] such as the Doran Air Force District, the Zerehi (armoured) Training Centre, and the Airborne District. Even the Takht Garden changed its land use to a military garrison.

Industrial and technological developments are other influential factors specific to the 20th century. The emergence of the aviation industry led to the construction of airborne and air force districts (with administrative or residential use for the workers in these organisations), as well as of the old and new Shiraz international airports. Moreover, Shiraz's wheat silo and the Fars Cement Factory were built outside the city as signs of modern architecture and industrial development.[82] Additionally, although traditional hospitals had existed long before in Shiraz, the first modern hospitals were built in the city during this period.[83] For example, the Namazi Hospital was constructed in the Kafshgar Garden lands in 1955. Nevertheless, it is undeniable that the most influential impact of modern technologies was making broader roads and bridges over the Dry River and constructing higher buildings and vaster neighbourhoods in a short time (see fig. 25).

With the building of Shiraz University, the former Pahlavi University, upon a hill, the role of contemporary scientific education was evident more than ever in the silhouette (see fig. 25).[84] Additionally, the emergence of the modern lifestyle of Shirazi residents demanded new land use for leisure and sport. While the trees of the polo field (later the Imam Hosein Garrison) were evident from a distant location, Shiraz's first stadium, Hafezieh Stadium, was also visible at the macro level. Moreover, Luna Park, the amusement park, was built on the northeastern hillside of Shiraz.

The cultural contributions, however significant, did not appear dramatically in the macro landscape. A wide range of repair projects for heritage assets and historical buildings such as the Nov Mosque and the Shah Cheragh tomb helped preserve Shiraz's historic buildings for the next generations.[85] However, although conserved physically, many of those landmarks were not as visible as in old times on the skyline due to massive and uncontrolled urban growth. Nevertheless, the trend to redesign the tombs of national figures such as Hafez, Saadi, and Khwaju Kermani, inspired by Iranian architectural principles, impacted the silhouette.[86]

Last but not least, the impact of environmental factors was significant on the landscape of Shiraz from 1925 to 1979. While the old gardening tradition was still visible in making the Dehqan, Khalili, Minou, and Minouye Salar gardens, the new trend of creating parks emerged in the 20th century. The Persian Gardens, now inscribed in the UNESCO World Heritage List,[87] was historically mostly off limits to the general public (though exceptions existed) and had specific design principles. By contrast, the parks were built for the use of all people, and they did not necessarily follow the design principles of the Persian Gardens. For example, traditional Iranian pavillions were not built within the newly established parks of Shiraz. The parks of Melli, Azadi, Bahar, Morvarid, and Valiahd (later Valiasr) were designed as non-traditional public green spaces. However, it was not the creation of gardens and parks that made the environmental

25 Shiraz's macro landscape from the Gahvareh Did (Div) view during the Pahlavi times depicts the remarkable effect of rapid urban development. Many old landmarks have been lost in the mass of buildings ever since.

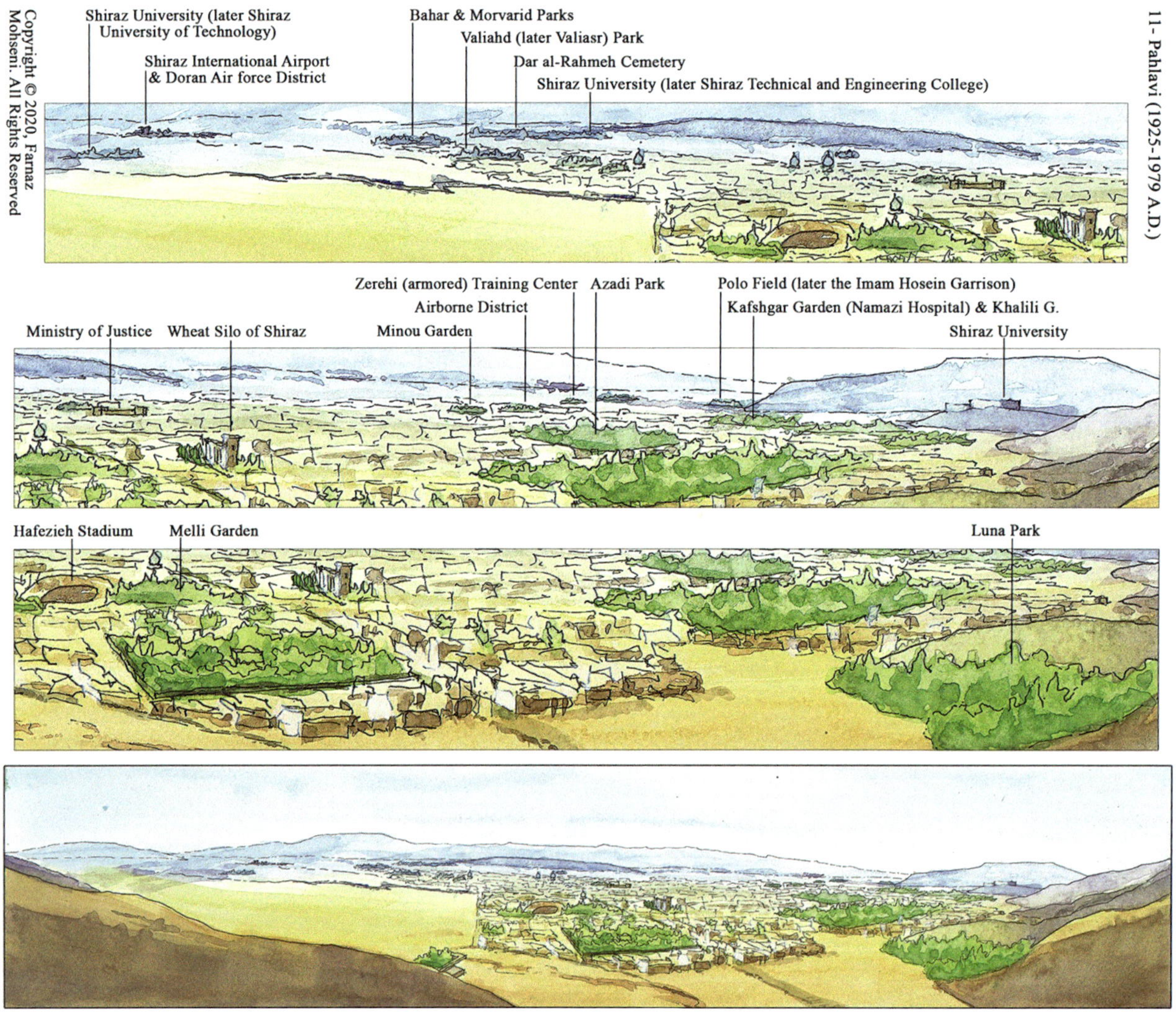

factor the most influential driving force. According to the location of the scattered new landmarks (see fig. 25), it may not be accurate to conclude that the monumental new establishments, such as the modern entertainment, healthcare, and education buildings, solely led the direction of the development. However, the northwest direction of Shiraz's urban development, which continued after 1979, was mostly led by environmental considerations. The northwest of Shiraz generally has more moderate and pleasant weather, due to its higher elevation and the proximity of the Qasr od-Dasht Gardens. The pleasure of fresh air and green spaces directed Shiraz's urban growth towards the northwest while putting the attraction source, the gardens, at high risk. Vast green areas and fields covered with gardens alongside the Dry River and the old replica of the Safavid Charbagh were slowly replaced by houses and neighbourhoods.[88] Therefore, by 1979, Shiraz was in general significantly less green in comparison to the Qajar period.

From 1979 AD to 2019 AD: Islamic Republic Period

Only a year and a half after the Islamic revolution, the eight-year-long Iran–Iraq war started and changed the whole country's demographic balance, including that of Shiraz. A migration flow of evacuees from in-risk regions to more central cities, such as Shiraz, was one of the most influential driving forces of rapid urban development.[89] Many migrants settled in Shiraz after the war. On the other hand, the centralisation of capital in big cities like Shiraz accelerated the migration from rural areas. During recent decades, global warming and the low level of underground water in many regions in Iran altered the country's previously agriculture-based economy even more. Nowadays, the majority of Iranians reside in urban areas. Shiraz became one of the five most populated urban metropolises in Iran, with a population of more than 1.5 million.[90] The city's area is now about forty times bigger than its original Qajar-era historical core from a century before (fig. 26). Additionally, being subjected to even more massive urban growth after 1979, it is no wonder that the balance of the macro landscape was drastically altered between the end of the 1970s and the present.

First of all, the number of old landmarks, which were still part of Shiraz's silhouette during Pahlavi times, has diminished. The domes of Shah Cheragh, Seyyed Alaoddin Hossein, and Ali bin Musa, which were hardly visible in the mass of new neighbourhoods built during the Pahlavi era, are nowadays even less distinguishable in the urban fabric. High-rise apartments block the view to the Karim Khan Citadel, and the vaults of the Vakil Bazaar are barely recognisable from the surrounding buildings (fig. 27). The list goes on, and the emergence of new skyscrapers makes the case more complicated. It is important to clarify again that this study only lists landmarks constructed in modern times, regardless of any bias against their architectural value or location. Many readers may assess some of the following buildings as not visually pleasing or located inappropriately in the city. However, this chapter limits its focus to the distinguishability of landmarks in the macro landscape.

Nowadays, the economy plays an integral role in shaping the macro landscape of Shiraz. The tourism industry has propelled the construction of high-rise hotels such as the Shams, the Aseman, the Chamran, and the Shiraz Grand Hotel. According to a survey[91] conducted by the author in 2020, many of these buildings are easily distinguishable in the silhouette at first glimpse. Some even block the view of a historic landmark. As the historic monuments are tourist attractions, the tourism industry's economic engine sometimes works against the capital that it has to attract tourists. From 1995 until 2010, the Bein al-Haramain project in Shiraz has resulted in the demolition of seven hectares of the city's historic fabric, including 87 historic houses, a school, a mosque, and even nationally listed monuments. Approval has also been given for the demolition of an additional 57 hectares of the fabric of the historic centre

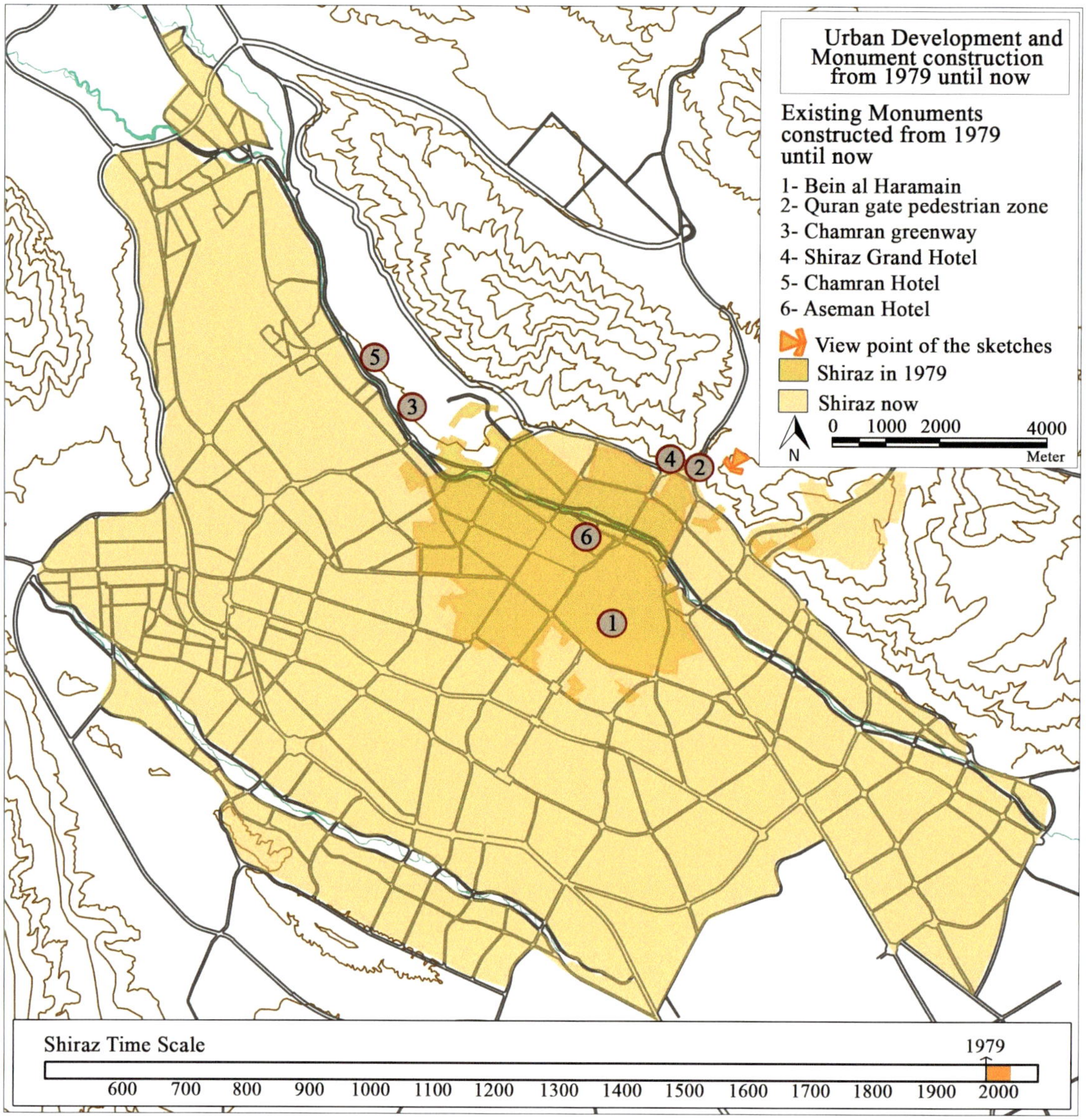

26 Shiraz during the Islamic Republic.

to be replaced by a hotel, shopping centres, and religious facilities.[92]

Constructed outside Shiraz's municipal borders but visible at the skyline, the Persian Gulf Complex is another example of commercial land use that impacts the silhouette. Also, the spiritual factor still plays an essential role in the macro landscape of Shiraz. Religion is a driving force behind the Bein al-Haramain project, which connects the two shrines of Shah Cheragh and Seyyed Alaoddin Hossein.[93] Moreover, the Nov Mosque, which dates back to the Atabak period, was and still is used as the central mosque for Friday Prayers in Shiraz. Consequently, the vast courtyard of the mosque was covered by a metallic roof for the convenience of the worshipers.[94] Today, the metallic roof is the only barely visible structure of the mosque on the silhouette.

The Parseh Stadium, the second sports complex of Shiraz, was built in the southwest of the city, while the National Library of Fars was constructed in the north-east, close to the Quran Gate, catering for the cultural and leisure needs of Shirazi residents in the 21st century. Both constructions play the role of new landmarks on the skyline. Transport needs are also influencing Shiraz's landscape significantly. The Valiasr bridge is the first cable-style bridge of Shiraz visible in the silhouette. Moreover, the Allaho Akbar Valley, where the Quran Gate is located, was broadened in 1988. The design of the main north entrance to the city was chosen through an architectural competition. Until 1986 and before the Allaho Akbar Valley's new design, cars used to pass under the Quran Gate. Nowadays, the gate is a monument on the side of the road surrounded by a pedestrian zone.

27 Shiraz's macro landscape from the Gahvareh Did (Div) view in 2018 shows the city filling out the Shiraz Plain. As a consequence of rapid urban growth, many historic landmarks are no longer distinguishable from the new urban fabric.

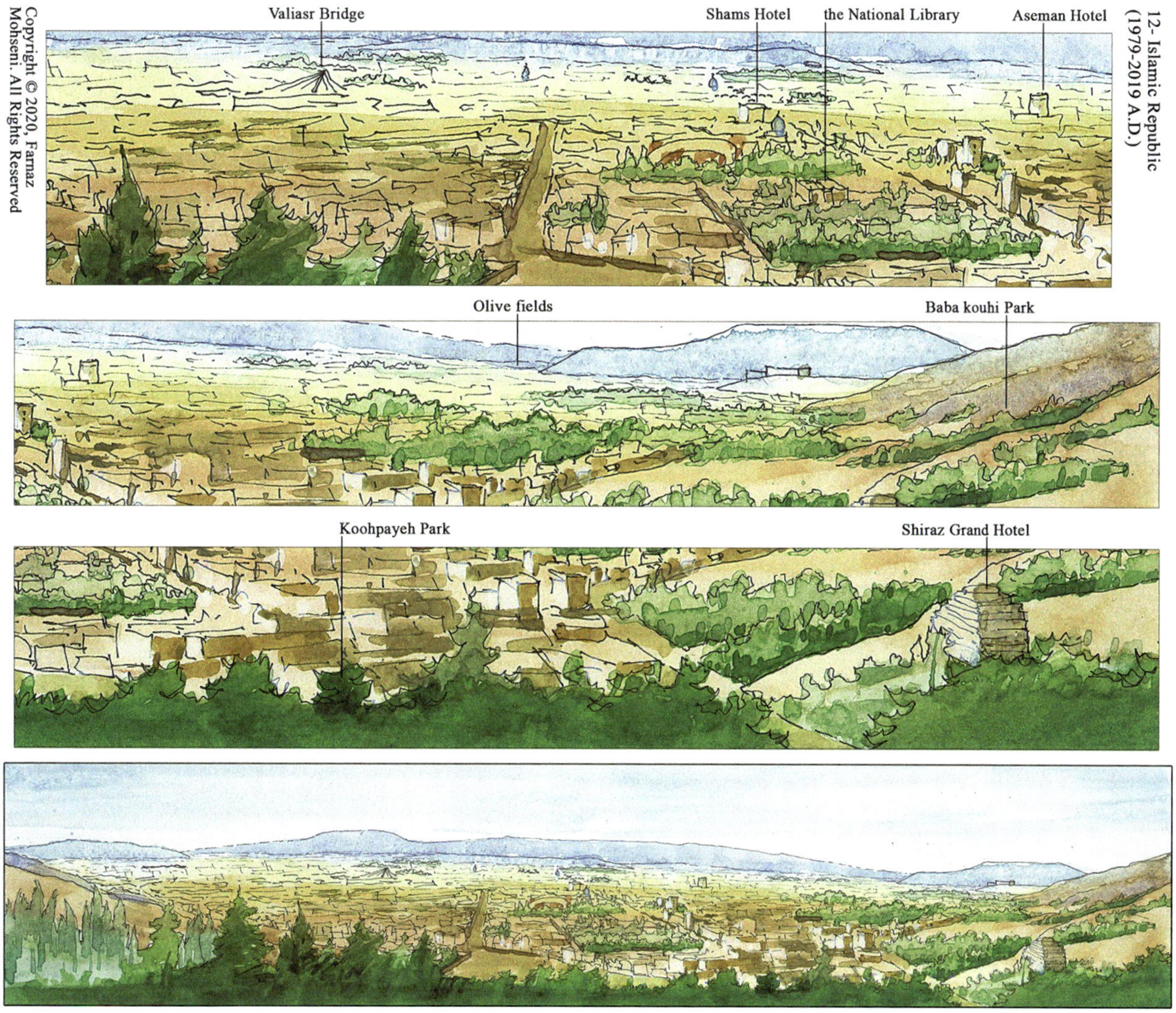

Simultaneously, a new trend has been noticeable over the past decades in many Iranian cities. The recent approach of greening the hillsides seems quite popular in Shiraz, a city surrounded by mountains. The Baba Kouhi, Koohpayeh, and Koohestan parks are among the examples that changed the city's general view (see fig. 27) and are viewed favourably by the public, according to a survey conducted by the author in 2020. These parks not only have a positive visual effect on the silhouette; they also provide residents with opportunities for hiking. Additionally, some old landmarks on the verge of invisibility in the massive scale of modern Shiraz have become more recognisable. The Baba Kouhi tomb, the ruins of Bandar Fortress, and the Gahvareh Did watchtower would have been barely seen at the macro level. However, the new parks built around small historic landmarks make them more visible without adding controversial extensions to the original buildings. This new trend is a continuation of the long gardening tradition and culture of Shiraz.[95] Also, the olive fields of the Bash Garden in the west of Shiraz and the design of the Chamran Greenway in the north are examples of green spaces influencing the skyline.

Despite the plantation and greening efforts, especially in Shiraz's marginal areas, the city's vastest green asset is at extreme risk. The historic Qasr od-Dasht Gardens in the northwest have diminished in size drastically and have been swallowed up by residential neighbourhoods in recent decades. Although many plans were proposed with the aim of preserving these gardens, this gigantic greenfield lost the majority of its area over a century. Scholars have different opinions on the original size of the gardens. However, according to various references, the gardens have lost at least two-thirds of their area, approximately 2,000 hectares.[96]

It can be argued that the most influential factors in the disturbed balance of the urban landscape in modern times are urban regulation and management. There are several management and legal gaps that pose an obstacle to the integration

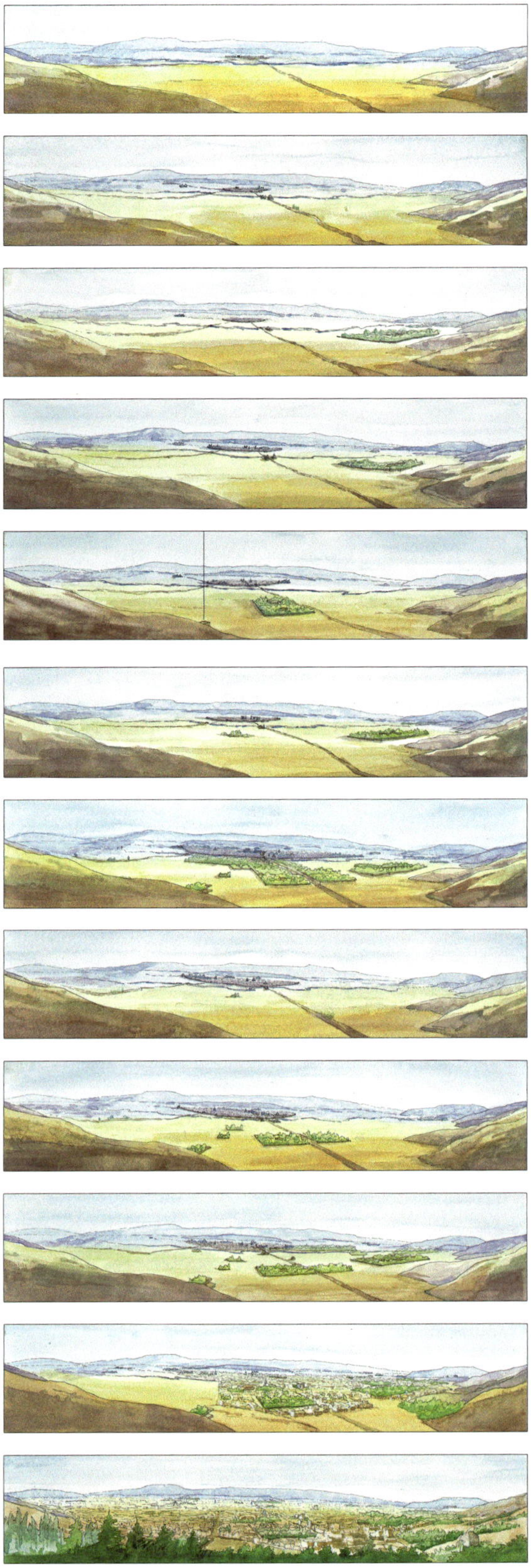

28 The evolution of Shiraz's skyline from 639 AD until today.

of urban planning and historic landscape conservation. Hence, there are not only problems in preservation rules, but the more significant challenge of the lack of an urban planning mechanism confining high-rise developments to specific zones. Nevertheless, to prove this hypothesis, an in-depth and comprehensive investigation of the legal and administrative challenges over the past century is needed. Such study would certainly be an essential topic for future investigation.

Discussion and Conclusion

This chapter discusses and illustrates the macro landscape development of Shiraz over time (fig. 28) while linking the city's skyline shifts with multi-dimensional driving forces. It uses a systematic visualisation method based on historical evidence to recreate the skyline of the city during different periods. The chapter argues that in different historical periods, political, economic, environmental, societal, religious, military, cultural, health, transport, legal, industrial, and educational factors shaped Shiraz's macro landscape and were reflected in the skyline. Nevertheless, massive urban development was the biggest influence on the macro landscape during the past century. This growth resulted in the reduced visibility of old monuments and the emergence of new landmarks that are debatably not aesthetically pleasing and disturbing in the skyline.

In the decision-making process for Shiraz's macro landscape management, it is of premium importance to consider environmental factors as the most influential driving force.[97] This is because Shiraz has long been admired as the city of Persian gardens, and gardening has been considered an old cultural tradition in Shiraz. Moreover, the survey conducted by the author in 2020 further verifies that green spaces are still the most valuable landmarks within the city rather than buildings due to the value of green gardens in the collective image of the Shirazi people. Consequently, the author suggests prioritising the preservation of current parks and gardens, especially the Qasr od-Dasht Gardens. Also, the recent initiative of building parks around smaller historic landmarks on hillsides could be encouraged. Future investigations of the opportunities and applicability of this approach for other historic buildings on hillsides, like the ruins of Abu Nasr Castle, should be undertaken.

Finally, as shown in the illustrations, the Shiraz macro landscape confronts two main questions in the 21st century. Where to build and where not to build? Undeniably, the economic factor would eventually lead to the construction of high-rise buildings. It is neither possible nor advantageous to ignore the powerful engine of development. Consequently, it is only by regulation and development codes that a balance between development and conservation can be achieved. Despite many efforts, a wide range of development plans has not successfully addressed this problem. An investigation of the legal and administrative gaps demands more comprehensive research. Nevertheless, to save the aesthetics and historic greenery in the skyline of Shiraz, the new codes and regulation system should be capable of reaching a balance between the demands of modern life and the preservation of the old.

This chapter is derived from the author's PhD thesis, completed at the Chair of Urban Management at BTU Cottbus-Senftenberg, see Mohseni 2023.

1 Afsar 1974.
2 Nasr 2004.
3 Chizfahm Daneshmandian et al. 2020.
4 Macro here refers to being large in scale or scope, i.e, covering the entirety of the city's landscape.
5 Mohseni et al. 2020b.
6 Downes/Lange 2015.
7 Liu/Nijhuis 2020.
8 Downes/Lange 2015.
9 Cybulski et al. 2020.
10 An/Powe 2015; Liu/Nijhuis 2020.
11 Kullmann 2014; Tobias et al. 2015; Liu/Nijhuis 2020.
12 Lovett et al. 2015; Tobias et al. 2015.
13 Bruyn 1718; Fraser 1834; Brugsch 1886; Herbert 2004; Dieulafoy 1887.
14 Mohseni et al. 2020a.
15 Mohseni et al. 2020b.
16 Chizfahm Daneshmandian et al. 2020.
17 Herbert 2004, 70; Loti 1904.
18 An/Powe 2015.
19 Kullmann 2014.
20 Chardin 1735; Niebuhr 1792.
21 Koch 1992.
22 Khubnazar 2002.
23 Pakzad 2011, 187.
24 A grand mosque or Friday mosque is a mosque used for the Friday prayers or the Eid prayers. The number of grand (*Jame*) mosques in one city has been very limited.
25 Dar al-Khalifa was a castle where political power was based during the Islamic period.
26 Afsar 1974, 42.
27 Afsar 1974, 34.
28 Khubnazar 2002.
29 Al-Muqaddasī 1982, 429–449.
30 Mustaufi 2002, 114.
31 Zarkoub Shirazi 1971, 36.
32 Khubnazar 2002, 187–197.
33 Mansouri/Arabsolghar 2016.
34 Zarkoub Shirazi 1971, 63–70.
35 Aryanpour 1986.
36 A Khanqah is a spiritual building designed for gatherings of a Sufism community.
37 Pakzad 2011, 303.
38 Zarkoub Shirazi 1971, 197–199.
39 Zarkoub Shirazi 1971, 71–72.
40 Aryanpour 1986.
41 Afsar 1974, 85–87.
42 A *ribat* was a traditional inn along the road, in which the voyagers recovered from their journey.
43 Afsar 1974, 89–91.
44 Zarkoub Shirazi 1971, 112.
45 Ibn Battuta 1997, 202.
46 Ibn Battuta 1997, 194.
47 Afsar 1974.
48 Afsar 1974, 97.
49 Aryanpour 1986.
50 Ibn Battuta 1997, 194.
51 Afsar 1974, 118.
52 Afsar 1974, 18.
53 A *caravan* was a group of travellers, often for the purpose of a trade expedition.
54 A *caravanserai* was the traditional inn where caravaners could recover from their journey.
55 Chardin 1735; Afsar 1974, 158–167.
56 Tavernier 1957, 654–667.
57 Afsar 1974, 167.
58 Shiraz1400 News 2016.
59 Bruyn 1718; Chardin 1735.
60 Tavernier 1957, 654–667.
61 Daulier Deslandes 1673; Chardin 1735.
62 Fasāʾī 2003, 168.
63 Afsar 1974, 154.
64 In many Iranian sources drafted by contemporary scholars, the «Hotaks» are referred to as «Afghans». Hotaks originate from lands that are a part of today's Afghanistan, which later became an independent country during the 18th and 19th centuries. At the time when Hotaks put an end to the Safavid Empire, Iran and Afghanistan were one country. A feudal tradition was important in the region for centuries. According to this tradition, one dynasty took control of the land and the other houses obeyed for a while by paying tribute until the next house rebelled and established the new kingdom. This was the case for many other dynasties such as the Afsharids, Zands, and Qajars. As it is a tradition in historical studies to identify the country's ruler by the name of the dynasty, the author holds the view that the same naming system should apply to the Hotaks, regardless of the separation of countries in later decades. Utilising the generalised term «Afghan» on the other hand would be scientifically less precise, considering the colourful ethnic makeup and history of Afghanistan. Last but not least, given the sensitivity of ethnic and racial issues in the 21st century, the author holds the view that the term «Hotak» is a more appropriate alternative for historical studies.
65 Khubnazar 2002, 799–800.
66 Hamidi 1997.
67 Afsar 1974, 190.
68 Aryanpour 1986, 295.
69 Chardin 1735.
70 Afsar 1974, 181–219; CHHTM of Fars 2019a, 2019b.
71 Waring 1807, 34–45.
72 Afsar 1974, 232.
73 Curzon 1892, 570–580.
74 Navab Shirazi 1992; Fasāʾī 2003, 307–308.
75 Aryanpour 1986.
76 Nasr 2004, 17–19.

77 Nasr 2004, 40.
78 The White Revolution was a series of fundamental reforms proposed by Mohammad Reza Shah, resulting in massive changes in Iran's legal, social, and economic status. The reforms undertaken over many years covered various articles, including land reforms and abolishing feudalism, privatisation of government-owned enterprises, nationalisation of forest and water resources, extensions of women's rights, etc.
79 Nikkar 2005.
80 Sane 2001.
81 Nikkar 2005.
82 Nasr 2004, 50–51.
83 Nikkar 2005.
84 Nasr 2004, 120–121.
85 Nasr 2004, 75–81.
86 Nasr 2004, 52–62.
87 UNESCO 2011.
88 Aryanpour 1986.
89 Nikkar 2005.
90 Statistical Center of Iran 2011.
91 The interviews with a total number of 385 Shirazi people included a combination of open- and close-ended questions. The interviewees were asked to identify valuable and disturbing landmarks in the skyline and provide reasons for their choice.
92 Mehr News Agency 2010.
93 Yadollahi 2020.
94 CHHTM of Fars 2023.
95 There may be some arguments about the environmental risks of such green spaces in terms of the amount of water consumption. It is of crucial importance to consider the ecological limitations in the design of hill parks. Adapting technologies that consume less water and selecting plant types according to the context would be necessary not only for the hill parks but also for all the green spaces in Shiraz.
96 Jamshidi 2004; Hajipoor et al. 2016; Sadeghi et al. 2019; Amood 2021.
97 Mohseni et al. 2020b.

Afsar 1974
کرامت الله افسر: تاریخ بافت قدیمي شیراز.
K. Afsar: The history of the old fabric of Shiraz (Tehran 1974).

Al-Muqaddasī 1982
شمس الدين المقدسي: أحسن التقاسيم في معرفة الأقاليم.
S. Al-Muqaddasī: The Best Divisions for Knowledge of the Regions (Tehran 1982).

Amood 2021
ضوابط و مقررات طرح تفصیلی محدوده استحفاظی باغ های قصر الدشت شیراز.
Amood Urban Planning and Architecture Engineers: The Criteria and Regulations of the Detailed Plan of the Qasr od-Dasht Gardens Preservation Zone in Shiraz. The office of Conservation Zone of Qasr od-Dasht Gardens of Shiraz Municipality. Shiraz [online, 2021], https://baghat.shiraz.ir.

An / Powe 2015
K. An / N. Powe: Enhancing ‹Boundary Work› Through the Use of Virtual Reality: Exploring the Potential within Landscape and Visual Impact Assessment. Journal of Environmental Policy & Planning 17, no. 5, 2015, 673–690, https://doi.org/10.1080/1523908X.2015.1012757.

Aryanpour 1986
A. Aryanpour: A General Survey of Persian Gardens and an Investigation of the Historical Gardens of Shiraz (Tehran 1986).

Brugsch 1886
H. Brugsch: Im Lande der Sonne. Wanderungen in Persien (Berlin 1886), https://archive.org/details/bub_gb_L75GAAAAIAAJ (19 January 2025).

Bruyn 1718
C. Bruyn: Voyages de Corneille Le Brun par la Moscovie, en Perse, et aux Indes Orientales (Amsterdam 1718), https://archive.org/details/gri_33125008232130/page/n7 (19 January 2025).

CHHTM of Fars 2019a
شناسنامه مدرسه های ثبت شده میراث فرهنگی، اداره کل میراث فرهنگی، صنایع دستی و گردشگری استان فارس.
Ministry of Cultural Heritage, Handicrafts and Tourism of Fars: The List of Inscribed Heritage Schools. Ministry of Cultural Heritage, Handicrafts and Tourism of Fars. Shiraz [online, 2019], http://www.farschto.ir (5 August 2019).

CHHTM of Fars 2019b
شناسنامه مسجد های ثبت شده میراث فرهنگی، اداره کل میراث فرهنگی، صنایع دستی و گردشگری استان فارس.
Ministry of Cultural Heritage, Handicrafts and Tourism of Fars: The list of Inscribed Heritage Mosques. Ministry of Cultural Heritage, Handicrafts and Tourism of Fars. Shiraz [online, 2019], http://www.farschto.ir (5 August 2019).

CHHTM of Fars 2023
مسجد نو، اداره کل میراث فرهنگی، صنایع دستی و گردشگری استان فارس.
Ministry of Cultural Heritage, Handicrafts and Tourism of Fars: The Nov Mosque. Ministry of Cultural Heritage, Handicrafts and Tourism of Fars. Shiraz [online, 2023], http://www.fafarschto.ir/att.html?ln=fa&at=104 (19 March 2023).

Chardin 1735
J. Chardin: Voyages du chevalier Chardin en Perse et autres lieux de l'Orient (Amsterdam 1735), http://resolver.sub.uni-goettingen.de/purl?PPN688540732.

Chizfahm Daneshmandian et al. 2020
M. Chizfahm Daneshmandian / M. Behzadfar / S. Jalilisadrabad: The efficiency of visual buffer zone to preserve historical open

spaces in Iran. Sustainable Cities and Society 52, 2020, http://dx.doi.org/10.1016/j.scs.2019.101856.

Curzon 1892
G. Curzon: Persia and the Persian question (London 1892), https://archive.org/details/bub_gb_IuxtAAAAMAAJ/page/n1 (19 January 2025).

Cybulski et al. 2020
P. Cybulski / Ł. Wielebski / B. Medyńska-Gulij / D. Lorek / T. Horbiński: Spatial visualization of quantitative landscape changes in an industrial region between 1827 and 1883, Case study Katowice, southern Poland. Journal of Maps 16, no. 1, 2020, 77–85, https://doi.org/10.1080/17445647.2020.1746416.

Daulier Deslandes 1673
A. Daulier Deslandes: Les beautez de la Perse; ou, La description de ce qu'il y a de plus curieux dans ce royaume, enrichie de la carte du païs, & de plusieurs estampes dessignées sur les lieux (Paris 1673), https://archive.org/details/lesbeautezdelape00daul/page/n98/mode/2up (19 January 2025).

Dieulafoy 1887
J. Dieulafoy: La Perse, la Chaldée et la Susiane (Paris 1887), https://archive.org/details/ldpd_6885554_000/page/n5 (19 January 2025).

Downes / Lange 2015
M. Downes / E. Lange: What you see is not always what you get: A qualitative, comparative analysis of ex ante visualizations with ex post photography of landscape and architectural projects. Landscape and Urban Planning 142, 2015, 136–146, https://doi.org/10.1016/j.landurbplan.2014.06.002.

Fasāʾī 2003
حاج میرزا حسن حسینی شیرازی فسائی: فارسنامه ناصری.
H. Fasāʾī: Naseri's Book on Fars (Tehran 2003).

Fraser 1834
J. Fraser: Historical and descriptive account of Persia (New York 1834), https://archive.org/details/historicaldescr00fras/page/n10 (19 January 2025).

Hajipoor et al. 2016
حاجی پور خلیل/ حسین پور محمد/ فاضلی سارا / امان زادگان الهام / زارعی گیلدا: مفاهیم، چالش ها و اصول یکپارچه سازی فضای سبز شهری. نشریه شباک.
K. Hajipoor / M. Hossainpour / S. Fazeli / E. Amanzadegan / G. Zarei: Concepts, Challenges, and Principles of Urban Green Space Integration. Shebak Journal 4, no. 11, 2016, 30–39.

Hamidi 1997
ملیحه حمیدی: استخوان بندی شهر تهران - جلد ۳.
M. Hamidi: The main structure of Tehran, vol. 3 (Tehran 1997).

Herbert 2004
T. Herbert: Travels in Persia, 1627–1629 (London 2004).

Ibn Battuta 1997
ابن بطوطه: سفرنامه ابن بطوطه.
Ibn Battuta: Ibn Battuta Travels in Asia and Africa (Tehran 1997).

Jamshidi 2004
محمود جمشيدي: اراضی باغهای قصرالدشت شیراز یک فرصت مکانی تاریخی. نشریه جستارهای شهرسازی.
M. Jamshidi: The lands of Shiraz Qasr od-Dasht Gardens, a Spatial-cultural Opportunity. Jostar haye Shahrsazi 10, 2004, 43–52.

Khubnazar 2002
H. Khubnazar: A History of Shiraz (Tehran 2002).

Koch 1992
H. Koch: Es kündet Dareios der König. Vom Leben im persischen Grossreich (Darmstadt 1992).

Kullmann 2014
K. Kullmann: Hyper-realism and loose-reality: the limitations of digital realism and alternative principles in landscape design visualization. Journal of Landscape Architecture 9, no. 3, 2014, 20–31, https://doi.org/10.1080/18626033.2014.968412.

Liu / Nijhuis 2020
M. Liu / S. Nijhuis: Mapping landscape spaces: Methods for understanding spatial-visual characteristics in landscape design. Environmental Impact Assessment Review 82, 2020, https://doi.org/10.1016/j.eiar.2020.106376.

Loti 1904
P. Loti: Vers Ispahan (Paris 1904), https://archive.org/details/versispahan00loti/page/n7 (19 January 2025).

Lovett et al. 2015
A. Lovett / K. Appleton / B. Warren-Kretzschmar / C. von Haaren: Using 3D visualization methods in landscape planning: An evaluation of options and practical issues. Landscape and Urban Planning 142, 2015, 85–94, https://doi.org/10.1016/j.landurbplan.2015.02.021.

Mansouri / Arabsolghar 2016
منصوری سیدامیر/ عرب سلغار ندا: سیر تحول رابطه ساختاری باغ و شهر در سازمان فضایی شیراز از سده چهارم تا دوازدهم هجری قمری. نشریه مطالعات معماری ایران
S.A. Mansouri / N. Arabsolghar: The Evolutionary Process of Structural Relationship between Garden and city in the spatial structure of Shiraz. Journal of Iranian Architecture Studies, no. 8, 2016, 5–20.

Mehr News Agency 2010
۸۷خانه تاریخی در شیراز تخریب شد. خبرگزاری مهر.
The Mehr News Agency: 87 historic houses were demolished in Shiraz, 29 September 2010, https://mehrnews.com/xcJzP (19 January 2025).

Mohseni 2023
F. Mohseni: Safeguarding the Visual Integrity of the Historic Urban Landscape (HUL) through Contextualised Instrument Development: The Case Study of Shiraz (Doctoral Thesis). Brandenburg University of Technology (Cottbus 2023).

Mohseni et al. 2020a
F. Mohseni / S. Lotfi / M. Shole: Proposing an adapted visibility analysis methodology for the building height codes of the Shiraz development plan. Sustainable Cities and Society 61 [online, 2020], https://doi.org/10.1016/j.scs.2020.102347.

Mohseni et al. 2020b
F. Mohseni / S. Weidner / M. Kloos: A historical analysis and the identification of driving forces behind the evolution of the urban macro skyline of Shiraz, Iran. Journal of Cultural Heritage Management and Sustainable Development 10, no. 4, 2020, 413–427, https://doi.org/10.1108/JCHMSD-09-2019-0110.

Mustaufi 2002
حمد الله مستوفي: نزهة القلوب.
H. Mustaufi: Strolling of Hearts (Qazvin 2002).

Nasr 2004
T. Nasr: Architecture and Urbanism of Shiraz: In the Pahlavi Period (1922–1978) (Tehran 2004).

Navab Shirazi 1992
علی اکبر نواب شیرازی: تذکرهٔ دلگشا.
A. Navab Shirazi: Memorandum of Delgosha (Shiraz 1992).

Niebuhr 1792
C. Niebuhr: Travels through Arabia and other countries in the East (Edinburgh 1792), https://archive.org/details/travelsthrougha00conggoog/page/n9 (19 January 2025).

Nikkar 2005
مجید نیک کار: مرکز شهر شیراز در گذر زمان. نشریه جستارهای شهرسازی.
M. Nikkar: Historic Core of Shiraz in the course of time. Jostar haye Shahrsazi 12, 2005, 52–67.

Pakzad 2011
J. Pakzad: History of Iranian City, From beginning to Qajar Era (Tehran 2011).

Sadeghi et al. 2019
علي رضا صادقي/ فريال احمدي/ مهسا چيزفهم دانشمنديان: بهرهگيري از روش ارزيابي اكولوژيكي در فرآيند طراحي زيباييشناسانه منظر شهري طبيعي مورد پژوهي: كناره رودخانه خشك شيراز. مطالعات ساختار و كاركرد شهري.
A. Sadeghi / F. Ahmadi / M. Chizfahm daneshmandian: Application of Ecological Assessment in Aesthetic design of Natural Urban Landscapes Study Area (Khoshk River, Shiraz, Iran). Urban Structure and Function Studies 19, 2019, 7–26. https://doi.org/10.22080/shahr.2019.15041.1638.

Sane 2001
منصور صانع: بیاد شیراز، عکسهای شیراز قدیم.
M. Sane: In the Memory of Shiraz, Pictures of Old Shiraz (Tehran 2001).

Shiraz 1400 News 2016
شیراز ۱۴۰۰: قبرستان تاریخی دارالسلام، سند افتخار شیراز.
Shiraz 1400 News: The Historic Dar al-Salam Cemetery, the Proof of Honour for Shiraz, 18 June 2016, https://shiraz1400.ir/?p=28357 (19 January 2025).

Statistical Center of Iran 2011
گزیده نتایج سرشماری عمومی نفوس و مسکن ایران ۱۳۹۰، مرکز آمار ایران.
Statistical Center of Iran: Gozide-ye Natayej-e Sarshomari-e Omoomi-e Nofoos Va Maskan-e Iran 1390 [The National Population and Housing Censuses of Iran 2011]. Statistical Center of Iran. Tehran [online, 2011], https://www.amar.org.ir/ (9 August 2019).

Tavernier 1957
J. Tavernier: Les six voyages de JeanBaptiste Tavernier, chevalier baron d'Aubonne, qu'il a fait en Turquie, en Perse, et aux Indes (Tehran 1957).

Tobias et al. 2015
S. Tobias / T. Buser / M. Buchecker: Does real-time visualization support local stakeholders in developing landscape visions?. Environment and Planning B: Planning and Design 43, no. 1, 2015, 184–197 [online 2015], https://doi.org/10.1177/0265813515603866.

UNESCO 2011
UNESCO: The Persian Garden [inscription files from 2011], https://whc.unesco.org/en/list/1372/ (19 January 2025).

Waring 1807
E.S. Waring: A Tour to Sheeraz, by the Route of Kazroon and Feerozabad (London 1807), https://books.google.de/books?id=kc1NAAAAMAAJ&pg=PA60-IA2.

Yadollahi 2020
S. Yadollahi: Tracing the Identity-driven Ambitions of the Iranian Urban Conservation Apparatus. In The Historic Environment: Policy & Practice 11, no. 1, 2020, 56–75, https://doi.org/10.1080/17567505.2019.1637081.

Zarkoub Shirazi 1971
احمد زرکوب شیرازی: شیرازنامه.
A. Zarkoub Shirazi: The Book of Shiraz (Tehran 1971).

Image Sources

1 Chardin 1735.
2 The author.
3–28, Table 1 The author, based on Mohseni 2023.

A ‹Mental Map› of Aleppo
The City's Urban Evolution and its Architectural Styles

Zeido Zeido

The Syrian conflict has brought the world's attentions to Syria. The images of destruction and human suffering have been the centre of this attention since the beginning of the conflict in 2011. The different media outlets have reintroduced several Syrian cities to the world, and with this renewed interest, several organisations and institutes started to produce research and recommendations in anticipation for future reconstruction efforts.

A Gap in Understanding the City

Aleppo, one of the oldest cities in the world, became a hot spot in recent years for the conflict in Syria. While this development has debatably shed more light on the city in world news and the academic field,[1] I argue that there is still a gap in understanding the city for researchers.[2] One piece of this gap is the inadequacy of the map for the old city used by Syrian authorities and UNESCO, which is only concerned with the part of Aleppo inside the borders of the designated World Heritage Site (fig. 1).[3] Another piece of the gap is the failure of existing maps to clarify the different urban spaces and the growth of Aleppo. Many researchers follow the example and use the materials of Jean Sauvaget,[4] the orientalist and historian who prepared several maps[5] showing the expansion of Aleppo over different periods such as Byzantine, Mamluk, early Ottoman, and 18th and mid-19th centuries. Heinz Gaube, a geographer and a historian, followed a similar approach by tracing historic maps of the city, explaining that the oldest map of Aleppo was created by Carsten Niebuhr in 1766.[6] Although full of misrepresentations and inaccuracies as Gaube explains, Niebuhr's map shows clearly the main features of the city at that time. Other key maps used by historians are the 1811 map by Vincent Gemain, which was edited in 1818 by the French consul in Aleppo at the time, Jean-Baptiste Rousseau.[7] The map co-authored by the chief architect of Aleppo, Charles Chartier, and Raghib Bey,[8] the son of the Ottoman *wālī* (governor) in 1899/1900,[9] which was published later in 1912 with French names in Baedeker's Handbook,[10] is another key map to read the city. This map is considered important as it shows a new pattern of planning the «modern» neighbourhood that appeared in the 1860s in comparison to the older parts of the city.

As Gaube explained, the only accurate maps of Aleppo that followed a precise survey and in which each property included the built and non-built sections are the colonial French maps of 1930–1931.[11] I analyse and explain in a previous study that these French maps, although later added to and edited, are still the base for the detailed cadastral maps available for Aleppo.[12] Gaube counted two maps that were produced later, one dating to 1951 by Antoine Sabbagh and Sons Publishing House / Orient Library in Aleppo, and another to the early 1960s published by the tourist information office. I suggest that Gaube, at the time, did not find the map that was compiled in 1941 by the US army.[13] The maps that Gaube himself produced later based on a 1975–1979 survey,[14] are attached to his book, of which

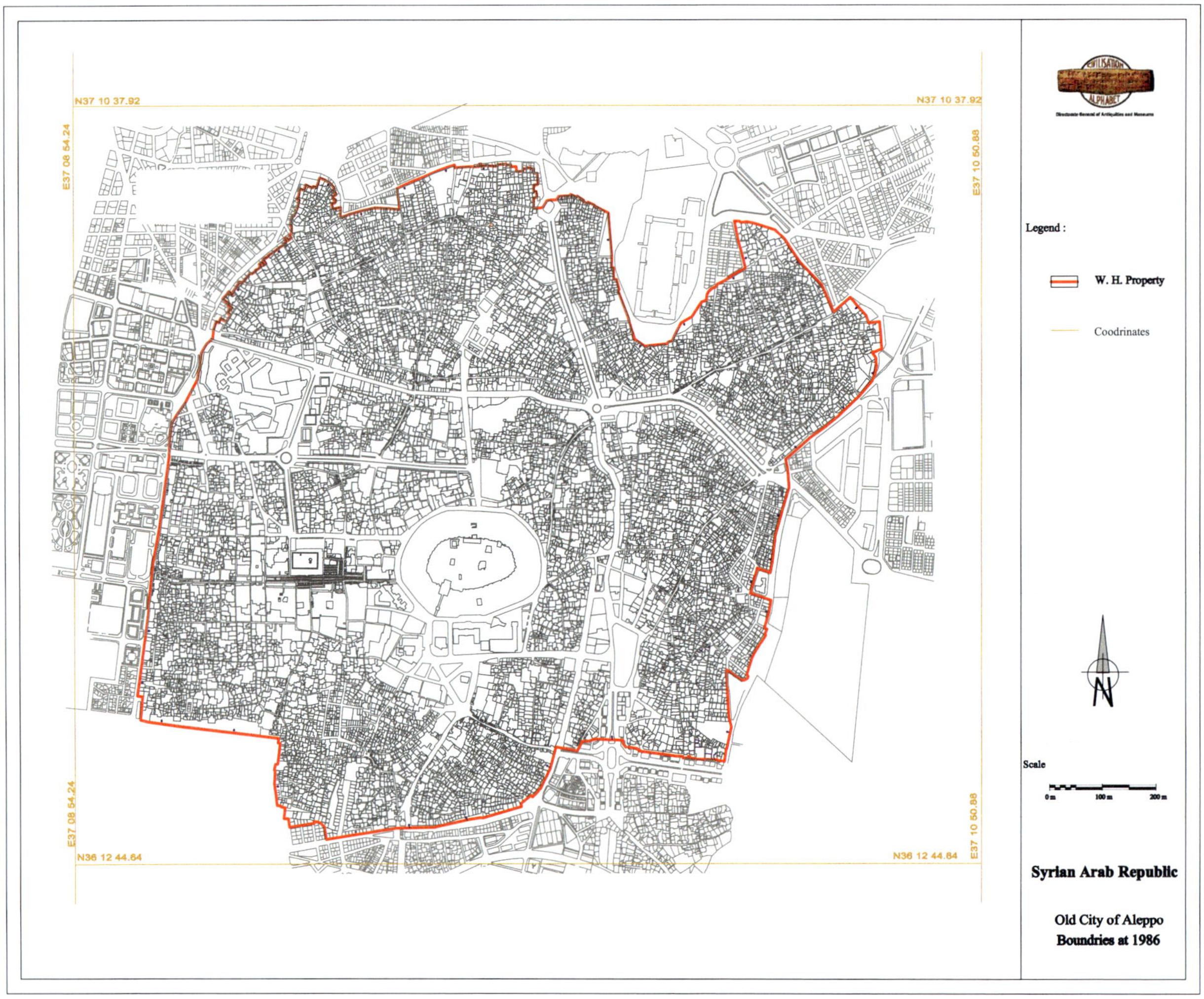

1 The map entitled «Ancient City of Aleppo» on UNESCO's website.

the first addition was published in 1984.[15] Gaube's maps would have been available shortly before the Russian army map[16] of Aleppo, which bears the date 1985. Notably, a rather low-quality satellite image of that year is available in the free public access satellite service Google Earth. The next available map in this service goes back to the year 2000, but the details of the streets and buildings are clearly visible in the satellite maps from that year onward. It should be noted that the previously mentioned maps are not the only ones available for Aleppo, but rather they are the key maps spaced over periods of time and often referred to by researchers who want to examine the expansion or urban development of the city. Hence, in other words, I argue that tracing the available maps produced over time has been a prominent method to understand the urban development of the city. This method is even traced in recent publications such as a book by the Aleppine historian Alaa Alsayed.[17]

Illustrations of the expansion of the city over the centuries are important. Nevertheless, they do not always highlight the shifts of urban character nor reflect how these spaces of the city are understood by its dwellers, especially in today's context. Therefore, instead of following a traditional method to show the growth of the city, this chapter provides a map that aims to offer a perspective on how Aleppines comprehend their city and its different urban spaces and architectural styles.

I would like to note here that this chapter was preceded by another publication that I co-authored with Nura Ibold, a heritage specialist, which discussed several issues relevant to Aleppo, including the heritage approaches of the Syrian authorities and the difference between what authorities and Aleppines define as «heritage».[18] In summary, on the one hand, the Syrian antiquity law does not identify buildings less than 200 years old[19] as heritage, with a few exceptions. On the other hand, the World Heritage Site of the old city of Aleppo is also approached as protected heritage regardless of the age of the buildings. Nonetheless as this earlier publication pointed out, there were many contradictions in the heritage protection laws and a lot of legal transgressions. For example, according to a shop owner in the old city, interventions for open courtyard houses, which in some cases can be less than 200 years old or with an unknown construction date, typically require the permission of both DOCA (the Directorate of the Old City of Aleppo) and DGAM (the Directorate General of Antiquities and Museums). By contrast, it seems that reconstruction or maintenance for post-1960s high-rise buildings inside the World Heritage Site typically requires only an approval of DOCA, as DGAM does not intervene in these cases.

In summary, interventions for structures within the World Heritage Site, which covers most of the old city, almost always need the approval of DOCA while DGAM does not intervene for buildings that it does not deem historic even in the World Heritage site. Hence, in practice, DGAM's criteria for protection inside the World Heritage site are not only limited to its own 200-years-old rule, but apparently they also include the type or style of the building considered historic, such as open courtyard houses. As discussed in my previously mentioned publication, the heritage and antiquity laws can be ambiguous and unclear, and breaking them can have no significant consequences.

Additionally, and importantly, what Aleppines understand as built heritage is not confined to the World Heritage Site of the old city, nor to buildings more than 200 years old. While I argue that there has been a shift in attitude towards historicist, and to a lesser degree modernist, socialist, and post-modernist architecture, among other styles in Syria, these architectural styles are seldom researched. Debatably, the lack of interest, documentation, but perhaps primarily the difficulties in obtaining data from Syrian public institutions, are key contributors to the problem.

For these reasons, I would like to highlight two issues. The first issue is that the old city of Aleppo, as it is defined by the World Heritage Site borders, has often been examined as an island and outside the context of its relation to the rest of the city. Notably, the UNESCO webpage devoted to Aleppo is one of many examples of how the World Heritage Site's two similar maps from 1985 and 2012 are introduced alone, without offering any context drawn from their surroundings (see fig. 1).[20] The theoretical definition of a World Heritage Site and the criteria for selecting a city or part of a city as such a site are rather vague.[21] In the case of Aleppo, the virtual line created to define the old city of Aleppo (see fig. 1) was specific and had tangible affects, such as the creation of DOCA, an authority[22] to deal with this explicitly defined part of the historic part of Aleppo. By default, as I argue, with the exception of a few buildings, the rest of the city outside these virtual red borders on the map (see fig. 1) receives almost no legal protection. This lack of protection extends to neighbourhoods with a similar urban fabric to that of the World Heritage Site. An example is the historic neighbourhood of Al-Masharika, mostly consisting of open courtyard houses, which this chapter will discuss later. Additionally, areas with different forms of urban fabric, such as the «modern» neighbourhoods that go back to the late 19th century (see fig. 4 later) with their unique historicist architecture, did not fall under the 200-years-old rule, nor inside the virtual borders of the old city, and thus they receive no state protection or care.

The second issue, supported by the list of available maps above, is the absence of available

2 ‹Mental Map› of Aleppo.

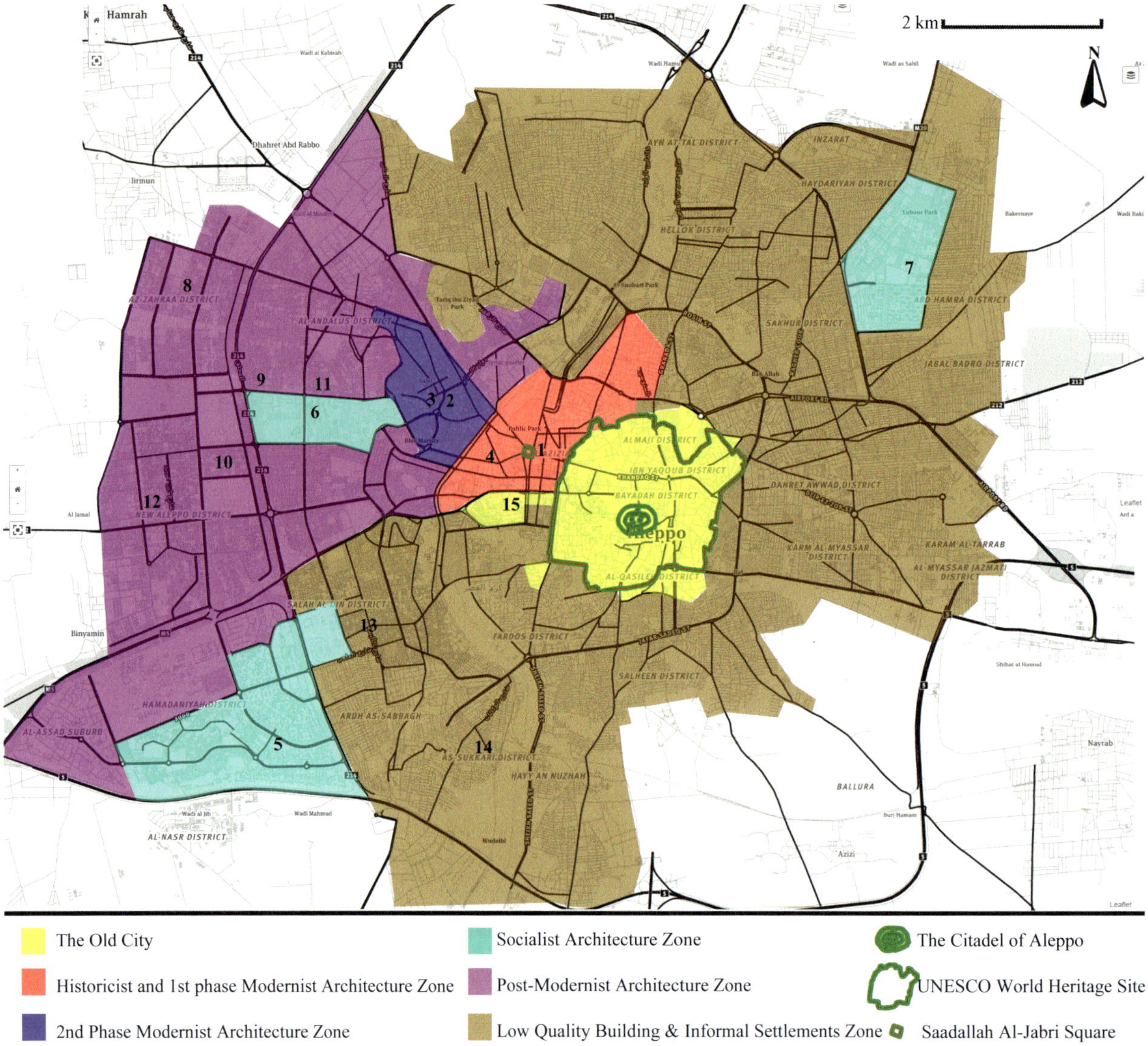

1. Al-Azizye
2. Al-Sabeel
3. Al-Muhafaza
4. Al-Jamiliye
5. Al-Hamdaniye
6. Dorms of Aleppo University
7. Madinet Hanano
8. Jamaeyat Al-zahraa
9. Jamaeyat Al-Jamiaa
10. Jamaeyat Al-Muhandseen
11. Al-Shahaba Al-Kadima
12. Halab Al-Jadida
13. Sayf Al-Dawleh
14. Al-Sukkari
15. Al-Masharika

resources to clarify which buildings are historic, to which period do they belong, and where are they concentrated in the city. Nonetheless, the chapter presents a point of view of the city and attempts to keep the discussion about the built heritage and different architectural styles of Aleppo going. It does this by providing a simplified yet clear understanding of the urban spaces and history of the city of Aleppo prior to and during the war in Syria. Thus, this chapter criticises the rigid and exclusivist definition of the historic part of Aleppo that is still adopted by authorities, emphasised by international organisations,[23] and recycled by several academics.

The chapter uses Kevin Lynch's[24] concept of «districts» of a city to create a map for Aleppo as viewed by – at least – a small group of its dwellers. The map highlights the different urban zones of the city that share common dominant architectural characteristics. The chapter also elaborates on the methods used to create this map and its limitations. Moreover, this study provides a timeline for selected significant urban events in Aleppo (see fig. 18 later) and relates some historic events and six time periods to the six coloured urban zones on the mental map (fig. 2). By using this map, the timeline of selected events, interviews, and different reports and secondary resources, the chapter discusses different relevant aspects of Aleppo's built heritage, such as the «value» attributed by locals to each architectural style and zone of the city, in addition to the division of Aleppo that occurred during the conflict in Syria.

A ‹Mental Map› of Aleppo: An Alternative Method

Lynch, an urban theorist,[25] argues that the residents of the same place share a certain image of their towns, and generally understand their surroundings and city components in consistent ways, forming what he called a ‹mental map›. A mental map could be the personal point of view or the perception of one person of his city. According to Lynch's theory, the inhabitants of a city understand the city through five elements: paths, edges, nodes, districts, and landmarks.

For this research, I joined a group composed of five people from Aleppo to focus on the concept of ‹district› and worked together with these individuals to highlight the different areas that share similar architectural characteristics on a map of the city. The map in this case was a satellite image that clarified the different street names and neighbourhoods. After the completion of the map so that it highlighted the distinctive urban zones (fig. 2), the map was displayed to twenty other individuals from Aleppo, who also agreed that the map conforms – to a great extent – to the way that they perceive the city. The twenty Aleppines were interviewed between 2016 and 2019. The interviews generally consisted of semi-structured questions, mostly conducted through an online call with some people contacted more than once as more questions emerged. Here, I must point out a potential unintentional shortcoming,[26] which is that the five persons selected to co-draw the map and the twenty interview subjects were, although not by design, all from west Aleppo.

As a reminder, this map is meant to be reductive in order to communicate a simplified point of view. Thus potentially more attention was given to west Aleppo, but further studies are required to account for the complexity of the areas coloured in brown (see fig. 2).

The Old City

The shared view of the group was that «old Aleppo» is comprised of the historic neighbourhoods dominated by traditional courtyard houses and narrow alleyways (fig. 3). Even some neighbourhoods that had lost most of their traditional fabric, but were arguably well known to Aleppines as «historic» by their names and location, were still

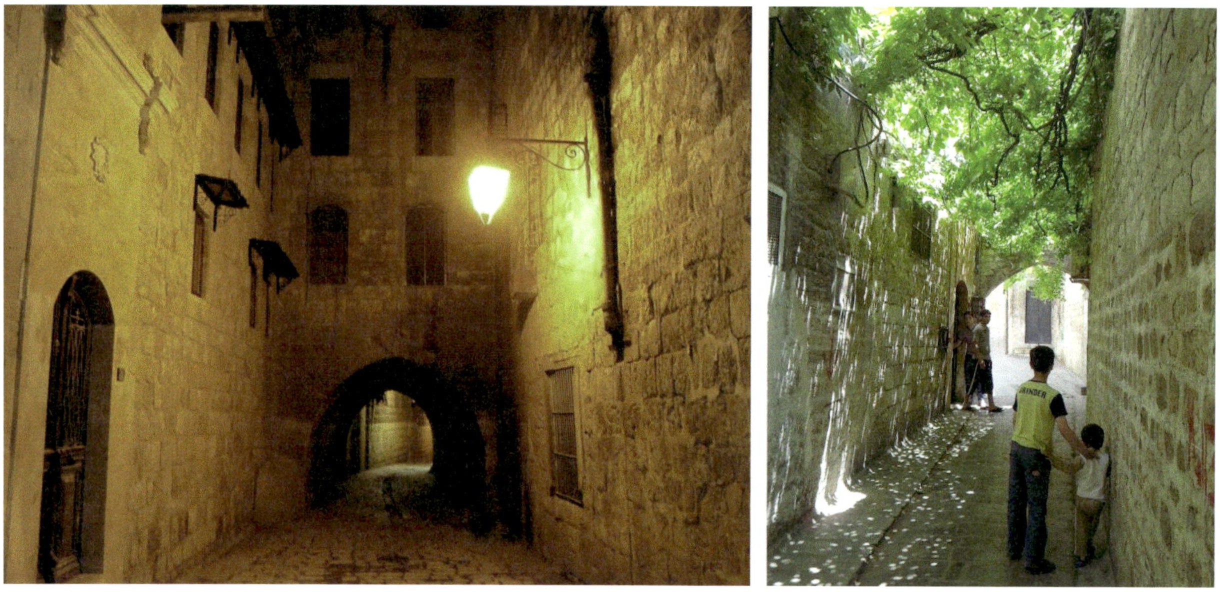

3 Example of traditional narrow alleyways in Old Aleppo.

conceived as part of «old Aleppo». This included for example Al-Masharika (see fig. 2), a neighbourhood that possessed eighty-three «historic» houses in the 1920s[27] and that once had a fabric similar to the rest of the old city, with narrow winding alleyways and historic houses with open courtyards. The neighbourhood, which was not included as part of the World Heritage Site, was partially bulldozed in the early 1980s and again in the early 2000s[28] and has lost almost all of its older historic fabric. Furthermore, the World Heritage Site borders that define the old city, which were added to the map later, had no significance in terms of how or what people viewed or defined as historic, worthy, or part of the old city. This part of the fabric of the city includes all the areas that date back to before the first new «modern» neighbourhoods appeared in 1868, starting with Al-Aziziye.[29] Despite the many different combinations of civilisations and styles that influenced this area, which are discussed in more detail in the timeline section in this chapter, «old Aleppo» was viewed as one homogenous part of the city. This zone is highlighted in yellow and named «the old city» on the map (see fig. 2).

Historicist and 1st Type Modernist Architecture

The group assigned the «modern» neighbourhoods that appeared in the late 19th and early 20th centuries as another distinct zone. This part of the city was viewed by the initial group as dominated by the historicist architectural style (fig. 4) and earlier modernist architecture (fig. 5). Many areas of these neighbourhoods have lost much of their distinguishing characteristic buildings for development and commercial projects, given a lack of authoritative protection. Nonetheless, historicist and earlier modernist architecture were still perceived as the defining character of this zone, with historicist architecture seen as the focal image of this zone.

Historicism in a western context usually refers to the revival or the recreation of historic styles.

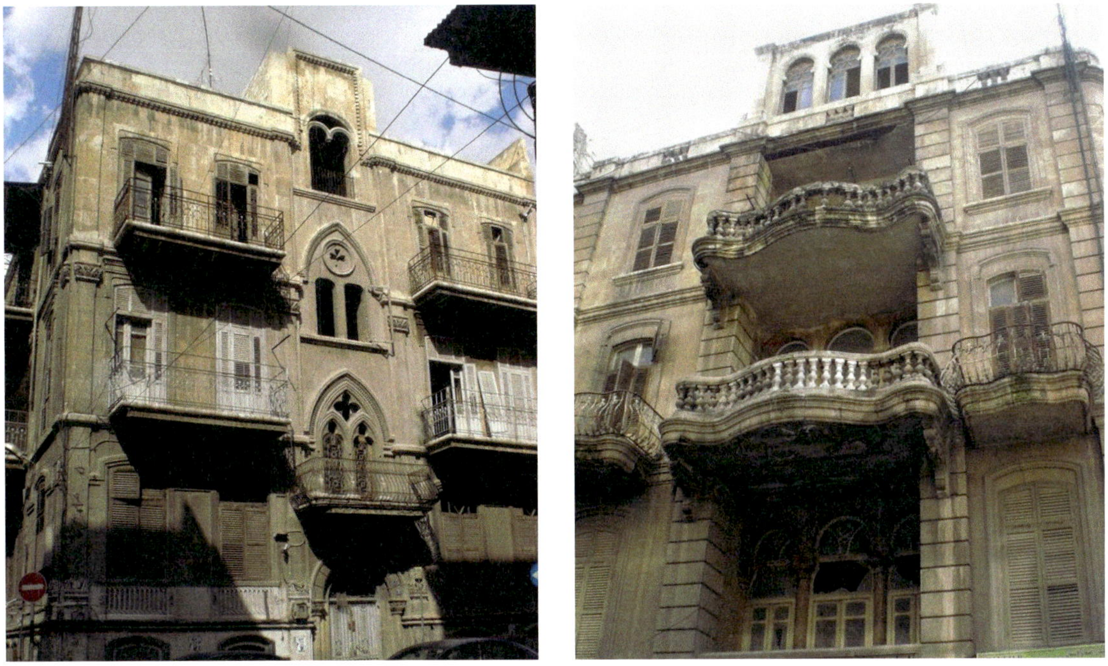

4 Example of historicist architecture in Aleppo in the Al-Aziziye neighbourhood.

5 Example of 1st type modernist architecture in Aleppo in Al-Telal.

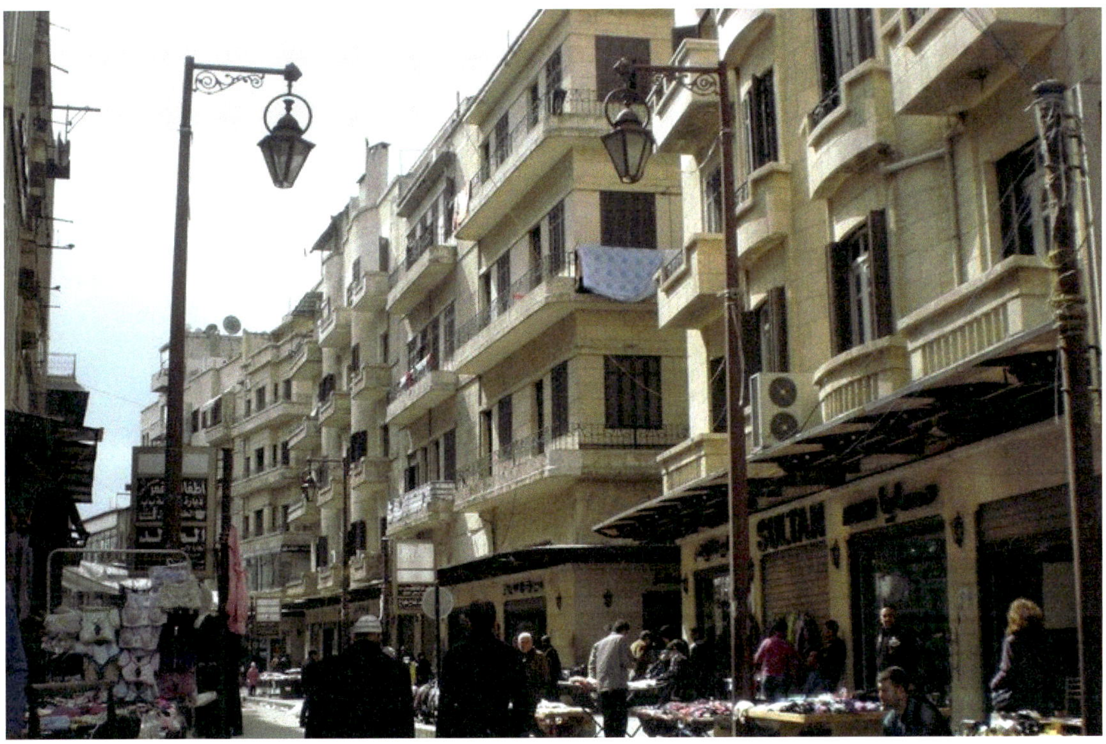

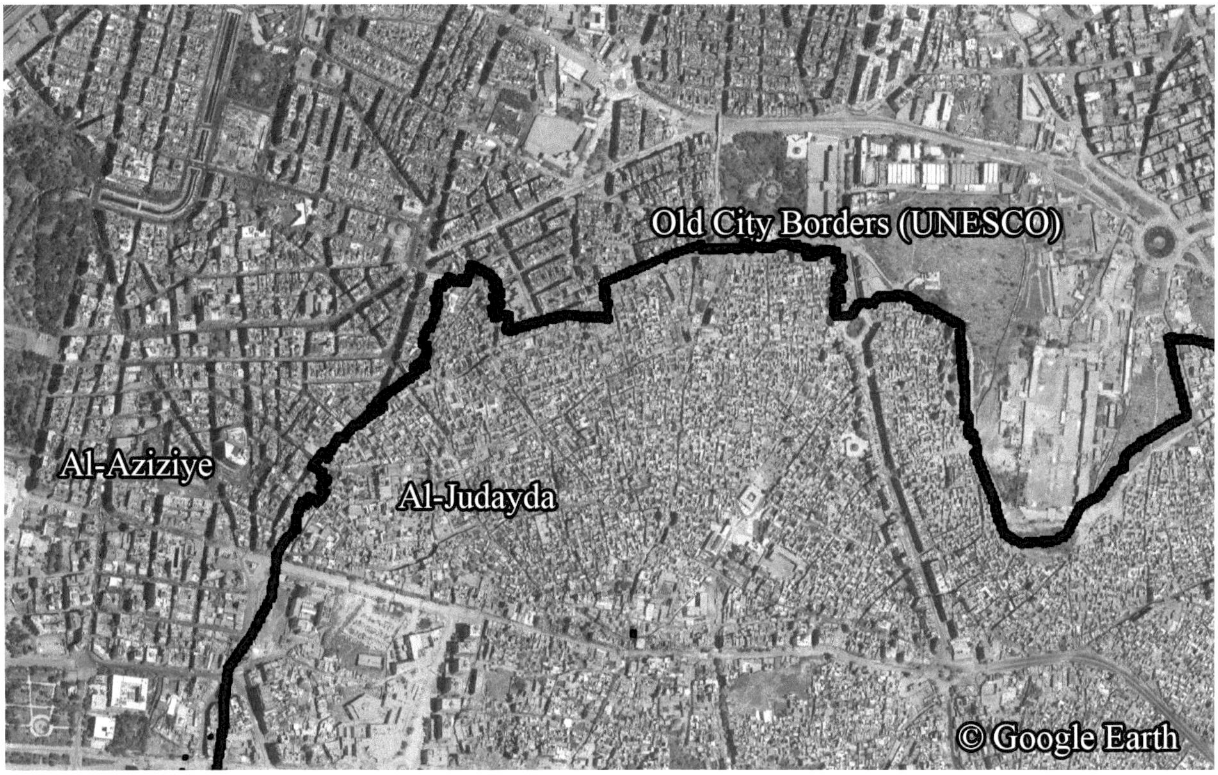

6 The organic urban fabric of the Old City vs. the planned fabric of the «modern» neighbourhoods.

Therefore, the terms «historicism» and «historicist architecture» are debatable in the case of Aleppo, because they are used to refer to a style more influenced by European historicism rather than characteristics associated with local historic architecture. The group who worked on the map could not separate the areas of early modernist architecture from the historicist ones. One reason for this might be that the historicist neighbourhoods that appeared after 1868 were followed shortly by the modernist architecture of the first half of the 20th century, filling the spaces in the «modern» neighbourhoods (fig. 6) and expanding them. This zone is highlighted in red and named «historicist and 1st type modernist architecture zone» on the map (see fig. 2). Furthermore, the replacement of the historicist architecture by modernist architecture was not of course sudden, but more likely a gradual phenomenon that occurred in the first half of the 20th century. Here it should be again noted that Aleppo's historicist architecture emerged in the 1860s,[30] decades before the period of French colonial rule over Syria (1920–1946).

2nd Type Modernist Architecture

The group distinguished a 2nd type of modernist styles in Aleppo, which dominates neighbourhoods such as Al-Sabeel and Al-Muhafaza (see fig. 2). This other style of modernism was associated with buildings that had a unique form of façade designs and exterior stones, and spacious balconies. In this chapter, I refer to this style as the 2nd type of modernist architecture to distinguish it from the 1st type of modernist architecture

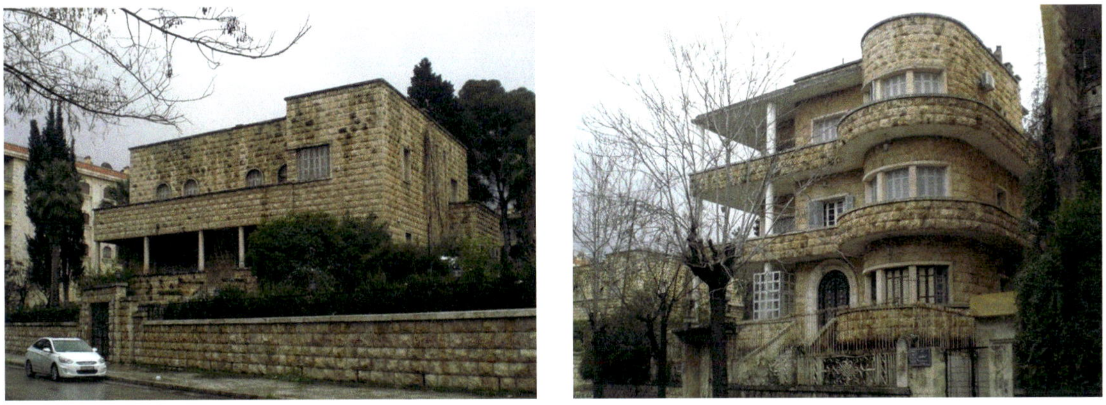

7 Example of 2nd type modernist architecture in Aleppo in Al-Sabeel neighbourhood.

discussed above. While presumably 2nd type modernist architecture followed 1st type chronologically as it dominates a newer expanded part of the city, a comparison of data, including the construction dates of buildings from both styles, is needed.[31] The difference between the two styles might not be entirely attributable to chronology, but rather also involve the nature of the neighbourhoods where the two types of architecture were built. For example, the 1st type of modernist architecture mostly dominates mixed commercial and residential areas, whereas the 2nd type dominates what is mostly strictly residential areas. Thus, certain distinguishing characteristics, such as bigger balconies (fig. 7) can be attributed to function rather than the time period of construction per se. Another way to look at this issue is to examine the work of modernist Aleppine architects. While not a lot of sources are available, Mustafa Hikmat Al-Yaziji is one of the few architects whose designs were collected and published, as he was perceived as a renowned architect by the Engineers Syndicate in Aleppo. This architect started his work in the early 1940s designing modernist buildings in Al-Jamiliye,[32] which can be considered as examples of 1st type architecture. Notably, Al-Jamiliye is a mixed commercial and residential area. However, Al-Yaziji also designed other buildings that can be attributed to 2nd type in residential areas such as Al-Sabeel.[33] Regrettably, the book published by the Engineers Syndicate in Aleppo[34] did not include the dates of construction for the different designs of Al-Yaziji, who passed away in 1998. Thus, having a celebrated Aleppine architect designing according to what is perceived as two styles of modernist architecture can indicate a shift that occurred because of function, or even building materials, rather than the emergence of a new style.

On the map, the 2nd type of modernist architecture zone is highlighted in dark blue (see fig. 2). Although the time of this zone's early development corresponded with French control of Aleppo (1920–1946), there seems to be no evidence of a direct French influence on this style or other styles, but rather modernism in Aleppo appears to be a product of the exchange of ideas and cultural influences. For example, despite the fact that the Franciscan School and Church (fig. 8) was inaugurated in 1934 in the presence of Comte Damien de Martel, the French High Commissioner, the project was funded by Mary Aswad, a prominent Aleppine woman at the time.[35] Thus, this well-known landmark in the city, which is one of the earliest structures in this zone, was not a French project. Notably, the use of protruding yellow stones for

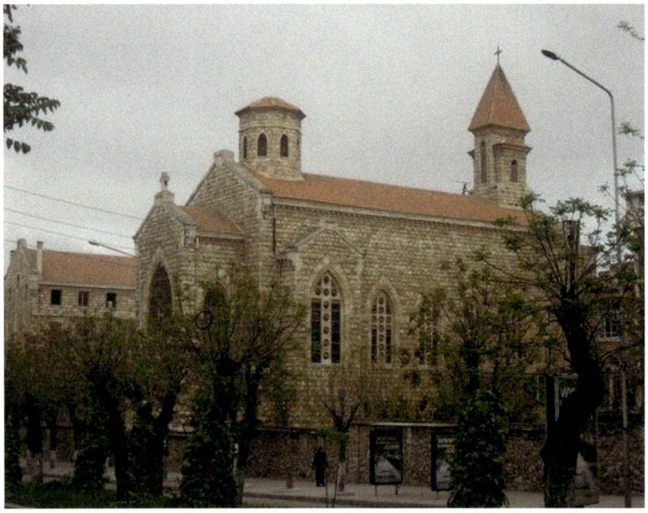

8 Franciscan School and Church in Aleppo.

the church's exterior[36] is a defining character of the buildings in this part of Aleppo.

Similarly, many notable modernist buildings in this zone of Aleppo were designed by prominent Aleppine architects.[37] In fact, a study by Mahmood Faysal Al-Rifai, a former dean of the civil engineering faculty in Aleppo University, gathered all the names of university-graduate engineers in Aleppo from the beginning of the 20th century until 1950. It listed the names of the 51 pioneering engineers in the city.[38] The study used the records of the Engineers' Union and the Syndicate of Engineers in Aleppo, in addition to information obtained from the engineers' families. It found that out of these 51 engineers, twenty received their degrees from St. Joseph University in Beirut, nine from Paris, six from Cairo, five from Istanbul, three from Grenoble, two from Stuttgart, one from London, two from Belgium, one from the USA, and one Yugoslavian civil engineer, Branimir Branko,[39] who received his degree from Zagreb. Here, two points should be noted. Firstly, that Al-Rifai's study establishes that all engineers apart from Branko were Syrians. The names he lists correspond with names used in Aleppo, whether Arabic, Armenian, or French names used by the Christian community. Many last names are recognisable as belonging to prominent Aleppine families.

The second matter to point out is that these engineers are listed as civil, mechanical, electrical, civil–electrical, and civil–sanitary engineers, with only two architects, the first of whom graduated in 1948. Nevertheless, it is important to note that at the time there was no clear separation between civil engineering and architecture as the same study calls attention to several names from the 51 pioneers, who graduated as civil engineers, as the designers of prominent buildings in Aleppo. This list includes Al-Yaziji for example, who despite having graduated as a civil engineer, is celebrated as a prominent Aleppine architect.[40] Thus, civil engineers would have acted as architects and designers of buildings. In fact, the study names a few examples and suggests that many of these engineers, especially in the first half of the 20th century, would have cooperated with the experienced professional craftsmen who traditionally acted as engineers and architects in Aleppo at least until the end of the 19th century. The Ottoman Salnames (Ottoman yearly books) of Aleppo, which were produced in the late 19th and early 20th centuries, mentioned an Ottoman Engineering Department,[41] with staff and titles of specialised engineer and architect.[42] What probably happened to change the role of these craftsmen is that laws in that period obliged having an architect or an engineer working on every single new building. The 1930 French-mandate Syrian law, the third article of decree 2390, required the submission of an architectural drawing of each floor of the building in addition to façade drawings and a site plan. Moreover, the law required providing the address of the architect and engineers if deemed necessary.[43] Imposing a similar law meant that traditional craftsmen, regardless of their experience, could no longer work without licensed architects or engineers.

This Al-Rifai study might have missed the names of a few engineers, and it indicates that not all practising engineers or architects at the time had joined the union, as was the case for two foreigners who worked during the French colonial period, Shalom Tobi and Alper Olaloski.[44] However, the study shows that Aleppines, while still under French rule, created an engineers' union in 1933.[45] The union was headed by Wajih Sameh Al-Jabri. Thus, there are no sources or evidence to suggest any major French interventions or that French architects reshaped architecture in Aleppo on a city-wide scale. Instead, the exchange of ideas, and especially education in western universities, played a notable part in the creation of Aleppine modernism. Another feature that distinguishes modernist architecture in Aleppo is the very thick interior and exterior walls, especially in buildings built up until the 1940s. I argue that one important reason is that cement in Syria was exclusively imported up until the first factory opened near Damascus in 1931, and then near Aleppo in 1948.[46] Thus, in the first half of the 20th century, Aleppine architecture not only evolved new styles of modernism and new methods of construction, but also changed from a traditional profession to one that required a formal education.

Socialist Architecture

Another distinguished part of the city was the socialist architecture zone, which contained districts such as Al-Hamdaniya, the buildings of Aleppo University, and Madinet Hanano.[47] Key distinguishing characteristics of these areas were the socialist architecture and the urban planning of generous street sizes and public spaces in comparison to the other parts of the city. Maan Chibli, a former professor of architecture in Aleppo University and the former mayor of Aleppo, points out that Al-Hamdaniya district was one of the projects of the Establishment of Military Housing,[48] the single largest engineering and construction firm in Syria and responsible for many large-scale projects since its founding in 1975. Although public space was accounted for in Al-Hamdaniya, the district was designed to house 5,087 units, including 1,400 units for low- to mid-low-class inhabitants in comparison to 1,200 units for upper-income residents.[49] The targeting of low-income residents, and the design of the flats' areas and quality to reflect the requirements of this demographic, in addition to the rigid forms of socialist architecture, partially explain why these areas were debatably perceived as unfavourable by the well-off part of the Aleppine community. This zone is highlighted in light blue on the map (see fig. 2). It is remarkable to note how in some cases, as in Al-Hamdaniya, simple ornaments were added to the façades in an attempt to affirm an Arabic character for these rigidly socialist buildings (fig. 9). In this sense, the Establishment of Military Housing, the government construction agency, affirms the «Arab» and «Socialist» characters, which were an integral part of the name of the Arab Socialist Ba'ath Party, the ruling party of Syria since 1963, which would declare itself the sole ruling party of the country in 1973.

Another important example of socialist architecture is the university dormitories, at Aleppo University, which was established in 1958 as a separate entity from the Syrian University and is today known as The University of Damascus. The first two units of the university dorms were built in 1967, and look different in design[50] from their later counterparts. The next three units were built in 1977, and in 1985 a decree was issued to establish six more units. The dorm units 17 and 18 were built in 1991, and by 2007 the university had twenty dorm units.[51] It is important to note that apart from the dorms, not all the buildings of Aleppo University display a rigid socialist style, but perhaps the structures' massive sizes and the visibility of several prominent buildings near main roads, such as the dormitories of the university (fig. 10) and the medicine faculty with its unmistakably socialist mural (fig. 11), give an overall feeling of a socialist space.

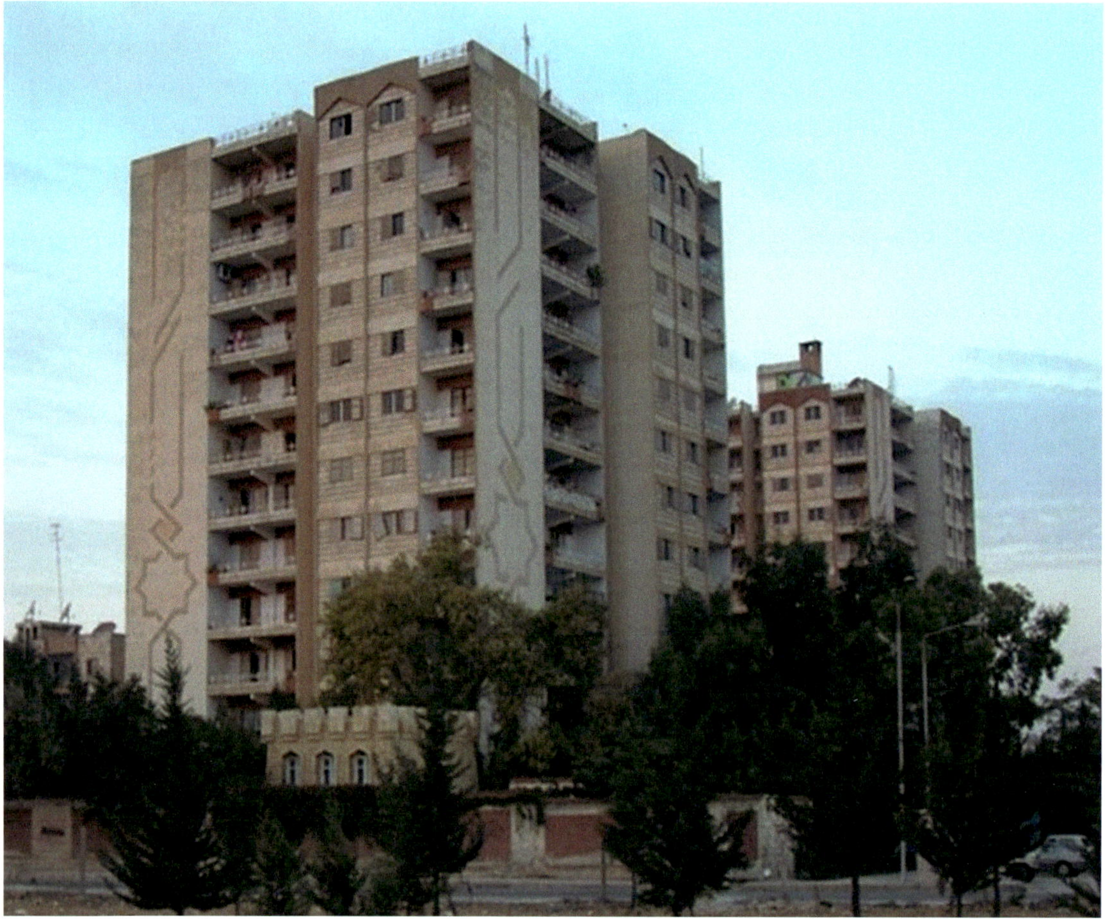

9 A building in Al-Hamdaniya.

10 Example of socialist architecture in Aleppo: the dormitories of Aleppo University.

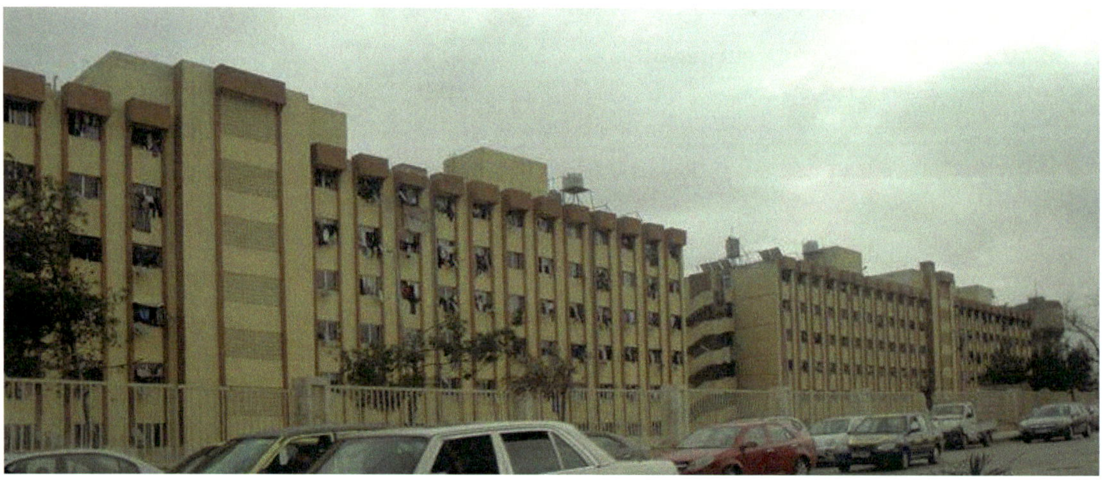

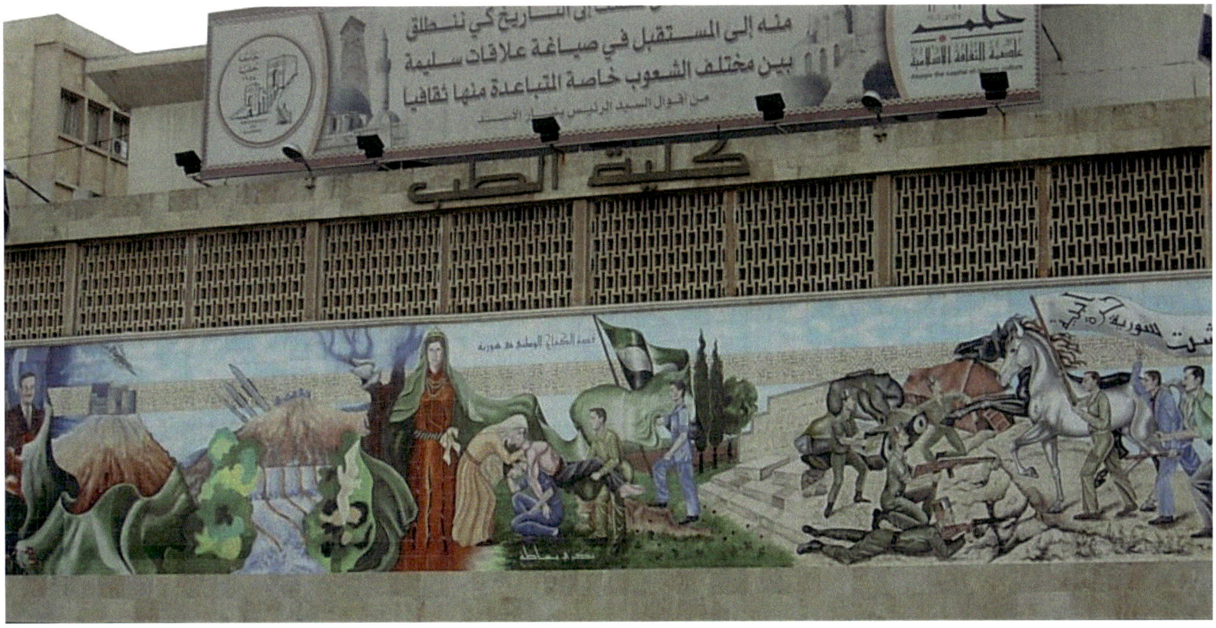

11 Socialist mural, Medicine Faculty of Aleppo University.

12 Socialist planning of Al-Hamdaniya in Aleppo including the stadium.

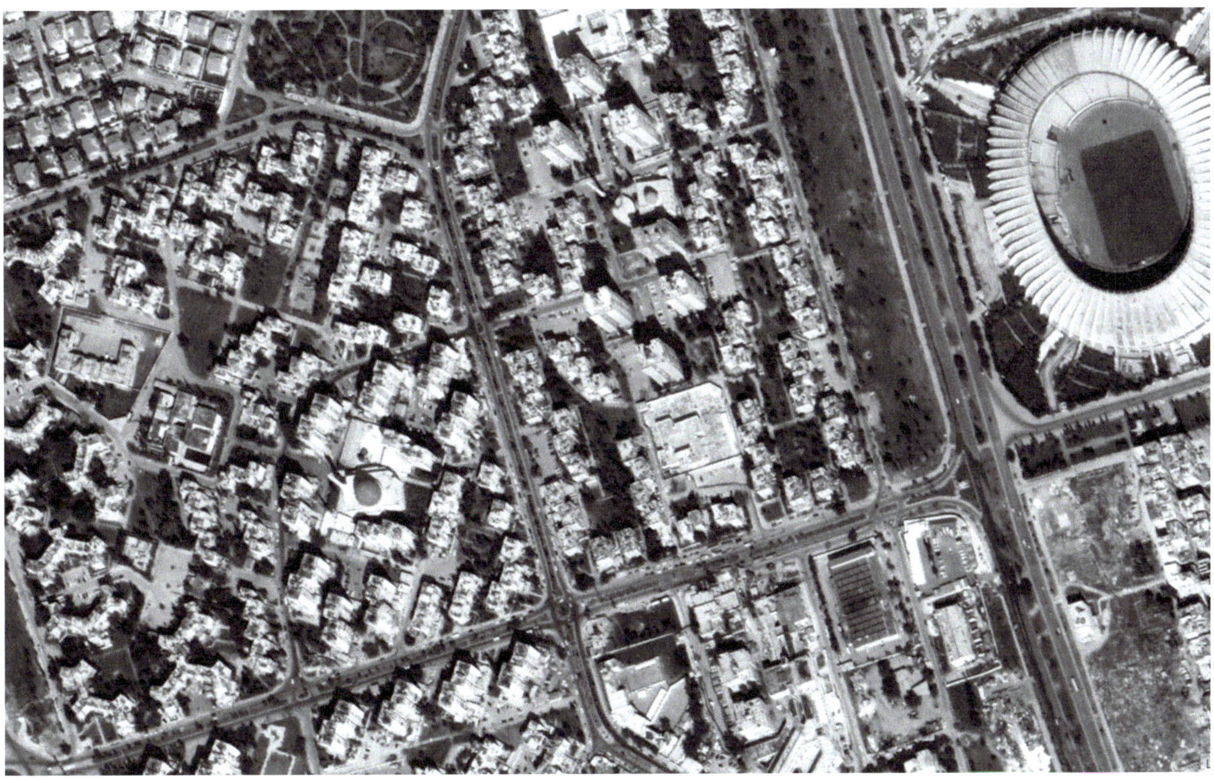

The Establishment of Military Housing does not mention any of its earlier projects on its website, but it does confirm that it was responsible for building a socialist-style landmark, the stadium in the Aleppo sports city in Al-Hamdaniya (fig. 12).[52] Nonetheless, Al-Thawara, an official Syrian newspaper, mentions that the Establishment of Military Housing indeed established the Al-Hamdaniye suburb and that it was responsible for building some university faculties in Aleppo.[53] While there is no information on their official website, the style of buildings of the dorms of Aleppo University and Madinet Hanano are most likely to be a product of a state construction entity, whether it is The Establishment of Military Housing or one of its peers[54] such as The Public Establishment of Housing.

Greco-Roman Post-Modernist (Contemporary) Architecture in Aleppo

Aleppo's contemporary architecture for the middle and upper middle class, or what could be called post-modernist architecture, was perceived as another distinctive zone. The term «post-modernist architecture» is another controversial term in the case of Aleppo. Unlike modernist architecture, ornaments are used again in this style. Still, the post-modernist style was very much uniform, lacked complexity, and debatably did not express – at least loudly – any cultural or ideological statements. In many cases this architecture tries to copy the motifs of Greco-Roman architecture (fig. 13). However, I argue that several elements still create a clear distinction between Aleppo's post-modernist buildings and its historicist buildings of the late 19th and early 20th century. Most notably, observable façade motifs in the post-modernist buildings are influenced by modern stone carving machines and technology. Another feature is that unlike historicist architecture, post-modernist buildings typically feature bigger balconies, like the 2nd phase modernist architecture. However, unlike the 2nd phase modernist architecture, post-modernist structures overall have more rectangular confirmative boundaries that try to make the

13 Examples of Greco-Roman Post-Modernist architecture in Aleppo in Al-Furkan neighbourhood.

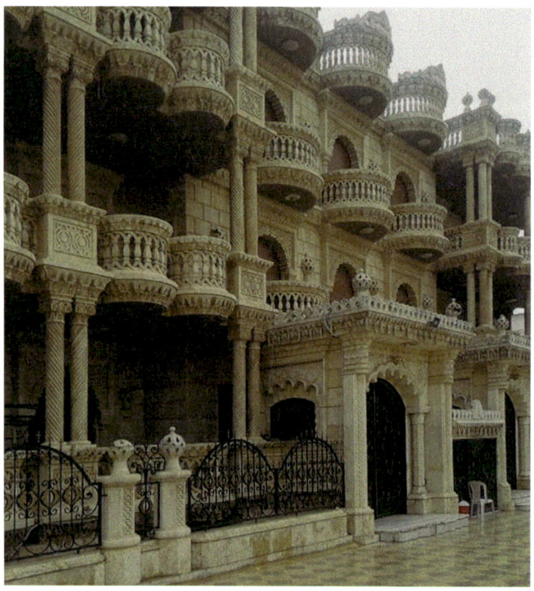

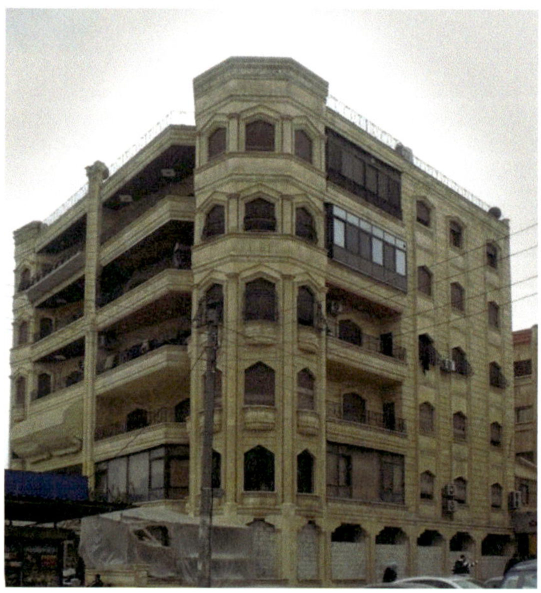

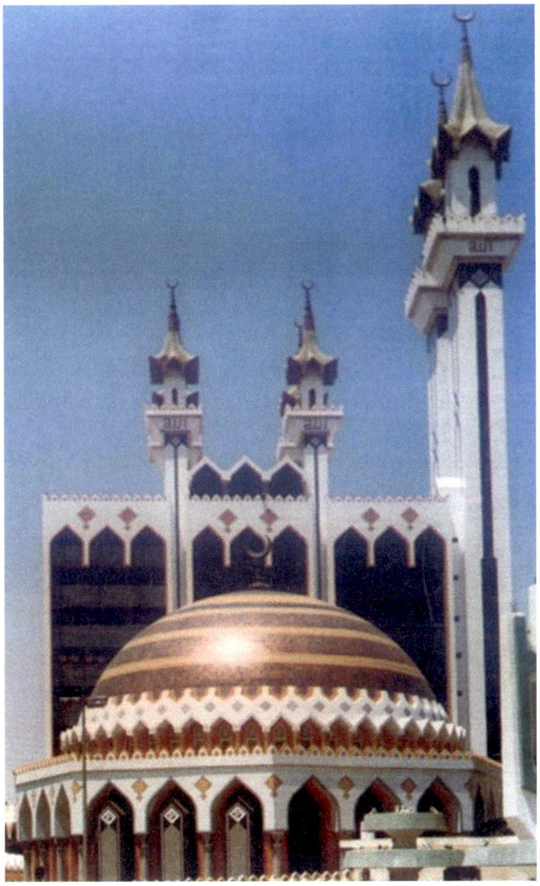

14 Al-Rahman Mosque in Aleppo.

most of the expensive land plots. For the abovementioned reasons, post-modernist architecture remains a controversial term in this case of Aleppo, and I use it to reference a period rather than building features.

This post-modernist zone is highlighted in purple on the map (see fig. 2). I argue here that Aleppo's architecture, although a subject of admiration, can feel very consistent and familiar, at least for its residents. For this reason, Al Rahman Mosque (fig. 14) feels like one of the few works, if not the only work, of post-modernism in the city due to its alien elements such as far-east-Asian style minarets, bright white exteriors, and the popping-coloured dome in the pale-colour city of facades built out of local stone. Nonetheless, the book issued by the Engineers' Syndicate of Aleppo that collected the work of Bashir Al-Mohandes, the Aleppine architect who designed the mosque, offers another narrative, claiming for example that «The golden colour on the dome is a reminder of the Dome of the Rock». Additionally, «As for the white colour, it prevails over most of the rest of the external cladding of the project, being the favourite colour of the Umayyads to express peace, purity and absolute order». Additionally, the book describes the «Fatimid inscriptions» on the interior of the dome. Thus, despite describing the structure as belonging to the category of religious creativity and a monument with Islamic contemporary character, the text published by the Syndicate of Engineers in Aleppo provides background on the roots and traditional origin of the unusual style of this mosque. I argue, however, that although the mosque might have some elements inspired by, or that could be interpreted to have a relation to other styles, it remains nonetheless unfamiliar and hard to pin down as relatable to other periods or other structures.

Notably, the text mentions that the party donating the land stipulated that another facility be built on it for the public good, giving this as a reason to why there is a hospital building next to the mosque where a yard would typically be found. The hospital did not open until the present day, although the study for this project started in 1976 and the mosque was inaugurated in 1994.[55] Notably, the book shows different photos of Al-Mohandes's works, which arguably belong to the categories of modernist, Aleppine post-modernist, and possibly even socialist architecture.

An important aspect of the city's urban development, most especially in this zone of Aleppo, is the housing associations that founded several neighbourhoods. According to article 2 of the Legislative Decree No. 13 of the year 1981 in

Syria, housing associations can be created with a minimum number of participants who commit to installed payments. Associations receive help from the government, such as obtaining lands to build on, in exchange for providing housing for cost price to its members. According to article 25 of the same decree, the joint association has the right to permit construction of residential buildings, supervise implementation, and equip the buildings with facilities and public services.[56]

Notably, many neighbourhoods in Aleppo have the word Jamaeyat (association) in their names, such as Jamaeyat Al-zahraa, Jamaeyat Al-Jamiaa (The University Association), and Jamaeyat Al-Muhandseen (Engineers Association). Associations in some cases, as their name indicates, conditioned or prioritised members of certain professions. According to the Aleppo National Archives – Digital Historical Document House, a project to document Aleppo's history and heritage, the oldest housing association in Aleppo was founded in 1959.[57] Furthermore, according to Al-Jamahir, an official Syrian newspaper, Aleppo had 506 housing associations before the 2019 regulations that enforced the merger of some housing associations.[58] Tishreen, another official Syrian newspaper, reported in 2015 about the failure and corruption of these associations in the past few decades. While blame was placed on the General Union for Housing Cooperation,[59] which was established in 1961 and organised the work of housing associations, the latter blamed unclear governmental policies, pointing specifically to the issue that no new lands to build on had been provided for the associations during the past 25 years.[60] In 2019, The General Union for Housing Cooperation was dissolved and replaced by The Ministry of Public Works and Housing.[61]

Architecture in Low Standards of Living Areas and Informal Settlements

The rest of Aleppo was highlighted as districts with low standards of living and informal settlements, locally known as Al-Manatek Al-Sha'bia[62] (figs. 15 and 16). This zone is highlighted in brown on the map (see fig. 2), and notably the size of this zone on the map is almost double that of all the other zones combined. The map suggests that this area formed almost two thirds of the city, demonstrating that Aleppo was physically polarised even before the Syrian conflict, as this chapter will discuss further later. To summarise, I would like to argue that the rise of this zone can be attributed to two major reasons: the economic crisis

15 Example of informal settlements in Aleppo in Ansari Gharbi district.

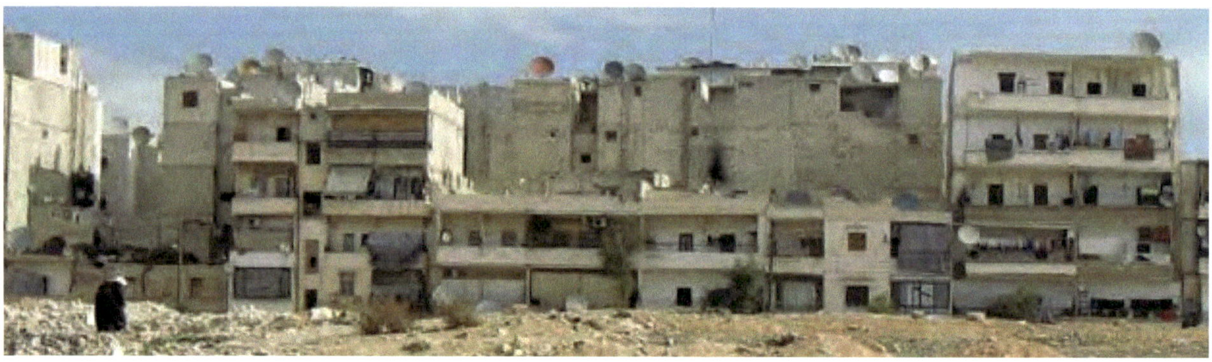

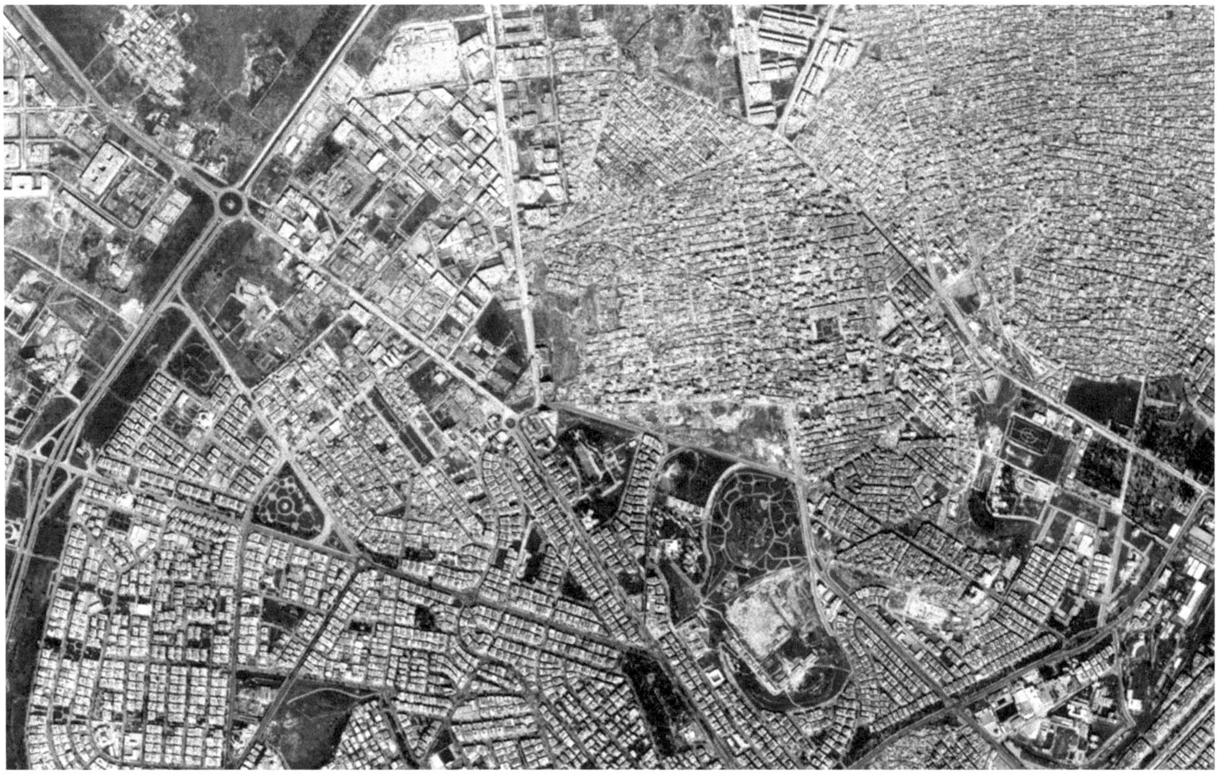

16 A segment from West-North Aleppo: Planned modernist and post-modernist neighbourhoods (bottom left) vs. low standards of living and informal settlements planning (upper right).

and policies in Syria which led to waves of internal migrations from rural areas to the cities, a pattern that has especially intensified since the 1970s, and the lack of any adequate governmental reaction to provide a proper city development plan or to deal with the housing crisis.[63]

Remarks on the ‹Mental Map›: Limitation of the Method

In this case, I must emphasise the fact that this map expresses the point of view of a small group of Aleppines, and that it reflects to an extent my personal perspective at the time as I was a part of the initial group. Moreover, it should be noted that the map is extremely generalising. For instance, there is debatably a big gap between the richer neighbourhoods of Al-Shahba Al-Kadima and Halab Al-Jadida, which are both placed in the post-modernist architecture zone. Similarly, in the zone of low-standard areas of living and informal settlements, the neighbourhood of Sayf-Al-Dawleh has by far much better living conditions than Al-Sukkari (see fig. 2). Furthermore, while the twenty people who were shown the map agreed that it reflects Aleppo as they understand it, most of them suggested slight edits such as minor modification of the zone boundaries.

In reviewing the map, Alhakam Shaar, a specialist in Aleppo's heritage, pointed out a few important aspects of the city that this map does not reflect, noting that it missed out on the complexity of east Aleppo, which might indicate an unconscious bias, not only by the group that helped formulate the mental map, but also in

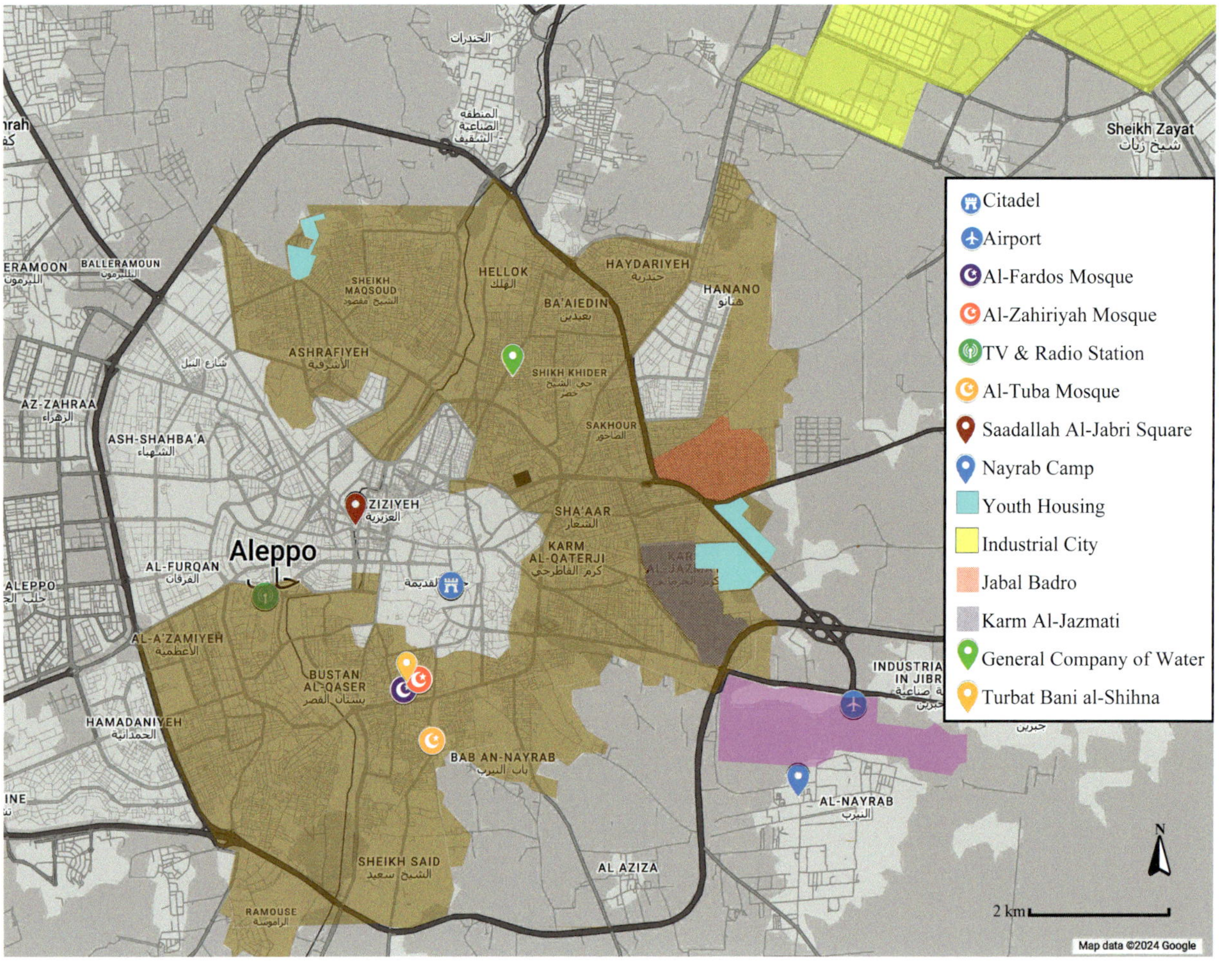

17 Remarks on East Aleppo.

the way that many residents of the city, especially those from its western part, perceive its eastern parts. For example, while sparse urbanism connects these areas to the rest of the city, the airport, the Al-Nayrab Palestinian refugee camp, and Sheikh Najjar (the industrial city) are on the east side of Aleppo. To be noted, some other institutions such as the General Water Company are also located east of the city (fig. 17). Moreover, as pointed out by Shaar and other researchers,[64] several buildings with protruding stones, similar to the buildings that this chapter designates as 2nd phase modernist, can be spotted elsewhere in Aleppo, for example, the area behind (west and north of) the TV and radio station (see fig. 17).

Noticeable in satellite images, on the very edge of north and east Aleppo (see fig. 17) are small areas planned in a socialist manner and named as «Youth Housing».[65] These areas were first constructed between 2000 and 2004,[66] with the exclusion of a small part in the east, which precedes the year 2000. Furthermore, like much of east Aleppo, areas such as Karm Al-Jazmati and Jabal Badro are mostly crowded and informal, yet unlike other areas, they encompass mostly one- or two-storey low-rise housing.[67]

Just like Al-Masharika and Al-Kallaseh, which were highlighted as a part of old Aleppo in the mental map because their names still resonate as «historic» with Aleppines, other historic areas such as Al-Fardos and Al-Maqamat lost most of their historic character. However, dispersed historic monuments can still be found there. Examples are Al-Zahiriyah Madrasa (1219/1220),[68] Al-Fardos Mosque (1235/1236),[69] and mausoleums such as Turabt Bani Al-Shihna.[70] Not only this area, but other dispersed monuments can still be found elsewhere such as Al-Tuba mosque, which dates to 1442/1443,[71] further south (see fig. 17).

It is important to point out that an architectural style of a certain period does not usually influence only a certain zone of the city, but rather adds a new layer to its older parts. For example, many socialist buildings can be found in the old city zone and in the zone of historicist and 1st type modernist architecture. Similarly, contemporary/post-modernist structures can be found in the 2nd type of modernist architecture zone, and so on. Moreover, not all structures in Aleppo can be clearly defined or confined to the seven architectural styles that are suggested in this chapter. Many buildings are on a cusp in between two styles or periods.

When asked about the «value», «worth», or «importance»[72] of the urban zones, most of the twenty interviewees selected the old city, the historicist and 1st phase modernist architecture zone, the 2nd phase modernist architecture zone, and the post-modernist architecture zone.[73] However, most of them referred to the old city as the most significant zone and pointed out as well that these zones have different levels of value and importance. The historicist-style buildings in the historicist and 1st phase modernist architecture zones were specifically pointed out as «valuable» in addition to the old city by most of the twenty interviewees. Socialist architecture was viewed unfavourably by most of the group. However, notably, the low standards of living and informal settlements areas were deemed as of no significant physical cultural value.

Timeline for Selected Significant Urban Events in Aleppo

The following timeline presents some selected significant urban events in the history of Aleppo. It especially highlights the civilisations that crossed the city, and some events that are related directly or indirectly to significant urban changes in Aleppo. As shown in figure 18, the graph connects each of the previously suggested architectural styles, and their corresponding zones in the «mental map», to an estimated rough period of the city's history. For example, I would like to propose 1868, the year of the formation for Al-Aziziye, the first «modern» neighbourhood, as a marker point in the city's urban transfer from the traditional fabric of the open courtyard houses to historicist-style architecture. Modernist architecture has received very little attention in Syria in general, and Aleppo in particular, and therefore it is hard to pinpoint a date or a building that can be attached to this movement. Therefore, I suggest the early 20th century as a rough estimate for the 1st phase of modernist architecture. While I could not obtain accurate information on the 2nd phase of the history of modernist architecture in Aleppo, some senior residents of the city suggested the 1940s as the time when these neighbourhoods started to see significant development. This is consistent with the findings in the earlier mentioned map compiled in 1941 by the US army,[74] which demonstrates that only very few buildings were constructed in the 2nd phase modernist architecture zone, including the Franciscan School and Church in Aleppo. The rise of socialism in Syria can be linked to 1973 when the Arab socialist Ba'ath Party became the sole ruling party of the country. It can also be linked to the introduction of a new constitution in 1973,[75] and the creation of the Establishment of Military Housing in 1975.[76] Although the early 1970s was a period when informal settlements intensified in Aleppo, several formal but low-standard living areas preceded this time. Additionally, the sprawl of informal settlements is linked to the post-independence

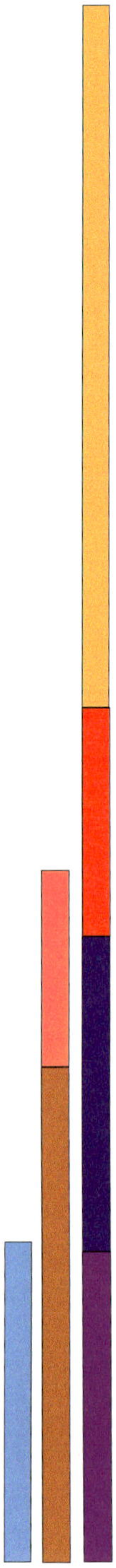

9000 BC Evidence of Human settlement near Aleppo.
333–323 BC Greeks, Alexander the Great.
312–383 BC Seleucid Empire.
64 BC Romans. | 395–637 Byzantines.
637–661 Rashidun Caliphs. | 661–750 Umayyads.
750–886 Abbasids. | 886–905 Tulunids.
905–936 Abbasids restore their direct rule.
936–944 Ikhshidids. | 944–1004 Hamdanids.
1024–1080 Mirdasids. | 1087–1117 Seljuks.
1117–11127 Artuqids. | 1127–1174 Zengids. | 1174–1260 Ayyubids.
1260–1382 Bahri Mamluks. | 1382–1516 Burji Circassian Mamluks.
1516 Ottomans. Selim I wins in the battle of Marj Dābiq and takes Aleppo.
1832 Aleppo is under the control of the army of Ibrahim Pasha.
1839 The edict of Gülhane initiates the Tanzimat period.
1841 Ottomans in control again.
1850 Kawmet Ḥalab.
1856 France is officially the protector of the Christians of the Ottoman Empire.
1866 Al-Majlis Al-Baladi [the municipality] is established in Aleppo.
1868 The formation of Al-Azizye, arguably the first «modern» planned neighbourhood.
1904 Train station is inaugurated in Aleppo.
1914 Start of WWI.
1918–1920 Faysal's Kingdom of Syria.
1920 French army occupies all of Syria, Lebanon, and Cilicia.
1939 Sanjak of Alexandretta known also as Hatay is ceded by France to Turkey.
1946 Evacuation Day (Independence Day) on 17 April.
1946–1971 Syria witnesses several military coups and several presidents.
1948 Arab-Israeli war and the Palestinian Nakba.
1950 Non-planned settlements first spring up.
1958–1961 The United Arab Republic is formed by Syria and Egypt.
1963 The Arab Socialist Ba'ath Party takes over the reins of government.
1967 The Arab-Israeli war.
1971 Hafez Al-Assad becomes the president.
1975 The Military Housing Establishment is founded.
1880 Bab Al-Faraj area in the old city is destroyed.
1980–1981 Clashes between the government and the Muslim Brotherhood.
1986 Old city of Aleppo is declared a World Heritage Site.
2000 Hafez Al-Assad dies, and his son Bashar Al-Assad takes over the presidency.
2011 The beginning of the conflict in Syria.
2012–2016 In July of 2012, Aleppo is devided to east, west and a Kurdish-controlled area.
2024 In December, the fall of the Assad regime.

18 Timeline for selected significant urban events in Aleppo.

period.[77] For this reason, I marked the early 1950s as the period of the rise of the low standards of living and informal settlements zone. It is difficult to pinpoint exactly when and why Aleppo moved from modernist to post-modernist architecture, apart from speculating that this seems to have happened around the middle of the second half of the 20th century.

The dates and events that the author selected to highlight major event and shifts of the city's history are the following:

- 9000 BC | Evidence of human settlement near Aleppo.[78]
- 4000–3100/2900 BC | Uruk Period.[79] Emergence of Mesopotamian civilisation.
- 2900–2330 BC | Sumerians. Era of independent city-states.[80]
- 2330–2180 BC | The Akkadian Empire.[81]
- 2000–1600 BC | Amorites, Yamhad Dynasty, and Yamhad (Aleppo) appears as an important centre.[82]
- 1595–1200 BC | Hittite dominance; in 1595 BC taking Aleppo marks the end of the Kingdom of Yamhad.[83] Also in this period, the rise of the Mitanni Empire and its competition with Egypt to control what is today Syria[84]
- 1200–1100 BC | Neo-Hittite; Aleppo possibly comes under the principality of Bit-Agusi.[85]
- 853–612 BC | Assyrians; in 853 BC King Shalmaneser III takes Aleppo.[86]
- 625–560 BC | The Neo-Babylonian (Chaldean) Empire.[87]
- 533–330s BC | Achaemenid Persians.[88]
- 333–323 BC | Greeks, Alexander the Great.[89]
- 323–312 BC | Generals of Alexander the Great fight over his empire. Syria is left with his general Antigonus, who dies in 301 and his domain is absorbed by Seleucus I Nicator, Alexander's *satrap* (governor) of Babylon.[90]
- 312–83 BC | Seleucid Empire; Seleucus I Nicator, reconquest of Babylon and solidification of his empire.[91]
- 83–64 BC | Armenian Kingdom; Tigran the Great takes Syria, after the last of the Seleucids rulers dies, until he is defeated by the Romans.[92]
- 64 BC | Romans; Pompey controls upper Syria and turns it into the Roman province of Syria.[93]
- 270–273 AD | Palmyra's expansion to Egypt and Syria and its demise.[94]
- 395–637 | Byzantines;[95] Theodosius the Great dies. His son Arcadius rules the eastern part of the empire with Constantinople as its capital, while his son Honorius rules the western part of the empire with Rome as the capital.[96] During this era, Aleppo is besieged by Sasanian Persians in 540 AD during the Byzantine–Sasanian wars of 540s, and they occupy Syria between 611 and 628.[97]
- 637–661 | Rashidun Caliphs.[98]
- 661–750 | Umayyads.[99]
- 750–886 | Abbasids.[100]
- 886–905 | In 886 Tulunids' rule over Syria is recognised by the Abbasids.[101]
- 905 936 | In 905 Abbasids restore their direct rule.[102]
- 936–944 | Ikhshidids; Muhammad Ibn Tughj Al-Ikhshi, who had governed Damascus and Aleppo since 905, establishes his own dynasty when he controlls Egypt in 936.[103]
- 944–1004 | Hamdanids; Sayef Al-Dawlah only comes to full power in 974. In 962 and again in 968 the Byzantines attack and ravage Aleppo.[104]
- Early 11th century | Constant disputes between the Faimids, the Byzantines, and the Banū Kilab tribe. By 1017, the Fatimids have a loose grip on Aleppo, challenged by the Banu Kilab under Salih Ibn Mirdas, who take Aleppo in 1024.[105]
- 1024–1080 | Mirdasids; in 1070 Aleppo leaders acknowledge the Seljuk ruler.[106]
- 1080 | Control of Aleppo moving between Seljuks and Uqaylids.[107]
- 1087–1117 | Seljuks.[108]
- 1117–11127 | Artuqids.[109]
- 1124–1125 | Crusaders led by Baldwin II siege Aleppo for three months from November to January, until Bursuqi the Seljuk *atabeg* (governor) of Mosul marches to Aleppo[110] and «the Crusaders [make] further attempts to harass the city until 1127».[111]
- 1127–1174 | Zengids.[112]
- 1174–1260 | Ayyubids.[113]
- 1260 | Mongols seize Aleppo.[114]
- 1260–1382 | The Bahri Mamluks.[115] During this period, the Mongols (also Ilkhanids or Tatars) launch several offensives on Syria in 1281, 1299, 1300, 1303, and 1312.[116]
- 1382–1516 | The Burji Circassian Mamluks rule during this period, and the Tatars led by Timur invade Aleppo in 1400.[117]
- 1516 | Ottomans; Selim I wins the battle of Marj Dābiq and takes Aleppo; Al-Mutawakkil III, the last Abbasid caliph in Baghdad, concedes the caliphate to Selim I.[118]
- 1774 | Treaty of Küçük Kaynarca; Russia becomes the protector of the Orthodox subjects of the Ottoman Empire.[119]
- 1819 | Rebellion against Ottoman rule. The governor orders the destruction of the gates of the districts as they had hindered his recapture of the city.[120]
- 1822 | An earthquake hits Aleppo and destroys two thirds of its buildings and the city walls, which were already in a «state of disrepair».[121] Furthermore, two thirds of the city's inhabitants die, and according to some estimates the population shrinks from 235,000 inhabitants to 100,000.[122]
- 1826 | Istanbul witnesses Vaka-i Hayriye.[123] The Janissaries are abolished in the empire, and many are killed, exiled, or imprisoned.[124] Seemingly, they continue to function as an entity after they are dismantled in Aleppo,[125] possibly until the events of 1850.[126]
- 1832 | Aleppo is under the control of the army of Ibrahim Pasha, son of Muhammad Ali Pasha, the first of the Alawiyya Dynasty of Egypt.[127]

- 1839 | The edict of Gülhane initiates the Tanzimat period, which sees a set of reforms that include full equal rights to non-Muslims.[128]
- 1841 | Ottomans in control again.[129]
- 1850 | Kawmet Ḥalab,[130] a revolt against mandatory military recruitment and taxes that turns into sectarian looting and a struggle for power between the two leaders of Janissarys and Ashrafs.[131]
- 1856 | France is officially the protector of the Christians of the Ottoman Empire; this happens according to Al-Ghazzi after France assisted the Ottoman Empire against its war with Russia.[132]
- 1866 | Al-Majlis Al-Baladi (the municipality) is established in Aleppo,[133] and the State of Aleppo, independent from the State of Syria, is created.[134]
- 1868 | The formation of Al-Azizye, arguably the first «modern» planned neighbourhood with historicist[135] architecture, in contrast to the dominating traditional narrow alleyways and open courtyard houses;[136] shortly followed by other «modern» neighbourhoods, such as Al-Nayal in 1878, Al-Jamiliye[137] in 1882, and Al-Sulaymaniye in 1895.[138]
- 1882 | Municipality of Aleppo uses a German urban planner called Jung[139] as a consultant to help plan for the city.[140]
- 1904 | Train station is inaugurated in Aleppo.[141]
- 1907 (or early 1908) | Electric light in Aleppo's streets[142]
- 1910 | Mandatory military service for Christian and Jews, which drives many members of these groups to migrate, especially to the Americas.[143]
- 1914 | Start of WWI.
- 1915 | Many Armenians arrive in Aleppo because of the Armenian genocide.[144]
- 1916 | The beginning of «the Arab Revolt» and the Sykes–Picot secret agreement between France and Great Britain, putting today's Syria, Lebanon, and a part of Turkey under French control.[145]
- 1917 | Balfour Declaration.[146]
- 1918 | British and Arab armies enter Aleppo.[147] The Ottoman Empire surrenders to the Allies and the end of WWI.
- 1918–1920 | Faysal's Kingdom of Syria,[148] mainly governs Aleppo, Homs, Hama, and Damascus, and in Transjordan. The coast from north Palestine to Cilicia is under direct British then French control.[149]
- 1920 | French army occupies all of Syria, Lebanon, and Cilicia.[150] The French authorities divide their occupied territories into Aleppo state, Damascus state, Greater Lebanon State, and the Alawite autonomous territory.[151]
- 1921 | The treaty of Ankara, also known as the Franklin–Bouillon Agreement. France gives up her claim to Cilicia.[152] The borders between Turkey and France are redrawn and Aleppo loses a big part of its historic northern hinterland. Sanjak of Alexandretta[153] in Aleppo is turned into an autonomous region. As French troops withdraw, thousands of Christian refugees follow.[154] According to one estimate, 60,000 Armenians arrive in the 200,000-inhabitant city.[155]
- 1922 | The League of Nations approves the texts of the French Mandate for Syria and Lebanon.[156] Alawite territories become a «state».[157] After signing on to the text in 1921, the boundaries of the Jebel Druze state are announced and implemented.[158] The Syrian Federation, which includes the States of Damascus, Aleppo, and the Alawite State, but not Lebanon or the Jebel Druze state, is created.[159]
- 1923 | The migration and arrival of a big Syriac community from Urfa to Aleppo, initially staying in refugee sheds that later turn into the Syriac neighbourhood in Aleppo.[160]
- 1925 | The Syrian State – the states of Aleppo and Damascus are combined into one state. The Alawite state is separated from them; Lebanon and Jebel Druze state are also not incorporated into the Syrian state.[161]
- 1936 | The Alawite and the Jabal Druze states are formally incorporated into Syria.[162]
- 1939 | Sanjak of Alexandretta, known also as Hatay,[163] is ceded by France to Turkey.[164] The districts of Alawite state and Jabal Druze are separated from Syria again.[165]
- 1940 | The Fall of France in 1940 during WWII; a pro-Vichy General Commissioner in charge of Syria and Lebanon.[166]
- 1941 | Free French and British armies are in control of Syria and Lebanon.[167]
- 1942 | Alawite state and Jabal Druze districts are reunited with Syria again.[168] According to Hreitani, a heritage expert, many Jews of Aleppo start to liquidate their businesses and migrate to Lebanon to work there, and most of those who migrated to Lebanon eventually migrate to Europe.[169]
- 1945 | The French military bombs Damascus and causes heavy physical destruction that includes the parliament building; casualties include 400 dead and countless injured; the end of WWII.[170]
- 1946 | Evacuation Day (Independence Day)[171] on 17 April. The French armies depart Syria. Moreover, according to David, an urban geographer and historian, a sharp increase in the migration of the financially comfortable social class out of the old city to the more modern neighbourhoods west of the city while many rural populations move to inhabit the vacant houses in the old city and its northern and eastern surrounding suburbs.[172]
- 1946–1971 | Syria witnesses several military coups and several presidents.
- 1947 | Israel is recognised by the United Nations; wide emigration of the Aleppine Jewish community.[173]
- 1948 | Arab–Israeli war and the Palestinian Nakba, after which many Palestinians become refugees, and the establishment of the Nayrab refugee Camp near Aleppo.[174]
- Late 1940s | Queiq river[175] stops passing through Aleppo, as its course regresses hundreds of metres;[176] this is because the river stems from Turkish territory and Turkish irrigation projects cut off the river from Syria.
- 1950 | According to the 1980 UNESCO report, «non-planned settlements first sprang up in 1950 and then surrounded the city on all sides, except in the west».[177]

- 1958–1961 | Aleppo is part of the United Arab Republic formed by Syria and Egypt; economic policies such as the nationalisation of land and factories lead to large-scale flight of capital and businesses to Beirut.[178]
- 1962 | Ein el Tal unofficial refugee camp, also known as Handarat, is established near Aleppo.[179]
- 1963 | The Arab Socialist Ba'ath Party[180] takes over the reins of government in a military coup.[181] New policies trigger more rural migration to the city.[182] Hafez al-Assad is one of the officers who overthrows the previous government.[183]
- 1966 | Hafez Al-Assad becomes the Syrian Minister of Defence.[184] Moreover, according to Hreitani, a committee is established to «freeze» Jewish properties, and their financial returns are put under the control of the Syrian ministry of foreign affairs.[185]
- 1967 | The Arab–Israeli war; according to Hreitani, the Jewish population in Aleppo notably diminishes.[186]
- 1971 | Hafez Al-Assad becomes the president.[187]
- 1973 | A new constitution is introduced, which dictates that the Ba'ath party is the sole ruling party of Syria.[188] New policies intensify the waves of migrants from the rural areas around Aleppo to the city and form formal and informal settlements.[189] October war with Israel.
- 1975 | The Military Housing Establishment is founded, the single chief construction company in Syria for large-scale projects.[190]
- 1979–1982 | Destruction[191] of a significant part of Al-Masharika district.[192]
- 1980 | Bab Al-Faraj area in the old city is destroyed. This area contained some of the historic Jewish neighbourhoods such as Bahsita and Al-Bandara.[193]
- 1980–1981 | Clashes between the government and the Muslim Brotherhood; protests and violence end up with historic massacres in Aleppo and other Syrian cities.[194]
- 1986 | Old city of Aleppo is declared a World Heritage Site.[195]
- 2000 | Hafez Al-Assad dies, and his son Bashar Al-Assad takes over the presidency.[196]
- 2001–2004 | Another part of the historic Al-Masharika district is destroyed.[197]
- 2011 | The beginning of the conflict in Syria.[198]
- 2012–2016 | In July 2012, Aleppo is split into government-controlled west and rebel-controlled east, in addition to a Kurdish militias-controlled area. In December 2016, Assad forces and allies take control of the east again except for the part controlled by the Kurdish millitias, which remained under their control until the fall of the Assad regime.[199] Fighting causes huge destruction of the old city and eastern Aleppo. Migration waves to other countries, but also inside the country to other cities, and within the city, typically from the east to the west of Aleppo, and the displacement of virtually all the residents of East Aleppo.[200]
- 2024 | In December, Aleppo is taken by the rebels.[201] In a matter of around a week, the rebels take Damascus and Bashar Al-Assad flees to Moscow.[202] At the moment of writing these lines tensions are rising with the Kurdish militias controlling east of Syria,[203] and Israel is expanding in the south of Syria and bombarding several locations in the country.[204]

Conclusion: Intervention Categories or City Zones to Safeguard the Built Heritage of Cities

When the division occurred in the city in 2012,[205] many people had a good understanding of what is east Aleppo and what is west Aleppo. The division of the city into two spheres,[206] or three counting the small Kurdish forces-controlled district, was not only social, but was also reflected in its physical attributes, especially architecture and urban spaces. A comparison between the «mental map» (see fig. 2) in this chapter and a map of how the city split into east and west[207] (fig. 19) provides some clues as to how Aleppines viewed their city, and why the short-lived east–west division of the city between 2012 and 2016 was easily understood by its inhabitants and will arguably remain significant in the foreseeable future. Therefore, understanding Aleppo's character and urban spaces is key to take forward steps to reunite the city and implement a plan to protect its architectural heritage, even the marginalised architectural styles outside the part inscribed as a World Heritage Site.

I have used my own interpretation and the aid of a small group of Aleppines to categorise the different architectural styles in Aleppo and then link them to an estimated period. Nonetheless, a survey for the remaining, and perhaps even destroyed, traditional courtyard, historicist, modernist, and possibly other styles of houses is much needed. An analysis of the architecture, neighbourhoods and components of the much-neglected eastern Aleppo is also necessary. Here, I argue that the methodology used in this chapter is applicable to other cities containing several areas or neighbourhoods with different distinctive characters. In many cases like Aleppo, different architectural characters

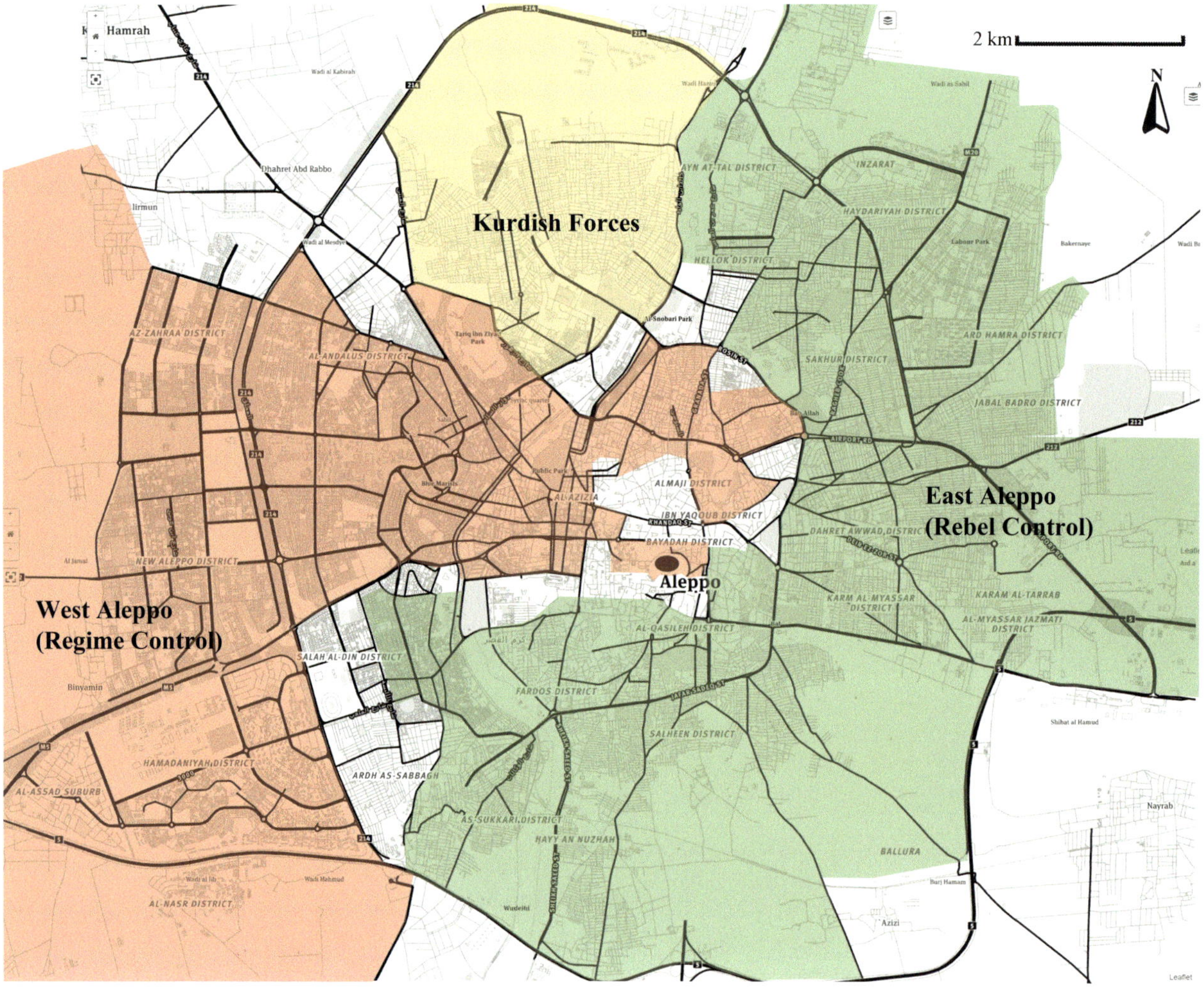

19 Division of Aleppo in 2013.

were created over time, or even by different key players, that morphed different typologies of architecture in different spaces of the city. Thus, older ideas and theories, such as Lynch's «Mental Map»,[208] can be alternatively developed to suit the unique circumstances of each city and make use of new available technology. Additionally, a «Mental Map» can be utilised to pinpoint not only the architectural styles, but also other characteristics of the city that are well known to its dwellers.

In different experts' meetings, I introduced the idea of adapting similar approaches to implement different protection regulations for different typologies of architecture or different zones in the city. For instance, after my input, the ideas mentioned above were discussed and revisited during a meeting of 26 international experts,[209] which resulted in the Cottbus Document. This document, which is concerned with safeguarding the cultural heritage of post-conflict cities like Aleppo, suggested the use of «Intervention Categories»: «In any city that has seen a long history there are areas of very different value, in heritage terms [...] In the belts around historic city centres, one often finds remarkable achievements of nineteenth and twentieth-century urbanism and architecture which deserve to be taken seriously in any reconstruction approach.»[210]

Another example is a publication produced by Stuttgart University, where, similarly, the idea was debated and reassessed by a group of researchers after I was able to present it. The meeting, which was concerned with Aleppo, produced a «City Zones» approach. In summary, this publication recommends dividing the city into different zones, each one with a unique set of characters and a specialised approach to deal with each zone's distinctive situation.[211] It is important to further note that many heritage experts, whether in the previously mentioned meetings or in other academic spaces, share similar ideas related to special zones and categories and that these ideas are part of an ongoing discussion rather than the sole intellectual property of one specialist.

Finally, the future (re-)construction of Aleppo should not be read only through the lens of foreign key players interventions,[212] or even the examples of other cities, but rather also through the local key players that shaped and continue to shape the city. International media and academic discussions often focus on a few ideas such as a «Dubaification»[213] scenario, where high-end towers might replace the old city of Aleppo as was the case of Beirut,[214] or even comparing the future Syrian situation to post-WWII Germany.[215] Nonetheless, domestic factors that might alter Aleppo are seldom discussed in media or academia. For example, withholding lands from housing associations and unaffordability might shrink the production of post-modernist buildings or any sort of new architectural styles in Aleppo. Similarly, a bigger takeover of all-governmental housing agencies might turn wider areas of Aleppo into socialist styles and forms. Notably, the Ministry of Public Works and Housing, which dissolved the General Union for Housing Cooperation and took over the housing associations, signed a cooperation memorandum with Russia in 2020. The memorandum applied to the «fields of rapid and prefabricated construction techniques and standardized building systems».[216] Most importantly, the lack of any governmental plans to provide sufficient housing for the population and the policy of ignoring informal settlements will only lead to their growth. The 2018 Aleppo «Development Plan», which was shared on social media by the Council of Aleppo City, includes some comments such as «unclear and incomprehensible plan as the previous time», and «the same as 30 years ago, nothing changed». Other comments on the same plan include the following: «We know this plan from a long time ago, nothing increased or decreased, we were expecting the boundaries of the city to expand» and «I swear, what I see is that the people who put the plan don't understand it, please specify the areas by name and what will change in each area.»[217]

In summary, heritage is not only something in the past to protect through the safeguarding of significant buildings, but also a subject that is being shaped and created right now in the present moment. In general, on the one hand, the passiveness towards protecting the city's heritage in the west of the city beyond a virtual boarder is a deliberate choice that is still causing several neighbourhoods in the favourable parts of the city to rapidly lose the buildings that define their character. On the other hand, overall, the practices discussed above have become so embedded in contemporary heritage politics led by the municipality that it is almost impossible to grasp the evidence of multiple urban transformation processes taking place beyond the better-off spaces in the city. Thus the discussion should cover the city as a whole. For most experts, the «Dubaification» of Aleppo is a horrible scenario if it were to replace the old city, but this is not necessarily the case for the areas of low standards and informal settlements, which in many cases have been levelled to the ground since the war started.

1 Karklis 2016; Ibold 2020.
2 The author is referring to the different conferences he attended that were organised for safeguarding the cultural heritage of Syria.
3 UNESCO 2012.
4 Sauvaget 1941.
5 The author is referring to the «Album» attached with the referenced book, specifically the illustrations Pl. LII, Pl. LIII, Pl. LIV, Pl. LVIII, Pl. LXII, and Pl. LXX.
6 Gaube/Wirth 2007, 87.
7 Raymond 2010.
8 Al-Ghazzi 1926, 450.
9 The year mentioned by Al-Ghazzi is 1317 Hijri. See the map of Chartier and Raghib in Gallica [1899/1900]; Lafi 2022, 218.
10 Baedeker 1912.
11 Gaube/Wirth 2007, 96.
12 Zeido 2023, 5–9; Zeido 2020, 98–131.
13 U.S. Army [1941] 1958. The map actually holds two dates: on the right side «Army Map Service, compiled 1941»; on the left side «Edition 2–AMS (...) Compiled in 1958 from Town Plans of Syria and Lebanon, 1:10,000, AMS, Aleppo, printed 1958.»
14 Gaube/Wirth 2007, 96.
15 To be noted, the referenced Arabic translation published in 2007 is a corrected and edited version of the original 1984 German version. In the introduction, the authors mentioned that these corrections will find their way to a new German edition, but until the date of writing this chapter, no second German edition has been published.
16 Russian Military 1985.
17 Alsayed 2015.
18 Zeido/Ibold 2019.
19 DGAM 2000.
20 UNESCO n.d.
21 Zeido/Ibold 2019, 87–90.
22 DOCA: The Directorate of the Old City of Aleppo.
23 See the referenced publication of Lafi, which provides important insight to the developments of heritage practices in Aleppo, Lafi 2017.
24 Lynch 1960, 46–72.
25 Lynch 1960, 46–90.
26 A peer reviewer has asked about this matter, pointing out that the prespective of this map might reflect only the views of residents from West Aleppo. Unfortunately, there was simply no time to conduct more interviews before the completion of this publication.
27 Al-Ghazzi 1923, 313.
28 See the references and further details in the section titled *Timeline for Selected Significant Urban Events in Aleppo.*
29 Al-Ghazzi 1923, 489.
30 Al-Ghazzi 1923, 489.
31 As mentioned in the introduction, this data, if available, is not currently accessible for the public and researchers.
32 A neighbourhood that belongs to the historicist and first type modernist architecture zone highlighted in red.
33 A neighbourhood that belongs to the second type modernist architecture zone highlighted in dark blue.
34 Syndicate of Engineers in Aleppo [1997], 5, 67, 70, 73, 124.
35 Taoutel 1964, 129, 135.
36 The Arabic term used in Aleppo for these stones, at least in some construction and academic circles, is: حجر صوري اصفر ناقء.
37 Syndicate of Engineers in Aleppo 1996; Syndicate of Engineers in Aleppo [1997]; Syndicate of Engineers in Aleppo n.d.
38 Al-Rifai 1996, 253–256.
39 The study spells the name in Arabic Alphabet; therefore, it might be spelled differently.
40 Al-Rifai 1996, 258–260.
41 Salname-yi Vilâyet-i Halep [1882/1883], 59; Salname-yi Vilâyet-i Halep [1884/1885], 132.
42 Salname-yi Vilâyet-i Halep [1895/1896], 147.
43 El-Acima 1930, 231.
44 Al-Rifai 1996, 270. The study spells all names in Arabic Alphabet; therefore, they might be spelled differently.
45 Al-Rifai 1996, 261.
46 Al-Rifai 1996, 270.
47 East to west in light blue in fig. 2 respectively.
48 Also translated to The Military Housing Corporation.
49 Chibli 2004, 115–116.
50 See page 277 for the pictures of the 1967 dorm units in Aleppo University 2008.
51 Aleppo University 2008, 35, 36, 39, 40, 49, 277.
52 The Establishment of Military Housing n.d.
53 Al-Thawra 2019.
54 See Al-Rifai 1996, 265–278, for more details on how socialism influenced the profession of architecture and engineering in Aleppo.
55 Yusuf 2013; Syndicate of Engineers in Aleppo 1998, 66–83.
56 General Assembly of Labor Unions 2011.
57 Aleppo National Archives 2014.
58 Al-Sajir 2019.
59 Arabic: الاتحاد العام للتعاون السكني.
60 Al-Hamdan 2015.
61 Arabic: وزارة الأشغال العامة والإسكان; SANA 2019.
62 Arabic: المناطق الشعبية. Mentioned as quartiers populaires in some sources.
63 Read more in detail about this issue in the referenced publication (Zeido/Ibold 2019).
64 This information was pointed out to the me by another researcher who did not want to be mentioned by name. Shaar also suspects that Al-A'arqoub area might contain several buildings with similar architectural style and features of 2nd phase modernism.
65 Arabic: مساكن الشباب.
66 The satellite images of Google earth showed nothing in 2000, and two visible buildings in 2004.
67 I could not confirm this information, but as a resident from Aleppo suggested, these areas were first inhabited by moving tribes and communities that lived in tents

and worked in raising cattle, unlike other areas that were settled by rural communities that lived in villages.
68 Al-Ghazzi 1923, 299.
69 Al-Ghazzi 1923, 389.
70 Al-Ghazzi 1923, 289; DAI n.d.
71 Al-Ghazzi 1923, 353.
72 It should be noted that the author did not use these exact terms as the questions were in Arabic.
73 In this study, twenty individuals from Aleppo were asked whether the mental map reflected how they viewed their city. They were also asked which parts or zones they saw as the most important, valuable, worthy, and aesthetically appealing. This survey took a semi-structured interviews form and the twenty people were asked these questions individually, not in one group. The interviews were conducted in a period between 2016 and 2019.
74 U.S. Army [1941] 1958.
75 BBC 2012.
76 Chibli 2004, 115–116.
77 Bianca et al. 1980, 21–22.
78 Akkermans/Schwartz 2003, 44–47.
79 Stiebing/Helft 2023, 41.
80 Stiebing/Helft 2023, 52.
81 Stiebing/Helft 2023, 74.
82 Stiebing/Helft 2023, 173.
83 Burns 2017, 11.
84 Stiebing/Helft 2023, 192.
85 Burns 2017, 18–20.
86 Stiebing/Helft 2023, 336.
87 Stiebing/Helft 2023, 397.
88 Stiebing/Helft 2023, 400.
89 Burns 2017, 26.
90 Burns 2017, 26–27.
91 Britannica 2024b.
92 Chain 2013, 238, 250.
93 Eder 2006.
94 Bryce 2014, 307–313.
95 Burns 2017, 72.
96 Leppin 2006.
97 Burns 2017, 69–70.
98 Burns 2017, 77.
99 Burns 2017, 77.
100 Burns 2017, 83.
101 Gordon 2012.
102 Burns 2017, 90.
103 Bacharach 1975.
104 Burns 2017, 90–93.
105 Eddé 2013; Burns 2017, 99.
106 Eddé 2013.
107 Basan 2010, 90.
108 Burns 2017, 107.
109 Burns 2017, 107.
110 Smail 1995, 135.
111 Burns 2017, 124.
112 Burns 2017, 124.
113 Burns 2017, 142.
114 Burns 2017, 169.
115 Burns 2017, 173.
116 Amitai-Preiss 2000, 58.
117 Burns 2017, 188.
118 Ágoston/Masters 2009, Introduction xxix.
119 Ágoston/Masters 2009, 615.
120 Arnaud 2008, 956.
121 Masters 1999, 65.
122 Alsayed 2015, 44, 113, 137. Alsayed, an Aleppine historian, questioned the accuracy of the numbers and argued that this was a meteor that hit a location near Aleppo.
123 Translated as «The Auspicious Incident», a rebellion of the Janissaries against the Sultan after the introduction of reforms to the army.
124 Ágoston/Masters 2009, 346.
125 Masters 2010, 293.
126 Masters 2010, 297–300.
127 Ágoston/Masters 2009, 205.
128 Ágoston/Masters 2009, 485.
129 Ágoston/Masters 2009, 294.
130 Known in Arabic as: قومة حلب.
131 Masters 1990, 3–20.
132 Al-Ghazzi 1926, 768.
133 Ayntabi/Othman 1993, 60.
134 Alsayed 2015, 42.
135 Arabic terminology: تاريخانية.
136 Alsayed 2015, 48, 59.
137 In official records the district was called «Al-Salimiye».
138 Alsayed 2015, 58, 116, 265.
139 Different spellings are a probability since the source spells the name in Arabic letters.
140 Maziak 1958, 190.
141 Al-Ghazzi 1926, 466.
142 Al-Ghazzi 1926, 468.
143 Alsayed 2015, 388.
144 Ágoston/Masters 2009, 54–55; Alsayed 2015, 478.
145 Hourani 1946, 44.
146 Hourani 1964, 46.
147 Hourani 1946, 49.
148 Khoury 1983, 80.
149 Hourani 1946, 50.
150 Hourani 1946, 53.
151 Longrigg 1958, 125–126; Hourani 1946, 172.
152 Khoury 1987, 50, 101.
153 Today's Hatay region in Turkey.
154 Longrigg 1958, 119.
155 Alsayed 2015, 480.
156 Hourani 1946, 55.
157 Longrigg 1958, 125.
158 Longrigg 1958, 127.
159 Hourani 1946, 173.
160 Arabic: حي السريان; Tuma 2024. To be noted, Shukri Tuma is the priest of St. George's Syriac Orthodox Church in Aleppo. The website is a documentation of the Syriac community history. According to Georgio Frick, another priest who participated in this work, the pieces on this

website are collected oral history open to the public for corrections and will be published in a book with the title من هجرة الى هجرة.

161 Khoury 1987, 59.
162 Khoury 1987, 59.
163 Arabic: هاتاي - لواء اسكندرون. The region included the city of Iskenderun, what was considered Aleppo's port to the Mediterranean.
164 Hourani 1946, 212.
165 Khoury 1987, 59.
166 Khoury 1987, 583.
167 Khoury 1987, 594.
168 Khoury 1987, 59.
169 Hreitani 2008, 161–162.
170 Khoury 1987, 616–617.
171 Arabic: عيد الجلاء.
172 David 1975, 19.
173 Hreitani 2008, 161.
174 UNRWA n.d. a.
175 Arabic: نهر قويق.
176 Alsayed 2015, 144.
177 Bianca et al. 1980, 21–22.
178 Podeh 1999, 143.
179 UNRWA n.d. b.
180 Arabic: حزب البعث العربي الاشتراكي.
181 Britannica 2024a.
182 Zeido / Ibold 2019.
183 Seale 2000.
184 Britannica 2024a.
185 Hreitani 2008, 90.
186 Hreitani 2008, 90, 162, 164.
187 Britannica 2024a.
188 BBC 2012.
189 Zeido / Ibold 2019.
190 Chibli 2004, 115.
191 No official report available on the date of destruction, this period is reported by pages on social media, which the author has estimated to be at least roughly correct based on collected statements and aerial photographs from different dates.
192 Arabic: حي المشارقة.
193 Arabic: بحسيتا والبندرة; Hreitani 2008, 101, 103.
194 Middle East Watch 1991, 14–15.
195 UNESCO 2012.
196 Britannica 2024a.
197 As can be seen by comparing online satellite imaging services such as Google Earth from 2000 and 2004.
198 Ibold 2019.
199 Tokmajyan 2017.
200 Shaar 2019, 30; Zeido / Ibold 2019, 94.
201 Bachega 2024.
202 Gebeily / Azhari 2024.
203 Sinico 2024.
204 Krever 2024.
205 As discussed in Zeido / Ibold 2019.
206 To be noted, in many cases, the part controlled by Kurdish rebels is considered its own space in the city and different from East and West Aleppo.
207 Chulov 2013.
208 Lynch 1960.
209 BTU News 2016, 22.
210 Schmidt 2017.
211 The IUSD Lab 2016, 85–88.
212 Ibold 2019.
213 The term refers to turning a place to a high-end glassed towers area, much like Dubai city.
214 Seif 2022.
215 Connolly / Bloch 2015; Ibold 2022.
216 Shaam Times 2020.
217 Council of Aleppo City 2018.

Ágoston / Masters 2009
G. Ágoston / B. Masters: Encyclopedia of the Ottoman Empire (New York 2009).

Akkermans / Schwartz 2003
P. Akkermans / G. Schwartz: The Archaeology of Syria: From Complex Hunter-Gatherers to Early Urban Societies (c.16,000–300 BC) (Cambridge 2003).

Aleppo National Archives 2014
أرشيف حلب الوطني - دار الوثائق الرقمية التاريخية: جمعيات التعاون السكني.
Aleppo National Archives – Digital Historical Document House: Housing Cooperation Associations. [Online 2014], https://www.facebook.com/digdoc.net/photos/a.456477554456706/456491274455334/ (28 February 2021).

Aleppo University 2008
جامعة حلب: ذاكرة جامعة حلب في عيدها الذهبي ١٩٥٨-٢٠٠٨. العيد الذهبي ٥٠. الجمهورية العربية السورية.
Aleppo University: Memory of the University of Aleppo on its golden Jubilee 1958–2008. 50th Golden Jubilee. Syrian Arab Republic (Aleppo 2008).

Al-Ghazzi 1923
كامل بن حسين بن محمد البالي الشهير بالغزي: نهر الذهب في تاريخ حلب، الجزء الثاني. المطبعة المارونية في حلب.
K. Al-Ghouzzi: The Gold River in the History of Aleppo, Part Two (Aleppo 1923).

Al-Ghazzi 1926
كامل بن حسين بن محمد البالي الشهير بالغزي: نهر الذهب في تاريخ حلب، الجزء الثالث. المطبعة المارونية في حلب.

K. Al-Ghazzi: The Gold River in the History of Aleppo, Part Three (Aleppo 1926).

Al-Hamdan 2015

هني الحمدان: التعاون السكني.. فشل أم إفشال..؟!.. آلاف الجمعيات السكنية مازالت تنتظر الأرض منذ ربع قرن.. واتهامات بالفساد لإدارات التعاون..! صحيفة تشرين.

H. Al-Hamdan: Housing Cooperation... Failure or Setting it Up to Fail...?! ... Thousands of Housing Associations are Still Waiting for the Land for a Quarter of a Century ... and Accusations of Corruption for the Cooperation Departments...! Tishreen Newspaper, 25 June 2015, https://mopwh.gov.sy/index.php?page=show&ex=2&dir=news&lang=1&nt=8&nid=478&act=383 (7 February 2025).

Al-Rifai 1996

فيصل الرفاعي: حلب بين التاريخ والهندسة. جامعة حلب، معهد التراث العلمي العربي.

M.F. Al-Rifai: Aleppo between History and Engineering (Aleppo 1996).

Al-Sajir 2019

عموري الساجر: حفاظاً على حقوق المواطنين دمج ١٠ جمعيات سكنية و٣١ قيد التنفيذ .. مشلح : تعثر العقود مع مجلس المدينة و إبرام عقد أولي مع الإسكان بخصوص ٨٢ برجية سكنية في الاشرفية. صحيفة الجماهير.

A. Al-Sajir: In order to preserve the rights of citizens, 10 housing associations are merged and 31 are under implementation. Mashlah: Contracts with the City Council have Failed, and a Preliminary Contract has been Signed with the Housing Regarding 82 Residential Towers in Al-Ashrafieh. Al-Jamahir, issue 15741, 16 July 2019, http://jamahir.alwehda.gov.sy/?p=46948 (10 September 2024).

Alsayed 2015

علاء نديم السيد: تاريخ حلب المصور أواخر العهد العثماني ١٨٨٠-١٩١٨ م. شعاع للنشر والعلوم.

A.N. Alsayed: Aleppo's photographed history in the late Ottoman period 1880–1918 (Aleppo 2015).

Al-Thawra 2019

مع نهاية القضاء على الإرهاب وبـدء مرحلـة إعـادة الإعمـار.. الإنشاءات العسكرية والإسكان العسكري وإدارة المشاريع الإنتاجية على جبهات العمل. الثورة أونلاين.

With the end of the Elimination of Terrorism and the Beginning of the Reconstruction Phase... The Military Construction, The Military Housing, and The Management of Productive Projects are on the Work Fronts. Al-Thawra, issue 17039, 1 August 2019, http://thawra.sy/index.php/pinvestigation/187170-2019-08-01-00-37-40 (13 February 2021).

Amitai-Preiss 2000

R. Amitai-Preiss: Mongol Imperial Ideology and the Ilkhanid War against the Mamluks, in: D.O. Morgan / R. Amitai-Preiss (eds.): The Mongol Empire and its Legacy (Leiden 2000), https://doi.org/10.1163/9789004492738_010.

Arnaud 2008

J. Arnaud: A. Tradition and Modernity in the Nineteenth Century: Modernization of the Cities of the Ottoman Empire (1800–1920), in: S.K. Jayyusi / R. Holod / A. Petruccioli / A. Raymond (eds.): The City in the Islamic World, vol. 2 (Leiden 2008) 957–981, https://doi.org/10.1163/ej.9789004162402.i-1500.257.

Ayntabi / Othman 1993

محمد فؤاد عينتابي / نجوى عثمان: حلب في مئة عام ١٨٥٠-١٩٥٠، ج١. منشورات جامعة حلب، معهد التراث العلمي العربي.

M.F. Ayntabi / N. Othman: Aleppo in a hundred years 1850–1950, vol. 1 (Aleppo 1993).

Bacharach 1975

J.L. Bacharach: The Career of Muḥammad Ibn Ṭughj Al-Ikhshīd, a Tenth-Century Governor of Egypt. Speculum 50, no. 4, 1975, 586–612, https://doi.org/10.2307/2855469.

Bachega 2024

H. Bachega: Inside Aleppo, the first city to fall to Syrian rebels. BBC, 12 December 2024, https://www.bbc.com/news/articles/c3wexlp91n4o (19 December 2024).

Basan 2010

O.A. Basan: Osman Aziz. The Great Seljuqs: A History (London & New York 2010).

Baedeker 1912

K. Baedeker: Palestine and Syria, with routes through Mesopotamia and Babylonia and the island of Cyprus, handbook for travelers (Leipzig 1912), https://archive.org/details/palestineandsyr01petegoog (10 September 2024).

BBC 2012

Profile: Syria's ruling Baath Party. BBC, 9 July 2012, https://www.bbc.com/news/world-middle-east-18582755 (9 September 2024).

Bianca et al. 1980

S. Bianca / J.C. David / G. Rizzardi / Y. Beton / B. Chauffert-Yvart: The Conservation of the Old City (Paris 1980), https://unesdoc.unesco.org/ark:/48223/pf0000042161.locale=en (10 September 2024).

Britannica 2024a

The Editors of Encyclopaedia Britannica: «Hafez al-Assad». Encyclopedia Britannica, [Online 2024], https://www.britannica.com/biography/Hafiz-al-Assad (10 September 2024).

Britannica 2024b

The Editors of Encyclopaedia Britannica: «Seleucid empire». Encyclopedia Britannica, [Online 2024], https://www.britannica.com/place/Seleucid-Empire (7 September 2024).

Bryce 2014

T. Bryce: Ancient Syria: A Three Thousand Year History (Oxford 2014).

Burns 2017

R. Burns: Aleppo: A History (New York 2017), https://doi.org/10.4324/9781315544076.

BTU News 2016

Post-Conflict Rebuilding: Guidelines and Toolkit for Safeguarding the Cultural Significance. BTU News 14, No. 46, September 2016, 22, https://www-docs.b-tu.de/presse/public/BTU-Zeitung/Ausgaben_2016/160831_BTU-News_Nr46_WEB.pdf (10 September 2024).

Chain 2013

M. Chain: The Kingdom of Armenia: A history (London 2013), https://doi.org/10.4324/9781315028804.

Chibli 2004

M. Chibli: Contemporary Architecture in Syria, in: J. Abed (ed.): Architecture Re-introduced: New Projects in Societies in Change (Geneva 2004) 114–119, https://archnet.org/publications/4783 (10 September 2024).

Chibli et al. 2009
M. Chibli et al.: Informal settlements in Aleppo: Rapid profiles of all informal settlements in Aleppo (Aleppo 2009), http://madinatuna.com/downloads/IS-Book_en.pdf (5 November 2018).

Chulov 2013
M. Chulov: Syria: the story behind one of the most shocking images of the war. The Guardian, 3 April 2013, https://www.theguardian.com/world/interactive/2013/mar/11/syria-bodies-river-aleppo-massacre (9 April 2013).

Connolly/Bloch 2015
K. Connolly / W. Bloch: The war is still raging, but the race to rebuild Aleppo has already begun. The Guardian, 12 March 2015, https://www.theguardian.com/world/2015/mar/12/war-rebuild-aleppo-syria-architects-reconstruction (10 October 2018).

Council of Aleppo City 2018
مجلس مدينة حلب: إقرار وتصديق المخطط التنظيمي العام لمدينة حلب. صفحة «مجلس مدينة حلب» على فيس بوك.
Council of Aleppo City: Approval and ratification of the development plan of the city of Aleppo. Council of Aleppo City Facebook Page. [Online 8 March 2018], https://www.facebook.com/Alpcity1/posts/2048578202045776 (10 December 2018).

DAI n.d.
iDAI.gazetteer: Turbat Bani al-Shihna. [Online n.d.] https://gazetteer.dainst.org/gazetteer-test/app/#!/show/2765788 (3 September 2024).

David 1975
J.C. David: Alep, dégradation et tentatives actuelles de réadaptation des structures urbaines traditionnelles. Bulletin d'études orientales 28, 1975, 19–50, http://www.jstor.org/stable/41604589.

DGAM 2000
DGAM: Antiquities Law – Passed in Legislative Decree #222 of October 26, 1963 with all its amendments. Syrian Arab Republic, Ministry of Culture, General Directorate of Antiquities and Museums, http://www.unesco.org/culture/natlaws/media/pdf/syrianarabrepublic/sy_antiquitieslaw1963_engtof.pdf (6 February 2018).

Eder 2006
W. Eder: Hellenistic states, in: Brill's New Pauly Online. Brill. [Online, 2006] https://doi.org/10.1163/1574-9347_bnp_e507080.

Eddé 2013
A.-M. Eddé: Aleppo (pre-Ottoman), in: K. Fleet / G. Krämer / D. Matringe / J. Nawas / D.J. Stewart (eds.): Encyclopaedia of Islam Three Online. Brill. [Online 2013], https://doi.org/10.1163/1573-3912_ei3_COM_24837.

El-Acima 1930
النشرة الرسمية للأعمال الإدارية – نظام العناية بطرق المدينة – القسم الأول – اجازات طرق وشواع المدينة – طلبات التخطيط. العاصمة.
Bulletin Officiel Bimensuel – Des Actes Administratifs. Official Gazette of Administrative Works – City Roads Care System – Part One – City Roads and Streets Permits – Planning Requests. El-Acima, issue 20, Damascus 1930, https://www.dig-doc.org/index.php?page=Ym9vaw==&op=ZGlzcGxheV9ib29rX2RldGFpbHNfdQ==&book_id=MTAzNA==&lan=YXI= (28 April 2025).

Gallica [1899/1900]
Gallica: Plan général de la ville d'Halep dressé par les ingénieurs des ponts et chaussées du vilayet Chartier, Raghid, Bekir. [1899/1900] https://gallica.bnf.fr/ark:/12148/btv1b52507324h (10 September 2024).

Gaube/Wirth 2007
هاينتز غاوبه / أويغن فيرت: دراسات تاريخية وجغرافية حول البنية العمرانية والتركيبة الاجتماعية والحركة. الاقتصادية لاحد مراكز التجارة الدولية في الشرق الأدنى. ج١.
ترجمة وتدقيق صخر علبي. وزارة الثقافة، الهيئة العامة السورية للكتاب.
H. Gaube / E. Wirth: Aleppo: Historische und geographische Beiträge zur baulichen Gestaltung, zur sozialen Organisation und zur wirtschaftlichen Dynamik einer vorderasiatischen Fernhandelsmetropole, vol. 1, edited and translated to Arabic by S. Olabi (Aleppo 2007).

Gebeily/Azhari 2024
M. Gebeily / T. Azhari: Syrian rebels topple Assad who flees to Russia in Mideast shakeup. Reuters, 9 December 2024, https://www.reuters.com/world/middle-east/syria-rebels-celebrate-captured-homs-set-sights-damascus-2024-12-07/ (19 December 2024).

General Assembly of Labor Unions 2011
القانون ١٣ لعام ١٩٨١ قانون الجمعيات التعاونية السكنية. الجمهورية العربية السورية، قانون الجمعيات السكنية.
General Assembly of Labor Unions: Housing Associations Law Legislative Decree No. 99 of 3/8/2011. [Online 2011], http://www.parliament.gov.sy/arabic/index.php?node=201&nid=6611&ref=tree& (24 June 2023).

Gordon 2012
M.S. Gordon: Ṭūlūnids, in: P. Bearman (ed.): Encyclopaedia of Islam New Edition Online (EI-2 English). [Online 2012], https://doi.org/10.1163/1573-3912_islam_COM_1250.

Hreitani 2008
محمود حريتاني: تاريخ اليهود في حلب. شعاع للنشر والعلوم.
M. Hreitani: History of the Jews in Aleppo (Aleppo 2008).

Hourani 1946
A. Hourani: Syria and Lebanon: Political Essay (New York 1946).

Ibold 2019
N. Ibold: Post-Conflict Syria: From Destruction to Reconstruction. Who's Involved and to Which Extent. Open House International 44, no. 2, 2019, 8–19, https://doi.org/10.1108/OHI-02-2019-B0002

Ibold 2020
N. Ibold: Perspectives for Aleppo: Towards an Integrated Approach for ‹Post-Conflict› Reconstruction of Cultural Heritage. Doctoral Thesis, Brandenburg University of Technology (Cottbus 2020), https://doi.org/10.26127/BTUOpen-5175.

Ibold 2022
N. Ibold: Infiltrators among Us: The Mundasīn in the Syrian Revolution. Middle East Journal of Culture and Communication 15, no. 4, 2022, 414–426, https://doi.org/10.1163/18739865-01504014.

Karklis 2016
L. Karklis: The destruction of Aleppo after five years of fighting. The Washington Post, 22 December 2016, https://www.washingtonpost.com/graphics/world/destruction-of-aleppo/ (4 February 2018).

Khoury 1983
P.S. Khoury: Urban Notables and Arab Nationalism: The Politics of Damascus 1860–1920 (Cambridge 1983).

Khoury 1987
P.S. Khoury: Syria and the French Mandate: The Politics of Arab Nationalism, 1920–1945 (London 1987).

Krever 2024
M. Krever: Israel strikes Syria 480 times and seizes territory as Netanyahu pledges to change face of the Middle East. CNN, 11 December 2024, https://www.cnn.com/2024/12/10/middleeast/israel-syria-assad-strikes-intl (28 December 2024).

Lafi 2017
N. Lafi: Building and Destroying Authenticity in Aleppo: Heritage between Conservation, Transformation, Destruction, and Re-Invention, in: C. Bernhardt / M. Sabrow / A. Saupe (eds.): Gebaute Geschichte: Historische Authentizität im Stadtraum (Göttingen 2017) 206–228.

Lafi 2022
N. Lafi: Urban infrastructure between local networks and the wider world: The tramway in Late-Ottoman Aleppo, in: Y. Ben Bassat / J. Büssow (eds.): From the Household to the Wider World: Local Perspectives on Urban Institutions in Late Ottoman Bilad al-Sham (Tübingen 2022) 207–221, http://dx.doi.org/10.15496/publikation-72248.

Leppin 2006
H. Leppin / K. Johne: Honorius, in: Brill's New Pauly Online. [Online, 2006], https://doi.org/10.1163/1574-9347_bnp_e517120.

Longrigg 1958
S. H. Longrigg: Syria and Lebanon under French Mandate (London 1958).

Lynch 1960
K. Lynch: The Image of the City (Cambridge MA 1960).

Masters 1990
B. Masters: The 1850 Events in Aleppo: An Aftershock of Syria's Incorporation into the Capitalist World System. International Journal of Middle East Studies 22, no. 1, 1990, 3–20, https://doi.org/10.1017/S0020743800033158.

Masters 1999
B. Masters: Aleppo: The Ottoman Empire's caravan city, in: E. Eldem / D. Goffman / B. Masters: The Ottoman City between East and West: Aleppo, Izmir, and Istanbul (Cambridge 1999) 17–79.

Masters 2010
B. Masters: The Political Economy of Aleppo in an Age of Ottoman Reform. Journal of the Economic and Social History of the Orient 53, no. 1–2, 2010, 290–316, https://doi.org/10.1163/002249910X12573963244520.

Maziak 1958
نديم مزيّك: تخطيط وعمران مدينة حلب. مجلة العمران. وزارة الشؤون البلدية والقروية، سوريا.
N. Maziak: Planning and Urbanization of Aleppo. Al-Omran Journal, vols. 20-21-22, Second Year, Aleppo 1958, 187–196.

Middle East Watch 1991
Middle East Watch: Syria Unmasked: The Suppression of Human Rights by the Asad Regime (New Haven 1991).

Podeh 1999
E. Podeh: The Decline of Arab Unity: The Rise and Fall of the United Arab Republic (Brighton, Portland 1999).

Raymond 2010
A. Raymond: Europeans in Bilad al-ShamAux origines du plan d'Alep par Rousseau: le plan de Vincent Germain de 1811, in: P. Sluglett / S. Weber (eds.): Syria and Bilad al-Sham under Ottoman Rule: Essays in Honour of Abdul Karim Rafeq (Leiden 2010) 497–512, https://doi.org/10.1163/9789004191044_027.

Russian Military 1985
Russian Military: Soviet City Plan of Haleb (Aleppo), Syria [electronic resource]: Digital Raster Graphics (DRGs) of Russian Military Topographic City Plan. [Online 1985], https://sierra.ceu.edu/record=b1186402 (6 February 2021).

Salname-yi Vilâyet-i Halep [1882/1883]
سالنامه ولايت حلب. دفعة ١٣.
Salname-yi Vilâyet-i Halep, no 13 (1300 Hijri [1882/1883]). Salname [Ottoman yearly book] of Aleppo, no 13. Halep [Syria]: Vilâyet matbaasında tab' olunmuştur, https://hdl.handle.net/2027/mdp.39015049569190 (10 September 2024).

Salname-yi Vilâyet-i Halep [1884/1885]
سالنامه ولايت حلب. دفعة ١٤.
Salname-yi Vilâyet-i Halep, no 14 (1302 Hijri [1884/1885]). Salname [Ottoman yearly book] of Aleppo, no 14. Halep [Syria]: Vilâyet matbaasında tab' olunmuştur, https://hdl.handle.net/2027/mdp.39015049569182 (10 September 2024).

Salname-yi Vilâyet-i Halep [1895/1896]
سالنامه ولايت حلب. دفعة ٢٣.
Salname-yi Vilâyet-i Halep, no 23 (1313 Hijri [1895/1896]). Salname [Ottoman yearly book] of Aleppo, no 23. Halep [Syria]: Vilâyet [Online], matbaasında tab' olunmuştur. https://hdl.handle.net/2027/mdp.39015049569133 (10 September 2024).

SANA 2019
مجلس الشعب يقر مشروعي قانوني إلغاء اتحاد التعاون السكني وتعيين المعيدين بالمؤسسات التعليمية الخاصة. سانا.
The Parliament Approves Two Legal Bills Abolishing the Housing Cooperation Union and Appointing Teaching Assistants to Private Educational Institutions. SANA, 18 December 2019, https://sana.sy/?p=1074364 (1 March 2021).

Sauvaget 1941
J. Sauvaget: Alep: Essai sur le développement d'une grande ville Syrienne des origines au milieu du XIXe siècle (Paris 1941).

Schmidt 2017
L. Schmidt: The Cottbus Document: Guidelines on Safeguarding Cultural Significance of Urban Structures Damaged by War and Aggression, in: P. Schneider (ed.): Proceedings: Fourth International Conference on Heritage Conservation and Site Management – Catastrophe and Challenge: Cultural Heritage in Post-Conflict Recovery (Cottbus 2017) 193–197, https://nbn resolving.org/urn:nbn:de:kobv:co1-opus4-43734.

Seale 2000
P. Seale: P. Hafez al-Assad – Obituary. The Guardian, 15 June 2000, https://www.theguardian.com/theguardian/2000/jun/15/guardianweekly.guardianweekly1 (24 October 2018).

Seif 2022
A. Seif: Beirut as a palimpsest: Conflicting present pasts, materiality and interpretation, in: E.K. Fowden / S. Çağaptay / E. Zychowicz-Coghill / L. Blanke (eds.): Cities as Palimpsests? Responses to Antiquity in Eastern Mediterranean Urbanism, vol. 1 (Oxford and Philadelphia 2022) 387–410, https://doi.org/10.2307/j.ctv25wxc84.25.

Shaam Times 2020
دمشق تصادق على مذكرة تفاهم سورية روسية في مجال الإسكان. وكالة أوقات الشام الإخبارية. وكالة أوقات الشام الإخبارية.
Damascus Ratifies a Syrian-Russian Memorandum of Understanding in the Field of Housing. Shaam Times News Agency. [Online 2020], https://shaamtimes.net/287447/ (19 February 2021).

Shaar 2019
A. Shaar: Reconstruction, but for whom? Embracing the role of Aleppo's displaced, in: Adopt a Revolution (ed.): Reconstructing Syria: Risks and Side Effects (Leipzig 2018) 29–32, [Online 2019], https://adoptrevolution.org/en/reconstructing-syria-risks-and-side-effects/ (26 August 2023).

Sinico 2024
S.M. Sinico: Fighting in Syrian Kurdish-held areas: What you need to know. Deutsche Welle, 13 December 2024, https://www.dw.com/en/fighting-in-syrias-kurdish-held-areas-what-you-need-to-know/a-71051390 (28 December 2024).

Smail 1995
R.C. Smail: Crusading Warfare 1097–1193 (Cambridge 1995).

Stiebing / Helft 2023
W.H. Stiebing / S.N. Helft: Ancient Near Eastern History and Culture (New York 2023), https://doi.org/10.4324/9781003163350.

Syndicate of Engineers in Aleppo 1996
نقابة المهندسين في حلب: أعمال الدكتور المهندس المعمار عبدالمنعم حربلي.
Syndicate of Engineers in Aleppo: The work of the Architect Doctor Abd Al-Moneim Hurbli (Aleppo 1996).

Syndicate of Engineers in Aleppo [1997]
نقابة المهندسين في حلب: أعمال المهندس المعمار مصطفى حكمت اليازجي. سلسلة أعمال المعماريين بحلب ٣. لجنة قسم الهندسة المعمارية.
Syndicate of Engineers in Aleppo: The works of the architect Mustafa Hikmat Al-Yaziji. The series of architects works in Aleppo 3 (Aleppo [1997]).

Syndicate of Engineers in Aleppo 1998
نقابة المهندسين في حلب: أعمال المهندس المعمار بشير المهندس.
Syndicate of Engineers in Aleppo: The work of the Architect Bashir Al-Mohandes, vol. 2. (Aleppo 1998).

Syndicate of Engineers in Aleppo n.d.
نقابة المهندسين في حلب: أعمال المهندس المعمار أحمد عدنان اخلاصي.
Syndicate of Engineers in Aleppo: The Work of the Architect Ahmed Adnan Al-Ekhlasi (Aleppo n.d.).

Taoutel 1964
فردينان توتل اليسوعي: وثائق تاريخية عن حلب أخبار اللاتين والروم وما إليهم ١٨٥٥-١٩٦٣. ج٤. المطبعة الكاثوليكية، بيروت.
F. Taoutel: Contribution à l'histoire d'Alep, Les documents Grecs Melkites et latins et leurs annexes 1855–1963, vol. 4 (Beirut 1964).

The Establishment of Military Housing n.d.
مؤسسة الإسكان العسكرية.
The Establishment of Military Housing, https://www.mod.gov.sy/index.php?node=554&cat=4016 (13 February 2021).

The IUSD Lab 2016
The IUSD Lab: «Scenarios for Post-War Reconstruction in Aleppo» Documentation. University of Stuttgart. [Online 2016], https://issuu.com/iusd.cairo/docs/02_doku_-_alp_06feb_mediumres_a (17 February 2021).

Tokmajyan 2017
A. Tokmajyan: Aleppo Conflict Timeline. [Online 2017], http://www.thealeppoproject.com/conflict-timeline/ (4 February 2018).

Tuma 2024
شكري توما: من هجرة الى هجرة.
S. Tuma: From migration to migration. 1924 - Urhoy - 2024, 27 August 2024, https://www.urhoy1924.com/fr_choukri_touma/.

UNESCO 2012
UNESCO: Ancient City of Aleppo. UNESCO World Heritage List, 2012, http://whc.unesco.org/en/list/21/multiple=1&unique_number=24 (5 February 2018).

UNESCO n.d.
UNESCO: Ancient City of Aleppo: Description. UNESCO. [Online n.d.], https://whc.unesco.org/en/list/21/ (2 August 2018).

UNRWA n.d. a
United Nations Relief and Works Agency for Palestine Refugees in the Near East: Neirab Camp. [Online n.d.], https://www.unrwa.org/where-we-work/syria/neirab-camp (27 August 2024).

UNRWA n.d. b
United Nations Relief and Works Agency for Palestine Refugees in the Near East: Ein el Tal (unofficial camp*). [Online n.d.], https://www.unrwa.org/where-we-work/syria/ein-el-tal-unofficial-camp (27 August 2024).

U.S. Army [1941] 1958
U.S. Army: [Aleppo] Alep 1958, 1:10,000, Edition 2-AMS, Series K922. U.S. Army Map Service, 1958, http://legacy.lib.utexas.edu/maps/world_cities/txu-oclc-13214823-alep-1958.jpg (6 February 2021).

Yusuf 2013
نضال يوسف: «جامع الرحمن».. متحف الفنون الحلبية.
N. Yusuf: «Al Rahman mosque»: Museum of the Aleppine Arts, 24 August 2013, http://esyria.sy/sites/code/index.php?site=aleppo&p=stories&category=places&filename=201308240035041 (29 October 2014).

Zeido 2020
Z. Zeido: Reclaiming the Architectural Heritage of Aleppo after the Syrian War (Doctoral Thesis). Brandenburg University of Technology (Cottbus 2020).

Zeido 2023
Z. Zeido: Attempting to document and rehabilitate Aleppo between 1994 and 2011: the ramifications of pre-conflict built

heritage mismanagement and the effects of the scarcity of documentation on options available for post-conflict conservation. Built Heritage 7, no. 3, 2023, https://doi.org/10.1186/s43238-023-00084-2.

Zeido / Ibold 2019
Z. Zeido / N. Ibold: The Division of Aleppo City: Heritage and Urban Space, in: S. Frank / M. Ristic (eds.): Urban Heritage in Divided Cities (London 2019) 87–104, https://doi.org/10.4324/9780429460388-7.

Image Sources

1 UNESCO 2012.

2 The author. A satellite image from http://www.aleppo-maps.ceu.edu was used as a blank canvas.

3 Photos by Mouhanad Aboudan, 2009.

4 left Journees.alepines (Social Media), https://www.facebook.com/journees.alepines/photos/a.421569481270982/421580274603236/?type=3&theater (3 November 2020).

4 right Journees.alepines (Social Media), https://www.facebook.com/journees.alepines/photos/a.419116214849642/419118581516072/?type=3&theater (3 November 2020).

5 Journees.alepines (Social Media), https://www.facebook.com/journees.alepines/photos/421229521304978 (16 March 2021).

6 Google Earth.

7 Journées.alepines (Social Media), https://www.facebook.com/journees.alepines/photos/a.452105341550729/452107558217174/?type=3&theater and https://www.facebook.com/journees.alepines/photos/a.452105341550729/452107481550515/?type=3&theater (3 November 2020).

8 Unknown Photographer, https://flickr.com/photos/samersawwas/3313911983 (3 March 2021).

9 Unknown, http://sy.worldmapz.com/photo/1858_fr.htm (3 June 2014).

10 Journées.alepines (Social Media). https://scontent-fra5-2.xx.fbcdn.net/v/t39.30808-6/462740796_8608057762622072_6624825584575554873_n.jpg?_nc_cat=109&ccb=1-7&_nc_sid=cf85f3&_nc_ohc=EzGc49DdFsMQ7kNvgEsBRjx&_nc_zt=23&_nc_ht=scontent-fra5-2.xx&_nc_gid=AelgY6MwQ6sjy69z4vo_bOa&oh=00_AYBcSKhFIh5iNw-FAPqY_KSVr_d-icjRA2a2yzEDnohIFw&oe=67B02F42 (3 November 2020).

11 Faculty of Medicine, University of Aleppo – Class 46 [Originally in Arabic: كلية الطب البشري جامعة حلب - الدفعة ٤٦]. (Social Media), https://www.facebook.com/photo/?fbid=449195847235952&set=a.449195797235957 (26 August 2023).

12, 16 Digital Globe.

13 left Photo by Majed Talustan, February 2020.

13 right Journeées.alepines (Social Media), https://www.facebook.com/journees.alepines/photos/a.426442874116976/426451897449407/?type=3&theater (3 November 2020).

14 Syndicate of Engineers in Aleppo 1998, 66.

15 Chibli et al. 2009.

17 The author, background from Google maps.

18 The author, based on the report and map from Chulov 2013.

Cairo
A Mosaic of New Capitals

Omar Abolnaga

In March 2015, only a year into the presidential mandate of Egyptian President Abdel Fatah al-Sisi, a unique international conference for economic development was organised in Egypt's resort city of Sharm El Sheikh. Despite being relatively forgotten today, that conference witnessed the launch of the highly promoted and anticipated New Administrative Capital (NAC) to take over Egypt's central bureaucratic and administrative role from Cairo. NAC is located just outside the eastern periphery of Greater Cairo, with the promise of being free from Cairo's infamous problems of traffic congestion, housing shortage, chaos, high energy consumption, and population influx. The government has assured the public that the new capital will be vaccinated for «all the diseases of Cairo».[1] Ever since its launch, the new capital has been advertised not only as a golden ticket towards strengthening the economy and upgrading the quality of Egypt's urban life but also as a solid nationalist foundation to establish a new modern state, or as President al-Sisi prefers to call it «the new republic».[2]

Today Egyptians and Cairenes eagerly await the opening of the first phase of the new capital. Hundreds of thousands of internet users meticulously watch the weekly video updates by bloggers and official channels on social media, checking on the construction of NAC.[3] People's scepticism about the state's ability to realise the promised city is shrinking, but the future of the project is still up in the air. Most doubts come from the project's massive scale and intent, and particularly from the unsuccessful history of similar state projects. Urban specialists and historians such as David Sims and Khaled Fahmy argue that the idea of a new capital has never been foreign to Egyptians.[4] Sims affirms that plans to relocate state buildings were announced under Sadat's regime in the 1970s and again under Mubarak in the early 2000s.[5] However, many commentators seem to forget a phenomenon described by Janet Abu-Lughod, a sociologist who was a keen observer of Cairo in the 1960s, where «every previous ruler of Cairo had his favourite section which therefore tended to absorb a disproportionate share of urban growth».[6] In fact, by carefully looking at the map of Cairo, one finds that most of the «formal»[7] parts of the city originate from the bits and pieces of land that were once intended by Egypt's rulers to become new administrative cores. However, those cities were annexed to Cairo over time.

Accordingly, this chapter explores and maps the cities now part of Cairo that were once intended to become strategic and administrative centres of wealth and power in Egypt. The chapter only focuses on Cairene cities built between the first half of the 19th century and the present day. This specific period has contributed most towards shaping the contemporary city of Cairo as we see it today. This chapter will discuss in turn the urban contributions of Mehmed Ali, Abbas I, Ismail, Tewfiq, Nasser, Mubarak, and al-Sisi, who all share similar but unequal ambitions to solidify their names in history by building new cities.

As we will see in this chapter, despite being built across three different centuries, those cities still share common cultural, urban, and political

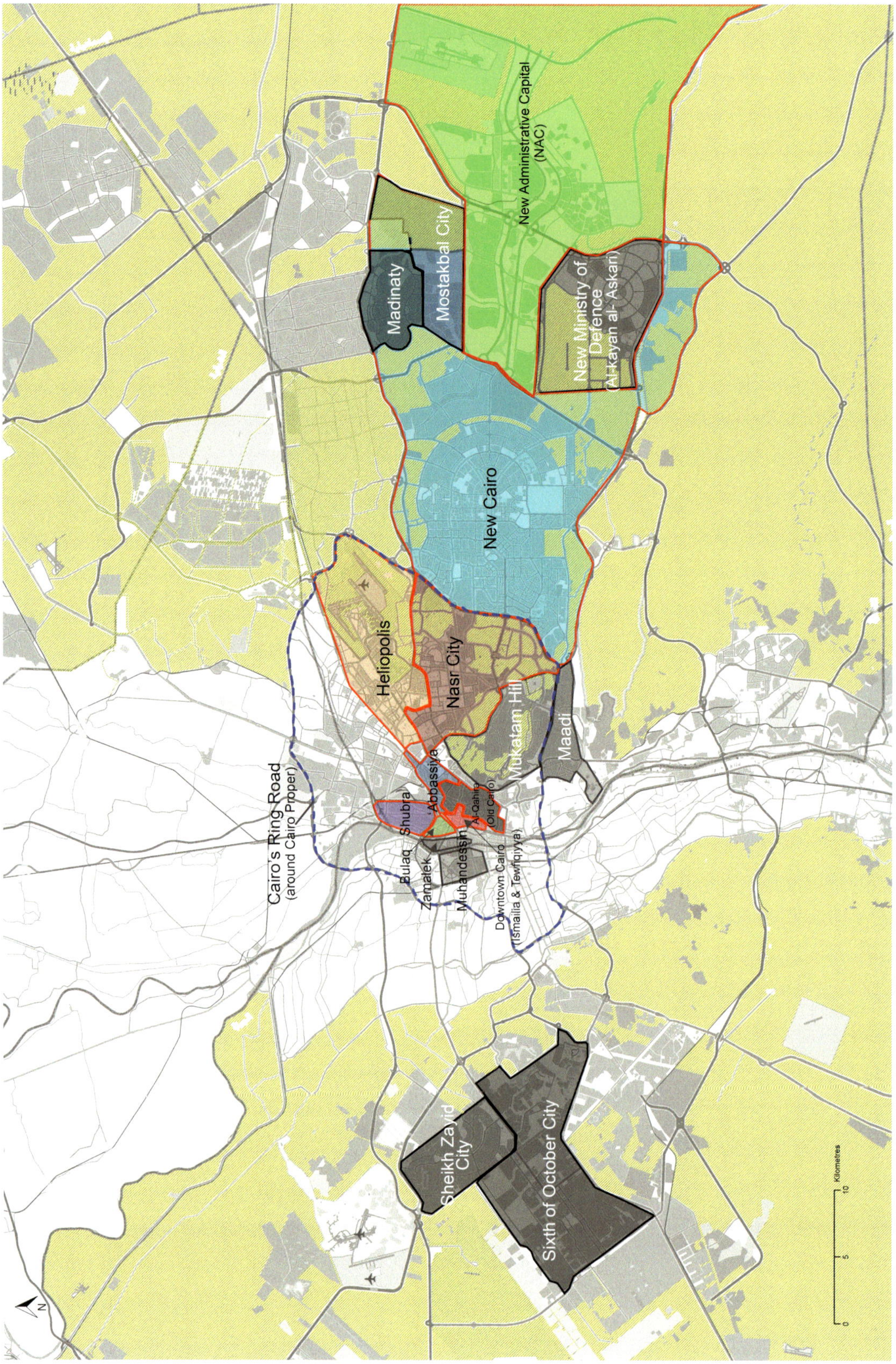

1 Overall map of Cairo at the present day, showing expansive desert land surrounding it (in yellow hatch).

attributes. This chapter explores those attributes by tackling the history behind the creation of each of the new cities, their political and historical influence, their relation to local Egyptian identity, and their interaction and engagement with their neighbouring areas today. In all cases, the chapter collects and uncovers scattered historical data of archived maps, memoirs, notes, and manuscripts to narrate the forgotten stories of the once-upon-a-time new capital cities, which, when viewed from above, make the formal city of Cairo resemble an incomplete mosaic (fig. 1).

This chapter does not attempt to create an architectural or urban guide to Cairo and its districts. Hence, areas known by observers and visitors of Cairo, such as Zamalek, Maadi, and Mohandessin, will not be discussed as they were never intended to be new capitals. Heliopolis and New Cairo, however, will be discussed even though they were not built as new capital cities. Heliopolis is crucial to this chapter as it was the first successful attempt to crash through the desert barrier away from the Nile valley. Several desert cities around Cairo have been arguably trying to replicate the success story of Heliopolis, including President al-Sisi's New Administrative Capital. Meanwhile, despite never being called a new capital officially, New Cairo was President Mubarak's personal project and received huge attention under his leadership.

Mehmed Ali's Three Nuclei

If it was the French who paved the road to modernising Egypt, it was without a shadow of a doubt Mehmed Ali (r. 1805–1848) and his dynasty who implemented modernity on the ground. When the Albanian Mehmed Ali was sent in 1801 by the Ottoman Sultan under the recommendation of Kavala's governor to repel *l'Armée d'Orient*, the French army in Egypt, little did he know that he was about to govern the whole country from a city distant from, if not the opposite of, its Islamic heyday. In fact, travellers to Egypt described Cairo at the beginning of the 19th century as «disgustingly filthy»,[8] something that was drastically altered under the rule of the Albanian governor. While Mehmed Ali had little impact on the physical borders of Cairo, he re-established the old habit of giving disproportionate emphasis to the urbanisation of particular areas of the city over others. This habit later became a recurrent driving force of the city's formal growth.

By the time Mehmed Ali was sent to Cairo, the city was unstable on both political and urban levels. Napoleon Bonaparte's army faced extreme opposition by Cairenes, with Cairo revolting against French rule not once but twice, and the French suppressing both uprisings with severe brutality. Abd al-Rahman al-Jabarti, an Egyptian Muslim thinker of the time, described the year 1798, when the French set foot in Cairo, to be «of successive suffering and turning times (...) of horrors upon horrors and contradicting conditions (...) of the dominance of destruction».[9] In an attempt to control Cairo, the French severely damaged large parts of the city, dismantled its gates, re-organised its administrative districts, and changed some of its «zig-zag» street patterns for military reasons.[10] As a result, Mehmed Ali's priorities for his first few years in Egypt were to consolidate his power, restore peace and order to Cairo, re-organise the governmental administration, and foster robust industrial and military development.

Before discussing Mehmed Ali's impact on Cairo, it is crucial to know the dynamics that influenced Mehmed Ali as a governor of Egypt. Such dynamics were influenced by his perspective towards Egypt and Egyptians on one side and the Sultan and the Ottoman Empire on the other. Mehmed Ali was a product of the Ottoman Empire: he was familiar with the Ottoman world; his language, culture, and manners were Ottoman; and he was well-informed about the power of the Sultan in Istanbul. At the same time, to Mehmed Ali, Egypt was not just a wealthy province of the

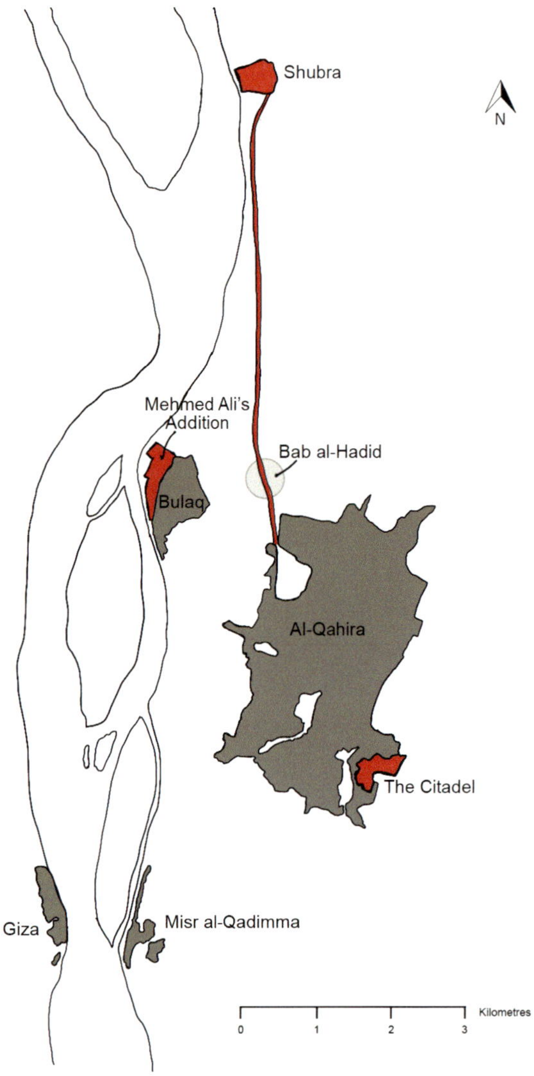

2 Three cores of Cairo and Mehmed Ali's additions.

Ottoman Empire. He believed that his fame and power would only be realised if he unleashed the potential of one of the most important provinces of the Ottoman world. He despised the Egyptian masses, calling them «wild beasts» and «animals», but he knew he would be powerless without Egyptians forming his army.[11] He believed that his organised management of Egypt would be translated into his gaining enormous wealth and power.[12] Overall, he cared about political and military power and wealth more than anything, not for their own sake but to immortalise his name and dynasty in history books. Hence, when he sought the national independence of Egypt from the Ottoman Sultan, he argued that «[this would] carve a place for my family and my dynasty's families in history to be remembered in four or five centuries' time».[13] Ultimately, Mehmed Ali's grip on Egypt paved the way for his dynasty, the al-ʿAlawiyya family, to be the actual rulers of Egypt, keeping Ottoman rule mostly nominal.[14] The al-ʿAlawiyya dynasty continued to rule Egypt until 1952 despite the dissolution of the Ottoman empire after the First World War.

Being a military man himself, Mehmed Ali admired Bonaparte and looked up to his military power and campaigns. He proved on many occasions that he fancied himself as displaying the strength and leadership of the Frenchman. Even Ali's «parasites», as the British army officer Charles Scott described Ali's admirers, «would fain persuade him that he [Mehmed Ali] is a second Napoleon».[15] Ali even ordered the translation and publication of a biography of Napoleon by the Egyptian governmental press in Bulaq.[16] Such admiration for military power, combined with his wish to solidify his memory in history, influenced Ali's attempts to create a modern army of his own in Egypt. These ambitions meant that he had to get rid of the old guard and build his own military legacy.

Though building a modern army might seem only slightly connected with the physical aspects of a city, it was Mehmed Ali's military plans that profited Cairo most, given that his forces happened to be concentrated in the centre of the capital. Before Mehmed Ali's rule, Cairo was documented by the French as having three distant cores: al-Qahira, Misr al-Qadimma, and Bulaq (fig. 2). Mehmed Ali's plans to reorganise the government and administration to build his army led to the urban expansion and development of Bulaq, and the founding of a new suburb of Shubra. Meanwhile, his attempt to get rid of the old guard made him superimpose his legacy on Cairo's historic Citadel, from

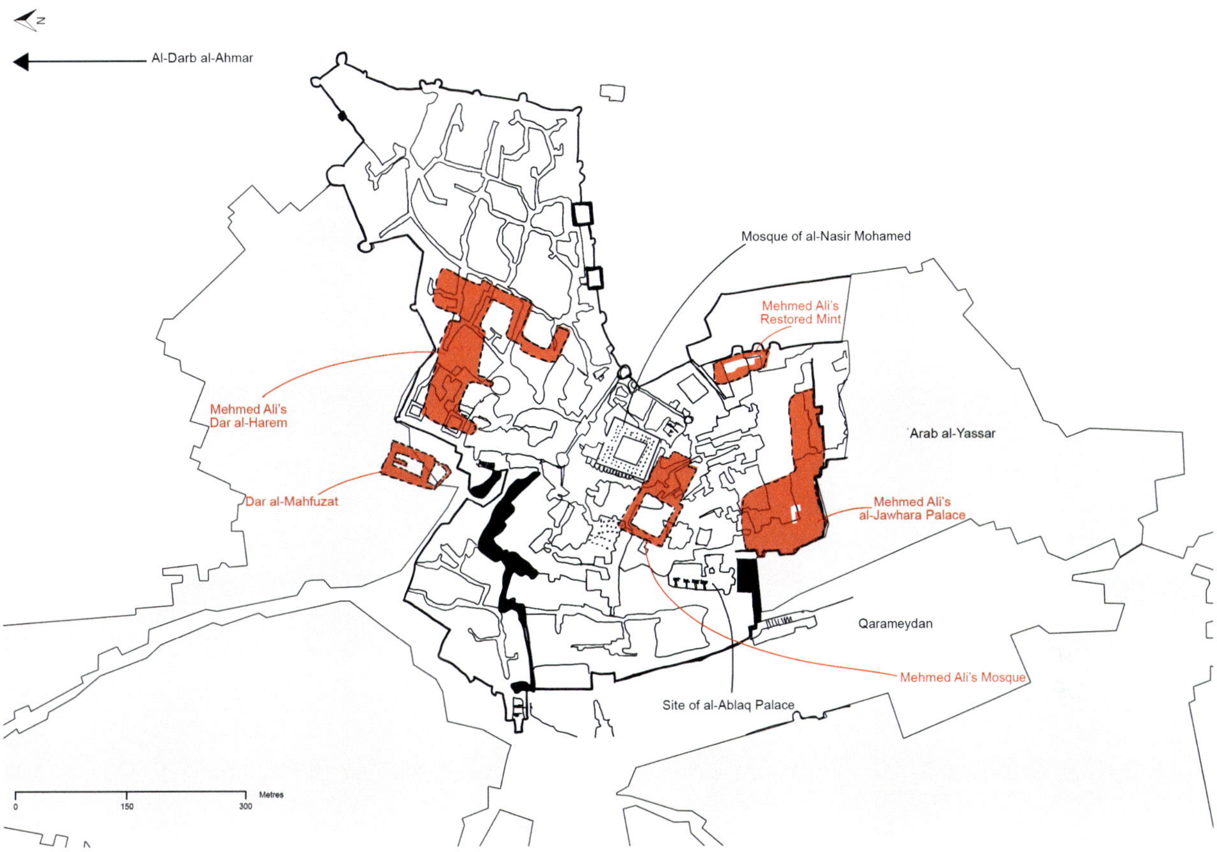

3 Mehmed Ali's modifications at the Citadel.

which Cairo had been governed since Salah al-Din. Hence, Mehmed Ali's legacy in Cairo can be tracked mostly through those three nuclei: Bulaq, Shubra, and the Citadel.

For Mehmed Ali as for earlier rulers, the Citadel had a crucial role in solidifying rule over the country. For centuries, the Citadel had been the headquarters of Egypt's rulers. Hence, the first urban impact of Mehmed Ali was inside the walls of the Citadel. To completely control his army, Mehmed Ali eliminated the Mamluk leaders who hindered his attempts to introduce new modern military tactics. Since the end of the 17th century, the Mamluks had held virtual control over the army and the government in Egypt as a result of the noticeable decline in Ottoman power. On 1 March 1811, Mehmed Ali invited the heads of all Mamluk households to attend a festive ceremony in the Citadel and ordered his Albanian troops to open fire on all his guests who were entering the Citadel through a narrow alley.[17] He tracked down and killed Mamluk leaders who managed to escape the Citadel massacre. He then cleared away all physical marks of the Mamluks, with a devastating impact on the urban and architectural Mamluk heritage of Cairo, and eventually on all of Egypt.

In the Citadel, Mehmed Ali ordered the construction and restoration of several buildings (fig. 3). In 1812, he built al-Jawhara palace on top of several small buildings that he demolished.[18] That palace was the official headquarters of governance during Mehmed Ali's reign. He also ordered the restoration of Dar al-Darb (the Mamluk mint) in the same year. In 1827 he built Dar al-Harem (the palace of the harem) to accommodate his wives and concubines. In 1828 he built Dar al-Mahfuzat (the national archives of Egypt) to store all the governmental papers and manuscripts. However, the most crucial building in Mehmed Ali's physical occupation of the Citadel was a mosque he named after himself, which was completed in 1848, almost a year before he died. How the mosque was commissioned and designed tells much about Mehmed Ali's views about the Citadel.

Mehmed Ali was clearly preoccupied with the idea of eternalising the memory of himself and his family. Physical occupation of the grounds of the Mamluk administration was his way of resisting the influence of the Mamluks and their legacy. Hence, in the 1820s, Mehmed Ali commissioned French architect Pascal Coste to design and construct a mosque in the Citadel, replacing the Hall of Justice, the Mamluks' former seat of power.[19] Coste was asked to design a massive structure that could be seen anywhere in Cairo. Mehmed Ali's robust intention of getting rid of the Mamluk influence over the city drove him to reject Pascal Coste's initial drawings as they alluded to Mamluk mosques. The final design for the constructed mosque avoided referencing any Mamluk visual characters even though they had been widespread in earlier Cairene mosques. Instead, Coste's approved design looked to establish visual links with the great Ottoman mosques of Constantinople. The massive scale of the new mosque of Mehmed Ali intentionally dwarfed the Mamluk mosque of al-Nassir Muhammad, which had been the main centre of religious ceremonies and public services in the Mamluk times.[20] Taking things to another level, Mehmed Ali ordered the transformation of the mosque of al-Nassir Muhammad into a food storage facility.

Mehmed Ali's plan to occupy the Citadel has gone the way he intended. Today, the Citadel is primarily associated with his mosque and palaces. The mosque is one of the most prominent landmarks in the whole city of Cairo. The Citadel remained the main grounds of government until its relocation to ʿAbdin Palace by Mehmed Ali's grandson, Ismail. Meanwhile, the relationship between the Citadel and its surrounding urban context has remained unchanged for decades. The walls of the Citadel have been too high for Cairo's urban sprawl to infiltrate. The residential area of ʿArab al-Yasar surrounds the Citadel from the southern side, while from the northern side, al-Darb al-Ahmar exists along with the cemeteries of Bab al-Wazir.[21] On the western side, there is a large square known during the reign of Mehmed Ali as the Qarameydan, which used to be the place where Ali addressed his local administration and military men;[22] however, that square was renamed after Mehmed Ali in the 19th century before its final renaming after Salah al-Din.

The second nucleus that Mehmed Ali invested in was the retreat of Shubra, particularly Shubra al-Kheima, located in the northern part of the city by the Nile. Construction of Ali's main palace in Shubra began in 1808 and was completed only one year later. This palace in Shubra is considered one of the earliest European-designed structures in Egypt's modern history. Shubra was a rural retreat at the time of the construction of the palace and remained almost devoid of any proper structures apart from the palace until the beginning of the 20th century. To connect the palace to Cairo, Mehmed Ali ordered the construction of a wide avenue flanked by trees on both sides. This avenue was only used by the Pasha to access his palace from al-Qahira.[23] British journalist and traveller James Augustus St. John describes the avenue as a grand one of trees in his travel book. He writes:

> Arriving at Shoubra [sic], we passed through the grounds of the Pasha's palace, and entered that grand avenue of trees which leads from thence all the way to Cairo. The road is here at least ninety or one hundred feet in breadth, and bordered on either side by a row of noble sycamores, acacias, mimosas, and tamarisks, whose branches, meeting above in many places, form a verdant arch, at all times impervious to the rays of the sun. The views on both sides are magnificent.[24]

Janet Abu-Lughod argues that this avenue was later used as an upper-class carriage promenade from the mid-19th century.[25] However, this thoroughfare lost its exclusivity at the beginning of the 20th century when it became the main artery that urbanised the agricultural fields in Shubra with the introduction of a new tramline in 1903. This new tramline connected Bab al-Hadid, the location of Cairo's central railway station, to Shubra using the same avenue that Mehmed Ali constructed. The whole network of tramlines developed at the turn of the 20th century (fig. 4) was the leading cause of urbanising Shubra and many places around Cairo. Many foreign investors would buy farmland on both sides of the proposed tramline for resale immediately after the extension of the line for immense profits. By the middle of the 20th century, large parcels of land around the tramline had already been urbanised, and urban sprawl, fuelled by the boom in informal construction on farmland, reached the palace by the 1970s.

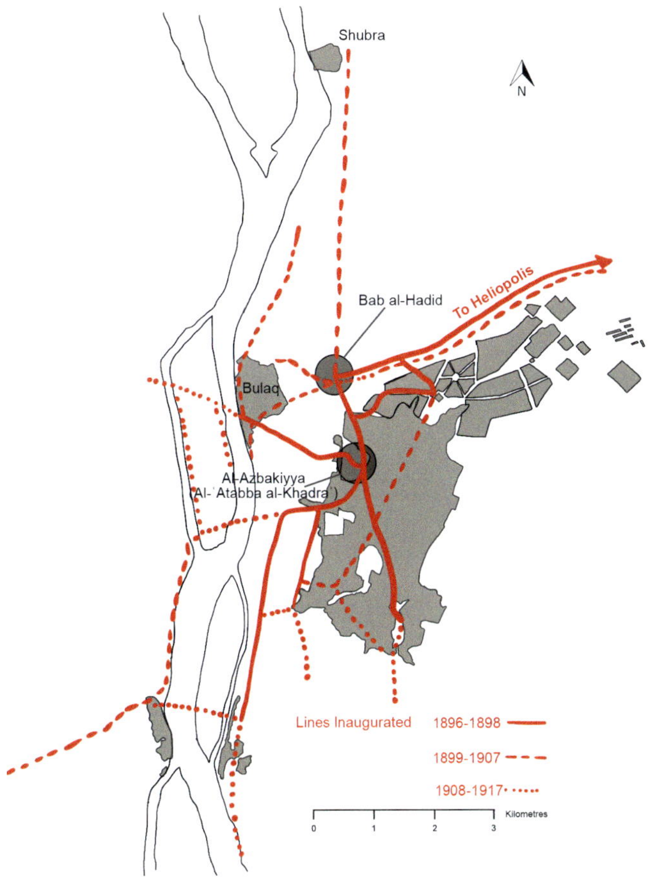

4 Cairo tramline network.

Mehmed Ali's third nucleus, Bulaq, broadly demonstrates his preference for the northwest corner of Cairo and negligence towards other parts of the city. In 1812 Bulaq «still bore marks of its destruction by the French during the siege in 1799».[26] However, only two years later it was reported by a traveller that «whilst Cairo appears neglected, Boolac [sic], its port, increases. New houses are built by merchants (...) some of them are large (...) it contains the naval arsenal and dock-yard of the Pasha.»[27] Bulaq was the site of most of Mehmed Ali's new establishments in Cairo in the following decade. There, he established textile factories for wool, linen, cotton, and a bleaching plant. In 1820 he established Egypt's first iron foundry, and only two years later, the new Bulaq press was in operation. Since Bulaq was a port, Mehmed Ali used local workshops to improve his naval installations and the performance of riverboat construction. Bulaq was also where he decided to locate his new secular schools. In 1821 a civil engineering school was opened, followed by other schools, such as the veterinary and agricultural schools, where all teachers were European.[28]

Akin to all the rulers that followed him, Mehmed Ali encouraged the wealthy elite to build their palaces between his two favourite spots, Bulaq and Shubra. The rich accepted the invitation because they did not want to disobey the Pasha and because the rest of Cairo was largely ignored and in continuous decay.[29] By the early 1840s, the trend of construction by the wealthy in the area between Bulaq and Shubra was well-advanced, as reported by travellers at the time.[30] Nevertheless, the area between Shubra and Bulaq was never fully urbanised until the 1970s.

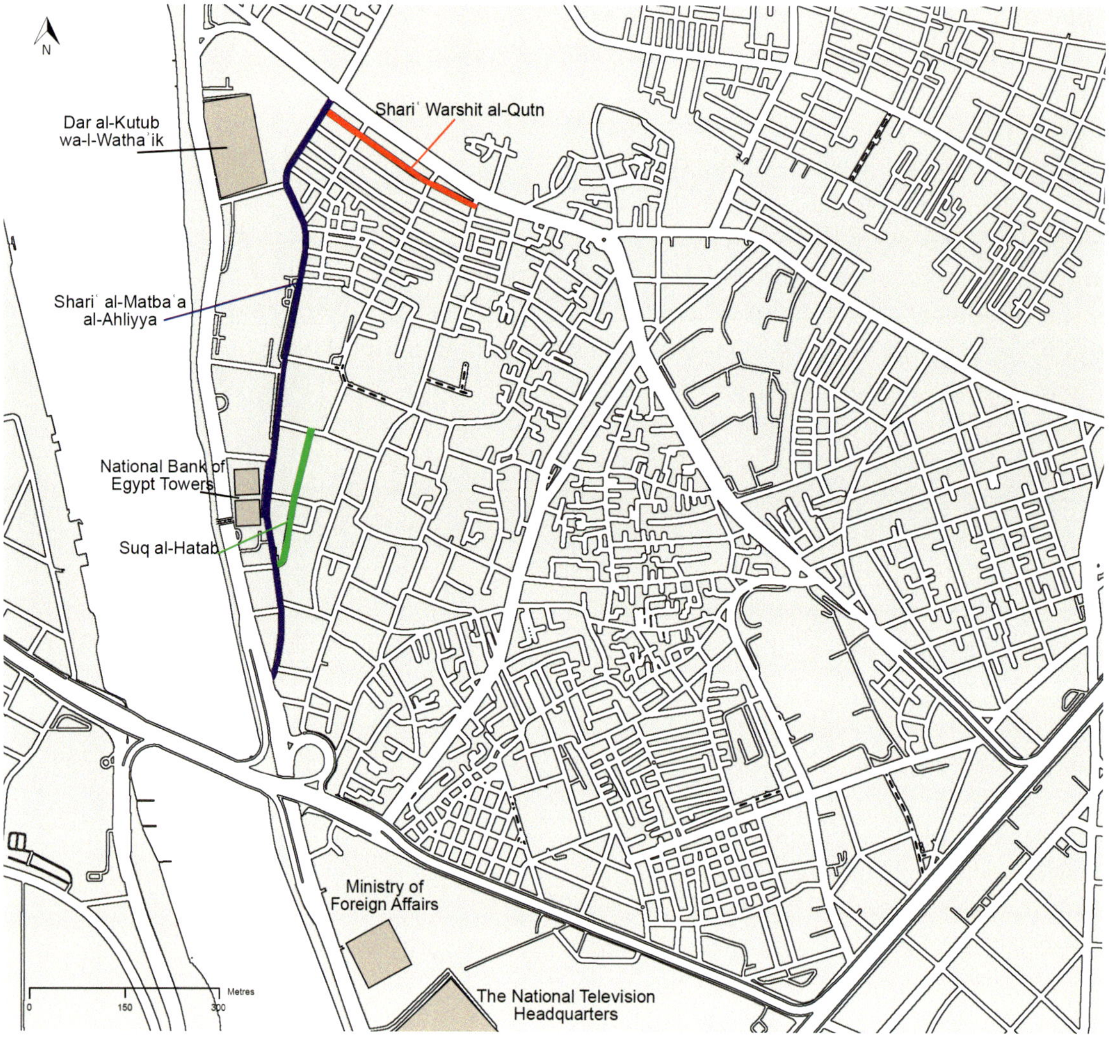

5 Map of Bulaq today.

Abu-Lughod writes:

> Būlāq [sic] had labored under a conflict between two incompatible land uses. One impulse had been to exploit the port functions fully (...) The other had been to take advantage of its riverine location and the fresh northerly breezes and keep Būlāq a pleasant, bucolic suburb.[31]

However, present-day Bulaq is different from how it used to be during the era of Mehmed Ali, when it was both a clean retreat and the centre of Cairo's commerce, manufacturing, and transport. Bulaq is now a densely packed neighbourhood with workshops and warehouses associated with light industries serving people from all over Egypt (fig. 5). Almost none of the factories built during Mehmed Ali's reign still exist. Only the names of roads associated with old plants, markets, and workshops, such as Shariʿ Warshit al-Qutn (Cotton Workshop Road), Suq al-Hatab (Firewood Market), and Shariʿ al-Matbaʿa al-Ahliyya (the National Press Road), can be found. The government workshops and the government press that used to occupy the Bulaq riverfront were demolished in the first half of the 20th century. Since then, upscale residential apartment buildings, along with hotels, commercial buildings, and some government buildings, such as the national television headquarters and the national archives (Dar al-Kutub wa-l-Watha'iq), have been constructed on Bulaq's riverfront. In the meantime, the eastern and northern parts of Bulaq were connected to other parts of the city, thanks to the urban boom that Cairo witnessed after the First World War and the completion of the tramline network.

Abbas Pasha's 'Abbassiyya

Mehmed Ali's health gave out in his final years, and he became senile. In March 1848, his son Ibrahim Pasha took over the daily affairs of the government, but this only lasted for a few months as Ibrahim died in November of the same year. Two months later, Ibrahim's nephew Abbas Hilmi I was appointed the new *vali*.[32] Abbas I (r. 1848–1854) is hardly celebrated in any literature that tackles his legacy. Louis Bréhier, a French historian who closely observed 19th-century Egypt, describes Abbas's reign as a disaster for all the progress of his grandfather's works. He sarcastically argues that «if this government [under Abbas I] had lasted longer [than the five years it did], Egypt was threatened to return to the beautiful Mamluk days».[33]

Unlike his grandfather, Abbas I preferred being protected by an army of Albanian soldiers instead of Egyptian peasants. There is no clear account of why Abbas reverted to imported troops; however, it is possible that Egyptian fellahin (peasants) saw an opportunity in the death of Mehmed Ali and his strong son to escape conscription, which Abbas's grandfather strictly enforced.[34] Only four days after becoming the *vali* of Egypt, the supreme council of the army, known as *diwān al-jihādiyya*, permitted only well-disciplined Egyptian soldiers to get married. There had been a history of incidents where «all soldiers abandon their military duties to get married».[35] Another possible reason why Abbas reverted to foreign troops was that he feared Egyptian uprisings due to his harsh policies, so he sought a foreign army to help him impose his iron fist over Egyptian villagers. According to Bréhier, Abbas used his imported army of 6,000 Albanians to «terrorise the countryside».[36]

Knowing the rebellious nature of imported Albanian troops, who once attempted to get rid of his grandfather and had a history of damaging and looting many properties in the city,[37] Abbas I stationed his army outside Cairo. He chose to locate the barracks of his troops in the desert of al-Haswa northeast of al-Qahira. At this time al-Haswa only had a palace, which Abbas bought from his grandfather in 1847. Although the official seat of government was still the Citadel, Abbas I

6 Map of 'Abassiyya by the end of the 19th century.

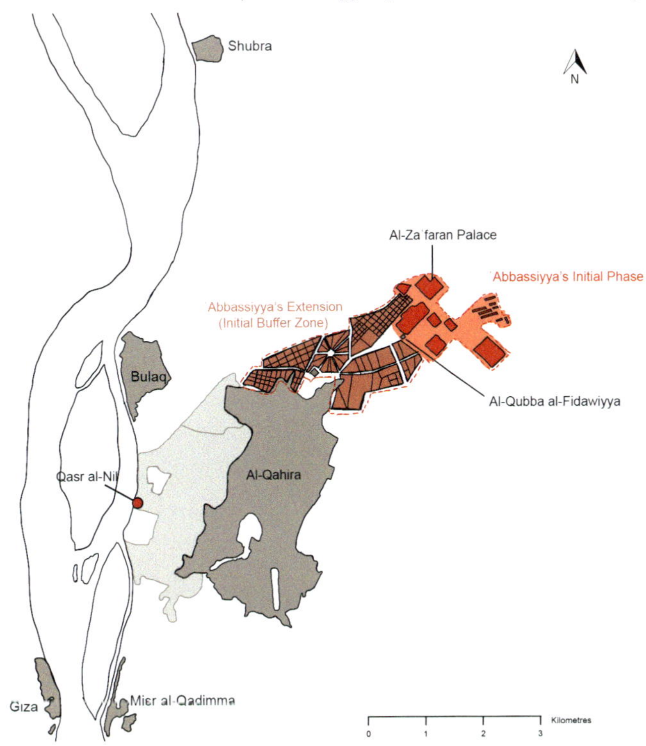

decided to build a «new capital» and name it after himself in that part of the desert.

The location of Abbas's new city in al-Haswa was mainly chosen for its strategic nature (fig. 6). Unlike the Citadel, al-Haswa was separated by a significant desert buffer from Egyptians and fellahin, whom Abbas greatly despised. Abbas knew he was not popular with either local Egyptians or his own family members; hence, living and ruling the country from the desert meant that his army could easily defy any threat coming from Cairo. Meanwhile, al-Haswa was still close enough to Cairo for his troops to repress potential uprisings. Another possible factor was the location of the new city on the pilgrimage route to Mecca. Al-Haswa was the first spot pilgrims stayed when travelling from Egypt to al-Hijaz.[38] Any other site meant that Abbas's new capital could miss *al-maḥmal*'s annual parade,[39] which was considered the most important ceremony in the city. The new city was also on the route of the railway to Suez. Besides, al-Haswa provided a clean and calm environment to its inhabitants, something that Abbas would later highlight while promoting the city to the wealthy elites of Egypt. Finally, the vast spaces of al-Haswa desert allowed Abbas to build multiple large palaces with enormous gardens. According to Ferdinand de Lesseps, the developer who had visited Abbas I in Cairo to present him with the concept of the Suez Canal, one of Abbas's palaces in the area was so massive that it had around 2,000 windows.[40]

Abbas I did not want to wait to move to his new city, so he rapidly built the barracks for the soldiers that would protect him.[41] But his troops and the desert buffer were not enough to secure his stay. Hence, he asked all the nobles and royals living in Egypt to build palaces in that area. He thought the calm environment, the healthy weather of al-Haswa, and buildings of a «modern style» would be enough to attract the wealthy nobles. However, a letter from Selim Pasha, head of the Egyptian Supreme Court, reveals that only three nobles answered the invitation and started building palaces during the first year. Under Abbas's orders, Selim Pasha threatened to penalise all the nobles and the rich who believed that «spending money to urbanise the desert is a loss».[42] Abbas wanted to introduce modern pumping and sewage systems to further attract the elite, who were considered an essential part of his personal security; nevertheless, due to high cost estimates, the sewage project was scrapped.[43]

In 1850, Abbas I renamed al-Haswa as ʿAbbassiyya to commemorate his name and legacy, yet the city remained an incomplete centre of power until his sudden death in 1854. Abbas lived in his city, attracting some of the wealthiest residents of Cairo. Elite army officers and tradespeople built a handful of residential and commercial buildings. ʿAbbassiyya at the time could be divided into two parts: one where the palaces and barracks were built, and the other for the residential and commercial units. Borders between both parts were clear and defined by a large avenue. Janet Abu-Lughod describes ʿAbbassiyya at the time of Abbas I as a «sort of royal suburb (...) [which] began to take shape».[44] However, Abbas's sudden death instantly killed his city's growth, which in any case had been limited to the area between al-Qubba al-Fidawiyya in the southwest and al-Zaʿfaran palace in the northeast (see fig. 6).[45] ʿAbbassiyya was almost forgotten for decades. During the era of Saʿid Pasha (r. 1854–1863), Abbas's uncle and successor, ʿAbbassiyya was even abandoned by military troops who were rehoused in the newly built barracks by the Nile in the Qasr al-Nil area (see fig. 6). In 1867 an English traveller to Egypt described ʿAbbassiyya as «a miserable memorial (...) of its founder (...) [which] in a few years (...) will be an unsightly mass of ruins».[46]

Things did not go the way the English traveller expected. Today, ʿAbbassiyya is neither a mass of ruins nor a miserable memorial of Abbas I. Indeed, most residents are not even aware of Abbas and the story of the city he built. There is consensus that ʿAbbassiyya has become an integral part of Cairo. ʿAbbassiyya is currently a focal point of the

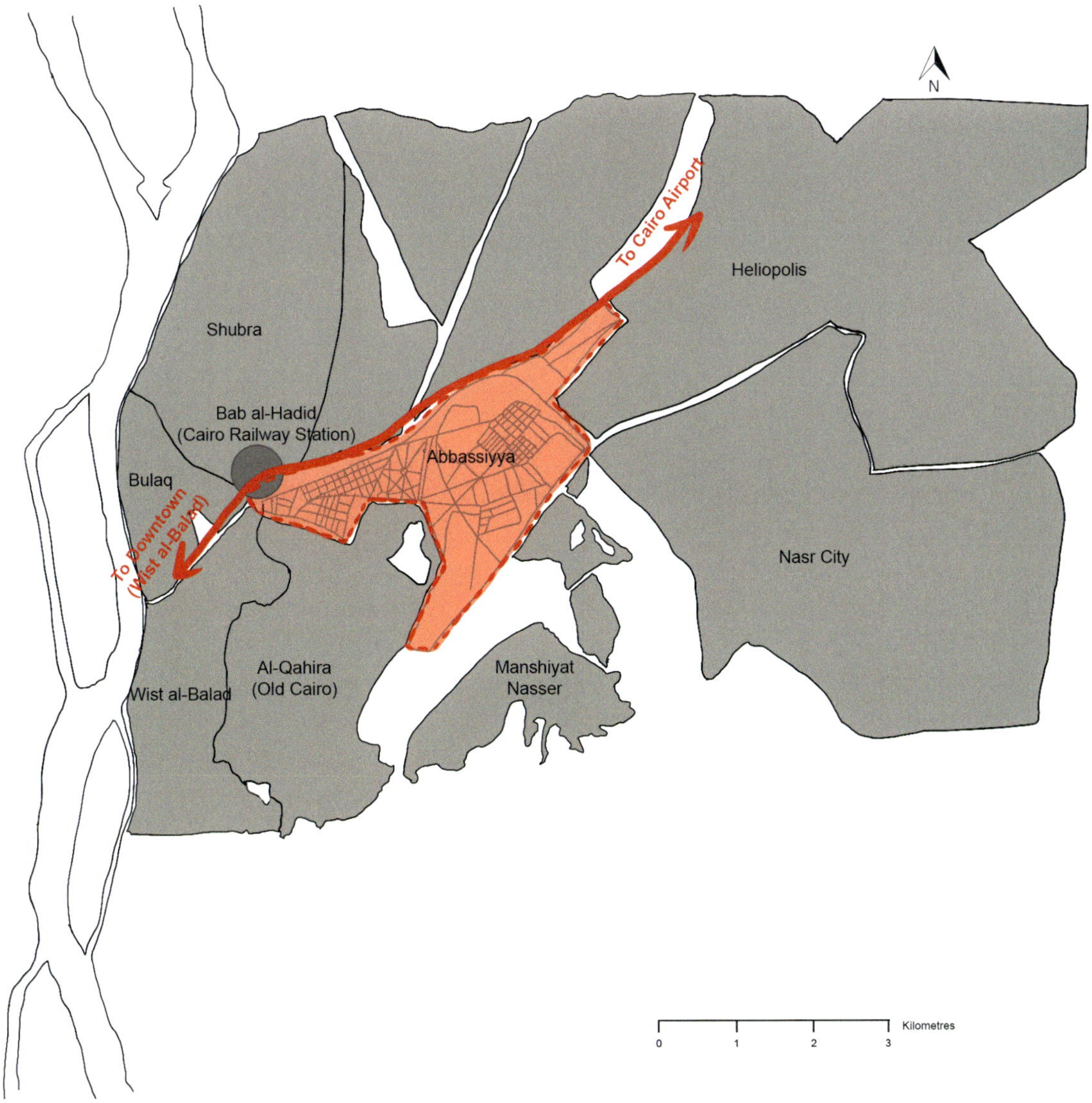

7 Map of ʿAbbassiyya today.

contemporary city of Cairo as it extends from Heliopolis in the northeast to Ramses Station (Bab al-Hadid) in the southwest (fig. 7). It has a population of about 80,000,[47] with many governmental and educational campuses.

Like Shubra and other parts of Cairo, ʿAbbassiyya's urban boom occurred immediately after the installation of the tramline from al-ʿAtabah al-Khadraʾ at al-Azbakiyya eastward towards ʿAbbassiyya in 1896, and then its extension from ʿAbbassiyya towards the Bab al-Hadid in 1898 (see fig. 4).[48] Maps drawn at the turn of the 20th century show that many palaces and villas were built during that time. One of these is the palace of al-Sakakini Pasha, who was a friend of Ismail Pasha, the developer of the downtown area of Cairo and the successor of Said Pasha. Al-Sakakini Pasha used his relationship with Ismail to urbanise the northern part of ʿAbbassiyya, commissioning the design of a master plan of a large parcel where his palace would be at the centre of a radial street system.

By the time of the Second World War, ʿAbbassiyya had become an upscale retreat for the rich, consisting mainly of luxurious villas and palaces, along with some state buildings such as the military barracks, a military school, a police school, and several hospitals. During the war, most wealthy people abandoned ʿAbbassiyya since the British used it as their main military base in Cairo. Fearing being targeted by the Axis forces, most of ʿAbbassiyya's residents moved east to the new town of Heliopolis, which had been gaining urban momentum due to the tramlines extended in its direction during its construction. On the other hand, the British used many abandoned palaces for military purposes. However, in 1955, a year before the complete withdrawal of British troops from Egypt, the Ministry of Education was given carte blanche by a presidential decree to transform the abandoned buildings into schools.[49] Accordingly, many abandoned structures were converted into schools and university buildings.

The city's dual characteristics that existed when it was founded have survived all alterations. Although ʿAbbassiyya today is considered a relatively small district of Cairo, it is still divided into two main sections: one is mixed-use, mainly residential, and the other is composed of military and educational campuses that serve all the residents of Cairo. The remaining palaces in the residential areas are either abandoned or used by the state for academic or administrative purposes. Meanwhile, large parcels of land are owned by the Egyptian military, which inherited them from Abbas Pasha and the British in the mid-20th century. Most campuses are located in the eastern and south-eastern parts of ʿAbbassiyya. Residential quarters are located in the western part of the district, joining Khedive Ismail's city, known today as Khedivial Cairo.

Since ʿAbbassiyya was developed over a long period, its urban fabric is fragmented. Each phase of development adopted a different form of urban logic. Hence, looking at today's map, one finds that each parcel has its own urban orientation. Different parcels are connected by main roads holding them together despite their fragmented fabrics. On the other hand, ʿAbbassiyya's strategic location has granted it the status of a transit city connecting the downtown area of Cairo to its eastern part. The presence of Ramses railway station, Cairo's main railway hub, just to its northwest, and Cairo's airport to its east, towards Heliopolis, has made ʿAbbassiyya a bustling transit district (see fig. 7). At the same time, the borders of ʿAbbassiyya are strongly defined by the main roads and highways which separate the district from the surrounding ones.

On the other hand, residents of the district today are no longer the wealthy or the elite, but mainly belong to the middle class. This demographic shift happened as a result of the migration of the population of low-income areas to the district, which at the time was seen as an opportunity to climb the social ladder as many of the original inhabitants had moved to Heliopolis and other places by the middle of the 20th century. Correspondingly, a shift in the uses of land as well as buildings has occurred. Many of the original bookshops, luxury shops, and workshops that used to serve the wealthy elite have been transformed into other shops with more practical uses that serve the less sophisticated residents. Hence, one finds that affordable sanitary stores have replaced old bookshops, and mechanical workshops have now taken the place of luxury department stores.

The old residential buildings still surviving in ʿAbbassiyya are in a state of decay. Several buildings are abandoned, and the remaining ones are not properly maintained. Some investors prefer to pay out the tenants in order to demolish these old buildings, and use the current laws, which allow developers to extend the building footprint to build taller newer buildings attuned to the unique demographics of the district, to generate substantial profit. In other cases, buildings owned by the state also suffer from little to no maintenance due to questions of jurisdiction among government bodies that commonly share responsibility but have opposing interests.[50] Overall, the district suffers from informal additions to either new or old buildings because of the demographic shift, making smaller and cheaper apartments more profitable than bigger ones. Hence, many apartments have been partitioned informally, and almost all rooftops have had informal extensions that generate significant profits for landlords. The only buildings provided with relatively proper maintenance are those belonging to religious institutions and the few prestigious schools and hospitals offering expensive high-standard services for families living in upscale areas in Cairo. These are mainly the French and English schools that made it through the waves of nationalisation in the 1950s and 1960s.[51]

Ismail's Ismailia and Tewfiq's Tewfiqiyya

Ismail (r. 1863–1879), the grandson of Mehmed Ali, inherited Egypt during a significant economic boom caused by a surge in cotton prices. Like his father Ibrahim, he loved urban embellishments, and it could be argued that he was the most prominent and influential of all Cairo's modern rulers in the mark he made on the city. Out of all the cities intended to become new capitals, Ismail's Ismailia quarter, located on the eastern bank of the Nile and westward to al-Qahira, is arguably the most successful. Ismail's new city is considered today as the actual administrative centre of the capital of Egypt.

The story of the Ismailia quarter is usually linked to Ismail's visit to the *Exposition Universelle* held in Paris in 1867, when he became fascinated by Baron Haussmann's planning for Paris. However, when Ismail said that «in the past thirty years Europe's influence has transformed Cairo. Now (...) we are civilized»,[52] he knew that his family's urban and cultural progress preceding his visit to the Expo had made Cairo physically prepared to enter a new era of modern European building. The overlooked fact in the Ismailia's quarter story is that Cairo in 1863 did not have the infrastructure sufficient to build «Paris Along the Nile».[53] Building on the Nile's banks, especially in the area where Ismail built his new city, would not have been possible without the engineering feats accomplished by Ismail during his first few years in power.

The most influential project that prepared the settlement of the new quarters of Ismailia was the construction of the Ismailia Canal, which connected Cairo to the Isthmus at Lake Timsah, located in the eastern part of the Nile Delta. In addition, French engineer M. Brocard, who oversaw the Ismailia Canal, was also responsible for the Nile embankment reinforcements in Cairo. This allowed the shoreline north of Bulaq, along with Jazirat Bulaq, known today as al-Zamalek, to be stabilised and made entirely flood-free.[54] Consequently, Birkat al-Azbakiyya, which had usually been filled with flood-water through a canal made by Mehmed Ali, became completely dry. Hence, the lands of al-Fajalla and Ismailia were ready for the development that was about to take place immediately after Ismail visited Paris in 1867 (fig. 8). Also, before the visit to the Paris Expo, Ismail attempted to provide Cairo with water and gas municipal utilities, which was becoming crucial for any modern European city.[55]

In 1867, the *Exposition Universelle*, Baron Haussmann's pièce de résistance, was held in Paris. It was designed to proudly display Paris's urban and architectural accomplishments. Haussmann was the planner who imposed the widely debated formal grid over the old streets of Paris. At the time, his way of planning Paris was considered a model to follow for many other European cities as the «Haussmannisation» of Paris was lauded by most of Europe's planners and architects. For a city to establish itself among the «elite» of cities, Haussmannisation was the model to follow. Hence, when Ismail received the invitation of Napoleon III to attend the Expo, he immediately accepted, not only to discuss Cairo's future with Haussmann but also to establish himself as a peer of European royalty, something that mattered a lot to him.[56]

André Raymond, an urban historian who focuses on the MENA region, argues that Ismail had considered modernising Cairo long before his trip to Paris; however, it was unquestionably at the *Exposition* and after he had been toured around by Baron Haussmann himself that he had his motivation renewed.[57] After Ismail visited Paris, he decided that he could not invite the crowned heads of Europe to Egypt for the opening of the Suez Canal while Cairo was seen to be in an «un-modern» state. The solution was to give Cairo a complete European makeover. Janet Abu-Lughod argues that Ismail was realistic in his demands as he knew that digging deep into the historic fabric of al-Qahira was too ambitious. He only wanted to provide Cairo with a European façade on its western edge where visitors' itineraries would stick to the new luxurious Ismailia that was planned to rival their European cities.

8 Ismail's modifications and urban projects in Cairo (in red).

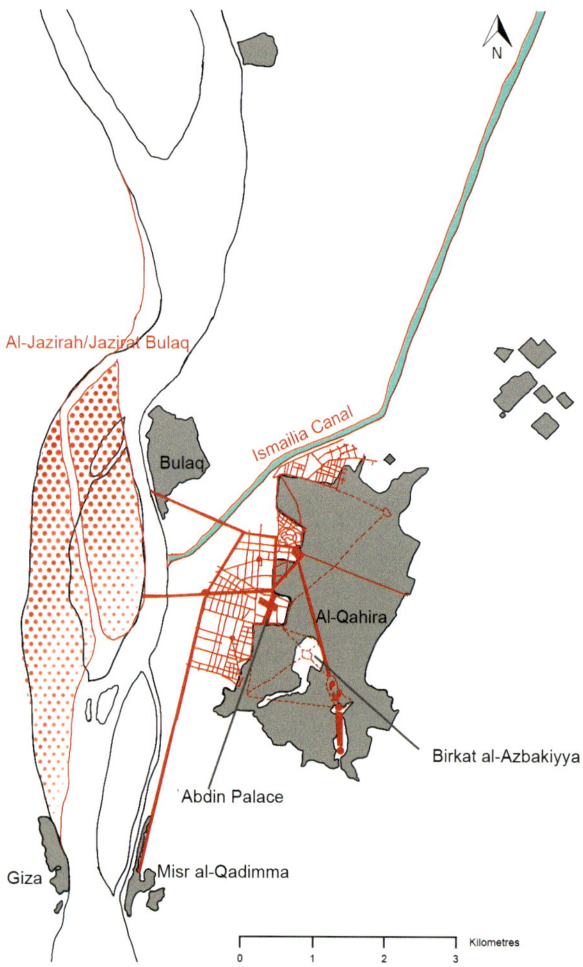

Ismail was fortunate to have at his disposal one of Egypt's most prominent European-educated modern figures in the country's history, Ali Pasha Mubarak. Mubarak was commissioned to draw up a master plan for the entire city following Haussmann's in-vogue style in the planning of Paris, supervise the execution of the plan in the Ismailia quarter, and redevelop the vacant lands peripheral to al-Azbakiyya.[58] Ali Mubarak drew up the master plan within months of Ismail's request. The project had elicited the support of Haussmann himself, yet it was reported that some contemporary architects and orientalists of the time lamented the plan's mechanical modernisation of Cairo.[59]

Once the plan was approved, Ismail offered parcels free of charge to the elite and members of the royal family in return for their building large villas with gardens to urbanise the new city quickly. Ali Mubarak states, «Ismail gave land to anyone willing to construct a dwelling worth at least 2000 Egyptian Pounds.»[60] To further encourage the wealthy to build, Ismail ordered the completion of public improvements before the opening date of the Suez Canal. However, the Ismailia quarter, as observed following the Suez Canal opening, was still largely underdeveloped. Foster Barham writes:

> for the space of about a square mile, laid out broad macadamized streets with broad trottoirs on each side, as if he were contemplating a European city, [but] (...) not much (...) has yet been done towards carrying out his grand designs, except around Ezbekiah [sic].[61]

Private demand proved not to be solely manufactured by Ismail's royal orders. After Ismail's displacement by the British in 1879 (discussed later), Ali Mubarak stated that the number of houses and palaces built by royals along the Cairene eastern bank of the Nile did not exceed 200.[62] Ismail focused his construction around al-Azbakiyya, where hard-surface streets were laid out, and a rare Haussmann-like thoroughfare was superimposed over the old urban fabric of al-Qahira, connecting al-Azbakiyya with ʿAbdin. In al-Azbakiyya, Ismail built the Comédie (also known as Théâtre Français) and the opera house.[63] At the same time, all buildings in that vicinity were whitewashed to welcome European visitors during the Suez Canal celebrations. As Janet Abu-Lughod notes:

> gaslights were installed along all adjacent streets [of al-Azbakiyya]; Shāriʿ Mūski was ‹upgraded› and Europeanized (...) and even the minarets of the nearby mosques were given gaily painted red and white stripes for the occasion.[64]

Besides, Ismail commissioned a famous French landscape architect to redesign al-Azbakiyya garden to compete with the same landscape architect's works in the Bois de Boulogne and the Champ de Mars.[65]

Ismail built a palace on the al-Jazira island (Zamalek today), which later hosted his most distinguished visitor during the Suez Canal ceremony, Empress Eugenie of France. He commissioned Barillet Deschamps, chief gardener of Paris during the reign of Napoleon III, to line a newly constructed avenue that connected Giza (the village) to the pyramids with shade trees. He also ordered the construction of two bridges across the Nile, including the Qasr al-Nil bridge, to provide Empress Eugenie with access to the apartments where she stayed on the al-Jazira island. However, neither of the bridges was completed in time for the Suez Canal ceremony.

Despite Ismail's new city being commonly described by Orientalists and nostalgists as «Paris Along the Nile», the master plan never followed an actual Parisian approach. Unlike Haussmann's Paris, Ismail's city did not erase historic Cairo off the map. The new city was built on vacant land. In contrast, a master plan for the native city was drawn by Ali Mubarak and was limited to creating new arteries through its urban fabric (see fig. 8). Although Mubarak's plan to superimpose a modern grid over old Cairo was heavily criticised by some planners of the time, it did not go anywhere near the practices of Haussmann's city planning.[66] The planning system imposed by Mubarak was composed of open spaces out of which avenues radiate, something that was efficiently carried out to plan in the tabula rasa of the new quarters, but not in the old city. Janet Abu-Lughod explains that difficulties in superimposing the modern grid over the old quarters were too overwhelming to implement.[67] Moreover, while buildings in Paris had a stringent code, the Ismailia quarter only had minimum building requirements to guarantee the speed of construction. According to urban researcher and curator Mohamed Elshahed, «the end result [in Cairo] is a much more eclectic rather than the fascist architectural uniformity of Haussmann's streets».[68]

A few important shifts in Egypt's history should be noted at this point. In the 1870s, Ismail could not meet his increasing debts, which largely financed his urban dreams in Cairo and Alexandria, causing «European economic and political penetration leading to the establishment of foreign control».[69] Ismail was displaced by the British in 1879 as he attempted to rouse national Egyptians against European foreign intervention. This event ushered in what can be called the «soft» occupation of Egypt by Britain. Later in 1882, Egypt was invaded by British forces under the pretext of protecting European lives and properties. This opened the door for Egypt to be directed by a «small number of Europeans backed by a British garrison».[70] According to historian Martin Daly, the Ottoman province was only «advised» by Britain, but this advice had to be followed.[71] Despite having Britain's representative operating in Egypt with the «lowly title of agent and consul-general»,[72] Egypt was in effect ruled by Britain. In December 1914, Egypt was declared a

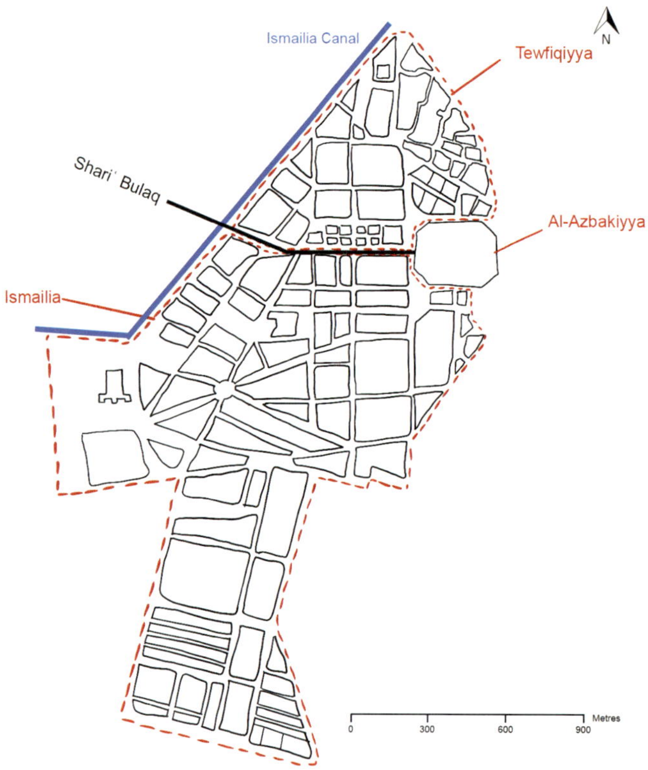

9 Map of Ismailia and Tewfiqiyya.

protectorate, putting it under formal British occupation. Egypt gained nominal independence from Britain in 1922, but British troops only withdrew from Egypt in 1956, following the terms of the Anglo-Egyptian treaty of 1936 and the nationalisation of the Suez Canal by President Nasser.

By 1879, the urban fabric of Cairo's Ismailia only had a few buildings. The city had to wait for the building boom that took place at the turn of the century; however, the street patterns laid out by Ali Mubarak have remained unchanged over the years. Under British control, Ismailia was becoming urbanised by the wealthy Egyptian elite and foreign entrepreneurs, who abided by the town planning drawn up by Mubarak and commissioned by Ismail. Also, the few buildings that replaced older ones in recent decades did not alter Ali Mubarak's urban plan.

The urban boom at the turn of the century made Tewfiq (r. 1879–1892), Ismail's son and successor, eager to engrave his mark on the city. He believed he could have his memory and legacy cemented in the history books by building his city. Hence, he ordered the exploitation of a large triangular pocket of a settlement located north of the Ismailia quarter and south of the Ismailia Canal (fig. 9). Encouraged by the steady urbanisation of Ismail's city, Tewfiq decided to drain and level the site of his new city to make it an extension of his father's quarters. When Tewfiqiyya was subdivided and put on the market in 1889–1890, many of the rich and entrepreneurs immediately bought land plots as the new city was an excellent opportunity that provided buyers with guaranteed and immediate profit due to its proximity to Ismail's city, which had become a busy business district for Europeans living in Egypt.

By the end of the 19th century and despite being geographically separated by an extensive avenue named Shariʿ Bulaq, Ismailia and Tewfiqiyya acted as one block that represented the westernised façade of Cairo while the old native city was left almost entirely intact from the pre-modern age. This situation gave rise to the dual nature of Cairo, which travellers documented mainly in the late 19th and early 20th centuries. Stanely Lane-Poole, for example, describes 19th-century Cairo as having European and Egyptian Cairos.[73]

Today Ismailia and Tewfiqiyya form most of what is known as Wist al-Balad (downtown Cairo). Although both cities were first intended to serve the wealthy and foreign ex-pats resident in the city, they do so for all classes today. Until recently, Egyptians from all over Egypt have travelled to Wist al-Balad to finish and lodge official paperwork, particularly in the infamous al-Mugamaʿ building, the beating heart of Egypt's civil service. Most ministries still have their headquarters in this area, providing Cairenes with almost all sorts of official services. Besides, most prominent companies, embassies, banks, and start-ups have their main headquarters in the same area. The central location of Wist al-Balad provides Ismailia and Tewfiqiyya with a central role in the lives of Cairenes and non-Cairenes. Whether travelling from the direction of Giza to the airport or vice versa, inhabitants of Cairo pass by the downtown area daily. In addition, the whole area contains Cairo's most valuable and intact modern architectural heritage. The majority of buildings in Wist al-Balad are listed as heritage buildings and are protected by law from demolition or vandalism.[74] Nevertheless, many buildings are not well-preserved since landlords do not get enough revenue from their buildings to maintain them due to the old rent control laws. Although a private company named Ismailia, after Ismail's city, has bought, renovated, and maintained twenty-five signature properties in the area, there is still a lot of space for enhancement to preserve Cairo's architectural treasures of the 19th and 20th centuries. The government has recently made partial changes to the old rent control laws, allowing landlords to get market rent values by 2027. Moreover, as the state plans to relocate its governmental headquarters to the New Administrative Capital, several of the buildings to be vacated will be converted for other uses. Al-Mugamaʿ, for example, has been emptied in order to be transformed into a luxurious five-star hotel.[75]

Overall, the promise of Ismail to Europeanise Cairo was fulfilled during the two decades following his exile in 1879. The native city of al-Qahira had been left relatively untouched, making the claims of Ismail building «Paris Along the Nile» not easy to validate. Although most written sources describing Cairo during the 19th and early 20th centuries note the existence of two Cairos «distinct in character (...) but slenderly divided in site»,[76] the Egyptian and European parts of Cairo in the present day have merged, making it difficult for visitors to differentiate between them. Except for their different histories and architectural and urban styles, the Oritentalists' «two [different] Cairos» cannot easily be spotted.[77] On the other hand, Tewfiqiyya's story is largely forgotten. Many Egyptians know the area of Ismail's founding of Wist al-Balad as his physical and historical marks are highly visible all over the city. The story of how Ismail went bankrupt to build his European image of himself and his city is still remembered and regularly narrated even by non-specialists, but this is not the case for Tewfiq and his story of extending his father's dream.

Heliopolis

Despite never being intended as a capital city, Heliopolis can be considered the first successful precedent in desert town planning in Egypt from a financial and social point of view. It has been claimed that most of Cairo's suburban cities today are based on the model of Heliopolis. Abu-Lughod describes the Heliopolis model as a «prototype for all to come later».[78]

Heliopolis was the dream of a Belgian industrial entrepreneur, Edouard Empain, who made a name for himself in Egypt when he introduced the first electrical tramways in the African continent at the end of the 19th century. He had already been involved in the business of electric transportation in Europe, with his company involved in establishing the Paris Metro. Building a desert city near Cairo appealed to Empain as it would benefit his electrical tram projects in the city. At the same time, Empain always dreamed of building a utopian city.[79] Whether for pure profit or romantic dreams, Cairo was a key city for Empain, armed as he was by his relationship with Boghos Nubar Pasha, the son of the late Prime Minister of Egypt, who gave him access to the Khedival court.[80]

Initially, Edouard Empain considered an empty area named Maadi, which stood between metropolitan Cairo and the winter resort of Helwan, southeast of Cairo, as the preferred location of his new town. However, when he failed to purchase the Metropolitan train line to Helwan in 1904,[81] Empain turned to an empty land in the desert northeast of ʿAbbassiyya to establish his urban dream. He was inspired by English urban planner Ebenezer Howard's Garden City concept. At the time, Howard's visionary plans for garden city housing were famous for their utopian social reforms. A garden city was a planned low-density urban development with large public green spaces for functions that were needed to keep the city self-sufficient. However, Empain was more interested in the concept of the garden city for its profit potential than for its utopian social potential. For Empain, a garden city near Cairo could be presented to wealthy foreigners as a desert oasis, distant from the pollution and hustle of Cairo, but at the same time easily accessible to Cairo's economic centre through an extension of the tramline.

In 1905, Empain's relationship with Boghos Nubar Pasha allowed him to buy 5,952 feddans of desert land located 12 km away from central Cairo for only one pound per feddan.[82] This low price and large amount of land made the concept of a garden city in the desert possible, as Emapin was not pressured to urbanise every square metre of his land for profit. Accordingly, Heliopolis's business model was established by buying land for very low prices, investing in the infrastructure and designs, connecting land to a vibrant city centre to create an economy, and then selling it to people.

The design of Heliopolis city started as two connected oases: an oasis for wealthy foreigners closer to central Cairo and another further away for lower-income Egyptians (fig. 10). Fortunately, Empain's Heliopolis Oasis Company, which owned the project, was affected by an international financial crisis, forcing him to change his approach to the project, focus on the first oasis, and bring more people to the city to prevent giving the impression that the city was a ghost town. Hence, a hippodrome, a luna park, an airport, and a grand hotel were all finished in a rush to attract foreigners (fig. 11). However, the most influential factor was the subsidised accommodation offered by the Heliopolis Oasis Company to the government at low prices, filling vacant buildings and starting an economy in the new town.

10 Map of the initial two oases of Heliopolis. Overlay sketch based on Illbert 1985.

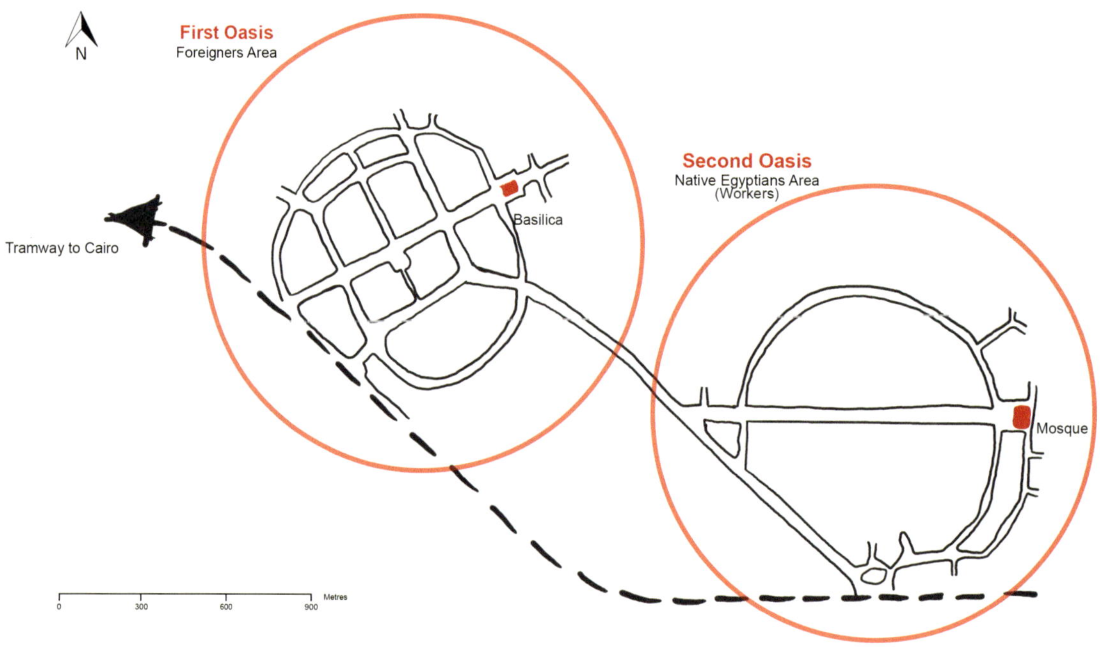

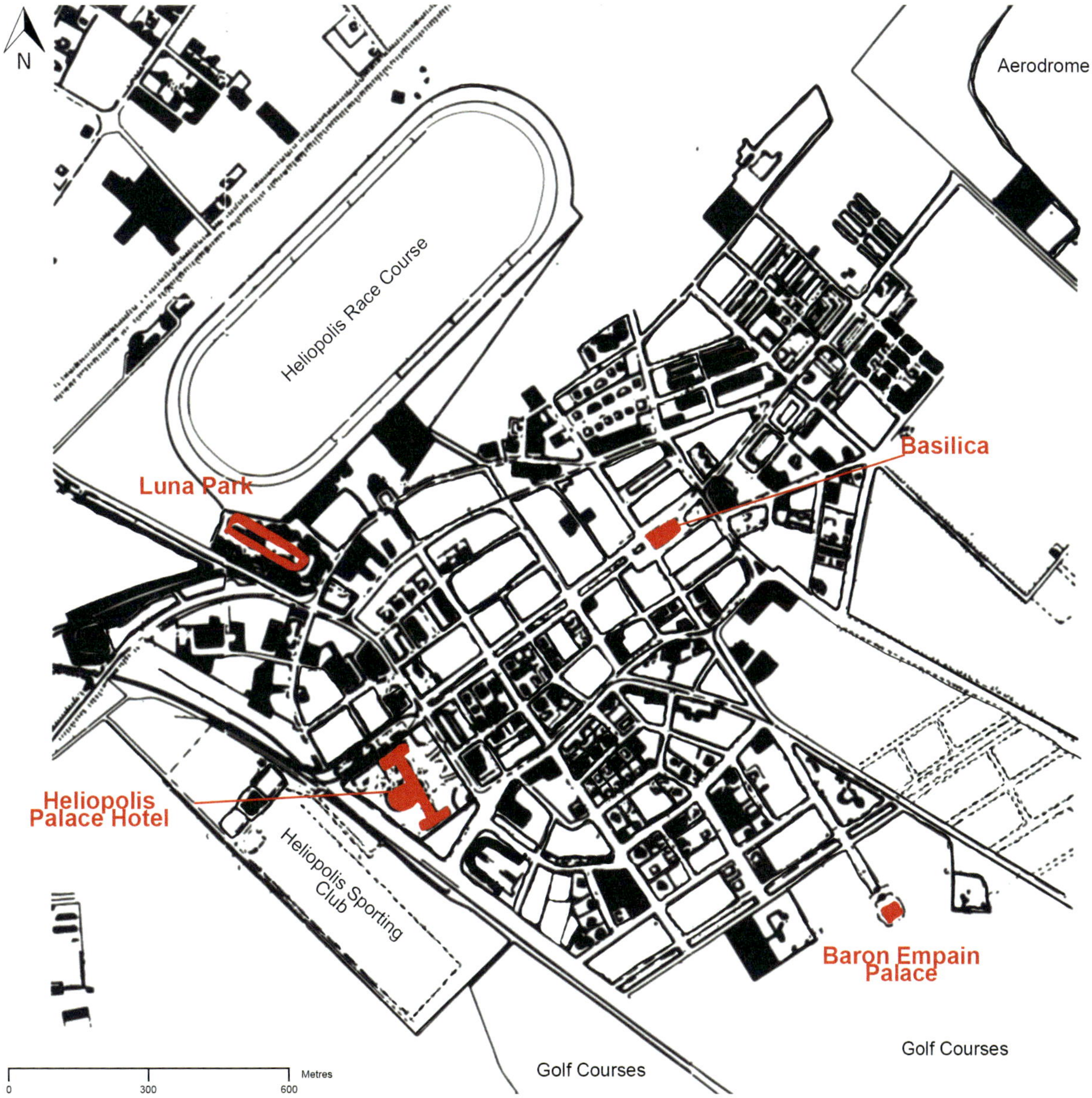

11 Map of Heliopolis in the 1920s.

Once the tramline was fully extended to Heliopolis in 1909, the city started to grow exponentially. In 1910, the Heliopolis Oasis Company purchased more land to reach a total holding of 7,500 feddans, and around 5,000 people had already moved there. During WWI, there was an overall stagnation in growth. However, after the war ended, economic growth started to boom. In 1928, there were more than 4,000 apartments in the city, and about 24,000 people lived there. By 1947, the number of Heliopolis inhabitants had doubled and reached 50,000 inhabitants.

The population of Heliopolis from the 1920s until the early 1950s was dominated by a Christian non-Egyptian majority, which was reflected in the architecture of the desert town. The centre of the first big oasis, intended for the Christian European population, was dominated by a large cathedral known today as the Basilique. Meanwhile, the other oasis, which Muslim Egyptians accommodated, had a mosque that was positioned in a less revealing form. In addition, churches, in general, outnumbered the mosques in the town.

The period which followed the coup d'état in 1952 saw an exodus of foreigners from Egypt, and Heliopolis started to lose its cosmopolitan nature. In 1960, the Heliopolis Oasis Company was nationalised, and a new approach to social housing in Egypt took over. The number of Egyptian inhabitants increased in Heliopolis until it reached 80,000 in the early 1960s. In the mid-1970s and during the open-door policy adopted by President Sadat (r. 1970–1981),[83] the urban and architectural features of the town started to change. Several villas were demolished and replaced by high-rise apartment buildings, which translated into immediate profit with huge margins.

During Mubarak's era (1981–2011), Heliopolis saw steady but relatively slow deterioration in its architectural and urban features. Nevertheless, Mubarak and his family lived in Heliopolis, which protected the area from the fast degradation that other similar regions of Cairo saw at that time. For example, gardens existed but were poorly maintained, and some villas were knocked down, but a 1983 law protected many historical buildings in the area. This degradation increased after Mubarak was ousted in 2011, a period in which Heliopolis witnessed unprecedented architectural and urban decay. Demolition of listed buildings was standard and informal construction started to spread.

Ultimately, the tramways and green corridors, two of the city's main features, were eradicated (fig. 12) within a few months during the reign of President al-Sisi, whose mandate began in 2014. These core changes were to make way for multi-lane traffic highways and flyovers that connect the metropolitan centre of Cairo to the cities of New Cairo and the New Administrative Capital. The walkability of Heliopolis, a crucial feature of any garden city, has been dramatically affected by such urban changes. According to several city inhabitants, crossing the newly widened Heliopolis Road has become almost impossible.[84]

Overall, the success story of Heliopolis is due to a lifeline provided by the expansion of the rapid electric tram connection to the economic heart of Cairo. The tram line from Bab al-Hadid to Heliopolis, passing through ʿAbbassiyya,

12 Heliopolis Square satellite imagery before (in 2009) and after recent developments (in 2022).

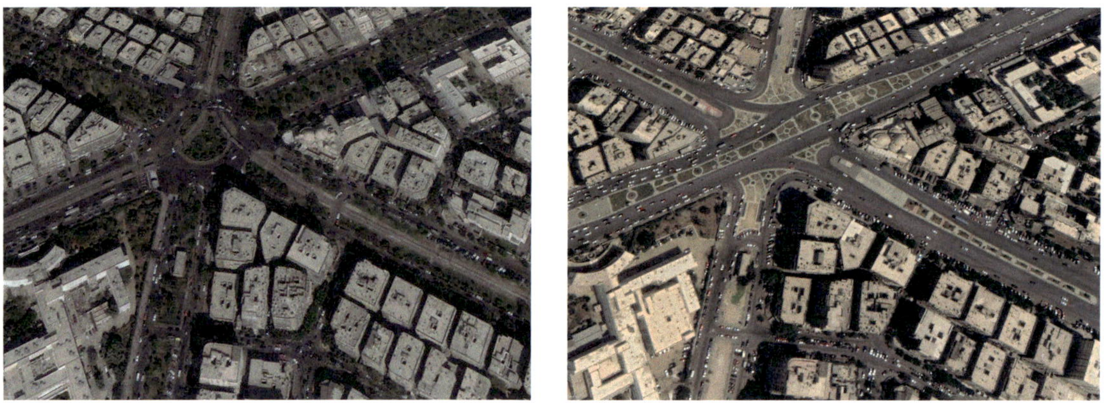

permitted the growth of both ʿAbbassiyya and Heliopolis. However, it was not only the tram that made Heliopolis, as Abu-Lughod describes, a winning «gamble».[85] A crucial factor was also the low price of land provided by the government, allowing the Belgian entrepreneur to subsidise the cost of a considerable number of Heliopolis units in order to attract Egyptian middle-class citizens and workers and kick-start a robust economy.

Despite the success of this model of urban expansion in the desert, few desert cities around Cairo followed a similar financial model. Bureaucratic legislation and the improvidence of some officials are the main obstacles to replicating the success of Heliopolis. For example, Egyptian tender and auction regulation law directs state land to be sold to the highest private-sector bidder. This puts the winning bidder in a position of cramping every inch of the purchased land, with units usually unaffordable to most of the population. In return, many desert cities end up being sold to a wealthy minority of investors willing to invest their savings in real estate, which generally holds its value against the often-devalued Egyptian pound. Moreover, many desert cities have remained ghost towns for decades without a local economy to kick-start their organic growth. Factors such as high walkability, green spaces, public transport, and subsidised housing are usually neglected against a backdrop of investors willing to buy properties and hold them against currency depreciation with time.

Nasser's Nasr City

In 1952, a successful bloodless coup d'état, planned and executed by a group of military officers, ousted the ruling King of Egypt, Farouk, the last ruling member of Mehmed Ali's dynasty. A new republic was announced the following year. Those military officers were led by a senior officer, Muhammed Naguib, and a young officer, Gamal Abdel Nasser, who declared that their mission was not only to seize power from the king but also to dismantle the British military occupation, eliminate foreign political influence, and eradicate corruption in Egypt's public life.[86] Nasser (r. 1954–1970), who became president in 1954 after getting rid of Naguib, was driven by socialist policies mixed with values drawn from pan-Arabism and nationalism.[87] «Nasserism» was a project reflected in Cairo's tangible and intangible forms. Driven by political, national, and social values, Gamal Abdel Nasser began developing Nasr city in 1958, a town initially announced only as an extension to Cairo but later given the status of Egypt's new capital as the «City of the Revolution».[88] To understand the intentions behind the building of Nasr city and the change in policies regarding its planning and purpose, one must first address the historical, political, and social contexts of the new republic established by the 1952 coup.

Coming to power through a coup, Nasser and his fellow junior officers knew that their only way to sustain and protect their legitimacy was by fully controlling all aspects of Egypt's governance. This was reflected in a new management framework that prioritised positioning people of trust, rather than people of experience, in senior positions within the government. For example, Nasser's closest friend, Abdel-Hakim Amer, was appointed as the head of the armed forces after being exceptionally promoted through several ranks in a short period.[89] As historian Khaled Fahmy argues, the Egyptian officers feared the scenario that had happened in Syria only three years before the 1952 coup, where a successful coup would be overthrown by another one within a short period.[90]

On the other hand, the officers behind the coup believed that another way to put things under total control was to gain, as Historian Sherif Younis calls it, *al-sharʿiyya al-injaziyya* (legitimacy through tangible achievements).[91] This was translated into the state taking decisions showing a clear bias towards the poor and the subaltern, in the meantime giving leverage for the officers to gain more power. One of the most controversial policies Nasser and his officers applied was nationalising and confiscating the property of all sorts of individuals or families with considerable wealth. Nasser himself believed that the old members of the social elite with substantial capital were an existential threat to the regime.[92] Hence, creating a «new society» that was loyal to the new military leadership was a key concept upon which the coup of 1952 built its legitimacy and power.

One of the pillars of the monarchy before 1952 was the established feudal system, in which only a few Pashas monopolised the ownership of the majority of Egypt's agricultural land in the Nile Valley and the Delta. The masses of people, in return, primarily fellahin, had been considered the property of the Pashas. The 1952 coup aimed first at destroying the old guard by toppling the head of the monarchy, the king, and his aristocratic elite to build the «new society». Only 45 days after the coup, the revolutionary officers issued the first land reform act, limiting an individual family's ownership to 200 feddans. Although Nasser and his fellow officers claimed that the fellahin who represented most of the population were Egypt's pride, in many cases, forms of contempt for the traditions, education, and even the looks of those fellahin were documented. The officers and their leader, Gamal Abdel Nasser, had a broad vision of the new ideal society they wanted to create; clearly, the fellahin's old life was not what Nasser was looking for.

A clear example of this attitude was when Nasser's Minister of Social Affairs declared that the goal of the revolution was to train the members of Egyptian society to be «civilised». He asserted that «it is impossible to build a society whose members were not trained to be good citizens (...) [the goal] is to have a well-trained society».[93] Such «good citizens» would have to get rid of their «chaotic» traditional costumes and instead only wear «modern and civilised» uniforms designed by the state to «put an end to the disorganised taste of fashion that gives an unthriving impression about our way of thinking».[94]

Accordingly, the earliest project that followed this mode of social engineering was Mudiriyat al-Tahrir, a massive agricultural land reclamation project in the Western desert near the Nile Delta. Mudiriyat al-Tahrir not only attempted to develop large-scale facilities producing fruit for export but also to reclaim «both people and the land».[95] To Nasser, the project was an instant success as it reclaimed large parts of the desert, producing agricultural products and «good citizens» that would be utilised to cement his rule. Only a year after the establishment of the project, Nasser used the workers of Mudiriyat al-Tahrir as a private army of civilians. In a power struggle between President Muhammad Naguib and Nasser in 1954, Mudiriyat al-Tahrir workers were urged to go to Cairo and join the National Guard and the Military Police to storm the Administrative Court and put an end to Naguib's attempts at democratic reforms.[96]

Moreover, through his land reform acts, Nasser essentially cut the wealth of many families of the previous elite. Even wealthy foreign entrepreneurs were pressured to leave the country. Nasser nationalised all the private companies, businesses, and factories owned by the foreign community that had lived in Egypt for decades.

Out of this context, a serious proposal to build a new capital appealed to the revolutionary government. First of all, the success of the Mudiriyat al-Tahrir project, which bred an army of civilians, coincided with a growing modern movement in relation to the urban environment that influenced many states around the world to build new cities from scratch.[97] Hence, there was an urgent need to shelter the new loyal social elite along with foreign diplomats in a new town that did not belong to the legacy of the demonised dynasty of Mehmed Ali.[98] Second, Cairo was already under many urban pressures and needed a new master plan to define its future growth, which was completed only within the first two years of Nasser's reign. Third, Nasser and his officers saw that building a new city would add to their portfolio of *al-sharʿiyya al-injaziyya*. Tangible achievements were considered a priority that would strengthen the officers' legitimacy and help promote the regime through state media. Finally, establishing a new capital and affiliating it with the regime had already been a recurrent habit of Egypt's rulers. Abu-Lughod calls this phenomenon the «long tradition of royal cities».[99] Consequently, it was about time for Nasser and his officers to put their names on the urban map of Egypt by building their new capital.

In 1959, President Gamal Abdel Nasser ordered the establishment of the Nasr City Society, which was responsible for building a new city near the desert of ʿAbbassiyya.[100] The Nasr City Society was founded to be self-financing through several strategies: selling parcels of land to buyers (mainly the new social elite), getting state loans guaranteed by the government, receiving bursaries and donations from different donors, and getting some funds from the national budget.[101] Construction of the new city was started jointly by the Ministry of Housing and the Ministry of Defence, with the latter more involved since it owned most of the land. The Nasr City Society was administrated by a board under the umbrella of the Ministry of Housing, while the Chairman of this board was exclusively chosen from the army corps of engineers. Meanwhile, the primary mastermind of the whole project was the architect Sayed Karim, who initially presented the idea of building a new capital to Nasser in his house in 1958.[102]

The location of Nasr City was chosen to fill the desert gap between the suburb of Heliopolis and ʿAbbassiyya (fig. 13). That location was chosen for three main reasons. First, the risks of invading the desert had already been minimised by the outstanding success of Heliopolis in the first half of the 20th century. Second, the proposal for developing Nasr City originally came from Sayed Karim, a prominent European-trained Egyptian architect of the time who already had outstanding experience in planning and designing desert cities such as Jeddah, Mecca, Riyadh, Kuwait City, Abu Dhabi, and Amman. Third, the 1956 Cairo master plan recommended that the future growth of Cairo be channelled into self-contained satellite cities located on desert sites instead of agricultural land to improve the symmetry of the elongated metropolis of existing Cairo.

The initial first phase of Nasr City covered an area of around 7,000 feddans located within proximity to highways and tramlines, connecting the colonial downtown area of Cairo to Heliopolis, and passing through ʿAbbassiyya (see fig. 13). That phase was subdivided into three zones that corresponded to three different uses. The first zone was planned to contain the official uses of the capital in which government offices, universities, ministries, international fairgrounds, parade grounds, an Olympic city, and a stadium were designed and built. The second zone, located in the south and west of the first zone, was used for industrial, institutional, and recreational uses. The Red Mountain, an elevated area rich with marble, sand, gravel, and other raw materials, was in this second zone. Many factories were designed and built to extract and process these resources. The third zone of the planned city was drawn to accommodate residential low-density villa communities.[103]

In general, Nasr City was designed to be affordable for the new military elite and the new middle class that gained relative wealth because of the policies that followed the 1952 coup. On the other hand, Nasr City did not accommodate enough social housing projects despite Nasser's socialist views. In the late 1960s, Nasser himself admitted that the state was not building enough housing for the poor.[104] The exceptionally few low-income housing units were only designed to separate the villa communities from the industrial and institutional zones. As for the military elite and high-ranking officials, an exclusive hilly area was selected to become a prestigious garden city to house their large villas with a minimum building plot of around one feddan.[105] However, this plan has never been realised, and today that area houses a large military-owned recreational complex.

Designed to be Egypt's new capital, Nasr City was planned to accommodate the headquarters

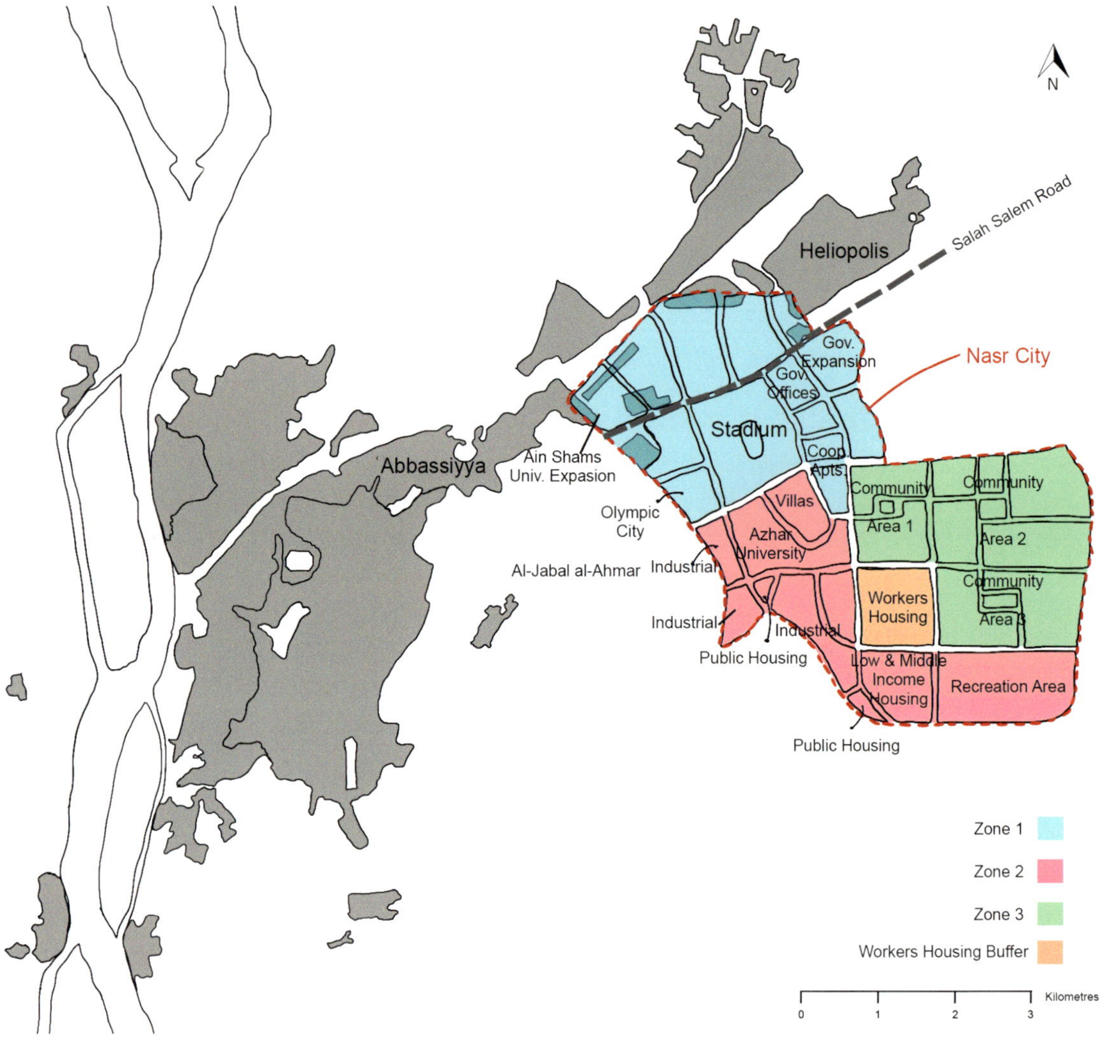

13 Map of Nasr City's Initial Phase.

of ministries, embassies, and residential houses for diplomats. Although many buildings were constructed for these purposes, only a few ministries and embassies made the actual move. Primarily for technical and bureaucratic reasons, the aim of moving all ministries to the new city was never realised. There was also not enough incentive for embassies located in the colonial downtown area to move only a few kilometres away to a new city. The few ministries that settled in Nasr City were those related to the new economy and the military. Hence, today one can find the Ministries of Petroleum, Energy, Tourism, Finance, Investment, and Defence in Nasr City. However, almost all other ministries, such as the Ministry of Interior and the Ministry of Education, kept their colonial downtown (Wist al-Balad) headquarters. Other official buildings, such as the Parliament, the presidential palace, and the municipality of Cairo, also remained in Wist al-Balad.

Despite the initial claims for Nasr City, the vision of «a capital inside the capital» was never

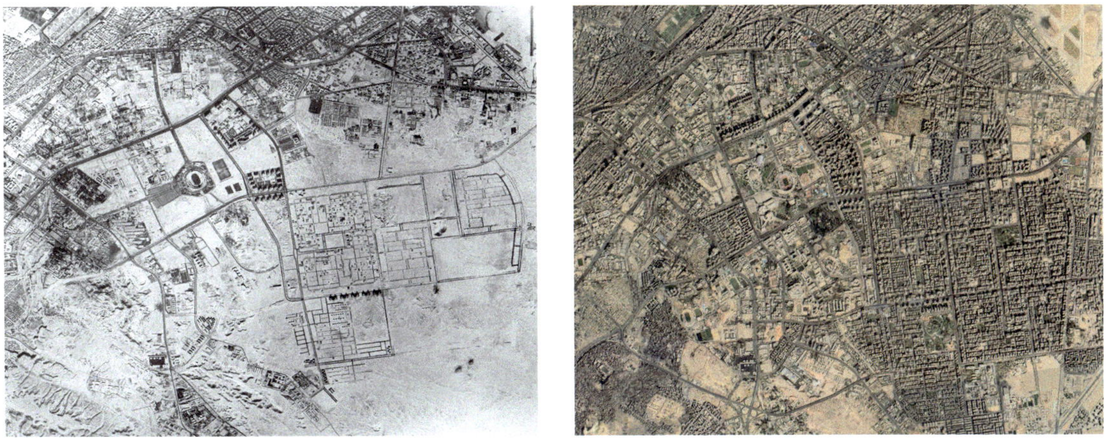

14 Nasr City Satellite Imagery in 1968 (left) and 2023 (right). Notice Nasr City's state as an incomplete desert city in 1968, only two years before the death of its founder, Gamal Abdel Nasser.

realised (fig. 14). The city was planned in an unapologetic modernist manner without a centre and with minimal services. This obliged its residents to stay connected with Wist al-Balad; hence, the whole concept of the capital or even an independent district had vanished by the 1970s. Nevertheless, Nasr City was growing horizontally, especially with the low-interest loans made possible by public companies and building cooperatives generating unprecedented demand, especially among the higher ranks of nationalist-era civil servants, military elites, and government employees. In 1971, a year after Nasser's death, his successor President Anwar al-Sadat issued a decree extending the city's boundaries to incorporate an additional 14,000 feddans (see fig. 1).[106]

The boom in oil revenues from the early 1970s until the late 1980s led to a substantial increase in wealth in Saudi Arabia and the Gulf. Many Egyptians, encouraged by the financial incentives of Gulf countries and the Egyptian open-door policy, which eliminated travel restrictions on Egyptians, flocked to the oil-rich countries to work in various sectors. Their income translated into a boom in Cairo's urban environment since real estate was considered a haven for investment. Besides, investing in real estate lifted a financial burden off the family members of Egyptian expats still living in Egypt who could not afford to buy apartments without the help of their relatives working abroad.

Usually, this economic shift is mentioned in the literature when discussing informal areas;[107] however, some formal areas, particularly Nasr City, were greatly affected as well. Throughout the 1980s and 1990s, Nasr City was highly densified. The intended political capital was forced to obey the demands of a new capitalist-driven economy. As a result of a large number of Egyptian returnees due to the Gulf War,[108] Nasr City adopted a new consumerist lifestyle. The main streets were commercialised, small walk-ups and villas were knocked down to be replaced by tall mixed-use apartment buildings, and large shopping malls started to appear for the first time in Egypt to cater for the returnees who had become used to spending their free time in shopping malls during the time they lived in oil-rich Arab countries.[109]

Today Nasr City is a busy district incorporated into other sections of Cairo. Its boundaries have mostly stayed the same since the extension order of 1971. On the northern side, the Salah Salem Road separates Nasr City from the districts of ʿAbbassiyya and Heliopolis (see fig. 13). The eastern boundary still has a large area of desert land (see fig. 1) separating it from Mubarak's New Cairo. This land currently hosts one new gated community developed by the Nasr City company, which was fully privatised in 2006.[110] On the western side, Nasr City touches Cairo's historic necropolis and Manshiyat Nasser, an informal area as old as Nasr City. On the southern side, Nasr City is surrounded by desert land and is currently getting urbanised at a relatively slow pace. Overall, it has very solid and clear boundaries. Except for very few areas on the northeast side where the city strongly engages with parts of Heliopolis, Nasr City is surrounded by wide streets that act as interim highways, preserving its robust boundaries. Since 2020, more interim highways have been created as a result of the state's controversial decision to widen all main roads in both Nasr City and Heliopolis, leading to the removal of all the green islands in those roads. Just as in Heliopolis, Nasr City's residents have become more dependent on cars to get around its different districts than at any other time.

Mubarak's New Cairo

New Cairo is one of the new desert cities built around Greater Cairo Proper after the 1973 October War.[111] No one can claim that New Cairo was ever intended to be a capital city. However, this new city was the personal project of ex-President Hosni Mubarak (r. 1981–2011), at least during the second half of his presidency. A disproportionate share of urban development funding was directed to New Cairo on top of other new towns built simultaneously under Mubarak's orders. Most government elites and businesspeople competed to buy land and build houses in these new developments, particularly in New Cairo. Mubarak's children, who had considerable political influence, chose New Cairo for their permanent residence. Moreover, large companies, brands, real-estate developers, and ministries were encouraged under Mubarak's policies to invest and open branches, if not headquarters, in New Cairo. Overall, it can be argued that New Cairo was set to become Egypt's financial and business capital under Mubarak's regime.

According to a classification made by Walid Bayoumi, an Egyptian specialist in urban and regional planning, Cairo's urban political economy can be divided into four different periods: a) The Arab Socialist Era (1952–1974), b) the era of the open-door policy (1975–1987), c) the era of the dissolving public sector (1987–2000), and d) the globalisation era (2001 to present).[112] New Cairo was established by the end of the open-door policy and blossomed during globalisation. Hence, it is essential to tackle this shift in the urban political economy of Egypt when writing about New Cairo.

The concept of creating new towns was initiated by President Anwar Sadat (r. 1970–1981, after Nasser and before Mubarak) in 1974, immediately after the 1973 October victory to «draw a new map of Egypt».[113] This map coincided with the open-door policy, which was considered a serious step towards transitioning Egypt's economy to a free market, although the state still dominated the housing sector. Sadat attempted to draw a new map of Egypt's population in which new towns were built in the desert to attract poor and low-income people away from overpopulated urban areas. Sadat even decided to make a new administrative capital of Egypt named after himself and move all the headquarters of ministries into this new city.[114] However, he was assassinated before that project was ever realised. When Mubarak came to power, the concept of new desert towns was still strong. Although many critics of this programme called for the winding up of the whole idea and a focus instead on improving the living conditions of people living in the «old» cities,[115] the state went on with the vision of the Minister of Housing, Hasaballah El Kafrawy, in establishing satellite cities in the desert.

In 1981, a new master plan for Cairo was launched and approved two years later, as part of which Mubarak's first Minister of Housing,

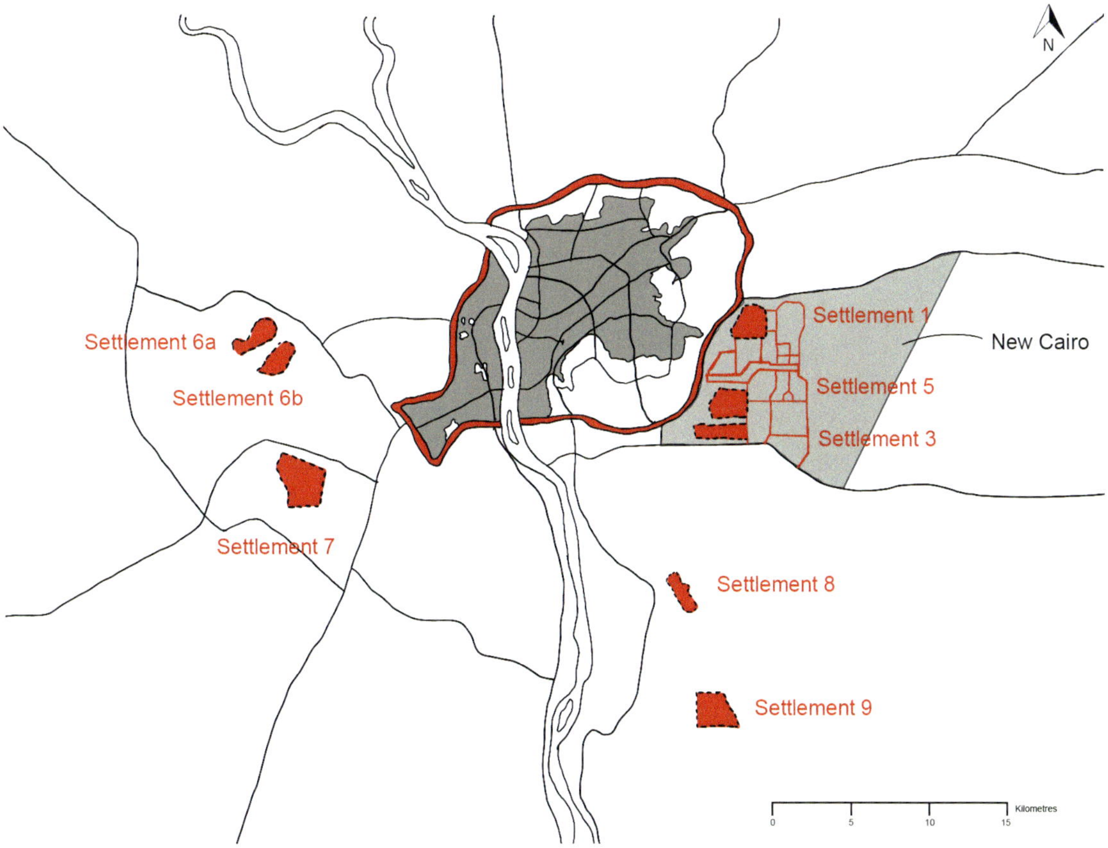

15 The master plan of Cairo, approved in 1983.

Hasaballah El Kafrawy, promoted desert settlements around Cairo. Throughout the 1980s, El Kafrawy backed new settlements by claiming they offered an alternative for those living in informal areas and for the urban poor who lived on expensive Cairene land parcels with high rent-gap values.[116] That vision was short-lived due to Egypt's poor economic productivity, which forced it in 1987 to reluctantly accept the financial pressures of the World Bank to restructure and reform the economy, adopting free-market enterprise as well as a general scheme of privatisation.[117]

Ironically, New Cairo was never planned to be a city of the wealthy elite. It was intended to be a socially balanced and independent new town to accommodate Cairo's urban low-income and poor overspills. New Cairo was generated from a plan to relieve Cairo from an urban crisis caused mainly by overcrowding in the metropolis and the appearance of informal areas. Informal construction had started to become a widespread pattern of housing when public housing spending was significantly reduced to fund the rebuilding of Egypt's military forces following Egypt's military defeat in the 1967 six-day war.

The master plan (fig. 15), which was approved in 1983, had four main objectives: first, it aimed to meet Cairo's growing population; second, it sought to protect agricultural land from urban sprawl by building ten new settlements around Cairo's desert; third, it attempted to reduce the concentration of the population of Cairo proper to enhance and restructure deteriorated historic areas; and fourth, it sought to create a ring road around Cairo to connect each of the planned new settlements.[118] However, in 1987, when the World Bank and other creditors forced Egypt not to use its urgently needed loans for housing and subsidies, the state was forced to reduce public spending and abort existing national programmes.[119] As a result, the initial plan to spend money on building new desert cities for the poor was partially scrapped.[120] Such cities were privatised by selling large land plots to private investors who saw this as an opportunity for massive influence and profit, given Cairo's prestigious status as the central economic and cultural hub of the Arab World. In the early 1990s, the 1983 master plan was modified so that some settlements were relocated, and others cancelled, giving way to the emergence of a new city called New Cairo, effectively merging new settlements one, three and five (see fig. 15).[121]

Mubarak was not keen on regulating private sector investment in the new towns. Socio-economic balance in the new cities, particularly in New Cairo, evaporated with the private sector's increasing interest in gaining maximum profits by contributing only to building upscale gated communities. This jeopardised the whole concept of resettling the poor in the desert. In New Cairo, profit margins were exceptional. According to a study published by *The Economist*, an investment of $ 250,000 in 1996 would yield $ 1,000,000 only ten years later. This huge profit margin was mainly due to the state's selling land parcels far below market value. An investor would buy the land, sell residential units based on preliminary schematic designs, start constructing a few buildings with the money collected, and then complete construction, gaining massive financial profit. Another way to profit, especially for individuals, was by holding small parcels for a considerable period in order to benefit once the state had expanded its services and infrastructure.

In this context, the building of gated communities, known in Egypt as «compounds», grew exponentially in New Cairo as it was highly suitable for investors wishing to quickly expand their capital. Investors would not need to wait for the whole city to be urbanised, which would take decades in normal circumstances. A private real estate developer could build the compound's roads, walkways, and infrastructure without relying on the government. A nearly completed compound would sell instantly for a substantial profit. In the case of New Cairo, buyers of the residential units of the gated compounds would either immediately move into their units once the compound was completed or put them on sale for instant profit. Overall, by following strategies of building and holding, New Cairo became a city of scattered gated communities full of upscale residential villas, penthouses, and townhouses with only a tiny strip of land dedicated to commercial and service usage (fig. 16).

Despite the failure of New Cairo and other new towns to achieve population resettlement, the state extended the new towns programme due to the immense profit gained from the wealthy who preferred to invest in real estate rather than hold cash in banks. Given Egypt's high inflation rates and the recurrent overnight hit to the Egyptian pound, which usually happened once a decade, real estate was considered a haven for the wealthy wishing to save the value of their capital. Driven by the consent of Mubarak himself, three updates to New Cairo's master plan were drawn up in 1995, 1999, and 2005 to accommodate investors' calls for more parcels to be allocated for their projects (see fig. 16).[122] Hence, New Cairo, which started as a combination of new settlements targeted to accommodate the urban poor, became a massive city driven by speculative demand for different types of land parcel. Gradually, gated communities conquered the city. Compound developers would appeal to wealthy clients by choosing foreign names for those gated communities and advertising them extensively on TV and billboards in English. Titles such as Lake View, Stone Park, Mountain View, and Eastown were carefully chosen to cater to wealthy Egyptians who wanted to experience a European-like environment away from Cairo itself, which had become widely associated with poverty and chaos.

By the end of Mubarak's thirty-year reign, New Cairo was steadily becoming Egypt's new financial capital. Prestigious ministries, sports clubs, and military and police institutes had already had their allocated parcels either wholly built or under construction. Perhaps the biggest is the Police Academy, known then as Mubarak's Police Academy. That academy was constructed on around 8,000 feddans on the city's western edge. In Mubarak's last decade, the Ministry of the Interior was the regime's cornerstone and having the academy in that area gave New Cairo a lot of attention and significance.

A significant shift towards presenting New Cairo as an official new capital city can be inferred from *Cairo 2050* vision, a $66 billion plan

16 The master plan of New Cairo in different stages. Note that the second stage of the master plan includes the initial three settlements.

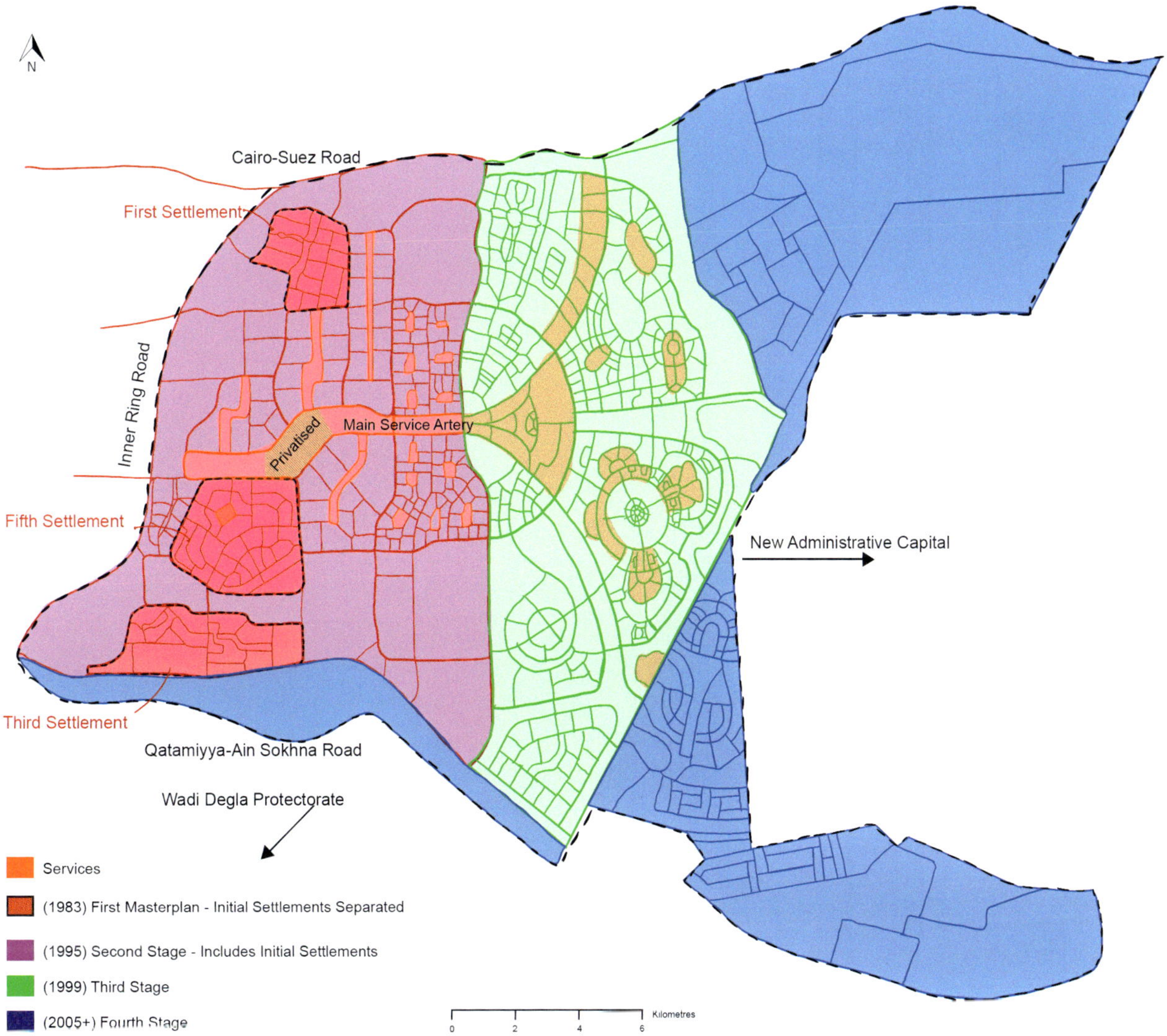

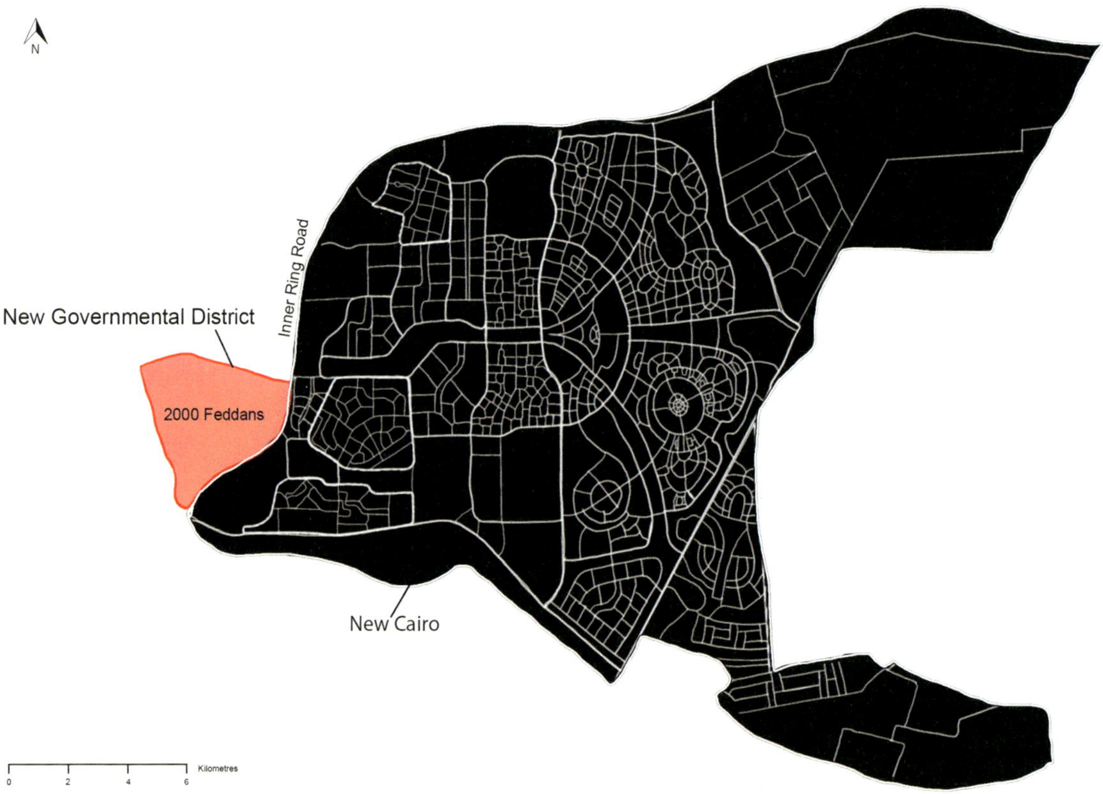

17 New Governmental District (New Cairo Trade Business Centre).

announced in 2008 by Gamal, the son of Hosni Mubarak, who was being groomed to succeed his father as Egypt's president. The vision, known in subsequent years as «Gamal Mubarak's vision for Cairo», aimed to transform the city into a global metropolis akin to Paris, London, and Tokyo.[123] In late 2008 the General Organisation for Physical Planning (GOPP), headed by the current Prime Minister Mostafa Madbouli, released a presentation that included a proposal for a new government district of 2,000 feddans located southwest of New Cairo (fig. 17).[124] The district, also referred to in the presentation as the «Cairo Trade Business Centre», was designed to include new headquarters for the parliament and senate, alongside residential areas for Mubarak's associates, within green spaces and expansive golf courses. In 2010, then Prime Minister Ahmed Nazif approved *Cairo 2050*, which continued to be championed by the Minister of Housing until 24 January 2011, the day before massive protests broke out, leading to the ouster of Mubarak and his government.[125] Following the 2011 revolution, the GOPP abandoned the entire *Cairo 2050* plan as it was deemed too expensive to implement. The announcement of the New Administrative Capital in 2015 confirmed the cancellation of any plan to build a government district southwest of New Cairo.

The area, initially dedicated to the governmental district of *Cairo 2050* and separating New Cairo from Nasr City, has seen a few constructions by the Ministry of Defence in the past decade and a half. In 2009, an Olympic city was built, and then in 2014 construction began in a state mosque named after the head of the Supreme Council of Armed Forces, General Hussein Tantawi. Subsequently, a substantial parcel was developed to become Cairo's new primary fairgrounds, stealing the spotlight from the former fairgrounds in Nasr City. The new fairgrounds have hosted several prestigious events, including the Cairo International Film Festival, which used to take place annually in the Opera House in Zamalek. Those tangible and intangible investments have shed more and more light on the new city, making it the number one destination for official events and potential investors.

New Cairo today is still surrounded by desert land (see fig. 1), despite the rapid urbanisation of Cairo proper. On the northern side, the city's borders are defined by the Cairo–Suez Road. On the western side, the edges are determined by the ring road. Wadi Degla's protected park is south towards Maadi, so supposedly no urban sprawl or extensions are expected anytime soon. On the other hand, the eastern part of New Cairo is only separated from the New Administrative Capital by Cairo's intermediate ring road. Once the New Administrative Capital is officially opened, the buffer between both cities should be filled up.

Currently, New Cairo consists of two sectors, north and south, divided by a main linear service centre. Each of the two sectors is divided into different districts, each with a centre that extends from the main city centre. However, most of the district centres today are still under-urbanised. They take the form of large urban deserted patches on New Cairo's map. Similarly, the large service centre that divides the city is also mostly deserted, except for a relatively large part that was privatised to become an upscale gated compound alongside a sports club. Most of the city's urban development is for residential purposes, whereas plans for industrial areas have been scrapped. The exploitation of land for upscale residential compounds, combined with the absence of public transport in residential districts, can be seen as a planned social barrier to keep the poor out of the city.[126] The city has grown by developing dispersed patches of gated luxury compounds, upscale housing, exclusive sports clubs, and educational facilities. The master plan of the city has made its roads very wide and horizontally dispersed, making commuting within the city almost wholly dependent on private cars, which contradicts the concept of the 1983 Cairo master plan (see fig. 15).

Al-Sisi's New Administrative Capital

The New Administrative Capital (NAC) of President Abdel Fatah al-Sisi (r. 2014–present) is the newest of all of Cairo's capitals. NAC is a mega-urban project currently under construction east of New Cairo between the newly constructed regional ring road, the Cairo–Suez Road, and the Cairo–Ain Sokhna Road (fig. 18). It is a mega-city that is intended to host the parliament, a presidential palace, 31 ministerial headquarters, 119 state offices, dozens of embassies and consulates, and eight residential districts to accommodate a target population of 6,500,000 by the date of completion.[127] Despite numerous financial and technical obstacles, which moved Prime Minister Mostafa Madbouli in January 2023 to suspend work on «projects that have not yet started», overall progress in NAC seems unaffected. In general, it can be argued that NAC is al-Sisi's biggest and most ambitious project out of numerous mega-projects launched since his presidential inauguration in 2014.

When NAC was initially announced in 2015 under the name *The Capital: Cairo*,[128] it was received with mixed views. Although building a new capital was not a novel idea to Egyptians, the announced project with «Cairo» in its title and the selected location near Cairo proper generated many questions regarding the intention behind the new city. Would the new city be part of Cairo as its title suggests, or would it be a completely new capital as it was initially presented?

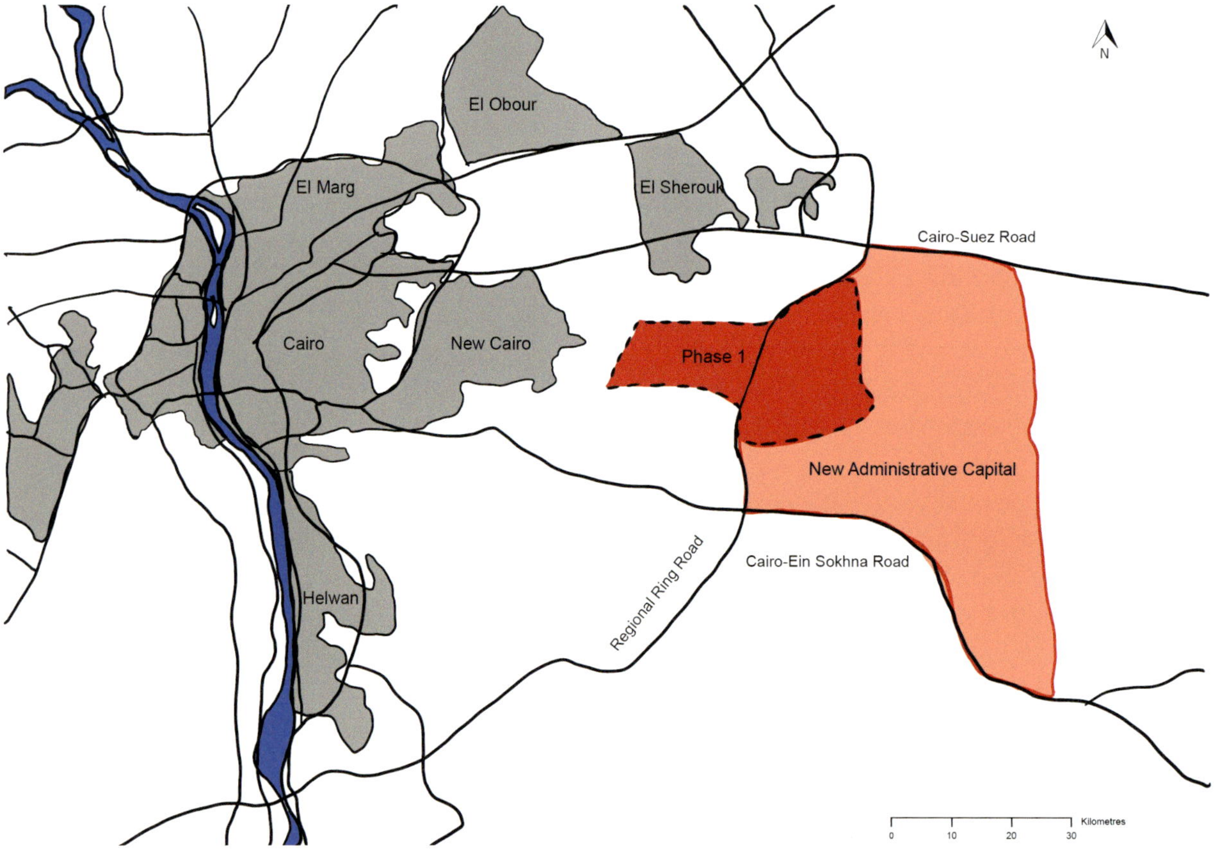

18 NAC's region on the map of Cairo.

NAC was announced via a presentation by the then Minister of Housing and current Prime Minister Mostafa Madbouli, who explained how this new city would attempt to solve Cairo's problems, particularly over-crowding. In the presentation, Madbouli focused on presenting *The Capital: Cairo* without reflecting on any parallel rehabilitation projects in Cairo. He noted that transport from Cairo to the New Capital would be enabled through high-speed trains and large highways, which Egyptians are not used to utilising within a single city. In addition, he added that the parliament, ministries, and other official offices would be relocated, again giving the impression of launching something distant from Cairo.[129] However, Madbouli cleared up the early confusion by announcing, «[NAC] is still part of Cairo and not a new city (...) according to the constitution, Cairo is the capital city of the country, so the new city will only be an administrative section within Cairo.»[130]

NAC took the public by surprise as people had never heard of the project despite Madbouli's words about the new city being an outcome of the state's long-term strategic planning. Indeed, announcing the establishment of NAC was one of several other announcements of mega-projects that the public only got to know about once officially launched. Another cause of confusion regarding NAC was its credibility, given Egypt's very weak economic viability at the time of its launch. The economic conference held in

Sharm El Sheikh, where NAC was announced, was an attempt to bring back foreign investments to Egypt after its financial and credit rankings were severely damaged by the turbulent political circumstances of the 2011 revolution. Moreover, it was unclear how this new capital city would abide by the announced promise of «being a city for everyone»,[131] especially since it was claimed to be a city of exceptional quality of life, «embracing all Egyptians regardless of their different classes».[132]

It can be argued that initially the new capital seemed to be another mega-project that al-Sisi wanted to announce and execute rapidly to «lift the spirit of Egyptian people», a goal that was set for an earlier project promoted as the digging of a «new Suez Canal».[133] This seemed possible, especially when al-Sisi promised to complete the whole city in a very tight timeframe. However, it became more apparent with time that NAC was more than just a spirit-lifting exercise. During its launch, Gulf royals were invited along with Emirati business tycoon and founder of Emaar Properties Mohamed Alabbar, who was set to be the actual developer of the new city. In an interview, Alabbar did not hide his scepticism about NAC, given its gigantic physical scale and budget; however, he declared that «Egypt's strong will and seriousness to execute this project fast» changed everything.[134] No information was provided about the exact time of introducing the concept of the new capital to the Gulf royals and Alabbar. However, according to the latter, the initial master plan for NAC was designed, reportedly by leading American planning firm SOM, only four months before the Sharm El Sheikh conference.[135]

Despite the proclaimed strong will of al-Sisi to complete NAC in a brief period and the ambitious plan portraying it as a golden nationalist solution that would solve Cairo's problems, the new city faced several financial issues that ultimately altered the initial goals announced in Sharm El Sheikh. According to the deal with Alabbar, Emaar was to fund the mega-project from its own capital. It was not clear how Emaar, a company known for its upscale luxury real estate projects, would fund a «city for everyone» in a country where most of the population is poor.[136] A few months later, the government declared that it would fund the residential units if the deal with Emaar collapsed.[137] A year later, Emaar withdrew from the agreement, and al-Sisi immediately ordered the establishment of a national company that would handle designing, constructing, and maintaining the new capital.[138] This meant that the state altered its initial plan of being only a moderator supervising the new capital city under private investors. According to the director of the newly formed national company, the deal with Emaar was cancelled as Emaar and the government could not agree on the profit split.[139] For similar reasons, a Chinese company, whose name was not publicly announced, withdrew from another deal to construct NAC.[140]

Although no further details were given about why the deals with Emaar and the Chinese company were cancelled, and why the state itself decided to change its plan and establish a national company that would construct and manage the new city, the way the state had been dealing with the project showcased a recurrent orientation towards city-making in Egypt. The nationalist theme of NAC was quickly altered a year into the city's establishment. As the project progresses today, NAC is viewed as a significant investment opportunity for Egyptians who prefer to invest their wealth in real estate to fight high inflation or for those who prefer a «Dubaiesque» experience rather than an Egyptian Cairene one. This can be seen mainly in the salient language used on public and commercial signs promoting NAC in Cairo. For months, billboards advertising the new city featured the statement, «Dubai in the Capital». Usually, NAC billboards feature a built environment characterised by carnival themes, absence of human integration, disintegration from the Cairene context, and non-Arabic names and language, emphasising spatial otherness that depicts a city catering to a minority of elite consumers.[141]

Such commodification of the new capital has also been reflected in the planning and parcelling of the city. Although Madbouli's presentation promised that NAC would be a new beginning for all Egyptians in which movement in and outside the city would depend entirely on public transport, the new city's significant commodification has altered this intention.[142] Except for a very few districts built by the Ministry of Housing, most of the land parcels in NAC are bought and developed exclusively by private investors who prefer to cater to the wealthy minority to guarantee high profit margins. Accordingly, residential units sold in NAC are built inside gated compounds, making the city not friendly to pedestrians or those using other transport methods such as bicycles and kick scooters. Also, due to a growing culture connecting private cars with the upper social classes, public transport in Cairo has become associated with the poor.[143] Hence the commodification of the new capital has given planners carte blanche to design a whole city where private vehicles are the primary method of transport. Even though mega-projects such as the monorail and light-speed trains are planned to connect Cairo to NAC, it is doubtful that they will be efficiently used by the residents of the new city given that residents of gated communities mostly use their cars to move in and out of their compounds. Even the wide avenues and spacious public spaces with minimal shading devices and vegetation suggest that transport in NAC will not differ much from Egypt's previous desert towns that followed Nasr City, such as New Cairo and Sixth of October City.

The main arteries of transport inside NAC are highways. The abundance of gated communities and the scarcity of affordable housing inside the city suggest that it might end up exactly like New Cairo, a city with an inconsistent urban fabric whose scattered gated compounds cater only for the rich, who can afford to commute using private cars. As a result, doubts about NAC taking over the administrative role of Cairo as Egypt's capital have been growing along with the commodification of the city. This has made several important diplomatic missions hesitant to relocate to NAC. According to one diplomat, «logic says that [diplomatic missions] relocation would make sense only after relocating the government and not before.»[144]

NAC's architectural and urban designs have also been criticised by professionals in the field. Urban planning and design consultant Mirette Khorshed and others explain how NAC is an output of the work of designers and architects who tend to serve an audience irrelevant to most Egyptians. They do so by importing «Western trends and ideals into their work to fit the general perceived idea of modernity (…). [For example,] many design elements have been transplanted without accounting for drastically different environmental conditions».[145] Chilean architect and Pritzker laureate Alejandro Aravena criticised the architecture of NAC at a conference in Cairo in 2019, noting that NAC's «designers [are] drowned in a sea of imagined nostalgia».[146]

Despite these criticisms, the Egyptian government seems committed to not halting or adjusting the proposed construction work in NAC, whatever the consequences. No official response has been given to technical criticism directed towards it. Despite Egypt's economic struggles due to the COVID-19 pandemic, the Russian invasion of Ukraine in 2022,[147] and the war on its eastern border in Gaza, work in NAC has been going nonstop.[148] It has been claimed that NAC is economically self-sustaining and hence there is no need to halt the ongoing work, especially since it is primarily publicised as the symbol of the «New Republic». Ahmed al-Tahry, former editor-in-chief of state-owned magazine *Rose AlYoussef*, declares that NAC will host Egypt's digital database in secure servers located 14 m underground. He explains, «NAC represents Egypt's new institutional phase of long vision planning unlike Nasser's ‹first republic› which took its decisions according to instantaneous reactions.»[149] Accordingly, Egypt's new capital is considered by officials to

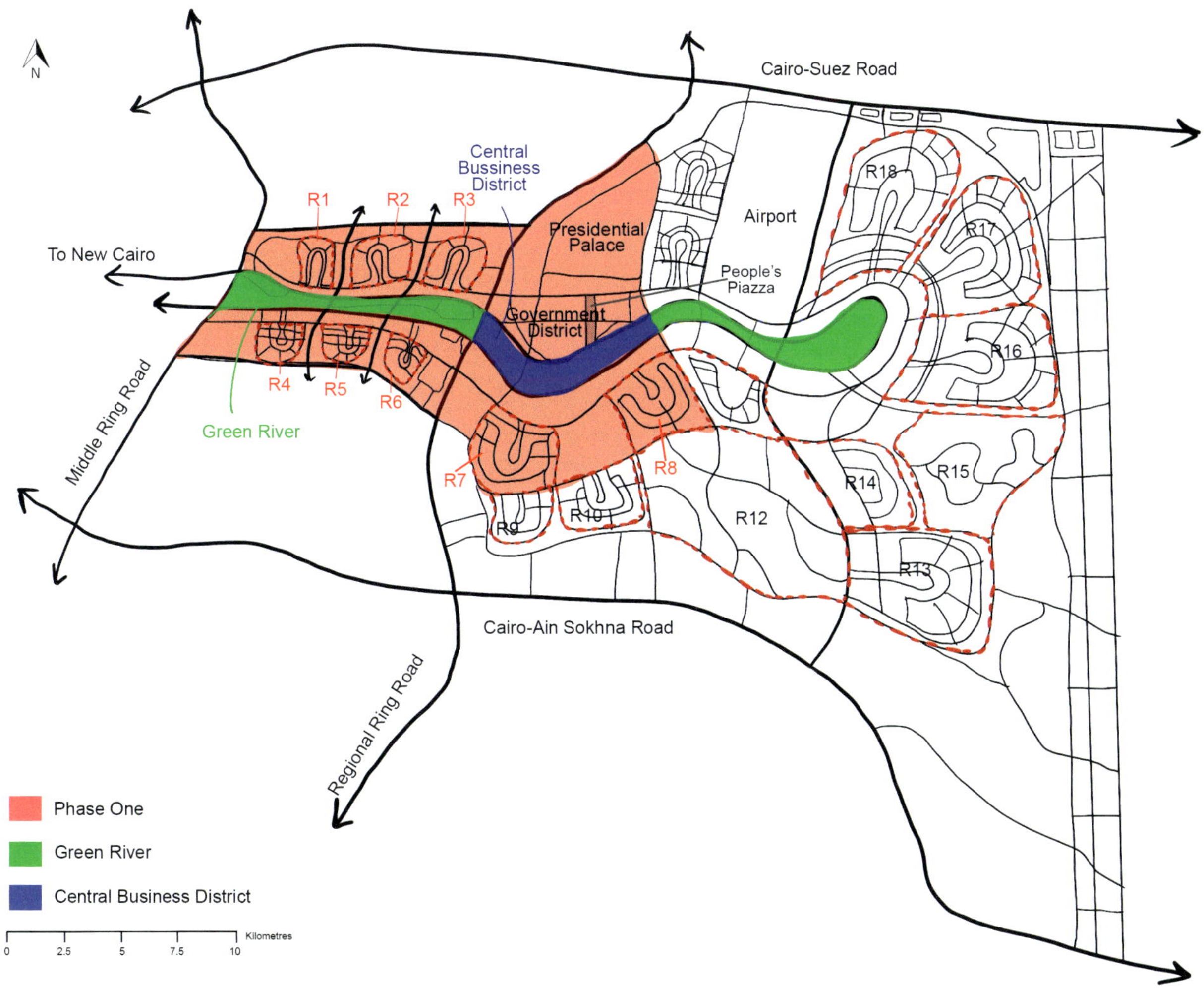

19 NAC's master plan.

be something that goes beyond the technical criticism of architects and urbanists.

Only the first phase of NAC is under construction today. This phase has eight residential districts named in English, from R1 to R8, located in the northern and southern parts, between the city's main gate on the western side and the eastern one (fig. 19). In the centre, a business district is being constructed midway into a stream-like park known as the green river, which also starts from the western periphery of the city going all the way towards the eastern end of the first phase. The green river is publicised as the city's main attraction, and the land value of plots increases as they are closer to the green river. Following the trend of comparing the new city against a backdrop of highly modern international metropolises, the green river is publicised in Egyptian state-owned media as «six times the size of Central Park and three times the size of Hyde Park».[150] In the northeastern corner of the first phase, a presidential palace of around 300 feddans is being constructed along with a governmental district that hosts the headquarters of the relocated ministries and the new building of the parliament. A large piazza separates the presidential palace from the ministerial buildings. Unlike the green river, the piazza looks to be used more as an official space for military parades than as a public space for the public's use.

Wide avenues that seem more like highways divide the city's first phase into isolated parcels of substantial size, dividing most residential and commercial districts from one another. Hence, the components of the city's first phase seem to suffer from detachment on the macro-scale by those highways and on the micro-scale by the existence of gated communities. Those wide avenues are planned to be extended into the subsequent phases of the new city. The next stages of NAC have not been widely discussed despite the publication of several maps that show the master plan of the entire city. The published master plan shows that NAC will have its own airport, a new mega-mall, and five more residential districts (see fig. 19).

NAC is currently surrounded by desert in all directions. However, that is set to change soon. The western side includes areas of New Cairo that are still under construction, while the northern side features another developing city, Mostakbal City, a fully gated community that, once completed, will connect the urban fabric of the new capital to Madinaty, another gated city (see fig. 1). To the south of NAC, a large gated complex of ten buildings will become the headquarters of the Egyptian Ministry of Defence. The complex is known as the military entity, al-Kayan al-ʿAskari. Each of the ten buildings is octagonal, and the whole complex is known as the Octagon, following the concept of the American Pentagon building. The surrounding area is to host other military buildings as well.

Overall, NAC is an example of Egypt's new dream of a new capital city. This city is highly inspired by Dubai's urban boom, which happened around two decades ago. Despite some specialists' protests, NAC continues to follow Dubai's trend of constructing «the biggest», «the longest», and «the widest» of everything. The logic behind those hopes is that it will work in Egypt just as it has in Dubai. Although an entirely new city, NAC has officially been declared part of Cairo.[151] There is potential for the new city to work as a new capital once the government relocates the ministries along with the governmental offices that currently jam Cairo proper. However, the idea of the new city fulfilling the promised dream of being a «city for everyone» is still in question. Despite offering residential units at relatively unaffordable prices, the government is keen on providing citizens with mortgage initiatives, which might make units slightly more affordable. However, there seems to be no clear intention for the non-wealthy to move into the capital under construction, at least for the time being.

Conclusion

There are common attributes when urbanising new plots in Cairo throughout Egypt's modern history. In the cases discussed above, each ruler chooses a new non-urbanised land area on which to build their new city from scratch. Most rulers have claimed a disproportionate amount of urban share to complete their own cities while the older parts of Cairo get ignored. Even in the case of NAC, which is purposely being built to fix what has gone wrong with Cairo, the announced plan does not mention particular upgrades in the central city, whether in parallel to NAC's construction or even once completed. Also, apart from the initial plan of New Cairo, all other cities have been designed and built to accommodate the wealthy and the elite. Gradually, demographics shift, making previous «royal cities» accommodate classes different from those primarily targeted. This has happened in Shubra, ʿAbbassiyya, Ismailia, Tewfiqiyya, and Nasr City, whereas New Cairo and NAC are still too relatively new to have experienced similar shifts.

Cairo's modern formal map looks like a scattered piece of mosaic where each component has been made with an entirely different logic. The lines upon which Ismailia and Tewfiqiyya have been drawn are altogether different from that of ʿAbbassiyya, which has been designed for exclusive palaces, or Nasr City, which is designed upon the principles of modernist planning, or New Cairo and NAC, whose compounds occupy most of their land parcels. Generally, this has resulted in the total fragmentation of the urban fabric of Cairo, even between parts of the same quarter. This is evident in the cases of ʿAbbassiyya, New Cairo, and NAC, where campuses and compounds form a city whose urban blocks appear oddly juxtaposed.

This chapter has tackled urban memory from two perspectives. On the one hand, the perspective of the majority of Egypt's modern rulers who tend to build new cities to engrave their legacies in history books. Naming cities after themselves explains that alone. Except for Mehmed Ali, Mubarak, and al-Sisi, «royal cities» have usually been called after the name of their founders. On the other hand, the public usually forgets the narrative upon which each city has been purposely constructed. Nasr City, for example, is only known today as a bustling district in East Cairo. The average person does not recall the story of how Nasser tried to build «the city of the revolution». Similarly, stories of how the other royal cities were built are also forgotten. This can explain why the literature has not widely tackled the phenomenon of Cairo's modern capital cities, notwithstanding its recurrence.

Overall, despite tackling the past of older quarters of the city of Cairo, this chapter has attempted to reflect on Cairo's future by presenting questions related to NAC. Given the repeated habit of building royal capitals, how would NAC differ from these previous ventures? Based on history, the only time a city became a functioning capital was when the core governance body was moved to it. This happened in Wist al-Balad, particularly in the blocks of Ismailia and Tewfiqiyya. Hence, if al-Sisi fulfils his promise to relocate the machinery of government to NAC, the output would likely be different from all previous desert towns. But NAC's main challenge remains in becoming a «city for everyone». If NAC continues to cater only to the privileged, it will eventually attract peripheral informal settlements. Otherwise, a major demographic shift is inevitable. As discussed, wealthy people usually move out of «royal cities» once they find a place that provides extra exclusivity. In my opinion, the million-dollar question is whether the current government will reconsider making NAC an inclusive city for everyone and disregard the idea of creating a «Dubai in the Capital». Or else, the story will most likely repeat itself, and we will one day witness the launch of another new capital promising to be devoid of the «diseases» of NAC.

1 Extra News 2015b.
2 Extra News 2021.
3 Egyptian Ministry of Housing 2019.
4 Sims 2018, xxxvi; Fahmy 2015.
5 Sims 2018, xxvi.
6 Abu-Lughod 1971, 90.
7 As in opposite to the «informal» or «ashwaʾi» as Egyptians call the parts of the city that have developed without formal planning.
8 St. John 1834, 140.
9 Al-Jabarti et al. 1994, 1.
10 For a full description of Cairo by the time of the French occupation, see Jomard 1809, 580.
11 His negative views on Egyptians are documented in his letters translated by Khaled Fahmy, see Fahmy 1997, 282.
12 Mehmed Ali's views can be documented through his own administrative letters. For example, in a letter, translated by Amin Sami Pasha, Ali declared that Egypt is much richer than other developed countries «since its agricultural land is cultivated twice and has the potential to be cultivated four times a year». See Sami 1928, 525–526.
13 Fahmy 1997, 284.
14 Mehmed Ali's family is formally known as the al-ʿAlawiyya family which should not be confused with the ruling ʿAlawi dynasty of Morocco, to which it has no relation.
15 Rochfort Scott 1837, 113.

16 Fahmy 1997, 79.
17 Fahmy 1997, 84.
18 Faraj 1946, 522.
19 Abolnaga 2020, 46.
20 Al-Asad 1990.
21 In the summer of 2023 ʿArab al-Yasar was completely eradicated, and its community was displaced to various locations around Cairo. The existing buildings were replaced by a theme park which includes bazaars, parking areas, fountains, and «decorative shapes». For the proposed plan, see Al-Khalafawy 2023.
22 Engel 2017, 204.
23 In 1805 after Mehmed Ali ousted the French from Egypt, he was given the title of *vali*, the Sultan's viceroy, while retaining the honorary rank of Pasha. Ali's successors from Ibrahim to Ismail inherited the title of Pasha until the Ottoman Sultan officially recognised Ismail as Khedive in 1867.
24 St. John 1834, 102.
25 Abu-Lughod 1971, 90.
26 Legh 1817, 35.
27 Light 1818, 22–23.
28 James 1968, 134.
29 Forbin 1820.
30 See footnote 25 in Abu-Lughod 1971, 91.
31 Abu-Lughod 1971, 91.
32 «*Wāli*» or «*vali*» was the administrative title given to designate governors of Ottoman provinces.
33 Bréhier 1901, 149.
34 Fahmy 1997, 99–103.
35 Sami 1936, 9.
36 Bréhier 1901, 150.
37 Fahmy 1997, 85.
38 Sami 1936, 22.
39 The *al-maḥmal* parade was a yearly celebration where the Egyptian government manufactured a new cover for Kaʿba and deliver it from Cairo to Mecca. It had been an annual tradition held in Egypt since the 13th century. See Saleh 2016.
40 De Lesseps 1887, 222.
41 An official letter, dated 1848, reveals that the barracks by then had already been built for a long time but not yet been roofed. This situation reflects how eager Abbas I was to move to his new city as soon as he was appointed as *vali*. See Sami 1936, 29.
42 Sami 1936, 21–22.
43 Mubarak 1886, 82; Sami 1936, 26.
44 Abu-Lughod 1971, 100.
45 Faraj 1946, 527.
46 Wilkinson 1867, 151.
47 CAPMAS 2018.
48 Abu-Lughod 1971, 133.
49 Al-Jaridda al-Rasmiyya 1955.
50 Herzog et al. 2010, 120.
51 Herzog et al. 2010, 102–105.
52 Raymond 2000, 312.
53 Although this descriptive expression is highly debated in the literature, it is usually used to describe the Ismailia quarter in Cairo, referring to Ismail's wish to build a city like Paris in Cairo after his visit to the Paris Expo in 1867. See Myntti 2014 and Elshahed 2011.
54 Abu-Lughod 1971, 103.
55 Abu-Lughod 1971, 103.
56 This appeared clearly in Ismail's comparative narrative that connected Cairo to other European cities.
57 Raymond 2000.
58 Abu-Lughod 1971, 105.
59 Abu-Lughod 1971, 109.
60 Mubarak 1886, 53.
61 Barham 1871, 405.
62 Mubarak 1886, 83.
63 Mestyan 2017
64 Abu-Lughod 1971, 107.
65 Abu-Lughod 1971, 107.
66 French architect Arthur Rhoné compares Mubarak's plan to modernise Cairo to «the eruption of an American city within the heart of a virgin forest». See Rhoné 1882, 1, translation by the author.
67 Abu-Lughod 1971, 110.
68 Elshahed 2011.
69 Hunter 1998, 195.
70 Daly 1998, 239.
71 Daly 1998, 240.
72 Daly 1998, 240.
73 Lane-Poole 1906, 1.
74 The urban fabrics and most buildings in Ismailia and Tewfiqiyya are protected according to the maps of the National Authority of Urban Harmony, established by presidential decree 37/2001.
75 Hosny 2022.
76 Lane-Poole 1906, 1.
77 Lane-Poole 1906, 1.
78 Abu-Lughod 1971, 138.
79 Willem 2015.
80 Raafat 1996.
81 Raafat 1996.
82 In 1905, it is reported that one Egyptian pound would buy one square metre in a cheap district in Cairo. One feddan equals 4,200 square metres.
83 The *al-infitaḥ* or the open-door policy was an economic system proposed by President Sadat following the 1973 October war, directing Egypt from an inward-geared economy to an export-oriented one that would «reintegrate the country with the world's developed market economies». See Weinbaum 1985.
84 According to a personal interview with several residents of Heliopolis overlooking Mirghani Street in 2020. For an overall report on the situation of safety of pedestrians in Cairo following projects that involve widening roads in residential areas, see Saad 2021.
85 Abu-Lughod 1971, 139.
86 Mansfield 1973, 19.

87 Mansfield 1973, 150–158.
88 Angélil/Malterre-Barthes 2018, 249.
89 Al-Jaridda al-Rasmiyya 1958.
90 Fahmy 2022.
91 Younis 2012.
92 Younis 2012, 380.
93 Quote translated by author. Younis 2012, 160.
94 Younis 2012, 161.
95 Younis 2012, 163.
96 Naguib 2010, 181–182.
97 Chandigarh, Brasilia, Salt Lake City, and other cities were influenced by the ideology of CIAM where new concepts of city planning were introduced, promoting rigid functional cities with residents housed in widely spaced tower blocks.
98 Angélil/Malterre-Barthes 2018, 249.
99 Abu-Lughod 1971, 233.
100 Al-Jaridda al-Rasmiyya 1959, 5.
101 Al-Jaridda al-Rasmiyya 1959, 5.
102 Elwakil 2019.
103 This zone was mainly composed of detached houses, known in Egypt as villas.
104 Shawkat 2020, 129.
105 Abu-Lughod 1971, 236.
106 Evin 1985, 106.
107 See for example Séjourné 2009, 16–19.
108 About one million Egyptian migrants were forced to return home from Iraq and Kuwait due to the Gulf war in 1991. See Zohry 2014, 75–98.
109 Frochaux/Martin 2010.
110 As of April 2023, Madinet Nasr (Nasr City) for Housing & Development Company announced its rebranding to Madinet Masr (Egypt City), in line with the company's strategy to expand nationally throughout Egypt.
111 «Cairo Proper» is the term used by David Sims to refer to the governorates of Cairo, Giza, and Shubra al-Kheima. On fig. 1, roughly including the area within the city's ring road, see Sims 2010, 6–7.
112 Bayoumi 2009, 17.
113 Elshahed 2015, 384.
114 For more information about Sadat City, see El-Shakhs 1994, 239–259.
115 Denis 1996, 7.
116 The term rent-gap was coined by the geographer Neil Smith in 1979 and it refers to the difference between the rent paid for a piece of land or a property at the present time and the potential achievable income under «higher and better» use. The rent-gap theory is central to gentrification, see Smith 1979.
117 Bayoumi 2009.
118 Sutton/Fahmi 2001, 137.
119 Bayoumi 2009, 7.
120 Bayoumi 2009, 1.
121 Sutton/Fahmi 2001, 138.
122 Bayoumi 2009, 9.
123 Tarbush 2012.
124 General Organisation for Physical Planning [2009].
125 Eldin 2011.
126 Formal public transport is available but does not cover the whole city. The transport system has mainly served those who work for the compounds' inhabitants. Networks usually end at the compound gates, where workers usually get picked up by compound owners. Otherwise, those workers would have to walk substantial distances to reach their destinations.
127 Mokhtar 2020.
128 CBC Extra 2015.
129 CBC Extra 2015.
130 Extra News 2015b.
131 Fawzy 2021.
132 Extra News 2015a.
133 Ehab 2018.
134 Ibrahim 2015.
135 Ibrahim 2015.
136 According to the Central Agency for Public Mobilization and Statistics (CAPMAS), the average annual income for a family of four was 44,190 EGP in 2015, equivalent to 5,000 USD at the time.
137 Abdelaty 2015.
138 Presidential executive order 57/2016.
139 Iskan Misr 2021.
140 Hassan 2017.
141 Fawzy 2021.
142 Extra News 2015b.
143 Sims 2018, 237.
144 Salem 2022.
145 Angélil/Malterre-Barthes 2018, 385.
146 Personal conversation with Alejandro Aravena during the Lafarge Holcim Conference at the American University in Cairo (4 April 2019).
147 Ukraine and Russia had been the main contributors to the tourism sector in Egypt. Also, Egypt relied heavily on importing strategic commodities, such as wheat, from both countries. This has largely affected foreign investment in Egypt and depleted its USD foreign reserves. For a detailed report, see IMF 2023.
148 Al-Sharq al-Awsat 2022a.
149 Al-Tahry 2021.
150 Ten TV 2021.
151 Youm7 2022.

Abdelaty 2015
محمد عبد العاطي: الإسكان: الدولة تنفذ العاصمة الإدارية إذا فشلت المفاوضات مع العبار. المصري اليوم.
M. Abdelaty: Housing: The State Will Implement the Administrative Capital If Negotiations with Alabbar Fail. Al-Masry Al-Yawm, 15 March 2015, https://gate.ahram.org.eg/daily/News/368605.aspx (30 July 2022).

Abolnaga 2020
O. Abolnaga: Influence of Post-Renaissance Ideology on Egyptian Post-Traditional Architecture: A Case Study of Cairene Islamic Religious Buildings. Unpublished MSc. Thesis, Cairo University (Cairo 2020).

Abu-Lughod 1971
J. Abu-Lughod: Cairo: 1001 Years of the City Victorious (Princeton 1971).

Al-Asad 1990
M. al-Asad: The Modern State Mosque in the Eastern Arab World. Unpublished PhD thesis, Harvard University (Cambridge MA 1990).

Al-Jabarti et al. 1994
A. al-Jabarti et al. (eds.): The History of Egypt, vol. 3 (Stuttgart 1994).

Al-Jaridda al-Rasmiyya 1955
تخويل وزير التربية والتعليم سلطة الاستيلاء على العقارات اللازمة للوزارة ومعاهد التعليم.
Authorising the Minister of Education to Seize the Properties Necessary for the Ministry and Educational Institutes. Al-Jaridda al-Rasmiyya, 30 October 1955, https://manshurat.org/node/41868 (3 February 2025).

Al-Jaridda al-Rasmiyya 1958
تعيين عبد الحكيم عامر قائدا عاما للقوات المسلحة. الجريدة الرسمية.
Abdel Hakim Amer appointed as Commander-in-Chief of the Armed Forces. Al-Jaridda al-Rasmiyya, 20 March 1958, https://manshurat.org/node/61881 (30 January 2025).

Al-Jaridda al-Rasmiyya 1959
أنشاء مؤسسة عامة لمدينة نصر بالعباسية بالقاهرة. الجريدة الرسمية.
Establishing a Public Institution for Nasr City in Abbassiya, Cairo. Al-Jaridda al-Rasmiyya, 21 May 1959, 5–6, https://manshurat.org/node/61377 (30 January 2025).

Al-Khalafawy 2023
ننشر مخطط تطوير منطقة عرب اليسار بمحيط القلعة بالسيدة عائشة. اليوم السابع.
S. al-Khalafawy: We Publish the Development Plan for ʿArab al-Yasar in the vicinity of the Citadel in al-Sayyida Aisha. Youm7, 4 November 2023, https://www.youm7.com/6361816 (5 November 2023).

Al-Sharq al-Awsat 2022
السيسي متمسك ببناء العاصمة الإدارية رغم الصعوبات و الانتقادات. الشرق الاوسط.
Al-Sisi Sticks to Building the New Administrative Capital Despite the Difficulties and Criticisms. 6 July 2022, https://aawsat.com/node/3743991 (6 August 2022).

Al-Tahry 2021
احمد الطاهري: الطريق الى الجمهورية الثانية: سيرة وطن.
A. al-Tahry: The Road to The Second Republic: Biography of a Homeland (Cairo 2021).

Angélil / Malterre-Barthes 2018
M. Angélil / A. C. Malterre-Barthes (eds.): Cairo Desert Cities (Berlin 2018).

Barham 1871
F. Barham: Egypt of the Pharaohs and the Khedive (London 1871).

Bayoumi 2009
W. Bayoumi: The Tale of the Unsettled New Cairo City-Egypt: A Review for the Implications of the Adopted Privatization and Laissez- Fair Policies on Excluding the Poor from Its Housing Market, in: The Annual Conference of Regional Studies Association, Leuven, 4 April 2009 (Leuven 2009) 1–17.

Bréhier 1901
L. Bréhier: L'Egypte de 1978 a 1900 (Paris 1901).

CAPMAS 2018
تقدير عدد السكان المصريين في الأقسام والمراكز وفقا للنوع ومحل الاقامة في ٢٠١٨\٧\١. جهاز التعبئة العامة والاحصاء.
Estimated Number of Egyptian Population in Boroughs and Centres According to Gender and Place of Residence on 1/7/2018. [2018], https://www.capmas.gov.eg/Admin/Pages%20Files/20181017124714shika1-2018.pdf (28 January 2025).

Daly 1998
M. W. Daly: The Cambridge History of Egypt, vol. 2 (Cambridge; New York 1998).

De Lesseps 1887
F. De Lesseps / C. B. Pitman (trans.): Recollections of Forty Years, vol. 1 (London 1887).

Denis 1996
E. Denis: Urban Planning and Growth in Cairo. Middle East Report, no. 202, 1996, 7–12.

CBC Extra 2015
د. مصطفى مدبولي وزير الاسكان يستعرض مشروع العاصمة الادارية الجديدة لمصر. سي بي سي اكسترا.
Dr. Mostafa Madbouli, Minister of Housing, Reviews the Project of the New Administrative Capital of Egypt. CBC Extra, [2015], https://www.youtube.com/watch?v=RuKzR2ieqlw (30 July 2022).

Egyptian Ministry of Housing 2019
العاصمة الإدارية الجديدة شهر يوليو ٢٠١٩. وزارة الإسكان.
Egyptian Ministry of Housing: The New Administrative Capital in July 2019. 29 July 2019, https://www.youtube.com/watch?v=jJLQ-kDnf2w (18 February 2023).

Ehab 2018
فادية إيهاب: بعد ٣ سنوات على افتتاحها.. قناة السويس الجديدة في أحاديث السيسي. الوطن.
F. Ehab: 3 Years after Its Inauguration… The New Suez Canal in Sisi's Speeches. Al-Watan, 6 August 2018, https://www.elwatannews.com/news/details/3575351 (2 August 2022).

Eldin 2011
هبة حسام الدين: «التخطيط العمراني»: مخطط القاهرة ٢٠٥٠ سيضع حدًا لكافة مشاكل العاصمة. اليوم السابع.
H. H. Eldin: Physical Planning: Cairo 2050 Will Put an End to All the Capital's Problems. Youm7, 4 January 2011, https://www.youm7.com/342604 (12 April 2023).

Elshahed 2011
M. Elshahed: Paris was Never along the Nile. Cairobserver, 14 December 2011, https://cairobserver.com/post/14185184147/paris-was-never-along-the-nile (14 August 2022).

Elshahed 2015
M. Elshahed: Revolutionary Modernism? Architecture and the Politics of Transition in Egypt 1936–1967. Unpublished PhD thesis, New York University (New York 2015).

El-Shakhs 1994
S. El-Shakhs: Sadat City, Egypt and the Role of New Town Planning in the Developing World. Journal of Architectural and Planning Research 11, no. 3, 1994, 239–159.

Elwakil 2019
M. Elwakil: Modernist Indignation: Two Architects on the Forgotten Legacy of Sayed Karim. Mada Masr, 16 February 2019, https://www.madamasr.com/en/2019/02/16/feature/culture/modernist-indignation-two-architects-on-the-forgotten-legacy-of-sayed-karim (20 June 2022).

Engel 2017
M. N. Engel: Ottoman Egypt in the Mid-Eighteenth Century: Local Interest Groups and Their Connection with and Rebellions against the Sublime Porte and Resistance to State Authority. Unpublished PhD thesis, University of Birmingham (Birmingham 2017).

Evin 1985
A. Evin: Cairo: 1800–2000 Planning for the Capital City in the Context of Egypt's History and Development, in: A. Evin (ed.): The Expanding Metropolis: Coping with the Urban Growth of Cairo (Singapore 1985) 91–120.

Extra News 2015a
فيلم وثائقي يستعرض مشروع العاصمة الادارية الجديدة لمصر. اكسترا نيوز.
A Documentary Film Showing the Project of the New Administrative Capital of Egypt. Extra News, [2015], https://www.youtube.com/watch?v=87q8VuaN10Y (8 August 2022).

Extra News 2015b
وزير الإسكان: مشروع العاصمة الإدارية الجديدة سيكون من اكبر المشاريع. اكسترا نيوز.
Minister of Housing: The New Administrative Capital Project Will Be One of the Largest Projects. Extra News, 14 March 2015, https://www.dailymotion.com/video/x5s9uln (30 May 2022).

Extra News 2021
السيسي: افتتاح العاصمة الإدارية الجديدة يساوي إعلان جمهورية تانية. اكسترا نيوز.
Al-Sisi: The Inauguration of the New Administrative Capital Equals the Declaration of a Second Republic. Extra News, 9 March 2021, https://www.youtube.com/watch?v=_dJSoGJM-vF4 (2 June 2022).

Fahmy 1997
K. Fahmy: All the Pasha's Men: Mehmed Ali, His Army and the Making of Modern Egypt (Cairo 1997).

Fahmy 2015
K. Fahmy: Chasing Mirages in the Desert. Cairobserver, 14 March 2015, https://cairobserver.com/post/113543612414/chasing-mirages-in-the-desert (17 November 2021).

Fahmy 2022
خالد فهمي: هزيمة يونيو المستمرة مع د. خالد فهمي – الحلقة ٤ – أثر الصراع بين عبدالناصر وعامر على أداء الجيش. الموقف المصري.
K. Fahmy: June's Continuous Defeat with Dr. Khaled Fahmy – Episode 4 – The Impact of the Conflict Between Abdel Nasser and Amer on the Army's Performance. 3 July 2022, https://www.youtube.com/watch?v=zG_TP3d3FHU (13 January 2023).

Faraj 1946
فؤاد فرج: القاهرة. الجزء الثالث.
F. Faraj: Cairo. Vol. 3 (Cairo 1946).

Fawzy 2021
R. M. Fawzy: Commodification of the Egyptian New Capital: A Semio-Foucauldian Landscape Analysis. Space and Culture, 26, no. 4, November 2023 [online 9 February 2021], https://doi.org/10.1177/1206331221991323.

Forbin 1820
L. N. P. A. de Forbin: Travels in Egypt, Being a Continuation of the Travels in the Holy Land, in 1817–18 (London 1820).

Frouchaux / Martin 2010
M. Frochaux / A. Martin: Nasr City, The Middle East Studio (Basel 2010).

General Organisation for Physical Planning [2009]
General Organisation for Physical Planning: Vision of Cairo 2050: Within a National Vision of Egypt. Cairo From Below, [2009], https://cairofrombelow.files.wordpress.com/2011/08/cairo-2050-vision-v-2009-gopp-12-mb.pdf (12 April 2023).

Hassan 2017
احمد حسن: بعد انسحاب الشركة الصينية من العاصمة الإدارية.. رئيس الاتحاد المصرى لمقاولى التشييد: شركات المقاولات المصرية قادرة على تنفيذ المشروع. اليوم السابع.
A. Hassan: After the Withdrawal of the Chinese Company from the Administrative Capital… The President of the Egyptian Federation of Construction Contractors: Egyptian Contracting Companies Can Implement the Project. Youm7, 12 February 2017, https://www.youm7.com/3097914 (3 August 2022).

Herzog et al. 2010
J. Herzog et al.: Abbasiya: A Forgotten Neighborhood. The Middle East Studio (Basel 2010), https://archive.arch.ethz.ch/studio-basel/assets/files/files/06_Abbasiya_web.pdf (28 January 2025).

Hosny 2022
H. Hosny: Egypt to Turn Ancient Government Building into Hotel. Al-Monitor, June 2022, https://www.al-monitor.com/originals/2022/06/egypt-turn-ancient-government-building-hotel (13 January 2023).

Hunter 1998
F. R. Hunter: Egypt under the Successors of Muhammad ʿAli, in: M. W. Daly (ed.): The Cambridge History of Egypt (Cambridge 1998) 180–197.

Ibrahim 2015
عزت إبراهيم: محمد العبار يتحدث الى الاهرام بعد التوقيع على مشروع العاصمة الجديدة: التخطيط لكايرو كابيتال استغرق ٤ شهور.. وسنبدأ العمل فورًا. الاهرام.
E. Ibrahim: Mohamed Alabbar Speaks to al-Ahram after Signing the New Capital Project: Planning for Cairo Capital Took 4 Months… And We Will Start Work Immediately. Al-Ahram, 15 March 2015, https://gate.ahram.org.eg/daily/News/368605.aspx (2 August 2022).

Illbert 1985
R. Illbert: Heliopolis: Colonial Enterprise and Town Planning Success, in: A. Evin (ed.): The Expanding Metropolis: Coping with the Urban Growth of Cairo (Singapore 1985) 36–42.

International Monetary Fund 2023
Arab Republic of Egypt: Request for Extended Arrangement Under the Extended Fund Facility-Press Release; and Staff Report. International Monetary Fund, 10 January 2023, https://www.elibrary.imf.org/view/journals/002/2023/002/article-A000-en.xml (28 January 2025).

Iskan Misr 2021
رئيس شركة العاصمة الإدارية يكشف أسباب استبعاد اعمار من تنفيذ المشروع.
The Head of the Administrative Capital Company Reveals the Reasons for Excluding Emaar from Implementing the Project. Iskan Misr, 16 February 2021, https://www.iskanmisr.com/55583 (3 August 2022).

James 1968
H. D. James: An Introduction to the History of Education in Modern Egypt (London 1968).

Jomard 1809
E. F. Jomard (ed.): Description Abrégée de La Ville et de La Citadelle Du Kaire, vol. 7, État Moderne II (Paris 1809).

Lane-Poole 1906
S. Lane-Poole: The Story of Cairo (London 1906).

Legh 1817
T. Legh: Narrative of a Journey in Egypt and the Country Beyond the Cataracts (Philadelphia 1817).

Light 1818
H. Light: Travels in Egypt, Nubia, Holy Land, Mount Libanon, and Cyprus, in the Year 1814 (London 1818).

Mansfield 1973
P. Mansfield: Nasser and Nasserism. International Journal 28, no. 4, 1973, 670–688.

Mestyan 2017
A. Mestyan: Arab Patriotism: The Ideology and Culture of Power in Late Ottoman Egypt (Princeton 2017).

Mokhtar 2020
هند مختار: الحكومة: انتقال ١١٩ جهة و٣١ وزارة للعاصمة الإدارية الجديدة. اليوم السابع.
H. Mokhtar: The Government: 119 Entities and 31 Ministries move to the New Administrative Capital. Youm7, 29 November 2020, https://www.youm7.com/5091087 (30 July 2022).

Mubarak 1886
علي مبارك: الخطط التوفيقية الجديدة لمصر القاهرة ومدنها وبلادها القديمة والشهيرة.
A. Mubarak: The New Tewfiq Plans for Egypt, Cairo, and its Ancient and Famous Cities and Country, vol. 1 (Bulaq 1886).

Myntti 2014
C. Myntti: Paris Along the Nile (Cairo 2014).

Naguib 2010
محمد نجيب: كلمتي للتاريخ.
M. Naguib: My Word for History (Cairo 2010).

Raafat 1996
S. Raafat: When Maadi Very Nearly Replaced Heliopolis. Egyptian Mail (Cairo 1996).

Raymond 2000
A. Raymond: Cairo (Cambridge MA 2000).

Rhoné 1882
A. Rhoné: Coup d'Oeil sur l'État Du Caire: Ancien et Modern (Paris 1882).

Rochfort Scott 1837
C. Rochfort Scott: Rambles in Egypt and Candia with Details of the Military Power and Resources of Those Countries, and Observations on the Government, Policy, and Commercial System of Mohammed Ali, vol. 2 (London 1837).

Saad 2021
اسلام سعد: هل تجاهلت الحكومة المصرية حق المشاه في مشروعاتها لتطوير الطرق؟ بي بي سي عربي نيوز.
I. Saad: Has the Egyptian Government Ignored the Right of Pedestrians in its Road Development Projects?. BBC Arabic News, 8 November 2021, https://www.bbc.com/arabic/middleeast-59178371 (1 January 2023).

Saleh 2016
F. Saleh: Egypt 100 Years Ago: The Ceremony of the Holy Carpet (Mahmal). Ahram Online, 16 July 2016, https://english.ahram.org.eg/News/232771.aspx (12 January 2023).

Salem 2022
عايدة سالم: سفارات تتبنى «انتقالًا بطيئا وجزئيًا» للعاصمة الإدارية الجديدة. مدى مصر.
A. Salem: Embassies Adopt a «Slow and Partial Move» to the New Administrative Capital. Mada Masr, 3 April 2022, https://www.madamasr.com/2022/04/03/feature/ةسايس/تارافس-ىنبتت-الًاقتنا-ائيّطب-يّئزجو/ (24 January 2025).

Sami 1928
امين سامي: تقويم النيل. الجزء الثاني.
A. Sami: The Nile Calendar, vol. 2 (Cairo 1928).

Sami 1936
امين سامي: تقويم النيل. الجزء الثالث.
A. Sami: The Nile Calendar, vol. 3 (Cairo 1936).

Séjourné 2009
M. Séjourné: The History of Informal Settlements, in: R. Kipper / M. Fischer (eds.): Cairo's Informal Areas: Between Urban Challenges and Hidden Potentials (Cairo 2009) 16–19.

Shawkat 2020
Y. Shawkat: Egypt's Housing Crisis: The Shaping of Urban Space (Cairo 2020).

Sims 2010
D. Sims: Understanding Cairo: The Logic of a City out of Control (Cairo 2010)

Sims 2018
D. Sims: Egypt's Desert Dreams: Development or Disaster? New Edition (Cairo 2018).

Smith 1979
N. Smith: Toward a Theory of Gentrification: A Back to the City Movement by Capital, not People. Journal of the American Planning Association 45, no. 4, 1979, 538–548.

St. John 1834
J. A. St. John: Egypt and Mohammad Ali: Or, Travels in the Valley of the Nile, vol. 1 (London 1834).

Sutton / Fahmi 2001
K. Sutton / W. Fahmi: Cairo's Urban Growth and Strategic Master Plans in the Light of Egypt's 1996 Population Census Results. Cities 18, no. 2, 2001, 135–149.

Tarbush 2012
N. Tarbush: Cairo 2050: Urban Dream or Modernist Delusion? Journal of International Affairs 65, no. 2, 2012, 171–186.

Ten TV 2021
اكبر حديقة في العالم... اول تصوير جوي للنهر الأخضر بالعاصمة الإدارية الجديدة. قناة تن.
The Largest Garden in the World... The First Aerial Photography of the Green River in the New Administrative Capital. Ten TV, 18 October 2021, https://www.youtube.com/watch?v=cO8tKuMvXUA (8 August 2022).

Weinbaum 1985
M.G. Weinbaum: Egypt's Infitah and the Politics of US Economic Assistance. Middle Eastern Studies 21, no. 2, 1985, 206–222.

Wilkinson 1867
J.G. Wilkinson: A Handbook for Travellers in Egypt (London 1867).

Willem 2015
T. Willem: A Colonial Enterprise That Became an Urban Success, 2015, https://www.academia.edu/16229519/HELIOPOLIS_a_colonial_enterprise_that_became_an_urban_success (26 December 2022).

Youm7 2022
ضم العاصمة الإدارية لحدود القاهرة. اليوم السابع.
Including the Administrative Capital to the Boundaries of Cairo. Youm7, 8 June 2022, https://www.youm7.com/5793644 (8 August 2022).

Younis 2012
شريف يونس: نداء الشعب: تاريخ نقدي للايديولوجية الناصرية.
S. Younis: The People's Appeal: A Critical History of Nasserite Ideology (Cairo 2012).

Zohry 2014
A. Zohry: Migration and Development in Egypt, in W. Sievers et al. (ed.): Migration from the Middle East and North Africa to Europe (Amsterdam 2014) 75–98.

Image Sources

1–9, 11, 13, 15–19 Maps by Omar Abolnaga.
10 Illustration by Omar Abolnaga after Illbert 1985, 37.
12 Satellite imagery from Google Earth 2009 and 2022.
14 Left: Satellite imagery from Center for Advanced Spatial Technologies, University of Arkansas / U.S. Geological Survey. Right: Satellite imagery from Google Earth 2023.

Tracing the Omitted Physical Transformations
Re-Narrating the Urban Development of Alexandria between the Mid-19th and Early 20th Centuries

Mirhan Damir

During the 19th and 20th centuries, Mediterranean port cities underwent considerable change, triggered by the industrial and commercial demands of European powers.[1] The port city of Alexandria in Egypt embodies rich and diverse layers of history, which can be (re)viewed differently as «heyday» and «setbacks». Commercial and industrial developments since the early 19th century contributed to reinstating the city's commercial role, both nationally and globally, as well as giving rise to urban transformation. According to Faruk Tabak, a specialist in economies and historical systems, Alexandria was a «a pale shadow of its former self», experiencing centuries of commercial, economic, and urban neglect around the second half of the 18th century. This evaluation is predominantly based on the level of commercial, economic, and industrial interchange with European countries at that time.[2]

However, the Middle East historian Michael Reimer argues that the city's commercial status, with its port and its Mediterranean and inter-Ottoman trade activities, was not eclipsed during this period.[3] In fact, André Raymond, an urban historian who focuses on the MENA region, showed in numbers that Alexandria's trade with Europe at the end of the 18th century constituted only 2.5% of its total trade. Thus he pointed out that evaluating the city's prosperity through the lens of its trade with Europe is misleading, as its maritime commerce was mostly with the Ottoman world and Morocco.[4] Nevertheless, most scholars agree that the first half of the 19th century witnessed Egypt's first steps towards modern development under the rule of Mohammed 'Ali (r. 1805–1848).[5]

The 19th century saw radical political transformations in Egypt influenced by the Ottoman Porte, the Mohammed 'Ali dynasty, and the British Empire. The year 1801 witnessed the end of the brief French conquest of Egypt (1798–1801) that – together with the Mamluk menace – interrupted the Ottoman hold over Egypt. The evacuation of French troops from Egypt was realised with the help of British troops.[6] Nevertheless, France continued to assist the Mamluks, who were a constant threat to Ottoman control in Egypt. In 1805, after rising in political power, Muhammad 'Ali was named as viceroy [*Wālī*] of Egypt. He succeeded in reinstating Ottoman sovereignty over Egypt by putting an end to the Mamluk political presence in Egypt in 1811.[7] This was part of his plan to gain trust from the Ottoman Sultan and hence consolidate political power in Egypt for himself and his descendants. Muhammad 'Ali's ambitions involved gradually making Egypt independent of the Ottoman Porte by redirecting Egypt's economic ties towards Europe and away from the provinces of the Ottoman Empire.[8]

The vision of a more European Egypt involved radical transformation of the country's internal administration by creating a military force, new commercial and industrial systems, and new urban planning models.[9] These changes were implemented via 'Ali's so-called «system of personal government»,[10] where all these systems and models in Egypt were placed under his personal control.[11] The Ottoman sultan and the British observed the rising threat from 'Ali's nascent military power and the fact that all of Egypt's commercial and industrial operations were transformed to run through him. Consequently, they forced 'Ali to abolish his monopoly system. After 'Ali's acceptance, the Ottoman Sultan 'Abd al-Majid granted Mohamed 'Ali, and his male descendants, heredity domain to Egypt.[12] According to Middle East historian F. Robert Hunter, the second half of the 19th century witnessed «the build-up of the dynasty state (Mohamed 'Ali)» and a growing material investment in Egypt facilitated through loans by European nations, especially France and Britain.[13] Thus, Mohamed 'Ali's rule can be seen as having two major consequences: the first was 'Ali's new dynasty in Egypt, even though the country was still nominally under the Ottoman Empire, and the second was European capitalist expansion – dominated by British interests and characterised by economic, commercial, and industrial investments.

By the 1870s, the viceroy Ismail Pasha (r. 1863–1879), the grandson of Mohammed 'Ali, could not meet the country's increasing debts, and as a consequence Egypt witnessed a «European economic and political penetration leading to the establishment of foreign control» and the disposition of Ismail Pasha. In 1879, 'Ali's developed system of personal government was put to an end and a system of political governance was established in Egypt that Hunter refers to as «a state within a state». Here, the state within a state refers to Egypt being governed by both the viceroy's government headed by Khedive Tewfik Pasha (r. 1879–1892) and an established international body of European bondholders referred to as the *caisse de la dette* (debt fund), controlled by Britain and France.[14]

The following decade witnessed growing anti-foreign sentiments as the country fell under French and, especially, British dominance. The precarious political situation was exacerbated in 1882, when Egypt came under British rule. During the British occupation, Egypt was directed by «a small number of Europeans backed by a British garrison» while remaining an Ottoman province officially ruled by the Mohamed 'Ali dynasty.[15] According to Near and Middle East scholar Martin Daly,

> Britain only ‹advised› the government of the Ottoman province, but its advice had to be followed; Britain's representative operated until 1914 with a lowly title of agent and consul-general, yet in effect ruled the country.[16]

Egypt was granted its nominal independence in 1922.[17]

While Cairo remained Egypt's administrative capital during the 19th century, Mohamed 'Ali realised Alexandria's potential as a commercial and defensive gateway to Egypt, and the nearest city to Europe.[18] Located on the Mediterranean Sea, Alexandria is an example of what architectural and urban historian Vilma Hastaoglou-Martinidis describes as an elevation of «coastal towns into all-important economic centers for their vast hinterlands».[19] Hence, Mohamed 'Ali reassigned the city's ancient role as Egypt's central commercial port city through functions such as hosting the country's European consuls and accommodating Egypt's main naval arsenal.[20]

Consistent with modernising Egypt, the country's first urban planning commission was established in Alexandria in 1834.[21] The so-called Conseil de l'Ornato was an early type of municipal institution mainly managed by a consortium of European merchants and consuls. The Ornato, originally a part of Mohamed 'Ali's health department, managed the urban development projects needed to serve its members' commercial and industrial aspirations. The Ornato had fourteen founding members: a president and a vice-president, six Ottomans, appointed by the viceregal government, and six Europeans, who were «either consuls or consular delegates».[22] The Ornato became a part of the Ministry of Public Works in 1878, where it remained until the establishment of the Alexandrian Municipality in 1890.[23]

The planning body established in Alexandria laid the ground for the city's physical and social growth. Between 1825 and 1840, Alexandria's population grew from 16,000 to 60,000.[24] As a result of the cotton famine during the American

Civil War in the early 1860s, the export of Egyptian cotton surged to become one of the primary sources for European and predominantly British mills. Egypt has since witnessed a cotton boom, becoming one of the leading global producers and exporters of cotton.[25] Contributing to a strategy of expanding exports of Egypt's commodities, Ismail Pasha gave concessions for development schemes for a chain of facilitative services. These included regulating structures on Alexandria's streets to plan a more defined warehouse complex from the 1860s onwards, and the rehabilitation of the port between 1870 and 1880.[26] These developments contributed to population influx from different social strata. Between the 1860s and 1880s, the city's population increased from 170,000 to over 232,000.[27] The increase included both internal and external migrants, enriching the interchange of ideas, skills, and global networking. This influx resulted in a continuous demand for urban development and, in turn, the realisation of commercial and industrial transformation.

The coastal city expanded predominantly along the Mediterranean coastline to the east and west, but also to the south. The literature analysing the city's urban development between the early 19th century and mid-20th century has focused mainly on the eastern and southern spatial interlinkages, while little work has dealt comprehensively with the city's westward expansion.[28] Some publications have offered a modest overview of the western city expansion up until the so-called al-Qabbarī area, while mentioning the western outskirts of ad-Dikhīlah and Burg al-'Arab (fig. 1).[29]

This chapter attempts to shed light on Alexandria's westward industrial development in the so-called al-Max area.[30] Despite al-Max's strategic location between al-Qabbarī and the city outskirts, no research has yet been conducted to analyse and uncover the area's spatial interlinkage as part of Alexandria's urban development.[31] The aim of this chapter is to fill this gap and trace al-Max's industrial transformations in the context of Alexandria's urban development. Mapping these transformations, this chapter will re-narrate the city's urban development between the mid-19th and early 20th centuries by revealing the untold story behind the westward industrial spatial development of al-Max in relation to the rest of Alexandria's eastern and southern expansion.

Following this introduction, the chapter first contextualises Alexandria's main geographic and urban characteristics in the mid-19th century. It then traces the told and untold narratives of the city's development through three sections, each based on an expansion direction: eastwards, southwestwards, and finally westwards in al-Max. This study was conducted mainly using primary data such as historical maps, photographs, and archival documents. Discontinuous archival

1 A 2022 map showing the western districts of Alexandria.

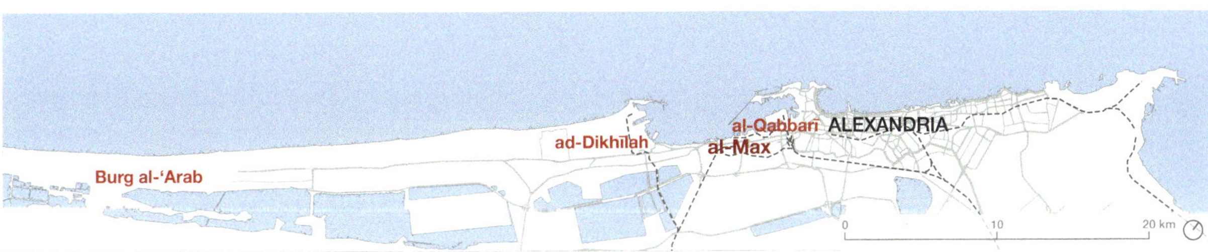

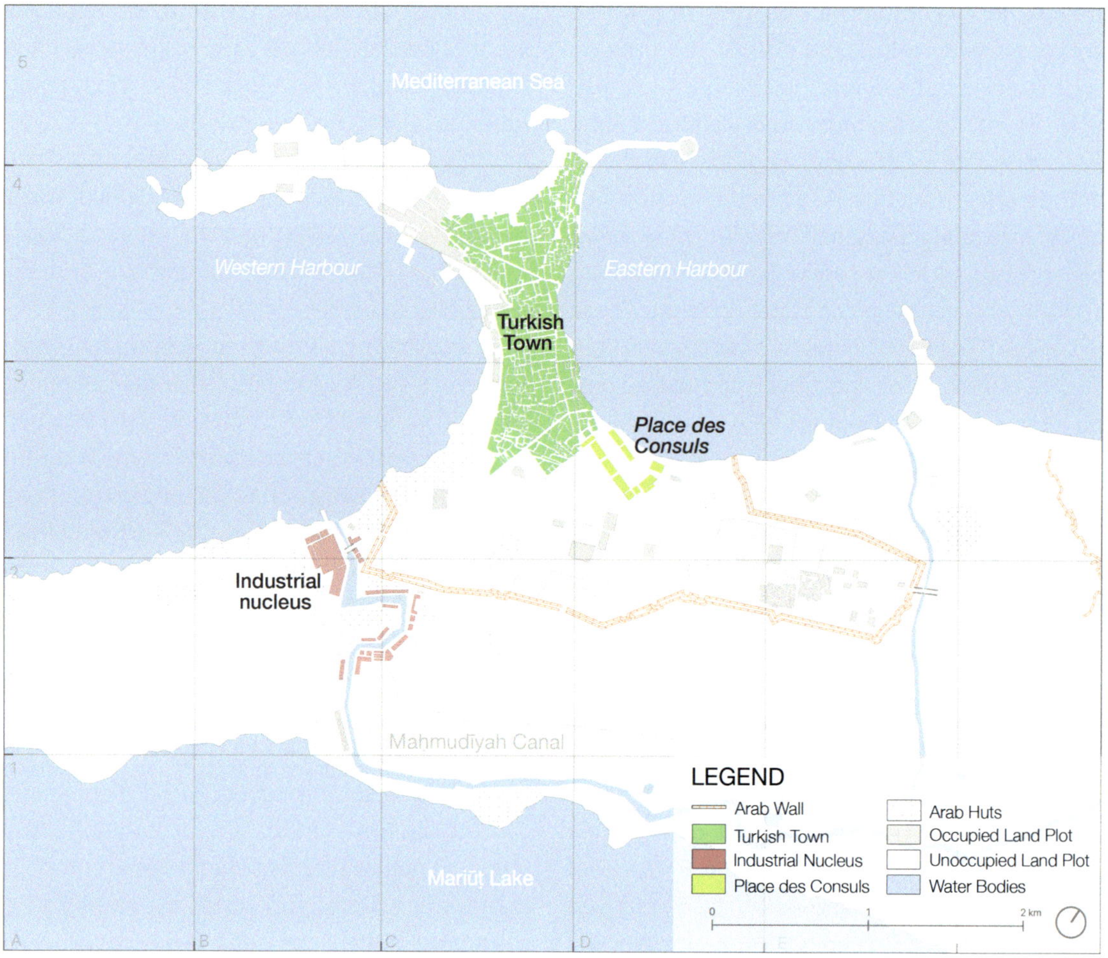

2 A map of Alexandria showing existing fabric around the mid-19th century.

visits in 2019 and 2021 were made to the Dār al-wathā'iq al-qaumīyah (DWQ) in Cairo and the Centre d'Études Alexandrine (CEA) in Alexandria, Egypt, and the Bibliotheque Nationale de France (BnF) in Paris, France; online archives and relevant secondary literature were also consulted.

Contextualisation

In the mid-19th century, Alexandria was characterised geographically by its waterscapes: the Mediterranean Sea, the Mariūṭ Lake, and the al-Maḥmudīyah Canal (fig. 2) connecting the city to the Nile.[32] At that time, the city comprised three built-up areas, which are here considered as the city's urban nuclei upon which the city's expansion was based.

The first urban nucleus was the peninsular called Turkish Town,[33] located between the crescents that formed eastern and western harbours, outside the Arab Wall.[34] This area developed to best serve the east and west sea-freight harbours and production activities. Turkish Town was a conventional Arab sinuous urban structure accommodating the city's core traditional crafts and housing for the poorer class. It was characterised by its spatial feature of accommodating commercial, trade, and residential uses.[35]

The second urban nucleus provided the genesis of the city's industrial area. It was characterised by its warehouses located *extra muros* next to the mouth of the canal and the western harbour (see fig. 2).[36] This expansion of this nucleus started with a granary, constructed by 1808 and defined as «the great warehouse of the Pasha»; the Pasha, here, referring to Mohammed 'Ali.[37] By 1830, more state-owned warehouses were constructed, elongating the western harbour between the canal and the Arab Wall.[38] Having already developed the associated functional characteristics, the area was assigned and planned as the city's industrial zone by the Ornato. The nucleus's expansion occurred during the reign of Wāli Abbas Hilmi I (r. 1848–1854), another grandson of Muhammad 'Ali, when state-owned land was offered to Alexandrians to build more warehouses to promote trade activities.[39]

Place des Consuls was the commercial and third nucleus of Alexandria.[40] The city's first commercial and business centre was also planned by the Ornato and placed next to the eastern harbour.[41] The rectangular-designed urban space comprised westernised buildings mainly built to host European consuls. Until the mid-19th century, Place des Consuls encompassed the Europeans' residences, consulates, banks, and company offices. Due to its extension the north-western enclosure of the Arab Wall was gradually removed by 1855.[42] As a result of the 1860s cotton boom, which caused an increase in the city's population, the city's bourgeois community promoted the city's extension to accommodate its commercial aspirations.

Going Eastwards: Residential Suburbia

By 1840, Alexandria's population of 60,000 people was mainly concentrated in the Turkish Town peninsular.[43] Looking west towards the industrial nucleus, Turkish Town overlooked the operating western harbour. To the east, Place des Consuls was surrounded by extensive countryside, while to the south were found ruins and traces of the ancient urban plan. Arab huts were scattered within and outside the city walls.[44] Emanating from Place des Consuls, three fashionable quarters developed to accommodate the city's bourgeoisie and middle class: the Latin Quarter, ar-Raml, and Moharram Bey (fig. 3).[45] Collectively, the three quarters were characterised by the introduction of a Westernised orthogonal urban plan, which developed into the city's main urban structure, ushering in a new chapter in the city's urban planning.

The street structure of the Latin Quarter radiated from Place des Consuls, thrusting its way both eastwards and southwards. Based on the 1845 map by Colonel Gallice Bey – director of fortification in Egypt at the time – the expansion involved the first gradual demolition of the north-western enclosure of the Arab Wall.[46] The orthogonal structure of the expansion was integrated with the re-traced urban plan of the ancient city. This was mostly visible in the reconstructed Canopic Road that ran longitudinally towards the eastern city gate.[47] The Canopic Road was the main street in the ancient grid plan of Alexandria, the spine of the city's ancient Hippodamian matrix.[48]

While the Latin Quarter grew inside the Arab city wall, both ar-Raml and Moharram Bey evolved *extra muros*. Their development was instigated by the establishment of khedivial countryside palaces (see fig. 3). The Moharram Bey suburb originated from Mohammed 'Ali's son-in-law, Moharram Bey, who had his palace constructed during the 1830s.[49] Located *extra muros* by the canal, the palace was connected to the city by a local road that pierced the southern enclosure of the Arab Wall by 1855. Later, by 1865, land divisions were planned along the roadsides to host the residences of wealthy families from all ethnic communities.[50] The suburb's growth eventually resulted in the demolition of the south-eastern enclosure of the wall between 1887 and 1895.[51] Shortly later, in 1902, a tram line was constructed on Moharram Bey road.[52]

Ar-Raml had its origins in the plan of Khedive Ismail (reigned 1863–1879) to set up his summer resort in the eastern countryside by the sea during the 1860s.[53] The construction of a new local road was authorised to make this possible.[54] Despite being remote to the city, ar-Raml soon developed into a residential banlieue, especially when a rail line was constructed next to the road in 1863, which pierced the eastern wall enclosure. Egypt's elite were soon encouraged to establish their summer houses by the sides of the road overlooking the sea. The land gap between the ar-Raml banlieue and the commercial nucleus was gradually filled with other residential districts. The development of these districts, as well as of the Latin Quarter, resulted in the demolition of the wall's eastern enclosure by 1917.[55]

In contrast to the ar-Raml rail line, which was established to serve the suburb solely via a one-directional linear course, the tramline that reached Moharram Bey was part of a tram project established in 1897 by the Tramway d'Alexandrie Company and referred to locally as «*tramways de la ville*», at that time.[56] Emanating from Place des Consuls, the tramline penetrated the established city fabric, moving towards the desired city extensions. One of the main characteristics of the city's tramline was its capacity to establish connectivity among the city's three nuclei, especially between the commercial and industrial nuclei. As it was difficult to penetrate the sinuous urban fabric of Turkish Town, the tramline route ran along the town's borders, overlooking the eastern and western harbours.

3 A map of Alexandria displaying the city's eastwards residential development around the second half of the 19th century.

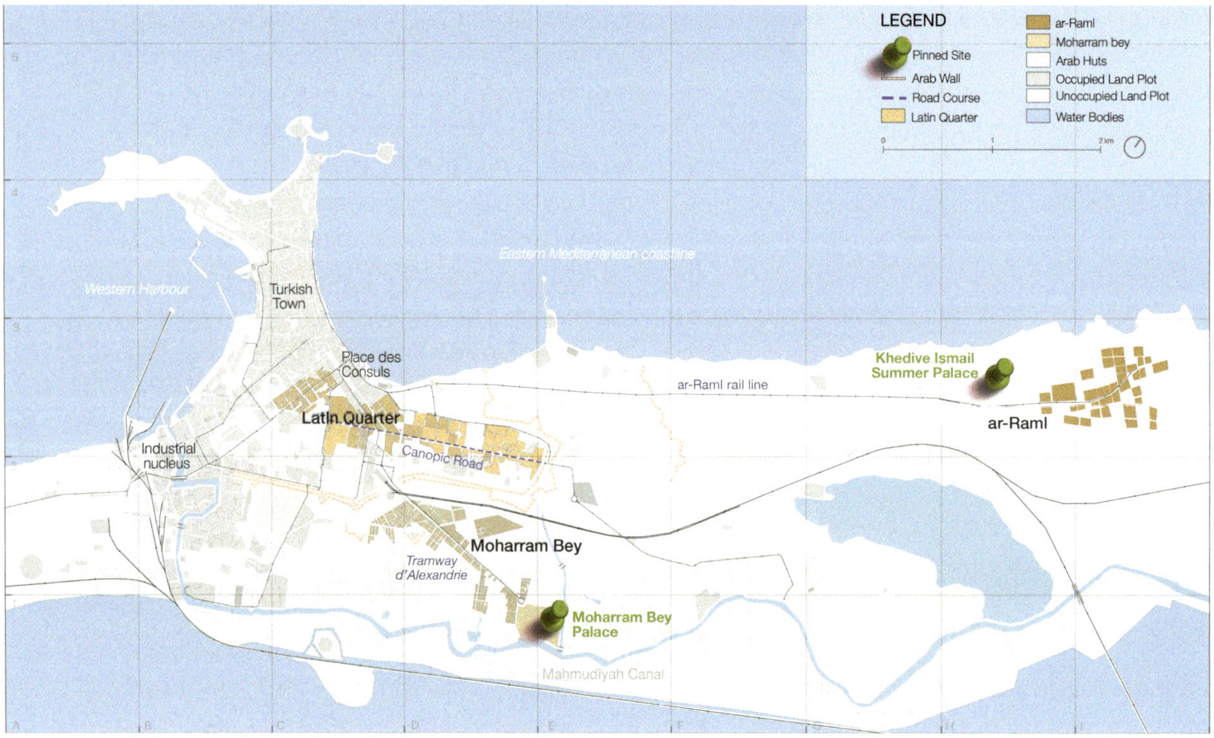

Going South-Westwards: Export-Pertinent Development

Alexandria's industrial nucleus, with its warehouses, represented Egypt's status as an exporter to the West. The strong interest in establishing more warehouses during the second half of the 19th century was closely related to the increased number of established cultivated commodities ready for export. This was also incentivised by the construction of a railway terminus at the south-western boundary of the industrial nucleus to facilitate the transport of export-oriented commodities from other cities to Alexandria (fig. 4).[57]

The industrial nucleus evolved in both Mina al-Baṣal and al-Qabbarī – two districts located adjacent to the western harbour along both sides of the canal mouth.[58] Both districts had long been inhabited by Arabs – the latter is named after Sheikh Al-Qabbari, who lived and worked in the area during the early 13th century.[59] The British traveller and journalist James St. John reported in 1834 that Arabs who worked in the state-owned warehouses were still residing there at that time.[60]

By 1855 the Turkish Town peninsula was fully built up, while the area to the east of the city was reserved predominantly for the city's bourgeoisie. Consequenttly, Mina al-Baṣal and al-Qabbarī were the best candidates to accommodate the city's lower-middle class and lower-class inhabitants.[61] Around that time, the industrial nucleus comprised a series of aligned warehouses along both banks of the canal.[62] While the Ornato was still coordinating the city's developments, the development of the industrial nucleus was mostly influenced by local and foreign[63] merchants and exporters, who incentivised the area's development to expand and ensure their business stability. Significantly, it was their initiative to establish La Commission du Commerce d'Exportation in 1869 to carry out the paving and draining of the warehousing roads in Alexandria, financed through voluntary taxes levied upon themselves.[64] The industrial nucleus extended along the canal, towards Place des Consuls, and along the western harbour. The connection between the industrial complex and Place des Consuls was enhanced, among other reasons, to link La Bourse and Le Marché aux Cotons. La Bourse (built 1861, rebuilt 1899) comprised Egypt's first constructed futures market for cotton and grains.[65] It stood in the commercial nucleus that hosted commercial and institutional structures of the «local-foreign» merchants. Le Marché aux Cotons (built 1872) involved all spot sales and arbitrating disputes for sales of cotton and grain.[66] It was constructed in the industrial nucleus by the Western port that hosted the country's main warehouses and workers' dwellings.[67] Significantly, the street connecting both the structures and their respective nuclei was the first in the city to be paved; it was named after Ibrahim Pasha (r. 1848), the eldest son of Wāli Mohammed 'Ali.[68]

Around the end of the 19th century, the industrial nucleus extended to include more warehouses constructed parallel to those aligned with the canal[69] and characterised by their chessboard-like arrangement. The industrial nucleus extended to an industrial complex; besides warehouses, it included sizable timber yards, cotton press factories, and worker residences. The extension by the canal banks led to the construction of bridges connecting Mina al-Baṣal and al-Qabbarī. As a result of the extensions emanating from the industrial nucleus and Place des Consuls, the south-western part of the city wall was demolished between 1856 and 1868.[70] By the end of the 19th century, the urban interstices between both nuclei were filled with middle to middle-lower class residents. The nuclei were in this way connected, amalgamating the industrial nucleus as part of the city.[71]

The high demand for commodity exports during the second half of the 19th century not only affected the expansion of the industrial nuclei, but also secured and accelerated connectivity to the port. The accommodation of a more affluent trade

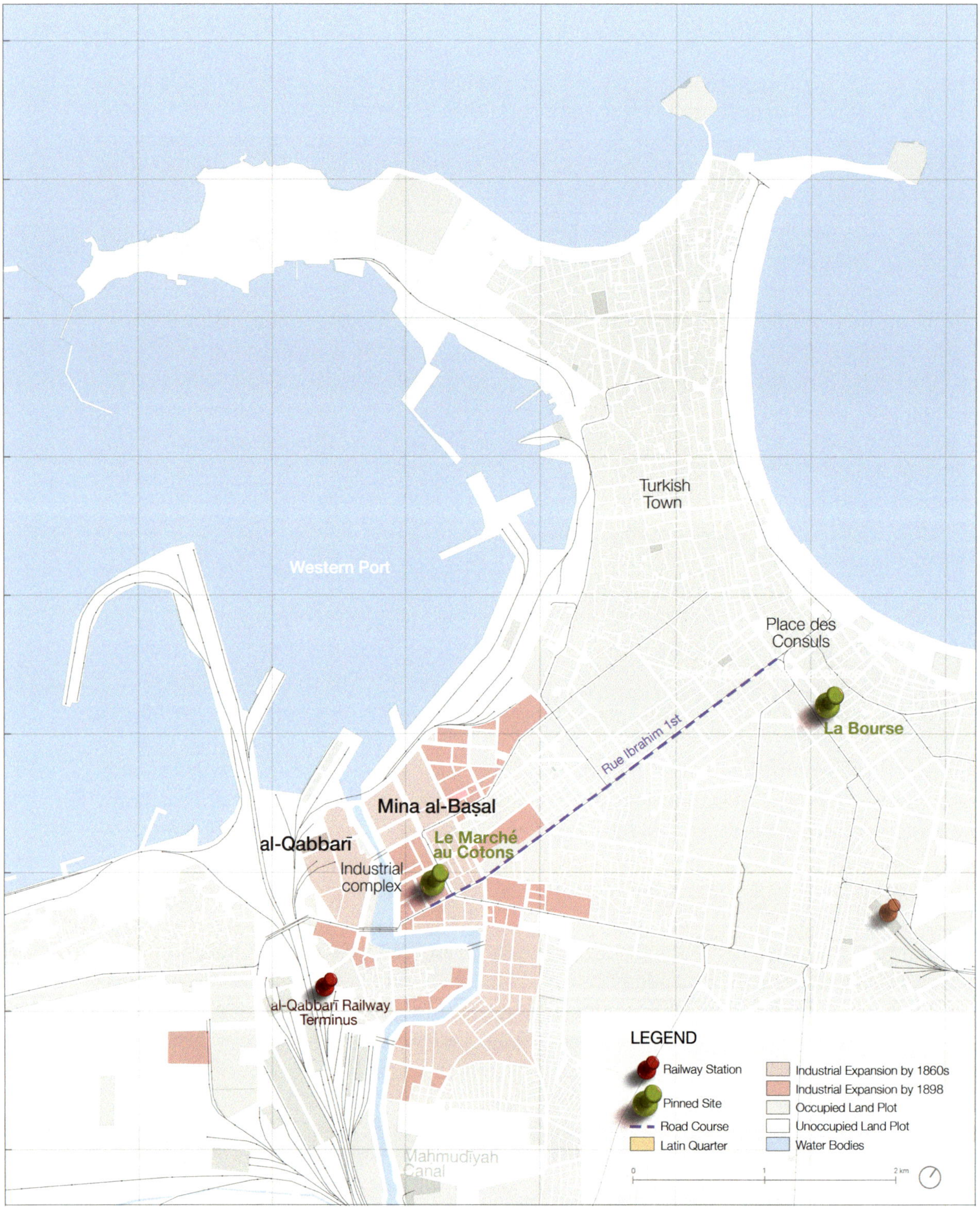

4 A map of Alexandria highlighting the development of the industrial land plots along the canal and towards Place des Consuls at the end of the 19th century.

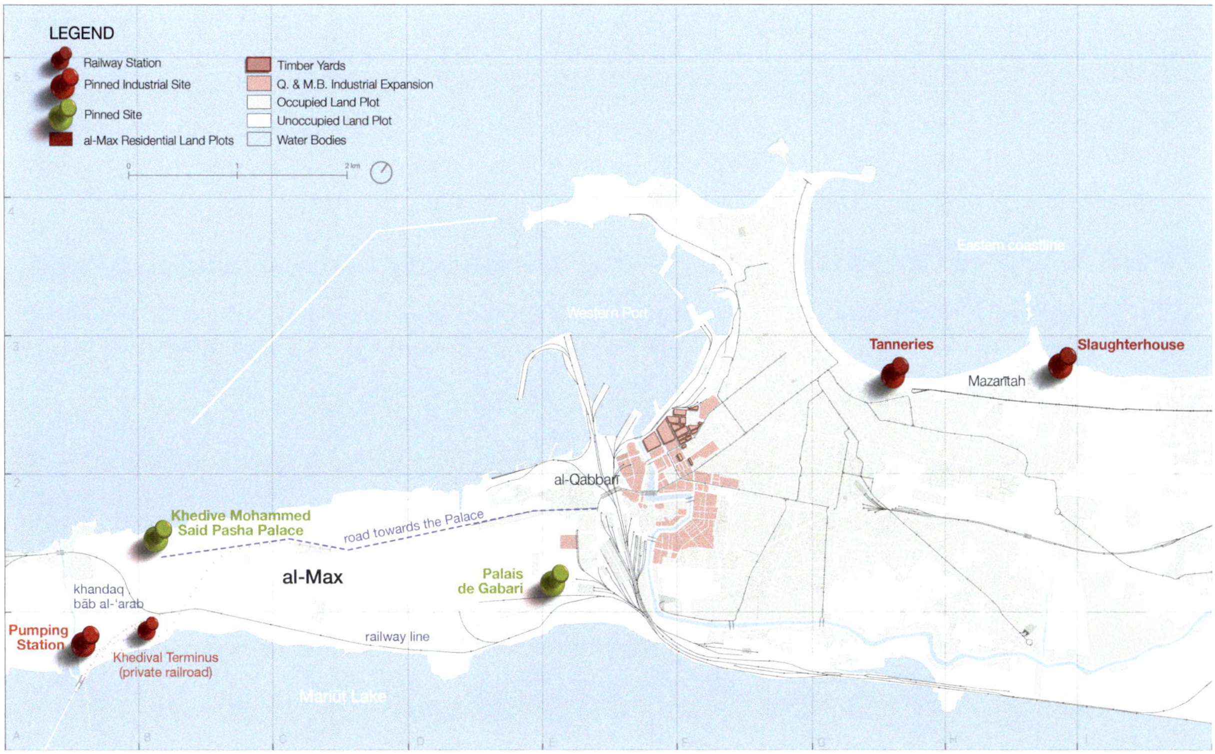

5 A map of Alexandria revealing the contextualisation of al-Max in relation to the city's urbanisation at the end of the 19th century.

infrastructure was realised in 1880 with the redevelopment of the existing western port, a project characterised as the «biggest foreign contract for the development of Alexandria» at that time.[72]

During the second half of the 19th century, the city was expanding from both the commercial and the industrial nuclei. Around the end of the 19th century, this development encountered existing and emerging challenges that stood in the way of proceeding with the desired city development. On the city's eastern side, the challenges encompassed existing industrial structures hindering residential development (see tanneries and slaughterhouse in fig. 5); these structures were later transferred westwards to the industrial complex (as explained later in this chapter). Regarding the industrial complex, the already densely built-up area faced the challenge of increasing demand for storage structures between the canal and the western harbour. These challenges were surmounted by extending westwards towards al-Max.

Going Westward: Industrial Suburbia

The area of al-Max was located west of al-Qabbarī. Al-Max was characterised by its longitudinal countryside landscape, overlooking both the Mediterranean Sea and the Mariūṭ Lake (fig. 5). Around the end of the 19th century, al-Max was mainly occupied by Bedouins, who undertook conventional agricultural activities.[73] By 1855 a hunting palace for Khedive Mohammed Said Pasha (r. 1854–1863) had been constructed in al-Qabbarī next to the Mariūṭ Lake.[74] The palace is referred to as «Palais de Gabari» on historical maps. First accessible via road from the north, it was later reachable via a khedival private railway from the south. The rail line extended westwards along the lake and ended in a terminus that was probably constructed by 1858.[75] By 1869, another palace was constructed for Said Pasha, located next to the Mediterranean Sea. Based on an 1882 map, the palace was referred to as «Palais de Vice Roi», referring to Khedive Tewfik Pasha (r. 1879–1892).[76]

Around the end of the 19th century, al-Max witnessed the implementation of two major engineering projects.[77] Both were part of other development projects in Egypt, conducted during the British occupation (1882–1922), and designed and implemented by British engineers and engineering companies. According to architectural and urban historian Nezar AlSayyad, Egypt was experiencing «an era of engineering».[78] These projects defined the core outlines that lay out al-Max as an additional development direction for the city. Besides serving the city's expansion, both projects responded to multiple demands for irrigation and port advancements on regional and national scales; additionally, they served several industrial developments. As a result of these projects, al-Max witnessed the laying out of the only large-scale industrial zone for the city's outskirts at that time. The new functions introduced by the projects led to the demolition of the khedivial palaces over a period of years: Palais de Vice Roi was demolished between 1882 and 1907 and Palais de Gabari between 1908 and 1914.[79]

The first project was part of several irrigation projects conducted in Egypt by the end of the 19th century, which encompassed re-digging canals and establishing several dykes, dams, and other irrigation structures.[80] These new structures, in turn, expanded agricultural areas and enabled an uninterrupted agricultural water supply and discharge all year long.[81]

6 A map of Alexandria displaying the industrial suburbia scheme in al-Max around the 1930s.

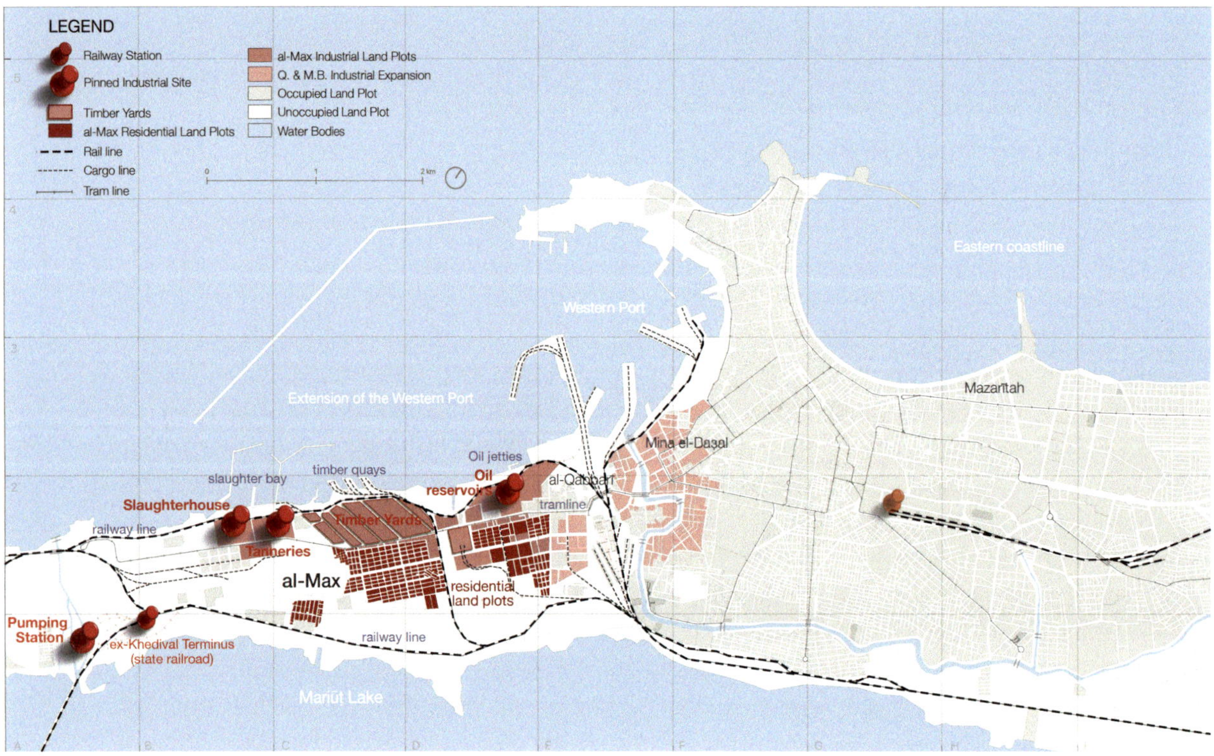

In Alexandria, British engineers contributed to the «khandaq bāb al-'arab» irrigation project in al-Max.[82] The project involved a man-made drainage cut dug between the Mariūṭ Lake and the Mediterranean Sea, probably in 1889–93, to discharge excessive water from the lake that flooded Alexandria's hinterland cultivation.[83] To maintain the water levels of the lake, the Irrigation Department constructed a pumping station next to the ditch mouth and the lake in al-Max. Constructed probably after 1892, this pumping station was described in 1935 by Naguib Ibrahim Bey, Egypt's director general of Projects at the Ministry of Public Works, as the oldest water pumping station in Egypt.[84] As the principal utility for Alexandria's hinterland, the site was only connected to Alexandria via unpaved roads. It was only later, in 1914, after the demolition of the second Khedivial palace, that the State bought the Khedival terminus, hence facilitating the site's reachability.[85] The course of the rail tracks extended to pass by the pumping station, thrusting its way towards Alexandria's hinterland. At the time of the construction of the al-Max pumping station, there was no municipal urban planning scheme for al-Max. The Irrigation Department therefore constructed *in situ* «workmen's houses» and residential villas for the station's engineers.[86]

The second project was initiated in February 1898, when the Egyptian government assigned the Khedivial Mail Company to proceed with further rehabilitation projects relating to the western port. The company conducted the project until 1906 from al-Qabbarī westwards towards al-Max (fig. 6).[87] The project included the construction of floating docks and quays, along with their adjoining service-related structures for the city's westward industrial seafront. Other than the irrigation projects, which contributed to serving Alexandria's hinterland, this project helped to solve spatial obstacles preventing the city industrial extension from penetrating the commercial and residential areas of the city at that time. For example, the port rehabilitation project contributed to accommodating transferred industries, which hindered residential development around the end of the 19th century. Alexandria's transferred industries at the time involved the timber yards as well as the tanneries and slaughterhouse (as discussed later in this section).

Al-Max was equipped with a transport infrastructure from around the end of the 19th century onwards, reflecting its position as seemingly remote from the city but open to both the sea and the lake. This infrastructure encompassed the former khedival railway along the lake, a cargo rail line along the sea established by 1907, and a tramline between both rail lines established by 1902. This, in turn, paved the way for al-Max's urban expansion.[88] The peripheral land vacancy of al-Max contributed to establishing a large-scale industry-defined suburbia west of the industrial complex. This first industrial suburbia was displayed on Bartocci's 1914 map.[89] The scheme comprised both industrial land plots arranged longitudinally along the rehabilitated western port as well as orthogonally planned residential land plots extending southwards towards the lake (see fig. 6).[90] Both industrial and residential land plots were divided longitudinally by the course of the tramline, facilitating the transfer of the industries mentioned above, along with the founding of new industries.

Around the end of the 19th century, the land plots in Mina el-Baṣal were densely occupied with industrial and residential buildings along the canal. In the aftermath of the cotton boom around the end of the 19th century, more warehouses were required to offer the necessary storage space. In the early 20th century, as part of the western harbour rehabilitation project, the decision was made to transfer the timber yards to al-Max. The 64,000 m^2 standing timber yards in Mina el-Baṣal were complemented by new timber yards occupying a sizable area of about 400,000 m^2. The owners of the timber yards in Mina el-Baṣal were offered a service with better facilities in terms of sizable storage areas,

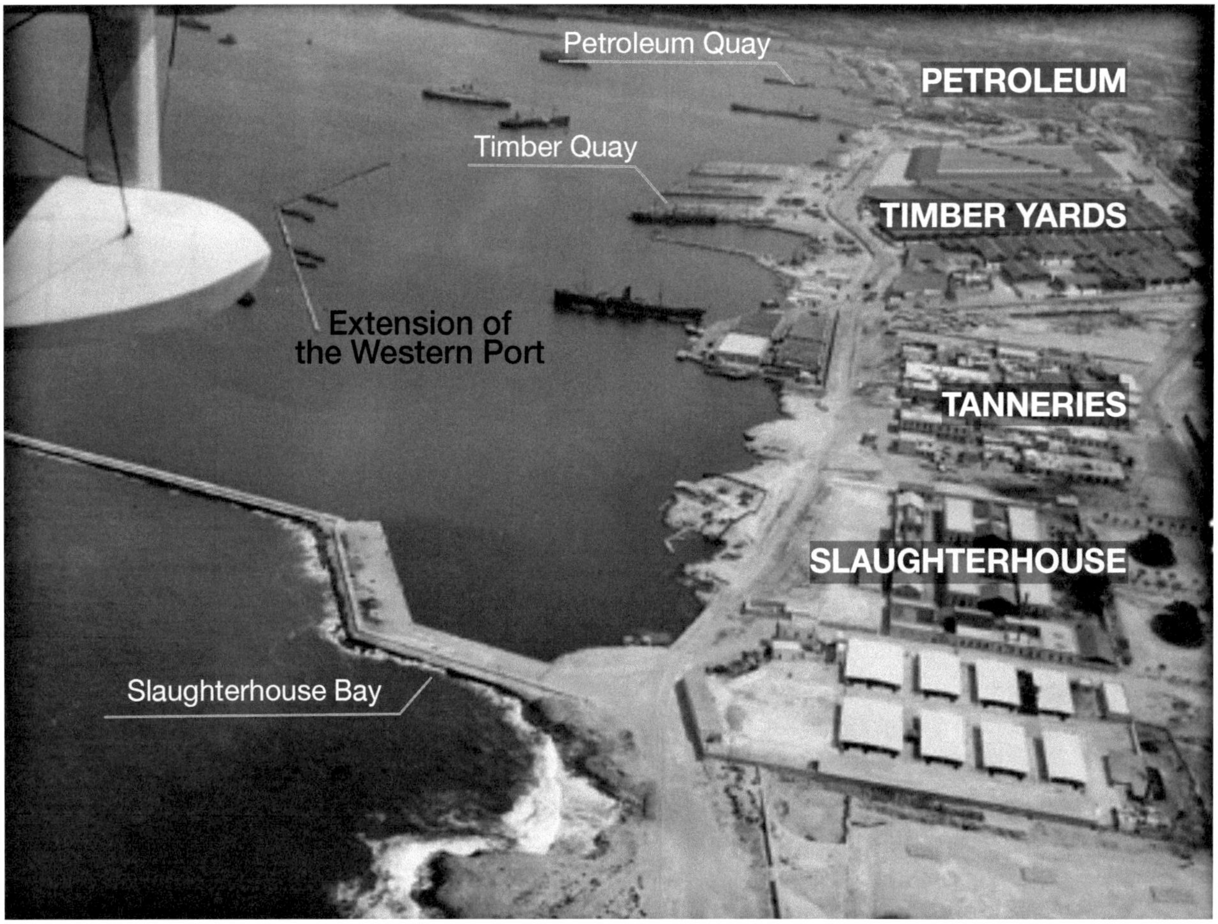

7 Aerial view of Alexandria's established industries in al-Max in 1932, viewed from the east looking westwards.

modernised construction materials, and a location overlooking designated timber quays. The final transfer of all timber yards to al-Max was realised during the 1930s.[91]

Along with the timber yards, the city's tanneries and the slaughterhouse were also transferred to al-Max. By the late 19th century, multiple tanneries were operating in Mazarītah overlooking the sea's eastern coastline (see fig. 6).[92] These tanneries were on the verge of becoming integrated spatially with the city's eastern extension. As these industries were inconsistent with the goal of modern residential city expansion, the Alexandria Municipality transferred them to al-Max, with the transfer completed in 1905.[93] All the city's tannery activities were contained in an area of approximately 9,000 m^2. Besides the tanneries, the slaughterhouse was also transferred to a new and sizable site in al-Max. The slaughterhouse overlooked its designated bay. The project was developed collaboratively by the ministries of Commerce and Agriculture (fig. 7).

In addition to reducing the operational load in Mina el-Baṣal and removing activities incongruous with the city's eastern expansion, the new industrial suburbia contributed to accommodating new industrial operations. The first was the petroleum industry. In Egypt, the petroleum industry developed abruptly between 1890 and 1909.[94] In al-Max, an area of 5,000 m^2 was specified to accommodate three oil import houses: the Russian Mantacheff Oil Company, French Worms et Cie, and American Soccony Vacuum.[95] As with the tannery, slaughterhouse, and timber yards, the reservoirs of each company overlooked the sea with their designated private jetties.[96]

Each constructed industrial operation was characterised by its direct connectivity with its privately constructed quay, which provided inland access through the railway course from the west and tram service from the east. The land gaps between the timber yards, tanneries, and oil import houses later accommodated further industrial and industry-related extensions (fig. 8). The 1914 orthogonal urban plan for the southern side of al-Max was later adapted as part of Alexandria's first city planning scheme published in 1919. The scheme was conducted by British civil engineer William Hannah McLean, the Engineer-in-Chief in the Municipality and Commissions Section of the Ministry of Interior.[97] Until the 1930s, al-Max was predominantly occupied by established industries. From the 1930s onwards, the schemed land plots were occupied predominantly with worker settlements, thus transforming the industrial outskirt of al-Max into an industrial suburbia.[98] No reliable source has revealed the involvement of the industry owners in planning their own workers' habitation in al-Max, except for the pumping station as discussed above.

Despite being marginalised inexplicably by scholarly work, the projects developed in al-Max between the end of the 19th century and early 20th century still, to a large extent, characterise its present urban structure and spatial identity (see fig. 8). Today, the westward city extension

8 Alexandria 2022: Tracing al-Max's extant industrial suburbia scheme.

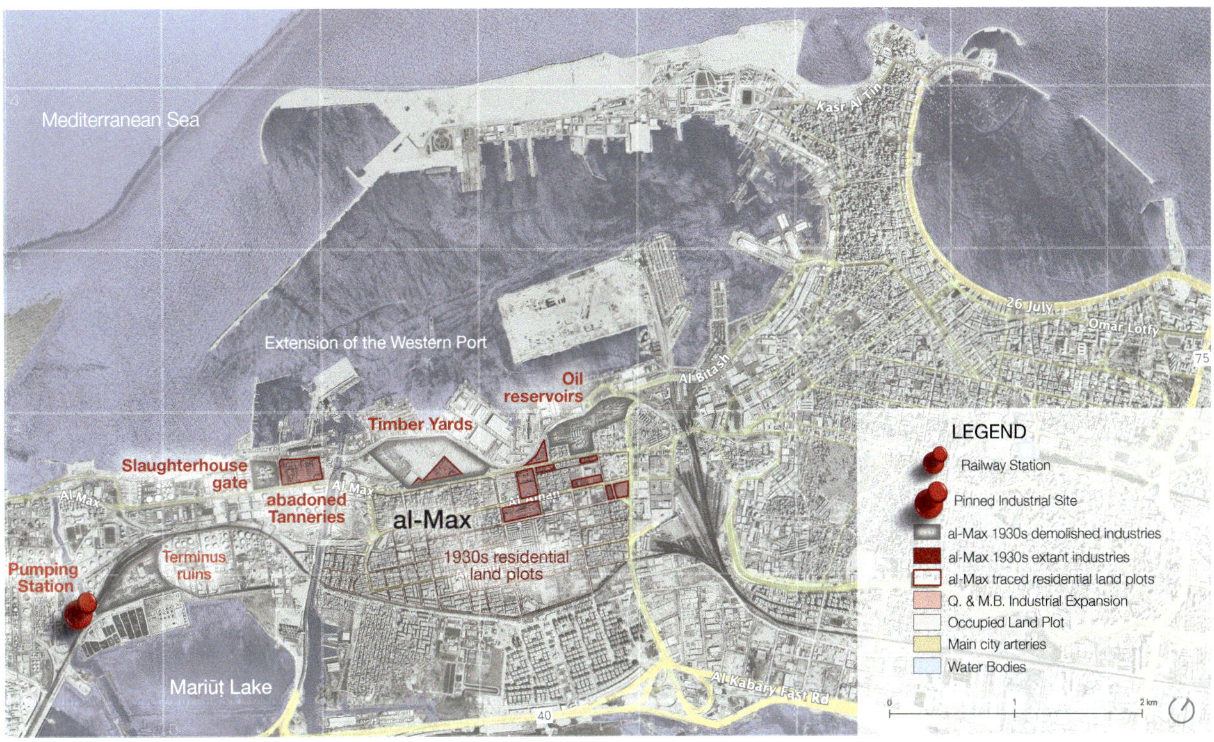

of al-Max has lost few of the industrial activities that operated during the first half of the 20th century. Nevertheless, some building elements still stand as a testimony to their former industrial activities, including the tanneries, which still stand abandoned today, the entrance gate of the slaughterhouse site, the disappearing ruins of the ex-khedivial terminus, and only about 1,500 m^2 of the once extensive area of the timber yards (400,000 m^2).[99] Still functionally uninterrupted with residential settlements, al-Max is today dominated by petroleum operations and minor timber activities, albeit now under new ownerships.

Conclusion: Alexandria's (Re)Visible Extension

The period between the mid-19th century and the early 20th century acted as a catalyst for the urban development of Alexandria, with the expansion emanating from the city's developed commercial and industrial nuclei at that time. The city expansion was mainly characterised by developments along the waterscapes of the Mediterranean Sea and the Maḥmudīyah Canal. Expansion to the east and the southwest filled the urban gaps between both waterfronts. This chapter has attempted to shed light on the rather neglected story of the city's westward development, which followed the desired urban plan by emanating predominantly from the city's commercial and industrial nuclei.

The westward extension was characterised by its relative proximity to the industrial nucleus of Mina el-Baṣal and al-Qabbarī. Nevertheless, its extensive area and functional operations, autonomous from the industrial nucleus, contributed operationally to its «independent» development. Presumably for this reason the industries established in al-Max have been marginalised in previous studies of Alexandria's urban history. Al-Max, with its industrial and industry-related zonings, endowed Alexandria with different types of heavy industrial operations.

Overall, looking westwards shows the historical development of a node of concentration for new industries as well as settlements to accommodate lower-class residents. On the one hand, the westward industrial expansion introduced an early urban form of zoning with specialised functions that enabled the modernised progression of Alexandria along the Mediterranean Sea and the Mariūṭ Lake. On the other hand, this expansion reduced the dense allotment of industries by the canal, allowing the establishment of industrial operations with direct connectivity to the extended western port.[100] Looking westwards contributes to linking the dots of Alexandria's (in)visible modern urban development. It also underlines the omitted industrial history of the city's (in)visible technical and industrial projects.

The westward expansion is a witness to Alexandria's industrial advancement, which demonstrated discernible spatial interlinkages with the city's eastward and southward urban growth. The city's morphological spatial characteristics are still mostly traceable. The eastward city expansion still predominantly contains upper- and middle-class residential neighbourhoods. South-westwards, the land use in both Mina al-Baṣal and al-Qabbarī still encompasses industrial and middle- to lower-class residential spatial characteristics. During the past decades, the westward city expansion in al-Mex has undergone noticeable physical transformations. Nevertheless, these transformed area retained their industrial and middle- to lower-class residential land uses. Although al-Max visibly preserves its identity as industrial suburbia, it is still largely neglected and invisible in terms of its history and extant heritage, seldom discussed by scholars or acknowledged by authorities.

This chapter contributes to a comprehensive understanding of how Alexandria's urbanisation, with its industrial and commercial transformations, integrated Egypt within the growing demands of European industries for agricultural and raw materials during the 19th and 20th centuries. The main argument of this chapter is that the still-standing though neglected traces of the historical westwards extension of Alexandria fostered modern industrial urbanisation, instituted new spaces for the making of the modern city itself, and is thus an integral part of the city's urban history. More work therefore needs to be conducted to shed light on the still untold narratives of the extant industrial structures and their associated socio-cultural characteristics to integrate them properly as part of the city's history and urban conservation strategies.

First, I would like to express my sincere gratitude to the editors of this book, Suna Çağaptay and Zeido Zeido, for the opportunity to share my contribution through this chapter in their esteemed publication and for their constant support during the reviewing and editing process. I am also grateful for the inspirational feedback of the esteemed reviewers, whose comments enriched the quality of this chapter.

1 Hastaoglou-Martinidis 2014, 80.
2 As the world was experiencing the upsurge of the Industrial Revolution during the second half of the 19th century, Ottoman rule in Egypt, which started in the 16th century, was often interrupted by the military elite of the Mamluk freedmen. A stable Mameluke political dominance was, nevertheless, not secured. Some literature refers to this period as Ottoman rather than Mameluke, reflecting the Mamluk's factionalism and its continuous warfare with the Ottomans. Cuno 1994, 1–2; Tabak 2010, 31.
3 Reimer 1994, 114.
4 Raymond 1991, 37.
5 Vatikiotis 1991; Crouchley 1938; Baer 1969.
6 According to historian Khaled Fahmy, the British, however, were «not prepared to occupy the province (Egypt) without the consent of the Ottoman Sultan» and thus brought Egypt back within the fold of the Ottoman Porte. This was realised with the treaty of Amiens (March 1802). Fahmy does not elaborate on the Britain's lack of colonial interest in Egypt at the time. Fahmy 1998, 140–141.
7 Muhammad 'Ali was appointed viceroy of Egypt under the Ottoman Empire in 1805. It took him, however, seven years to defeat the Mamluk freedmen and demonstrate his control over Egypt. See Cuno 1994, 2.
8 It all started during the early 19th century, when European countries were busy with the Napoleonic Wars while competitively expanding their colonial power in the Mediterranean region. Fahmy 1998, 140.
9 Awad 1996, 44–45.
10 Hunter 1998, 181.
11 The shortage in the grain supply for the British forces in Europe was a commercial opportunity seized by 'Ali. He imposed an administrative and commercial monopoly in the country by controlling Egypt's agricultural economy and increasing its commodities, not only to serve the British forces in Europe but also to further the «lucrative trade with Europe». Egypt's agricultural system was also under the control of 'Ali's monopoly system. This monopoly was also applied in the country's political, administrative, economic, and industrial systems. Fahmy 1998, 140–150.
12 Fahmy 1998, 139.
13 Hunter 1998, 180.
14 Hunter 1998, 195.
15 Daly 1998, 239.
16 Daly 1998, 240.
17 Reimer 1988, 531; Daly 1998, 239.
18 Clot-Bey 1840, 265–266. As part of the development of the western port, a summer residence for Mohammed 'Ali was also constructed in 1818 and was later extended in 1837. See Wiet 1959 in Awad 2008, 82.
19 Hastaoglou-Martinidis 2014, 80.
20 During the Ottoman period, from 1517, Egypt's port and naval activities were allocated in several port cities overlooking the Red and the Mediterranean seas. The former was occupied by the towns of Suez and al-Quseir, and the latter by Damietta, Rosetta, and Alexandria. Alexandria's port and naval activities were, however, eclipsed by Damietta and Rosetta, where the latter was signified as «Cairo's Mediterranean entrepôt» at the time. 'Ahmad/Al-'Abbadi 1997, 13; Reimer 1994, 113; Cuno 1994, 49.
21 The term «Ornato», derived from Italian, was suggested by the Italian civil engineer Francesco Mancini, who arrived in Alexandria during the 1820s. The idea of establishing this commission was probably inspired by similar commissions that had functioned in Italian cities such as Milan and Venice since 1807. The term was translated into Arabic in the archives as majlis al-urnātu. Founded in 1834, the Ornato council was linked to the Ministry of Public Works in 1878. See Illbert 1996, 109–110.
22 There is an information gap in Reimer's paper: despite elaborating on the member parties of all the Ornato's fourteen members, the paper still states that the founding Ornato members comprised only one local sheikh among the other non-local members. As it is unlikely that the local elite controlled the committee's presidency or vice-presidency, it is unclear whether the local sheikh

was included as one of the Ottoman subjects. Reimer 1993, 62–63.

23 Baer 1968, 118–40; Illbert 1996, 109–10.

24 Reimer 1993, 59.

25 With its increasing debt, the Ottoman Empire was influenced by the pull of the European market, especially during the 1860s. As a result of the cotton boom, Anatolia took over the distribution of Egyptian cotton seeds, before the role passed to Eyalet of Egypt. Exports increased considerably from 5,000 to 7,000 bales in 1860 to more than 80,000 bales by 1865. Owen 1993, 110–112; Earle 1926, 526–527.

26 Malaval/Jondet 1912.

27 Reimer 1988, 534.

28 Riad 1933; Awad 1987; Abdel-Salam 1995; Pallini/Scaccabarozzi 2016.

29 In Arabic: al-Qabbarī = القباري; ad-Dikhīlah = الدخيلة; Burg al-'Arab = بُرج العَرب. Locally, the three areas still hold the same name.

30 Locally, the area still holds the same name.

31 These structures are found in the Egyptian National Register List, published by the Alexandria Governorate in 2007.

32 In Arabic: Mariūṭ Lake = بُحيرة مَريوط; al-Maḥmudīyah Canal = ترعة المَحمودية. The lake is still known by the same name, but the canal only lasted until 2019, when the canal was silted up and transformed into a road, presently called al-Maḥmudīyah Road = مِحور المَحمودية

33 In Arabic: Turkish Town = الحي التُركي. Turkish Town is a settlement which changed its physical shape between the 6th and the early 19th centuries due to gradual inundation of the ancient Hellenistic Heptastadium that connected the Rhakotis, inland of Alexandria, with its adjacent island Pharos. Locally, it still holds the same name. Riad 1933, 240.

34 The Arab Wall dated back to the 13th and 14th century. 'Ahmad/Al-'Abbadi 1997, 10–12.

35 This was a traditional spatial feature that was found not only in other Egyptian port towns (e.g., al-Quseir on the Red Sea) but in commercial towns countrywide during the Islamic period.

36 Until the end of the 18th century, Alexandria's warehouses were probably located in Turkish Town next to the eastern and western harbours. See Beawes's definition of «proper places» in Beawes 1783, 762.

37 It was constructed when Mohammed 'Ali was granted the monopoly for grain export to supply the British army in both Malta and Spain during the Peninsular War. St. John 1834, 22; Cuno 1994, 104.

38 Girard 1822, 173.

39 Mubarak 1889, 62–63 in Reimer 1988, 536.

40 The square was originally named Place de Franks, later renamed Place des Consuls. In 1873 the state acknowledged Mohammed 'Ali's modernising role in the city's economic and commercial development with the renaming of the square as Place Mohammed 'Ali and the placement of an equestrian statue of 'Ali in the square. Today the square is locally known as Manshiyah Square = ميدان المَنشية. See Awad 1996, 43–45.

41 Reimer 1993, 60.

42 Hastaoglou-Martinidis 2014, 97.

43 Reimer 1993, 59.

44 Jondet 1921, map XXXIII.

45 In Arabic: Latin Quarter = الحي اللاتيني; ar-Raml = الرمل; Moharram Bey = محرم بك. Locally, the three quarters still hold the same names.

46 Gallice Bey 1845.

47 The ancient Canopic Road is now locally known as Fouad Street = شارع فؤاد.

48 The Canopic Road is referred to as the Rosetta Road in other publications, since it was the overland trade road connecting Alexandria with Rosetta. Awad 1996, 50; McKenzie 2007, 19–24; Ferro/Magli 2012, 381.

49 Moharram Bey was also appointed as the governor of Alexandria. Based on the 1845 map of Gallice Bey, Plan Alexandrie et environs, the Moharram Bey Palace stood next to the Maḥmudīyah Canal and its branch al-farkhah Canal, which ran north along the eastern city gate. Following the death of Moharram Bey, his estates were sold to new owners. Jondet 1921, map XXXVI; As-Sirūgī 2010, 181.

50 Jondet 1921, maps XXXV and XXXVI.

51 Jondet 1921, map XLVII; Hogarth/Benson 1895, map II.

52 The tramline was part of an infrastructural tram project established by the Belgian Tramway d'Alexandrie Company in 1897. More information about the tramline is presented in the following sections of the chapter. Jondet 1921, map L.

53 Ar-Raml is known in Arabic as الرمل, the Arabic word for «the sand»; in French-language publications, it was known as «Rámleh». As the name depicts, Rámleh was considered «la petite Riviera» for its sandy shore. The summer palace was originally built and owned by Mustafa Fazıl Pasha, the half-brother of Khedive Ismail, who acquired the palace shortly after its construction. The area in which the palace stood, however, retained its name as the Mustafa Pasha area, and is currently known as Mustafa Kamel Pasha after the Egyptian nationalist advocate. Pecnik 1901; Awad 1987, 100.

54 Mubarak 1889 in Reimer 1988, 537.

55 Jondet 1921, map LIII. The eastern side was the only remaining part of the Arab wall. Presumably, therefore, parts of the wall were preserved at that time. These wall ruins are still standing today.

56 Originally founded and operated by two separate companies, the ar-Raml rail line and the Alexandria tram were later incorporated under the Alexandria and Ramleh Railway Company. Today, they are owned and operated by the Public Authority for Passenger Transport. The historical routes are largely unchanged and operating. Van Pellecom 2010, 11; President au Ministre de l'interieur 1919.

57 The first section of the railway line, from Alexandria to Kafr al-'Īs, opened in 1853; the railway was later extended

to Cairo in 1855 and to Suez in the final phase. Nasr ElDin 2006, 22; Nasr ElDin / Gwyn 2016, 76; Silva 2016.

58 In Arabic: Mina al-Baṣal = مينا(ء) البصل; the literal translation of its name is the «onion harbour». In some literature, it is also referred to as «Minat al-Baṣal». Locally, the district still holds the same name. It is still locally famous with its volumetric warehouses. 'Ābid 2012, 57.

59 Al-Qabbarī is named after Sheikh al-Qabbarī, who lived in Alexandria during the early 13th century. Sheikh Al-Qabbarī is buried in a shrine that developed into a mosque in the district that still bears his name. Al-Qabbarī derives from the word «al-Qabbar» or «cabbage»; Sheikh Al-Qabbarī was a local merchant owning cultivation lands at the same location. 'Abd-Elbasit / ElSaiyd Hamdy 2014, 34.

60 St. John 1834, 22; Jondet 1921, map XXXIII.

61 Jondet 1921, map XXXV; Crinson 1996, 171.

62 Jondet 1921, map XXXV.

63 «Local foreigners» are a non-Egyptian community of foreign origin, who resided, or in some cases were born, in Egypt.

64 Baer 1968, 118–140; Wright 1909, 432.

65 Until its demolition, La Bourse was locally known as البورصة.

66 Presently, Le Marché aux Cotons locally holds the same designation; in Arabic = بورصة القطن.

67 Huri 1935, 81.

68 'Ali Pasha Mubarak (1889) reports that the paved street was called Ibrahim Street. The street was 1,000 m long and about 24 m wide and referred to as Rue Ibrahim 1st on historical maps. It was named after the eldest son of Wāli Mohammed 'Ali and the unrecognised Khedive of Egypt and Sudan. The street is presently known as-Saba' Banāt street [السَبَع بنات]. Mubarak 1889, 66.

69 Jondet 1921, map XXXVI.

70 Hastaoglou-Martinidis 2014, 97; Jondet 1921, XXXVI.

71 Jondet 1921, XXXVI.

72 The project works were entrusted to the London firm William Bruce Greenfield & Co. Malaval / Jondet 1912, 18; Reimer 2019.

73 De Cosson 1935, 179–180.

74 Based on Muller's 1855 published map, the palace was referred to as «Palais de Saïd Pacha». Jondet 1921, map XXXV.

75 De Cosson 1935, 89–90.

76 Jondet 1921, map XLIV; Collection Max Karkégi 1859, 318.

77 This is based on «Provisional Map of Alexandria & Environs», published by Survey Department Cairo 1907. The map was surveyed in 1889–93 and revised 1902–03.

78 Engineers like Sir George Kenneth Scott-Moncrieff, John Henry Garstin, Lieutenant-Colonel Ross, and William Willcocks, among others. AlSayyad 2019.

79 Ministère des Travaux Publics 1882; Survey Department Cairo 1907; Davies & Company 1901; Bartocci 1922.

80 For more comprehensive information regarding the British irrigation projects in Egypt, see Schuyler 1891.

81 This was part of the comprehensive plan to increase and secure the supply of raw materials, primarily cotton.

82 In Arabic: khandaq bāb al-'arab = خندق باب العرب. Locally, the ditch is presently referred to as al-Max canal.

83 This is exemplified, among others, in plantings of olives, barley, date palms, and most importantly the sizable vineyards of Fondation Gianaclis, located 25 km to the west of Alexandria. See Raafat 2010, 32; Survey Department Cairo 1907; De Cosson 1935, 90–91.

84 The station is still operating until present. Ibrahim Bey 1935, 114–119.

85 Anthony De Cosson mentions the «state» but does not reveal which «state» body undertook the acquisition. De Cosson 1935, 11–12. The palaces and railroads were private property of the Alawi family at the time.

86 Survey Department of Egypt 1911–13, sheets I–II and II–II.

87 The Khedivial Mail Steamship & Graving Dock Co. was founded in 1898. Its ships and docks were owned by various departments of the Egyptian Government. Malaval / Jondet 1912, 118.

88 Survey Department Cairo 1907; Municipalité 1902.

89 Bartocci was the director of the Greek–Roman Art Museum of Alexandria between 1904 and 1929. Known for his excellent painting skills, he contributed to producing one of Alexandria's best-known reconstitution maps of the ancient town, where synthetic archaeological results and historical hypotheses are overlayed on Alexandria survey map. Bartocci's map was published in 1922 by Evaristo Breccia.

90 Bartocci 1922. In her text, the author of this chapter is referring to the 20th-century base map displayed in Bartocci's map and not his archaeological mapping results.

91 The cadastral maps of Alexandria 1930s. The city map (scale 1:500) is devided over several sheets, held by the Libraries of the Faculty of Engineering and the Faculty of Education of Alexandria University, not digitised.

92 The district name Mazarītah (مزاريطة) derives from the French word «lazaret», which referred to the quarantine station for the maritime travellers established in the same area during the early 19th century during the reign of Mohamed 'Ali. The district Mazarītah is presently referred to as al-Azaītah (الأزاريطة). The slaughterhouse and tanneries are indicated on the historical maps of Al-Falaki (1865) as السلخانة (trans. al-salakhānah), of L. Barreau (1868) as «Abbatoir» and «Tannerie», and of D. G. Hogarth (1895) as «Slaughter house».

93 Chambre de Commerce Egyptienne d'Alexandrie 1951.

94 According to William A. Wescott, Mohamed Atta, and John C. Dolson, the exploration history of the oil industry was divided into six stages: the first extended from 1862 to 1921 in the Gulf of Suez area. Malaval 1911 states that petroleum imports were only 109,000 L.E. in 1890 and later reached 356,000 L.E. in 1909 for a tonnage of 96,000 tons. Wescott et al. 2016, 6; Malaval 1911, 29.

95 Until 1911, oil was used simply for heating and lighting; Malavel then anticipated the rapid increase in

consumption of petrol, with the use of unrefined petroleum engines in locomotives, factories, and ships' boilers and machinery. Malaval 1911, 29.

96 Politis 1930, 60.

97 Between 1913 and 1926, McLean laid out national and regional development plans, based on British town planning schemes. These encompassed about 50 Egyptian towns, including Alexandria. Home 1990, 9.

98 This is visible in Nicohosoff's 1937 map.

99 The first gradual dismantling of the timber yards started in June 2016 when part of the timber yard area was sold for other storage purposes serving the port. Based on the author's visit to the timber yards in January 2020, three timber yards were still standing, making a remaining area of 12,000 square metres (3 %) of the former 400,000 square metres established during the early 20th century. Since then, the empty area has undergone extensive physical changes to its historical footprint by further demolition of the timber yards and the placement of service roads on the resulting empty area for storage purposes. By October 2022, most of the remaining three timber yards had been dismantled; the last remains of the once extensive timber yard area – in terms of footprint and physical structure – now holds an area of almost 1,600 square metres.

100 Riad 1933, 247.

'Abd-Elbasit / ElSaiyd Hamdy 2014
محمد عبد الباسط / محمد السيد حمدي: ذاكرة الإسكندرية الفوتوغرافية. مكتبة الإسكندرية.
H. Abd-Elbasit / M. ElSaiyd Hamdy (eds.): The Photographic Memory of Alexandria (Alexandria 2014).

Abdel-Salam 1995
H. Abdel-Salam: The Historical Evolution and Present Morphology of Alexandria, Egypt. Planning Perspectives 10, no. 2, 1995, 173–198, https://doi.org/10.1080/02665439508725818 (10 October 2020).

'Ābid 2012
سوزان عابد: حكايات وروايات من مصر: وروايات من مصر: ميناء البصل .. حي الأعمال بالإسكندرية. ذاكرة مصر المعاصرة. مكتبة الإسكندرية
S. 'Ābid: Stories and Tales from Egypt: Al-Baṣal Port... the Neighbourhood of Businesses in Alexandria. Memory of Modern Egypt 10, July 2012, [56–59], https://archive.org/embed/26_20240218_202402 (17 March 2025).

'Ahmad / Al-'Abbadi 1997
عنتر إسماعيل أحمد / حسام العبادي: دليل موجز لآثار مدينة الإسكندرية. مؤسسة شباب الجامعة.
'A. I. Ahmad / H. Al-'Abbadi: Short Guide to a Historical and Archeological Site in Alexandria (Alexandria 1997).

Al-Falaki 1865
محمود الفلكي: خريطة الاسكندرية في سنة ١٢٨٢ هجرية.
M. Al-Falaki: Map of Alexandria in 1282 Hijri, Map Collection of archive of Centre d'Études Alexandrines, GRA_347, credit Collection J.Y. Empereur.

AlSayyad 2019
N. AlSayyad: Nile: Urban Histories on the Banks of a River (Edinburgh 2019).

As-Sirūgī 2010
أحمد السيد السروجي: الإسكندرية: قرائة من وحي أوراق الكهرباء ١٨٩٥-١٩٠٥. المطبعة الحديثة.
A. A. As-Sirūgī: Alexandria: A Reading based on the Electricity Documents 1895–1905 (Alexandria 2010).

Awad 1987
M. F. Awad: Le Modèle Européen : L'évolution Urbaine de 1807 à 1958. Revue de l'Occident Musulman et de La Méditerranée, no. 46, 1987 (Alexandrie, entre deux mondes, edited by R. Illbert), 93–109, https://doi.org/10.3406/remmm.1987.2193.

Awad 1996
M.F. Awad: The Métamorphoses of Mansheyah. Revue Mediterraneans/Méditerranéennes, no. 8–9, 1996, 42–58, https://doi.org/10.34847/nkl.1b0e24s2.

Awad 2008
M.F. Awad: Italy in Alexandria: Influences on the Built Environment (Alexandria 2008).

Baedeker 1877
K. Baedeker: Ägypten: Handbuch für Reisende (Band 1): Unter-Aegypten bis zum Fayûm und die Sinai-Halbinsel (Leipzig 1877).

Baer 1968
G. Baer: The Beginnings of Municipal Government in Egypt. Middle Eastern Studies 4, no. 2, 1968, 118–40. https://www.jstor.org/stable/4282239 (28 April 2020).

Baer 1969
G. Baer: Studies in the Social History of Modern Egypt (Chicago 1969).

Bartocci 1922
M. Bartocci: Alexandrie. Plan de la ville Ancienne et moderne, in: E. Breccia: Alexandrea ad Aegyptum (Bergame 1922). https://catalogue.bnf.fr/ark:/12148/cb445882121 (25 September 2021).

Beawes 1783
W. Beawes: Lex Mercatoria Rediviva: Or, The Merchant's Directory (London 1783), https://catalog.hathitrust.org/Record/001121349 (13 October 2020).

Clot-Bey 1840
A. B. Clot-Bey: Aperçu Général Sur l'Égypte, Tome I. (Paris

1840), https://archive.org/details/b22018992_0001/page/n7/mode/2up (13 October 2020).

Collection Max Karkégi 1859
Notes et documents sur la ville du Caire et l'histoire de l'Egypte contemporaine, 1859 (A) Palais du Gabary, près d'Alexandrie, résidence du vice-roi d'Egypte, Bnf_ Z-90 (2)-4, Collection Max Karkégi, Bibliothèque nationale de France (Bnf), Paris, France.

Crinson 1996
M. Crinson: Empire Building: Orientalism & Victorial Architecture (London 1996).

Crouchley 1938
A. E. Crouchley: The Economic Development of Modern Egypt (London 1938).

Cuno 1994
K. M. Cuno: The Pasha's Peasants: Land, Society, and Economy in Lower Egypt, 1740–1858 (Cairo 1994).

Daly 1998
M.W. Daly: The British Occupation, 1882–1922, in: M.W. Daly (ed.): The Cambridge History of Egypt, Volume Two, Modern Egypt from 1517 to the End of the Twentieth Century (Cambridge 1998) 239–251.

Davies & Company 1901
Davies & Company: Mediterranean Egypt, the Port of Alexandria, published at the Admiralty 15th March 1901, Hydrographic Office, printed in Great Britain in 1908. https://collections.lib.uwm.edu/digital/collection/agdm/id/8500/ (20 September 2021).

De Cosson 1935
A. De Cosson: Mareotis Being a Short Account of the History and Ancient Monuments of the North-Western Desert of Egypt and of Lake Mareotis (London 1935).

Earle 1926
E. Mead: Egyptian Cotton and the American Civil War. The Academy of Political Science 4, no. 4, 1926, 520–545, https://www.jstor.org/stable/2142228 (7 August 2022).

Fahmy 1998
K. Fahmy: The Era of Muhammad 'Ali Pasha, 1805–1848, in: M. W. Daly (ed.): The Cambridge History of Egypt, Volume Two, Modern Egypt from 1517 to the End of the Twentieth Century (Cambridge 1998) 139–179.

Ferro /Magli 2012
L. Ferro / G. Magli: The Astronomical Orientation of the Urban Plan and Alexandria. Oxford Journal of Archaeology 31, no. 4, 2012, 381–389, https://doi.org/10.1111/j.1468-0092.2012.00394.x.

Gallice Bey 1845
Gallice Bey: Plan Alexandrie et environs, 1845. Map collection of Centre d'Etudes Alexandrines (CEAlex), Alexandria, Egypt.

Girard 1822
P.S. Girard: Mémoire Sur l'Agriculture, l'Industrie et Le Commerce de l'Égypte (Paris 1822), https://gallica.bnf.fr/ark:/12148/bpt6k6213077f (19 October 2020).

Goad 1898
C. Goad: Insurance Plan Alexandria Egypt, 1898. Map Collection of archive of Centre d'Études Alexandrines, GRA_300, credit Collection J.Y. Empereur.

Hastaoglou-Martinidis 2014
V. Hastaoglou-Martinidis: The Cartography of Harbor Construction in Eastern Mediterranean Cities: Technical and Urban Modernization in the Late Nineteenth Century, in: B. Kolluoğlu / M. Toksös (eds.): Cities of the Mediterranean from the Ottomans to the Present Day (New York 2014) 78–99.

Hogarth / Benson 1895
D.G. Hogarth / E.F. Benson: Archaeological Report, 1894–1895: Report on Prospect of Research in Alexandria, 1895, https://www.jstor.org/stable/41932136 (19 October 2020).

Home 1990
R. Home: British Colonial Town Planning in the Middle East: The Work of W.H. McLean. Planning History 12, no. 1, 1990, 4–9. https://intlplanninghistorysociety.files.wordpress.com/2014/07/1990_vol-12_no1.pdf (4 August 2020).

Hunter 1998
F.R. Hunter: Egypt under the successors of Muhammad 'Ali, in: M.W. Daly (ed.): The Cambridge History of Egypt, Volume Two, Modern Egypt from 1517 to the End of the Twentieth Century (Cambridge 1998) 180–197.

Huri 1935
T.J. Huri: Alexandrie: Portique de l'Orient (Alexandria 1935) https://pfe.cealex.org/diffusion/PFEWeb/pfe_068/PFE_068_003_w.pdf (14 March 2025).

Ibrahim Bey 1935
N. Ibrahim Bey: The Development of Irrigation and Drainage in Egypt. Egypt Today, 1935, 115.

Illbert 1996
R. Illbert: Alexandrie 1830–1930: Histoire d'une Communauté Citadine, vol 1 (Cairo 1996).

Jondet 1921
G. Jondet: Atlas Historique de La Ville et des Ports d'Alexandrie. l'Institut français d'archéologie orientale (Cairo 1921).

La Chambre de Commerce Egyptienne d'Alexandrie 1951
La Chambre de Commerce Egyptienne d'Alexandrie (Alexandria 1951) Map collection of the Centre d'Etudes Alexandrines (CEAlex), Alexandria, Egypt, not digitised.

Malaval 1911
B. Malaval: Le Port d'Alexandrie, Conférence Faite Le 3 Juin 1911 à l'Université Populaire Libre d'Alexandrie Sous Le Patronage de l'Alliance Française (Alexandria 1911) https://bdd.cealex.org/diffusion/etud_anc_alex/LVR_000034_w.pdf (14 March 2025).

Malaval / Jondet 1912
B. Malaval / G. Jondet: Le Port d'Alexandrie (Cairo 1912), https://gallica.bnf.fr/ark:/12148/bpt6k9108696h.

McKenzie 2007
J. McKenzie: The Architecture of Alexandria and Egypt, c. 300 B.C. to A.D. 700 (New Haven and London 2007).

Ministère des Travaux Publics 1882
Ministère des Travaux Publics: Alexandrie, in: Atlas des

ports étrangers, 3e série (Paris 1882) pl. XVII, https://coilink.org/20.500.12592/bh7bx4 (16 March 2025).

Mubarak 1889
علي باشا مبارك: الخطط التوفيقية الجديدة لمصر القاهرة ومدنها وبلادها القديمة والشهيرة. المطبعة الكبرى الأميرية.
'A. P. Mubarak: Egypt's Plan of Cairo and Its Old and Famous Towns, vol. 7 (Cairo 1889), http://menadoc.bibliothek.uni-halle.de/ssg/content/titleinfo/1240600 (29 July 2020).

Müller 1855
C. Müller: Plan d'Alexandrie, comprenant toutes ses fortifications, rues et édifices publics, scale not given (Trieste 1855), https://gallica.bnf.fr/ark:/12148/btv1b8440801b (14 March 2025).

Municipalité 1902
Les Services Techniques de la Municipalité: Plan de la Ville d'Alexandrie, 1902. http://www.alexanderstomb.com/main/imageslibrary/maps/AlexMunicipality1902.jpg (17 March 2025).

Napier 1841
E. Napier: Plan of Alexandria and its neighbourhood, 1841. Map Private Collection of Dr. C. Shalaan. Centre d'Etudes Alexandrines – UAR 3134, Centre National de la Recherche Scientifique.

Nasr ElDin 2006
A. Nasr ElDin: Railroads in the Land of the Nile: The Story of Egyptian Railroads. Economic and Business History Research Centre 1, no. 3, 2006, 19–22.

Nasr ElDin / Gwyn 2016
A. Nasr ElDin / D. Gwyn: Early Main Line Railways in Egypt: The Tainted Gift, in: P. Cross-Rudkin (ed.): Early Main Line Railways: papers from the International Early Main Line Railways Conference (Clare 2016) 76–88.

Nicohosoff 1937
A. Nicohosoff: Plan General d'Alexandrie avec ses Embellissements Recents (Alexandria 1937).

Owen 1993
E. R. J. Owen: Middle East in the World Economy, 1800–1914 (London 1993).

Pallini / Scaccabarozzi 2016
C. Pallini / A. R. Scaccabarozzi: British Planning Schemes for Alexandria and Its Region, 1834–1958, in: C. N. Silva (ed.): Urban Planning in North Africa (Ashgate 2016) 161–70.

Pecnik 1901
C. Pecnik: Ramleh: La Riviera Eleusinienne et Alexandrie (Egypte) Manuels de Voyage Woerl (Leipzig 1901) https://bdd.cealex.org/diffusion/etud_anc_alex/LVR_000077_w.pdf (14 March 2025).

Politis 1930
A. G. Politis: L'Hellenisme et l'Egypte Moderne, Tomb II (Paris 1930) https://anemi.lib.uoc.gr/metadata/5/e/a/metadata-01-0001093.tkl (14 March 2025).

President au Ministre de l'interieur 1919
Lettre du President au Ministre de l'interieur au sujet des Tramways, 9 October 1919. Wathā'iq Abdīn, 0069-005354 (Cairo 1919). Dār al-wathā'iq al-qaumīyah (DWQ), Cairo, Egypt.

Raafat 2010
S. Raafat: The Egyptian Bourse (Cairo 2010).

Raymond 1991
أندريه ريمون: المدن العربية الكبرى في العصر العثماني. ترجمة لطيف فرج. دار الفكرللدراسات والنشر والتوزيع.
A. Raymond: Grandes villes arabes à l'époque ottomane (L. Faraj, Trans.) (Cairo 1991) https://archive.org/embed/1319p.d.f1224 (16 March 2025).

Reimer 1988
M. J. Reimer: Colonial Bridgehead: Social and Spatial Change in Alexandria, 1850–1882. International Journal of Middle East Studies 20, no. 4, 1988, 531–553, https://www.jstor.org/stable/163400 (18 October 2020).

Reimer 1993
M. J. Reimer: Reorganizing Alexandria: The Origins and History of the Conseil de l'Ornato. Journal of Urban History 19, no. 3, 1933, 55–83, https://doi.org/10.1177/009614429301900304.

Reimer 1994
M. J. Reimer: Ottoman Alexandria: The Paradox of Decline and the Reconfiguration of Power in Eighteenth-Century Arab Provinces. Journal of the Economic and Social History of the Orient 37, no. 2, 1994, 107–146, https://doi.org/10.2307/3632545.

Reimer 2019
M. J. Reimer: Colonial Bridgehead: Government and Society in Alexandria, 1807–1882 (London, New York 2019).

Riad 1933
M. Riad: Alexandria: Its Town Planning Development. The Town Planning Review 15, no. 4, 1933, 233–248, https://www.jstor.org/stable/40101080 (10 October 2020).

Schuyler 1891
E. Schuyler: Irrigation. Continent of Africa. Egypt, in: Canals and Irrigation in Foreign Countries: Report from the Consuls of the United States in Answer to Circulars from the Department of State, 255–300 (Washington 1891), https://books.google.de/books/about/Canals_and_Irrigation_in_Foreign_Countri.html?id=dOTyoC93l5IC&redir_esc=y (22 October 2020).

Silva 2016
C. N. Silva: Urban Planning in North Africa (London 2016).

St. John 1834
J. A. St. John: Egypt and Mohamed Ali; or Travels in the Valley of the Nile, vol. I (London 1834) https://archive.org/details/egyptandmohamme01johngoog/page/n378/mode/2up/search/store (20 October 2020).

Survey Department Cairo 1907
Survey Department Cairo 1907: Provisional Map of Alexandria & Environs. Sheet 1/2. Scale 1/50,000. Surveyed in 1889–1893. Revised in 1902–03. Egypt. Maṣlaḥat al-Misāḥah (Cairo 1907). Map at American Geographical Society Library Digital Map Collection, https://collections.lib.uwm.edu/digital/collection/agdm/id/3120/rec/23 (25 September 2021).

Survey Department of Egypt 1911–13
Survey Department of Egypt: Alexandria, scale 1:5,000, (Alexandria 1911–13). Map at Albright Institute of Archaeological Research, Jerusalem, Israel, https://aiar.org/wp-content/uploads/2015/05/Alexandria_1_5000.pdf (19 December 2020).

Tabak 2010
F. Tabak: Economic and Ecological Change in the Eastern

Mediterranean, c. 1550 1850, in: B. Kolluoğlu / M. Toksös (eds.): Cities of the Mediterranean from the Ottomans to the Present Day (New York 2010) 14–22.

Van Pellecom 2010
R. Van Pellecom: Alexandria & Ramleh Railway Co Ltd. AAHA – Amicale Alexandrie Hier et Aujourd'hui, no. 61, 2010, http://www.aaha.ch/cahiers/aaha-cahier-61-ronny.pdf (20 October 2020).

Vatikiotis 1991
P. J. Vatikiotis: The History of Modern Egypt: From Muhammad Ali to Mubarak (Baltimore 1991).

Wescott et al. 2016
W. A. Wescott / M. Atta / J. C. Dolson: A Brief History of the Exploration History of the Gulf of Suez, Egypt, poster presentation given at AAPG 2016 International Convention and Exhibition, Cancun, (Mexico, September 2016) 6–9, https://www.searchanddiscovery.com/documents/2016/30473westcott/ndx_wescott.pdf (30 August 2021).

Wiet 1959
G. Wiet: Mohammed Ali et Les Beaux-Arts (Cairo 1959).

Wright 1909
A. Wright: Twentieth Century Impressions of Egypt. Its History, People, Commerce, Industries, and Resources (London 1909), https://gallica.bnf.fr/ark:/12148/bpt6k9106163s/f9.image.r=industrial%20building%20company%20of%20alexandria (24 April 2020).

Image Sources

1 Open Street Map, www.mapz.com (8 August 2022). Edited by author, 2022.

2 Author, 2021, based on Napier 1841 and Müller 1855 (cf. Jondet 1921, map XXXV).

3 Author, 2021, based on Al-Falaki 1865; Baedeker 1887.

4 Author, 2021, based on Goad 1898; Hogarth / Benson 1895.

5 Author, 2021, based on Goad 1898; Hogarth / Benson 1895.

6 Author, 2021, based on Bartocci 1922; Nicohosoff 1937.

7 Library of Congress, Prints & Photographs Division, [reproduction number, e.g., LC-DIG-matpc-00718] G. Eric and Edith Matson Photograph Collection, [online n.d.] https://www.loc.gov/pictures/item/2019706705/ (10 October 2020). Edited by author, 2021.

8 The author used a blind map of the city as a blank canvas to colour and highlight the zone and city fabric. The blind map is based on Google Earth Pro (20 September 2021).

Redoing the Peripheries
Displacement, Segregation, and Urban Sprawl in Casablanca

Raffael Beier, Torben Dedring

Like many other cities within the Middle East and North Africa (MENA) region, Casablanca, Morocco's economic capital, is characterised by a strong legacy of colonial spatial segregation. Between 1912 and 1956, Casablanca belonged to the French protectorate in Morocco. During the protectorate's first years, French settlers started to build a *ville nouvelle* (new town) exclusively for Europeans and adjacent to the existing *ancienne médina* (old town), which in 1907 had a population of only about 20,000 inhabitants.[1] The spatial separation between the Moroccan old town and the European new town laid the foundation for the segregated urban planning that has marked the development of Morocco's biggest city, which currently has a population of around four million.

Today, the legacy of colonial spatial segregation is still easy to detect by taking a closer look at the city's layout on satellite images. In today's city centre, the walled *médina* with its narrow, winding roads is surrounded by the *ville nouvelle* with its vast boulevards and Art Deco houses. From the harbour along the northeastern seashore, early colonial industries developed into the current industrial corridor that has established Casablanca as Morocco's industrial centre. Historically, this has been the place of the city's large working-class neighbourhoods, the so-called *quartier populaires*, which started to develop in the mid-20th century through public housing schemes around the first shantytowns (*bidonvilles*), erected by Moroccan workers in response to a lack of alternative accommodation. On the other side of the city centre along the southwestern seashore, former European villa neighbourhoods have become today's places of residence for the urban elite, easily recognisable on a satellite picture by the large amount of greenery. Nearby recent developments such as the Morocco Mall – opened in 2011 as Africa's supposedly largest shopping centre – have reinforced the wealthy status of this area.

This rough morphological characterisation from above shows how colonial planning has irrevocably shaped the city's development. Yet, beyond this macro-level spatial segregation, Casablanca's urban planning since Independence in 1956 has continued to follow colonial pathways and has hardly challenged the city's legacy of colonial segregation – with certain parallels to Janet Abu Lughod's famous account of an «urban apartheid» in Rabat-Salé.[2] In this chapter, we focus on these continuities by highlighting three common threads, namely urban re-imagination, resettlement, and land speculation.

First, urban re-imagination means a drastic rethinking of what is «good» urbanism, as embodied by the construction of the European *ville nouvelle* as the «modern» antithesis of the *ancienne médina* under colonial rule.[3] Today, such re-imagination refers to the objective of transforming Casablanca from an industrial city with a rough working-class image to a shiny and attractive hub for international financial services.[4] The construction of new megaprojects – i.e., Casablanca Finance City and Casablanca Marina[5] – should help to spread Casablanca's renewed image as a world-class metropolis emancipated from its colonial industrial past.

Second, resettlement of *bidonville* dwellers has been a fundamental element of urban planning in Casablanca since colonial times.[6] Informally constructed *bidonvilles* were original parts of the colonial *quartiers populaires* (the «old» or «colonial peripheries»). However, authorities – from colonial times up until today – have perceived these shantytowns as a threat to orderly urban planning, public health, and social peace, and have initiated different resettlement projects that have moved them further away from the city centre since the 1930s. Starting in 2004, the national *Villes Sans Bidonvilles* (VSB, cities without shantytowns) programme has resettled *bidonville* residents in the name of «adequate housing» away from workplaces towards marginal and publicly neglected new towns (the «new peripheries»).[7]

Third, speculation based on expected land price increases has been a major driver of Casablanca's metropolitan growth. Recalling Casablanca's colonial history, the late anthropologist Paul Rabinow noted, «Speculation was the motor force of the city's birth and growth (…). The result was a spatial extension toward a continually receding periphery.»[8] Today, linked to resettlement projects, such somewhat uncontrolled «speculative sprawl»[9] drives the emergence of hardly integrated «new peripheries», fuelled by political economies boosting the construction sector.[10]

Based on these three common threads (and we do not claim this to be an exhaustive representation), this chapter uses cartography to show how current urban development trends in Casablanca sustain spatially the legacy of colonial planning. We argue that the re-imagination of Casablanca as a world-class metropolis since the turn of the millennium has been working once again as a driver for remaking socio-spatial segregation at the metropolitan level – through megaprojects and urban renewal, resettlement of marginalised urban dwellers, and a construction boom led by land speculation. Casablanca's image-driven transformation pushes long-term stigmatised, politically undesired, and socially marginalised population groups from the *quartiers populaires* – the «old peripheries» – towards the «new peripheries».[11] Seen as a burden to the city's international economic ambitions and its aspirational image, these people are expected to reside outside the perimeter of the imagined world-class city, symbolised by the growth of urban megaprojects. Thus, this chapter argues that current urban planning since the 2000s addresses urban deficiencies with roots in colonial planning (i.e., *bidonvilles*) by producing «new peripheries» in a way that resembles the creation of the «old peripheries» under colonial rule. While the core city is renewed and upgraded, the construction of new peripheries is driven by land speculation and population resettlement, lacking integrated urban planning at the metropolitan level.

In the remainder of the chapter, we will start by briefly summarising colonial planning practices in Casablanca before we show how the colonial peripheries (the old peripheries) – especially the informally constructed parts of these areas known as *bidonvilles* – have developed since Independence. The chapter's first map (fig. 1) visualises the colonial legacy of Casablanca as well as the spatial distribution of *bidonvilles* before the start of the VSB programme in 2004. This idealised[12] thematic map based on satellite imagery features specific urban developments that are of relevance to Casablanca's colonial urban planning legacy. The map's historic elements are based on historic maps of Casablanca as well as literature on Casablanca's colonial planning history.[13] For other map elements, we used data and knowledge from the first author's field research in Casablanca[14] as well as a detailed analysis of historic satellite imagery (Google Earth) (i.e., the spatial distribution of *bidonvilles* before the start of the VSB programmes).

Following this discussion, we describe how current metropolitan growth is driven by both business interests in urban sprawl and the political desire to build a «world-class» city. The chapter's second map (see fig. 6) visualises changes to

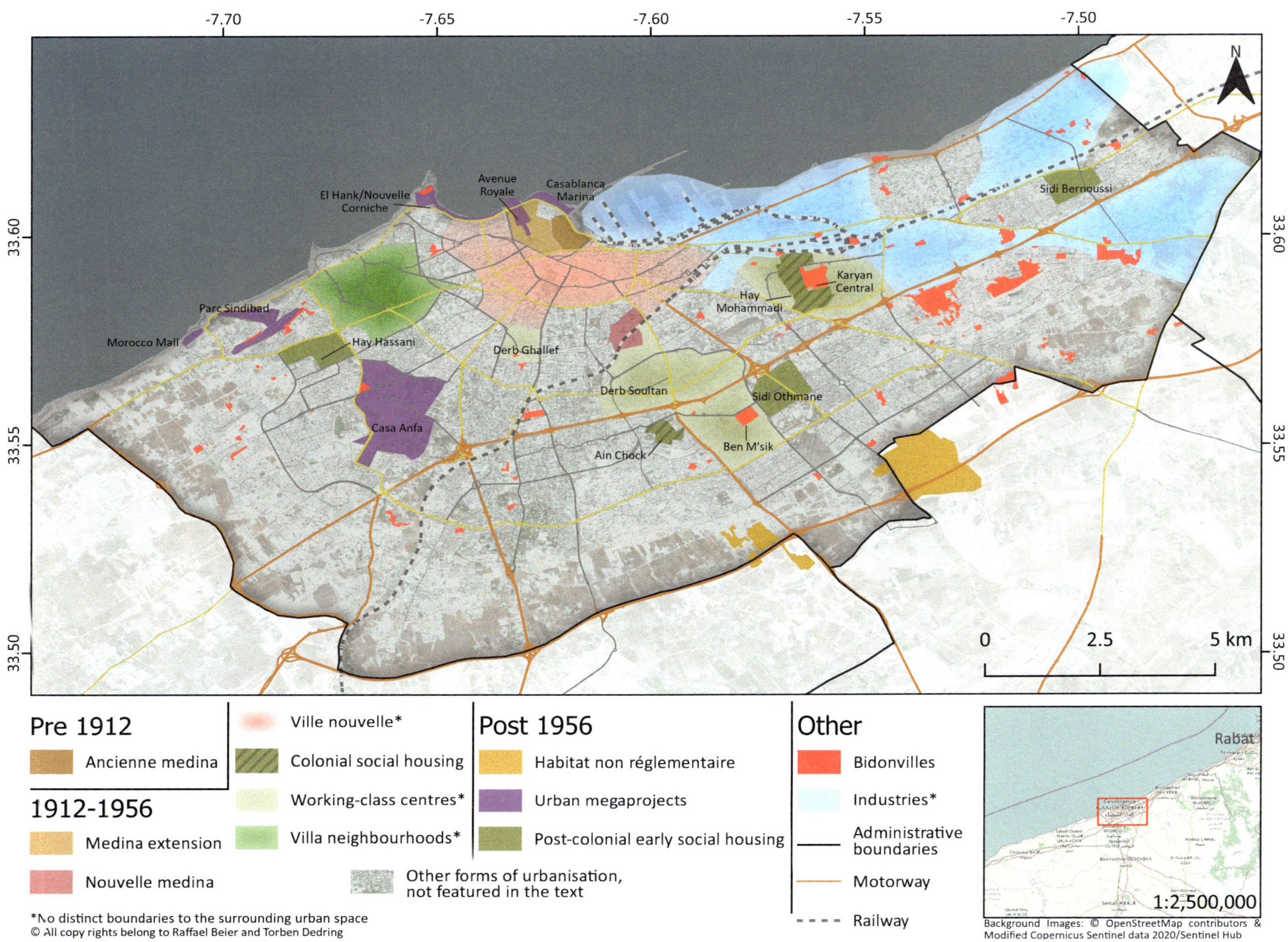

1 Casablanca's colonial urban planning legacy and the spatial distribution of *bidonvilles* around 2004.

the built-up area, showing Casablanca's *bidonville* resettlement sites and its urban sprawl since 1994. To locate the resettlement sites and to identify the precise resettlement projects, the authors build on the first author's interviews with displaced residents and other stakeholders,[15] online articles in local newspapers, and information available on the website of the leading housing and resettlement operator Al Omrane.[16] The urban sprawl since 1994 was reconstructed through cloud-free Landsat 5 (1994 & 2004), Landsat 8 (2014) and Sentinel 2 (2019) satellite images utilising a bi-temporal pixel-based random forest classification algorithm within the Google Earth Engine (GEE). This is a supervised classification algorithm, which assigns a class (e.g., urban or non-urban) to a pixel based on several decision trees with randomly selected reference sites.[17] The second map further emphasises VSB resettlements as major drivers of urban sprawl, but also highlights the spatial distribution of *bidonvilles* before the VSB programme (see first map) and individual resettlement projects and sites by using information from Al Omrane, newspaper articles, and the first author's own field research.

The Emergence of Casablanca's Colonial Peripheries

Before the French protectorate, which after the initial military occupation lasted from 1912 to Morocco's Independence in 1956, Casablanca was a tiny fishing town with a small but busy port. In 1907, only about 20,000 inhabitants – including about 5,000 Jews – lived in what is today the city's old town, the *ancienne médina* (see fig. 1). With the proclamation of the protectorate in 1912, General Lyautey, the first French resident-general in Morocco, started the construction of a new town (*ville nouvelle*), which was much bigger than the *ancienne médina* and exclusively intended for a European population that despite rapid growth never exceeded Casablanca's Moroccan population.[18] The *ville nouvelle* was located directly opposite the *ancienne médina*, separated from it by the old town wall and large boulevards (fig. 2). Although the *ville nouvelle* might look on maps like an extension of the old town, it was designed as a separate town in order to ensure strict residential separation of Europeans,

2 The spatial separation of *ancienne médina* and *ville nouvelle* in Casablanca, March 2015.

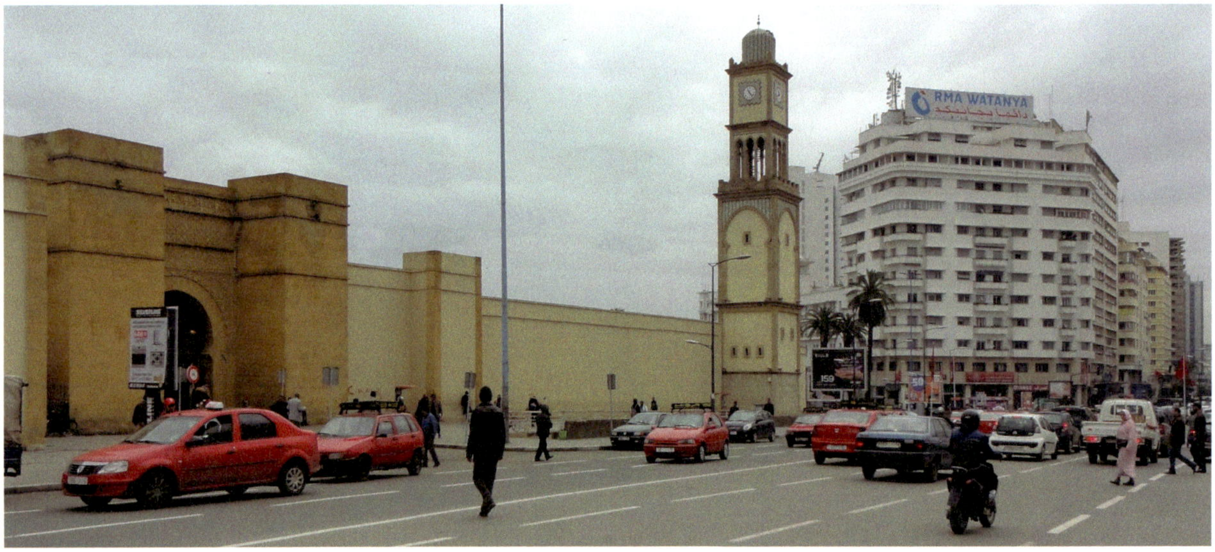

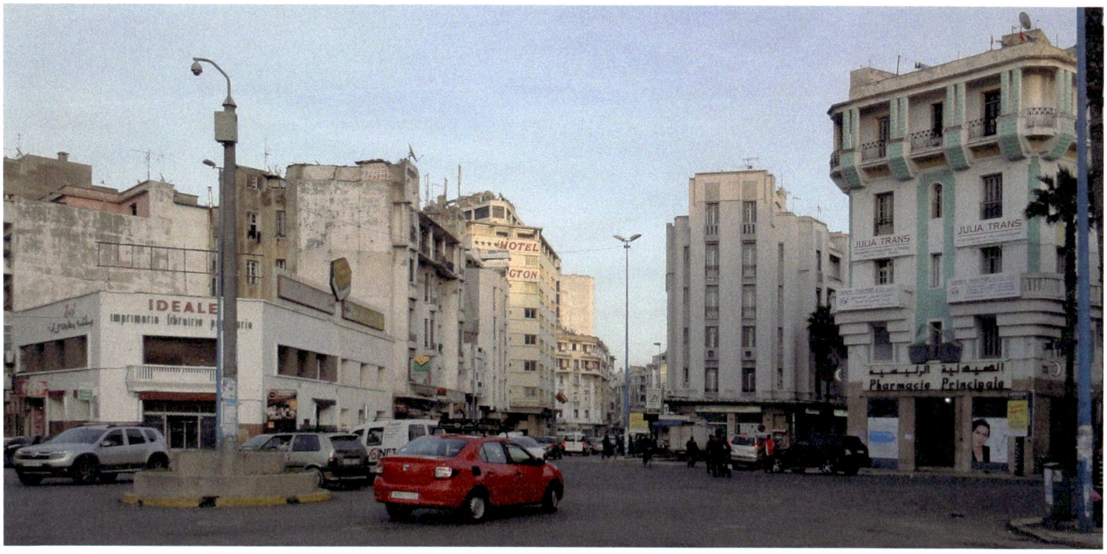

3 Art Deco architecture at Mers Sultan roundabout in Casablanca's *ville nouvelle*, February 2017.

who refused to cohabit with the Moroccans in the *ancienne médina* (see fig. 1).[19] Since its establishment, Casablanca's *ville nouvelle* has been a site for experiments with modern European urbanism – first inspired by Art Deco style and later by the ideas of Le Corbusier (fig. 3).[20] Its construction was largely driven by land speculation, which initially was one of the reasons for a severe housing shortage.[21] Today, vast boulevards and monumental apartment and office buildings with white, often generously decorated façades characterise this part of the city. The city administration has recently started to invest in the restoration of Art Deco buildings to promote this architectural heritage for touristic purposes.[22]

The *ancienne médina* represents to some extent an alternative version of city planning. Unlike the boulevards of the *ville nouvelle*, the street layout in Moroccan medinas may be confusing for outsiders, characterised by lots of narrow, winding alleys and cul-de-sacs that offer lots of shadow and semi-public spaces. High residential density is further complemented by numerous small shops and street markets that make Casablanca's *ancienne médina* a busier and more crowded place than the *ville nouvelle*. However, compared to the medieval old towns in Morocco's four imperial cities Marrakech, Fez, Meknes, and Rabat, Casablanca's comparatively young *ancienne médina* has little touristic appeal and has not experienced similar gentrification and touristification processes.[23] Still, Casablanca's *ancienne médina* and especially its western extra-mural extension represent working-class market centres and neighbourhoods.[24]

During the protectorate, the *ancienne médina* was one of the limited places where the growing Moroccan population of Casablanca could reside. Since the 1910s, more and more Moroccans from the countryside were attracted by the booming port city, not only to search for work in construction and industry, but also to escape rural droughts.[25] The shortage of housing for Moroccans caused overcrowding in the *ancienne médina*, which quickly led to a deterioration of infrastructure and housing conditions, ignored by the colonial authorities.[26] Furthermore, the *ancienne médina* expanded towards the west

– the only possible direction given the sea and the harbour in the northeast and the *ville nouvelle* in the south (see fig. 1, «medina extension»).[27] These extra-mural extensions developed in a somewhat unplanned way after the 1910s and mostly accommodated poorer working-class people.[28] Here, Moroccan land speculation was an important driving force, which led to extremely high densities and narrow streets, similar to the *médina* but with a more regular street grid.[29]

In the 1920s, driven by the construction of colonial industries close to the port, new peripheries emerged as the places of residence of the industrial labour force, who could not find a place to stay in the overcrowded *médina*. On the one hand, colonial authorities refused to provide shelter for the native working class in order to prevent Moroccans from settling in the city, but also because they were barely able to provide housing to the growing European population.[30] On the other hand, there was an urgent need for cheap labour close to the factories. Thus, the authorities tacitly tolerated auto-constructed neighbourhoods close to the industries as a «temporary» makeshift solution (see fig. 1).[31] This temporary tolerance allowed colonial authorities to occasionally intervene and restructure some of these settlements in case of hygienic concern or interest in occupied land.[32] Casablanca's most famous *bidonville*, Karyan Central (*Carrières Centrales*), which used to be the centre of Hay Mohammadi, was a result of colonial restructuring of scattered *bidonvilles* in the late 1930s (see fig. 1).[33] Initially, the *bidonville* houses were built out of available makeshift materials such as petrol tins (*bidons*), wooden planks, and corrugated iron sheets.[34] It is said that the French term *bidonville* – literally meaning a city built out of petrol tins – goes back to the first auto-constructed neighbourhoods in Casablanca.[35] In addition to the *bidonvilles*, some colonial companies, for example the sugar and the cement companies, also built their own workers' housing at the eastern peripheries to accommodate their factory workers. Examples are the *cité* COSUMAR and the *cité* SOCICA, which together with *bidonvilles*, formed the city's first industrial working-class neighbourhood, today known as Hay Mohammadi.

Finally, another Moroccan neighbourhood of the early colonial city developed in the south of the *ville nouvelle*. Unlike the other types of peripheral developments (in particular, *bidonvilles* and the medina extension), the so-called *nouvelle médina* was a more intentionally planned project of the colonial authorities (see fig. 1). The decision to build a *nouvelle médina* followed diverse rationales. First, it was a response to the housing shortage and hygienic concerns related to the degradation of the *ancienne médina*.[36] Second, it sought to keep segregation and domination, but to co-opt established Moroccan elites – including the Sultan.[37] The latter was allowed to use one part of the *nouvelle médina* to construct his palace and another to build his own neighbourhood – Derb Soultan – with dense housing mainly for his servants.[38] Through semi-planned land parcelling, Derb Soultan quickly expanded further towards the south, resulting in a very dense and badly equipped working-class commercial centre (see fig. 1).[39] Beside the market of Derb Ghallef, which, similar to other market centres, had developed in a somewhat unplanned way just outside the European *ville nouvelle*,[40] Derb Soultan became the second market centre for the Moroccan working class outside the *ancienne médina*. Later, a third market centre developed around the *bidonvilles* in Hay Mohammadi, mainly serving the industrial labour force.[41]

Employing a more general perspective, Casablanca's growth under colonial rule was driven by land speculation and urbanistic experiments. As such, the city grew in a dynamic and decentralised way that did not respect land-use plans in a rigorous way. While private European capital drove the expansion of villa neighbourhoods mainly towards the southwest and the south, small *bidonvilles* emerged at scattered locations in the east and were often home to construction and industrial labourers. In the 1940s, when about 19% of the city's population lived in *bidonvilles*,[42] colonial authorities felt urged to intervene – for hygienic purposes, but also to enhance the protectorate's legitimacy vis-à-vis the disadvantaged local population. The Moroccan sociologist Abderrahmane Rachik notes:

> On the eve of the Moroccan Independence, the mass housing production of the colonial authorities presented a desperate (and late) attempt to gain some kind of political legitimacy towards the nationalist movement and among popular classes.[43]

A first example of what we call colonial social housing in the first map was the construction of Aïn Chock in the mid-1940s as the first relocation site for former *bidonvilles* (see fig. 1). Although Aïn Chock eventually became more of a publicity strategy and never achieved its objective of rehousing a large number of *bidonville* dwellers, it marks the beginning of Casablanca's long-term tradition of housing and resettlement interventions.[44] In the 1950s, colonial authorities experimented with different forms of social housing in the district of Hay Mohammadi.[45] This included the construction of public housing estates inspired by Le Corbusier[46] and large-scale experimentation with sites and services. The so-called *trâmes d'Ecochard*, a form of sites-and-services housing scheme, provided low-income households with a modular house on an 8x8 grid, which allowed people to expand their houses incrementally over time according to their changing resources and needs.[47] This planning concept has significantly shaped the «old peripheries», such as the working-class neighbourhood Hay Mohammadi, and was even adopted after Independence.[48]

Colonial Peripheries after Independence: From Glory to Disgrace

When Morocco finally achieved its Independence in 1956, some of the glory of this moment was shared by the residents of Casablanca's largest *bidonvilles* Ben M'sik and Karyan Central (see fig. 1), which had been significant centres of the Independence movement.[49] On a tourist information signboard at the tramway stop «Hay Mohammadi», the following memorial information recalls Karyan Central's significant role (fig. 4):

> During the French protectorate, Karyan Central was an important centre of Moroccan resistance. Its inhabitants played a crucial role in the struggle for Independence. After Independence in 1956, King Mohammed V paid homage to people's loyalty, when praying in the neighbourhood's eponymous mosque.

Since the time of King Mohammed V's visit, the neighbourhood around Karyan Central has been called Hay Mohammadi (literally, Mohammad's neighbourhood). What the signboard does not

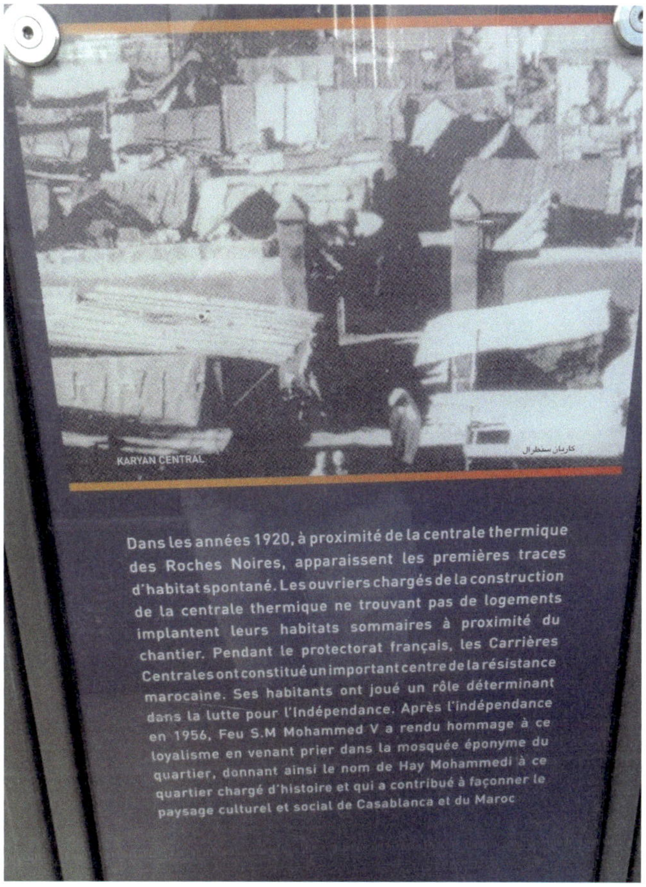

4 A memorial sign of CasaMémoire highlighting the history of Karyan Central, December 2016.

mention is that Karyan Central does not exist anymore (fig. 5). Between 2009 and 2016, the state resettled the residents of Karyan Central in the spatially disconnected new neighbourhood of Nouvelle Lahraouiyine (fig. 6), some 10 km away from Hay Mohammadi and outside the municipal boundaries of Casablanca. Although most of the approximately 30,000 inhabitants agreed to be resettled, the resettlement included, in March 2016, the forced eviction of about 450 remaining households, who were accused of illegal occupation of land.[50]

This brief introduction shows how Morocco's colonial peripheries, particularly its *bidonvilles*, have lost social status over the decades since Independence. Notwithstanding that *bidonvilles* were never considered a legitimate part of the city, stigmatisation has intensified over time, driving large-scale population displacement and resettlement. Once the home of the Independence movement, *bidonvilles* became the most stigmatised places of residence in urban Morocco. Today, large parts of the urban society as well as politicians on all levels consider *bidonvilles* as abnormal exclaves of the city, the evil part of urbanisation, and a burden to the state and its development and modernisation agenda.[51] *Bidonville* residents are stigmatised as poor, uneducated, and potentially criminal, stuck in their rural and traditional ways of life. They are discriminated against on

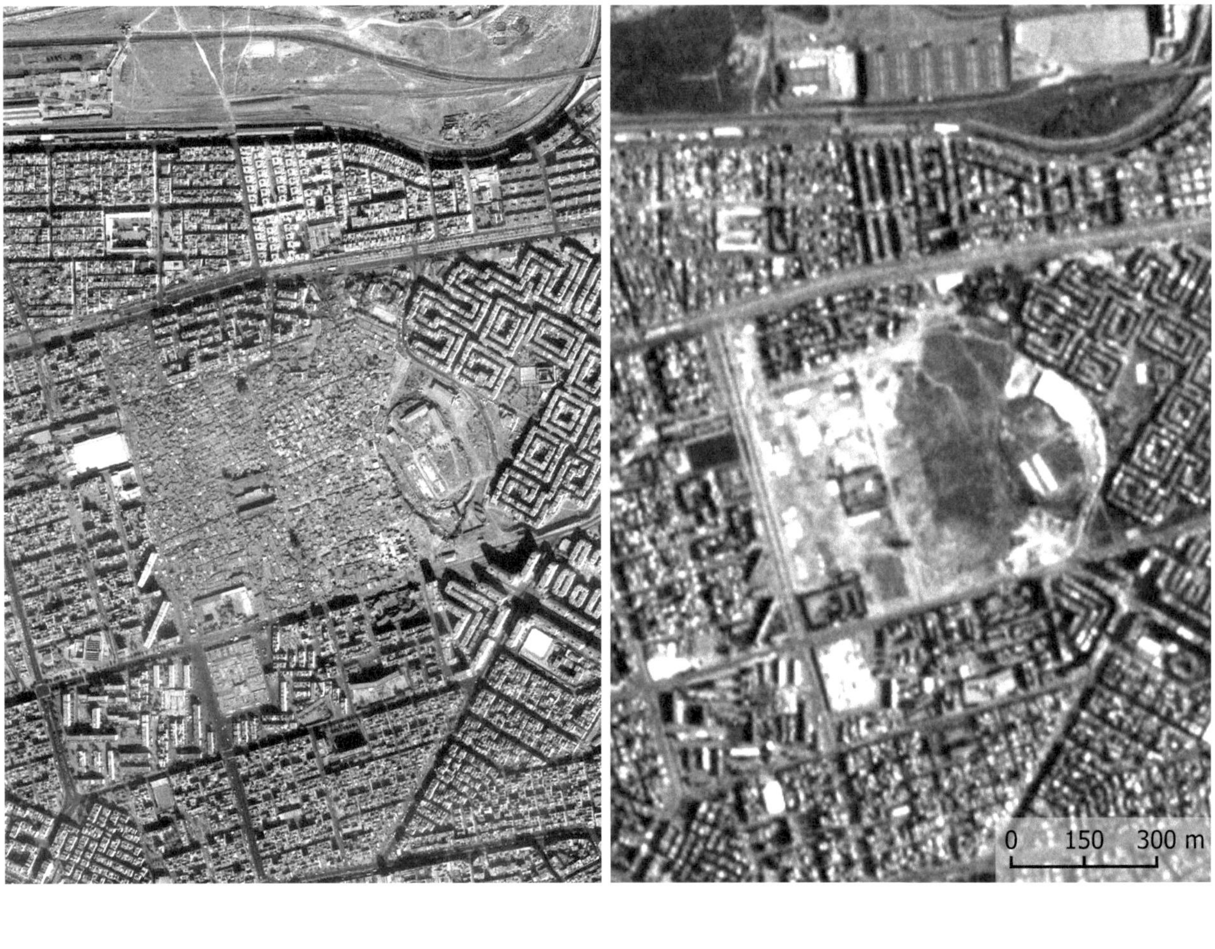

5 The *bidonville* Karyan Central, surrounded by other working-class neighbourhoods in Hay Mohammadi, before its demolition (left side, 2006) and today (right side, 2021).

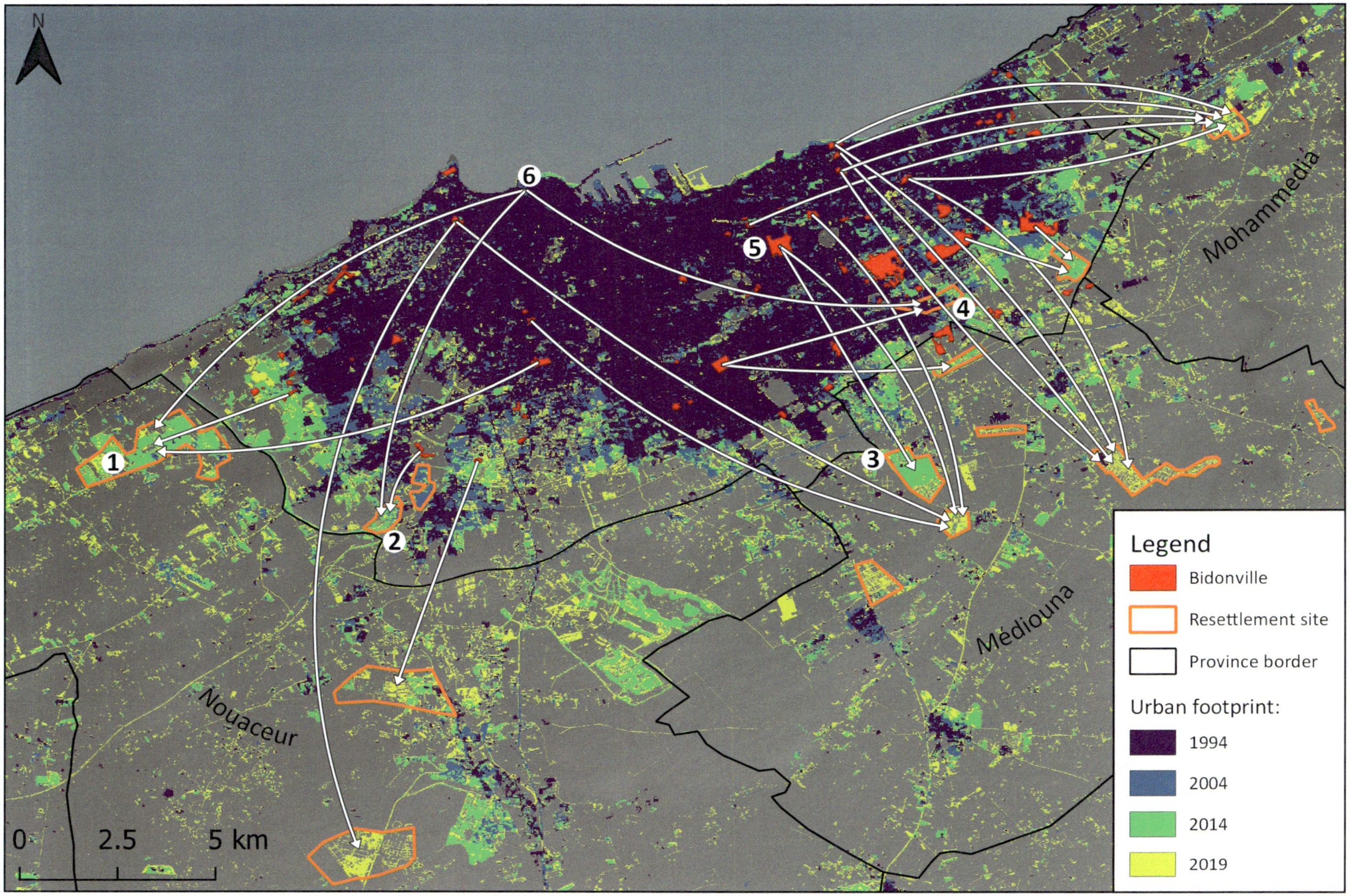

Overall classification accuracy (OA) in % based on n validation points

	1994	2004	2014	2019
n	900	900	900	1696
OA in %	91.22	93.89	91.78	96.99

Year of production: 2020 | Projection: WGS84; 4326

1: Er-Rahma
2: Nassim
3: Nouvelle Lahraouiyine
4: Attacharouk
5: Karyan Central
6: Medina Extension

6 *Bidonville* resettlement sites and the growth of sealed surface area from 1994 to 2019 in Casablanca's metropolitan area.

the job market, at school, and by police officers.[52] Stigmatisation has further increased since 2003 in reaction to suicide attacks launched by some *bidonville* dwellers in inner-city Casablanca. The attacks fuelled the image of these neighbourhoods as breeding grounds for religious radicalism and extremism.[53] We will come back to this at the end of this section.

Immediately after Independence, Morocco's new government continued with social housing projects similar to late-colonial policies.[54] This included the construction of the Hay Hassani neighbourhood at the end of the 1950s, which was inspired by the *trâmes d'Ecochard* and which replaced a few unauthorised settlements that were destroyed by a fire in the same area (see fig. 1). Several similar neighbourhoods constructed during that time at the city's peripheries were supposed to provide enough low-income housing to replace *bidonvilles*. However, on the one hand, continuous rural-to-urban migration led to the emergence of new *bidonvilles* and the growth of existing ones.[55] On the other hand, in the 1970s, middle-class residents, displaced from the former *ville nouvelle* and adjacent neighbourhoods due to rising land prices and rents, took over new housing in neighbourhoods such as Hay Hassani, Sidi Bernoussi, and Aïn Chock.[56] Moreover, in the 1960s and 1970s, the post-Independence government prioritised rural development over urban housing policies.[57] Today, Aïn Chock, Hay Hassani, and Sidi Bernoussi are predominantly middle-class neighbourhoods, even though they are partially characterised by overpopulation and deteriorating building structures.

In the same period, from the 1960s to the 1980s, the former colonial working-class peripheries became central due to continuous urban growth. Older *bidonvilles* such as Karyan Central and Ben M'sik quickly developed into spatially well-integrated neighbourhoods and market centres. Despite having no formal land tenure, inhabitants of *bidonvilles* started to invest in their housing environment, replacing tin with bricks and cement, establishing collectively organised sanitation systems through auto-construction, and claiming their right to basic infrastructure such as water and (later) electricity. In response to the latter claims, public authorities ensured *bidonvilles'* access to basic grids but continued to refuse the formalisation of their land tenure.[58] In the 21st century, the vast majority of houses in Casablanca's *bidonvilles* are brick houses with a tin roof, an indoor bathroom, and access to water and electricity.[59] Thus, the incremental development and consolidation process of *bidonvilles* followed typical pathways of auto-constructed neighbourhoods as described most prominently by the late British architect and theorist John Turner in Latin America.[60]

However, since the 1980s, the image of *bidonvilles* in Morocco has further worsened. Two events triggered important policy interventions: bread riots in 1981 and suicide attacks in 2003. In 1981, strikes against a price increase of staple goods turned violent with some of Casablanca's larger *bidonvilles* such as Ben M'sik being centres of protest.[61] These protests reinforced a stigma of *bidonvilles* as the «illegal» home of the rebellious «dangerous classes». In response, the government immediately dismissed the in-situ upgrading plans for Ben M'sik and returned to resettlement approaches.[62] Instead of further integrating the former colonial peripheries, relocation to more peripheral serviced sites for self-construction (*recasement*) became the dominant approach – similar to the late-colonial *trâmes d'Ecochard.* To clarify, *recasement* means that residents receive a plot of land at another, usually more peripheral, location for a low, subsidised fee, but have to pay for all construction costs.[63] Residents receive no compensation apart from the opportunity to buy a subsidised plot of land and to become a formal homeowner. This scheme offers the government the advantage of planning the new settlement from scratch, avoiding dense structures that may complicate security or even military intervention.[64] Thus, the 1981 riots marked a turning point that reinforced the political desire to eradicate shantytowns, making them – at least for some time – an urgent priority of urban planning.[65]

However, the new strategies did not prove to be effective. Many eligible people would rather sell their plot at the resettlement site and move to another *bidonville* because they could not afford the construction of the house and/or preferred to stay in their area and hence closer to the city.[66] After 1998, with the advent of the *gouvernement d'alternance* (leftist government), progressive joint academic and political initiatives called for more participatory approaches as well as in-situ upgrading.[67] However, major changes failed to materialise on a larger scale due to another change in government in 2002 and, most importantly, because of the 2003 suicide attacks in Casablanca's city centre. The attacks severely worsened the stigmatisation of *bidonvilles* and their inhabitants.[68] As Sami Zemni and Koenraad Bogaert, specialists in North African studies, put it,

> The attacks not only stigmatised the slums as a breeding ground for radical Islamists, but also negatively affected the city's ‹unique selling proposition› and its image as a reliable destination for investment.[69]

They seemed to confirm the views of King Mohammed VI, who had called *bidonvilles* in a speech from October 2002 «a source of frustration, exclusion, deviation, and extremism» and a threat to Morocco's progressive development.[70]

The attacks and related security concerns were the final trigger for the nationwide VSB programme with the objective of clearing away all shantytowns in Morocco.[71] Although at the beginning of this programme, in-situ upgrading was still an official option as well as resettlement to apartment housing and serviced sites (*recasement*), in fact the VSB programme marked a final break with in-situ upgrading.[72] Upgrading was never the preferred option and was silently abandoned after new attacks in 2006 and 2007. Once again, security concerns drove authorities to prefer the demolition of shacks and subsequent *recasement* to serviced plots for construction.[73] To speed up the eradication of *bidonvilles* and to avoid a reselling of plots (and hence resettling in another *bidonville*), authorities invented the so-called third-party scheme.[74] As is usual in *recasement* schemes, two *bidonville* households in this scheme together receive one plot in the new town at a subsidised price. They are requested to demolish their own house in the *bidonville* directly after having accepted the resettlement conditions. If they are not able to build the new house themselves, they transfer the duty to a third party, who then funds the construction of a four-storey house as well as temporary rent for the *bidonville* households. In return, the third party receives the two lower floors, while each of the two *bidonville* households becomes the owner of one of the upper-floor apartments. Notwithstanding severe shortcomings, the scheme has increased housing affordability for vulnerable population groups and accelerated the resettlement projects.[75] Thus, the VSB programme moved a large number of *bidonville* dwellers – among them the residents of Karyan Central – to Casablanca's distant peripheries.

To conclude this section, it is important to underline that we are not aiming to criticise the fact that the state intervenes to improve the situation of *bidonvilles*. In fact, many inhabitants are looking forward to state interventions such as the VSB programme, reflecting the successful political rhetoric framing them as social policies that help to lift people out of poverty by moving them towards socially more conducive environments.[76] Our critique focuses more on the *how*, as we will further elaborate in the conclusion. As shown, Moroccan housing policies after the end of colonial rule have slowly moved away from in-situ solutions that improve the living conditions of people where they live without major disruptions of social and economic lives.[77] Instead, multiple forms of stigmatisation and security concerns have led to a strengthening of resettlement approaches after 1981 and 2003. Thus, instead of breaking with the colonial past, large-scale population displacement towards the peripheries continues to reproduce colonial patterns of segregation at the metropolitan level. Even worse, resettlement approaches have become increasingly repressive since the 2010s. Whereas modest participatory elements were part of the VSB programme at the beginning,[78] more recently, forced evictions have become more widespread and violent.[79]

Urban World-Class Aspirations, Land Speculation, and the New Peripheries

Looking at the regional level of Greater Casablanca,[80] one may highlight two significant drivers of resettlement programmes in the 21st century: first, the politically motivated transformation of the city of Casablanca into a world-class metropolis and international finance hub[81] and, second, real estate business and land speculation in the hinterland, composed of the provinces of Nouaceur, Médiouna, and Mohammedia[82] (see fig. 6). These drivers matter significantly, alongside stigmatisation and the 2003 suicide attacks that functioned as a trigger of the VSB programme.

The political wish to develop Casablanca into a world-class finance hub is rooted in nationwide policies aiming at boosting the international competitiveness of Morocco's larger cities. The first signs of these politics date back to the 1990s and the end of the reign of King Hassan II (r. 1961–1999), who created his own monument in the form of the largest mosque in Africa. Today, the Hassan II Mosque is Casablanca's most impressive landmark, marking the beginning of Morocco's urban renewal policies, based heavily on urban megaprojects and global image construction.[83] Hassan II Mosque was followed by the construction of the Avenue Royal to link the monumental mosque to the colonial city centre.[84] Whereas these early megaprojects were mainly financed by public money, more recent megaprojects such as the waterfront project Casablanca Marina and the brownfield redevelopment project Casa Anfa (including Casablanca Finance City; fig. 7), located on the city's former airport, are increasingly driven by private capital following neoliberal logics.[85] These projects are emblematic of new political priorities in neoliberal urban development and

7 The construction of Casablanca Finance City as part of the brownfield development Casa Anfa, July 2019.

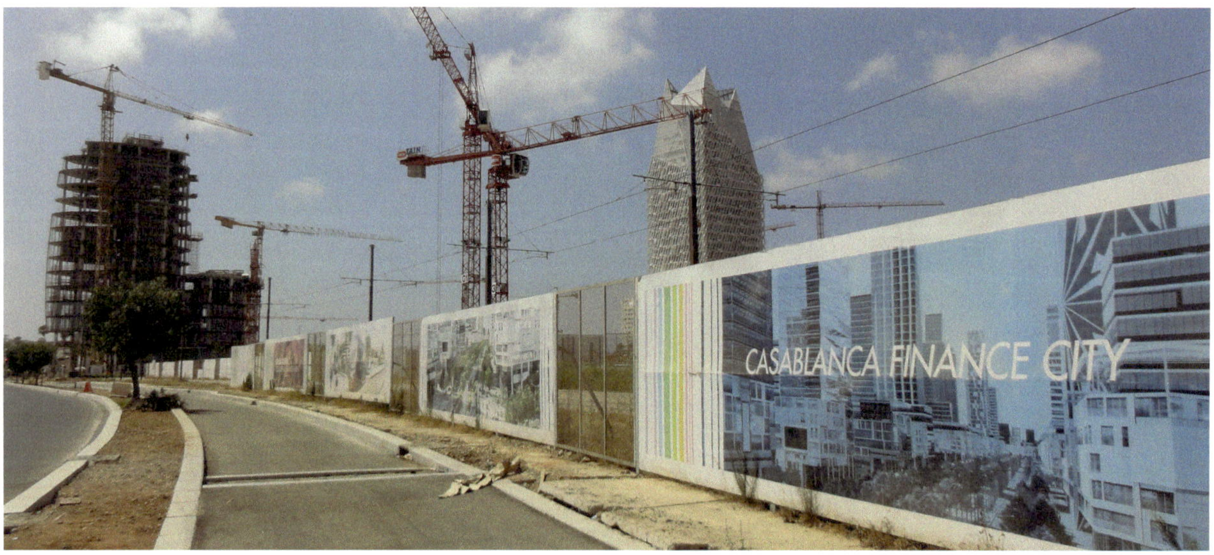

the promotion of «world-class» cities under King Mohammed VI (r. 1999–today).[86] Their main objective is to attract foreign direct investment, mainly in real estate, tourism, and finance – either directly through the participation of foreign donors in megaproject construction or indirectly through the international promotion of a new, powerful «modern» image.[87]

Megaprojects are closely related to the displacement and resettlement of *bidonville* dwellers. On the one hand, the construction of megaprojects is a direct reason for the displacement of marginalised population groups, whether in *bidonvilles* or other parts of the city. Most prominently, this is the case for the Avenue Royale, which cuts through the historic extension of the *ancienne médina*, requiring the relocation of more than 10,000 households to the peripheral resettlement sites of Nassim, Er-Rahma, and Attacharouk.[88] Similar direct displacements occurred in the context of the El Hank / Nouvelle Corniche waterfront redevelopment project, Casa Anfa, and the construction of the Sindibad amusement park (see fig. 1). On the other hand, the politically desired transformation of Casablanca from an industrial city to a shiny international finance hub also drives displacement in an indirect way, through discourses on aesthetics, image, and modernisation. In his book *Neoliberal Authoritarianism*, Bogaert describes this indirect reasoning in the following way:

> Urban spectacles such as Casablanca Marina will put Morocco's cities back on the world map (...). The promotional video of Casablanca Marina starts with a picture of the globe where, one after the other, Dubai, London, New York, and Casablanca appear as flashes of light (...). Thanks to the new megaproject, Casablanca is going to be among the great cities of the globe.

He concludes,

> slums, obviously, do not fit the particular picture of modernity advertised by [urban megaprojects such as] Casablanca Marina.[89]

Thus, the VSB programme follows economic logics too, seeing the *bidonvilles* as urban eyesores and a potential burden to the country's ability to attract tourists and investors and, hence, as a threat to its economic development.[90]

At the same time, displacement and resettlement of *bidonvilles* are drivers of an urban sprawl in the metropolitan hinterland of Casablanca (see fig. 6). However, it would be too simplistic to argue that urban expansion is just the *result* of resettlement. In fact, urban sprawl is an outcome of both political choice and the economic interests of semi-public real estate agencies such as Al Omrane and Idmaj Sakane, which *drive* resettlement.[91] Under the reign of King Mohammed VI, the renewed focus on the development of urban areas and economic investment led to the promotion of private and public real estate investment and the opening up of the rural neighbouring provinces for the urban expansion of greater cities.[92] The construction of low-income housing was seen both as a way to prevent the growth of informal developments (*habitat non-réglementaire*; see fig. 1) at the city's margins[93] and to boost the economy through construction. Through various fiscal and legal incentives, the reclamation of formerly non-urbanised land offers a lucrative opportunity for semi-public real estate agencies to generate rental income.[94] If they are involved in the resettlement of *bidonville* dwellers, the state provides them with public land for free, while allowing them to generate profit by using some of the land for commercial real estate developments.

For example, in the context of the resettlement of Karyan Central to Nouvelle Lahraouiyine, Al Omrane was in charge of the development of formerly vacant public land, including basic wastewater management, streets, and connection to basic grids. The total costs of about 130 million Dirham[95] were almost completely financed through fees that each of the 6,000 resettled households had to pay for their plots in Nouvelle Lahraouiyine.[96] In addition, the resettled residents were obliged to construct their own houses on their plots themselves. As explained above, if they were unable to afford the construction (including

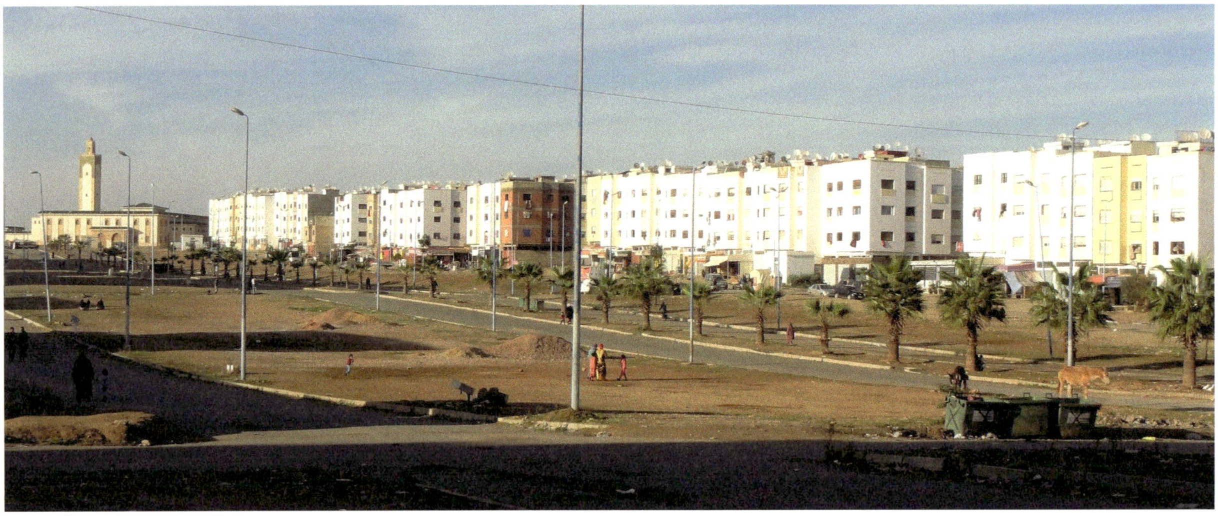

8 Undeveloped building plots in the resettlement town Nouvelle Lahraouiyine, December 2016.

charges for the plots), they could ask a third-party investor to build it for them in exchange of a partial transfer of property rights.[97] Al Omrane did not construct houses for the resettled inhabitants of Karyan Central but was allowed to construct five-storey houses on 200 additional plots within Nouvelle Lahraouiyine and to sell them at market prices.

Moreover, land adjacent to the resettlement site is fully developed by private developers. However, given modest demand and lower than expected market prices, the commercial real estate projects have developed at a much slower rate than the resettlement operation, with some plots still undeveloped in 2021 (fig. 8). Nonetheless, the mobilisation of public land for the resettlement of *bidonville* dwellers offers a unique business opportunity for real estate developers as it allows them to privatise public land and to monetise parts of the land value by selling additional plots in the resettlement towns at market prices. Hence, resettlement operations represent the anchors of a politically and economically desired urban sprawl marked by speculative interests (see fig. 6).

These factors explain how, with the coming into power of King Mohammed VI in the late 1990s, the extent of Casablanca's urban sprawl has remarkably intensified. Looking at population growth,[98] Casablanca's population increased at an annual rate of 1.1 % between the censuses of 2004 and 2014. During the same time, the two provinces Médiouna and Nouaceur (see fig. 6), which absorb most of Casablanca's peripheral growth, both grew in terms of population, almost eight times faster at an annual growth rate of 8.3 % (see fig. 6). Growth rates below the province level show even stronger contrasts. Some districts of Casablanca, such as Hay Mohammadi (-11.3 % in total) and Ben M'Sick (-19.1 %), lost population between 2004 and 2014 due to the demolition of *bidonvilles*. In contrast, the population of the municipalities of Lahraouiyine in the Médiouna province (164.3 %) and Dar Bouazza in the Nouaceur province (125.7 %) – both the location of important resettlement sites, namely Nouvelle Lahraouiyine and Er-Rahma – more than doubled in the same period.

Besides population growth, the sealed surface area[99] has grown significantly in the neighbouring provinces as well. Based on the spatial analysis visualised in the second map, we have calculated an increase of 146.4 % of the built-up area between 2004 and 2014 for the entire province of Médiouna.[100] At 135.7 %, the increase within the province of Nouaceur is of similar magnitude. To compare, in the same ten years, Casablanca's sealed area only increased by 9.5 %. Comparing the growth of the built-up area with the population growth, one can observe that land-sealing grew disproportionately faster than population. In the case of the province of Médiouna, the number of inhabitants per sealed square kilometre decreased by 26 % from 18,136 to 13,446. In the province of Nouaceur, the same value dropped by 22 % during the same period. Thus, Casablanca's urban sprawl, rather than being the result of deliberate migration flows, is significantly driven by political and economic interest in real estate investment and resettlement.

Looking at the second map (see fig. 6) and the spatial patterns of urban expansion, it becomes obvious that this expansion lacks integrated spatial planning. Instead, the «new peripheries» produce haphazard patterns following the availability of mainly public land.[101] The availability of land at the peripheries determines where exactly resettlement sites are built. Because of the modalities of the third-party scheme and the commercial sale of plots and houses on the same site, these resettlement sites attract additional population groups. However, the lack of urban planning leads to a development of different non-integrated, and non-connected, peripheral islands. Most remarkably, they are characterised by severe accessibility shortcomings, especially for people unable to use individual motorised transport. Whereas the city of Casablanca is currently renewing its public transport system through tramways and in line with its ambitions to become a «world-class» city, the neighbouring provinces are only slowly becoming part of this process.[102] In the early years after relocation, many resettled residents had to rely on informal bus services and car sharing, shared taxis, and three-wheelers (*triporteurs*) – providing less comfortable, reliable and safe transport options, and consequently feeding a feeling of marginalisation among inhabitants. Fortunately, the 2021 renewal of Casablanca's bus system has seen more formal bus lines serving the neighbouring provinces and its resettlement sites.

Colonial Planning Continuities and Disruptions: Some Concluding Thoughts

Casablanca's urban development has been significantly shaped by colonial planning – most obviously marked by the spatial juxtaposition of *ancienne médina* and *ville nouvelle*. Colonial planning strengthened spatial segregation and produced Casablanca's first urban peripheries, mostly located next to the industrial corridor in the northeast. These «old peripheries» were characterised by shantytowns (*bidonvilles*), workers' housing, and early social housing programmes. For a long time, notwithstanding occasional interventions that tended to reinforce colonial segregation, the «old peripheries» were not a priority of post-Independence politics. This changed significantly with the coming into power of King Mohammed VI in 1999, who made urban development a political priority. The aspiration to create a «world-class» city made the *bidonvilles*, the most visible remains of the colonial peripheries, for many reasons an undesired part of the city that should be eradicated. Through schemes that tend to continue colonial *recasement* policies, the resulting VSB programme has resettled *bidonville* dwellers to barely integrated peripheries, as shown by the second map. One may argue that the VSB programme addressed long-term ignored outcomes of colonial planning. However, instead of enhancing the integration of *bidonville* dwellers where they already live, the programme has reproduced patterns of segregation and inequality at the metropolitan level. Moreover, the resettlement of *bidonvilles* was used as the catalyst for an urban expansion that mostly suits real estate investors and semi-public agencies such as Al Omrane who profit from the release of public land. The outcomes are «new peripheries» that lack spatial integration and reinforce marginalisation. During colonial times, working-class Moroccans were kept physically outside the colonial *ville nouvelle*. Today, the hardly accessible and distant «new peripheries» keep undesired population groups outside the perimeters of the «world-class» city.

1 Rabinow 1989, 36.
2 Abu Lughod 1980.
3 Ennahid 2022, 361–362.
4 Aljem/Strava 2020, Barthel 2010, Chambre des Représentants 2013.
5 Casablanca Finance City is a high-end commercial development that aims at boosting Casablanca's status as an international finance hub by clustering financial industries and infrastructure. It forms part of a larger brownfield regeneration project called Casa Anfa, which is located on the grounds of Casablanca's former airport. Casablanca Marina is a luxurious real estate development – including a hotel and a mall – that has transformed Casablanca's seashore between the harbour and the Hassan II Mosque.
6 Rachik 2002. Casablanca is an emblematic case, taking into account that resettlement has shaped many Moroccan cities in fundamental ways, from the forceful implementation of colonial segregation (Abu Lughod 1980) up until today's slum resettlement and new town programmes (Harroud 2019, Rousseau/Harroud 2019).
7 For a detailed discussion of the VSB programme, refer to Beier 2019a, Bogaert 2018, Harroud 2019.
8 Rabinow 1989, 38.
9 Rabinow 1989, 38.
10 Rousseau/Harroud 2019.
11 Beier 2020b.
12 This term mainly refers to a simplified graphic representation of the *ville nouvelle*, villa neighbourhoods, colonial working-class centres, and the industrial belt.
13 Old maps (Larousse 1971, 2597; Chouiki 1997) as well as current satellite images were helpful to identify the rough limits of the *ancienne médina*, the *ville nouvelle*, the villa neighbourhoods, industries, and the working-class centres. Other literature supported the identification of neighbourhoods that are key to explain Casablanca's early urban development (*ancienne médina*, medina extension, and *ville nouvelle*: see Rabinow 1989, 34–38, Rachik 2002, 21–32; *nouvelle médina*: see Rabinow 1989, 41–43, Rachik 2002, 37–41; working-class centres: see Rachik 2002, 43–49, 54–56; colonial social housing: see Rabinow 1992, 56–57; Chaouni 2011; Rachik 2002, 56–58; post-colonial early social housing: see Chouiki 1997, 93–94; Rachik 2002, 72, 93–104). Furthermore, *bidonvilles* and *habitat non-réglementaire* were identified using satellite images from 2004 (start of the VSB programme) as well as our own field research. Finally, Casablanca's urban megaprojects are described by Aljem/Strava 2020, Barthel 2010, and Beier 2020b.
14 This refers mainly to the identification and history of *bidonvilles* and social housing in Hay Mohammadi and Sidi Moumen, where the first author conducted surveys and qualitative interviews to assess the impact of relocation. For detailed information on field research and methodology, see Beier 2019a, 69–100.
15 For a similar map, see Beier 2019a, 123.
16 These newspaper articles were a major source of information: Medias24 2018, L'Economiste 2014, L'Economiste 2015, and H24info 2018. In addition, the authors used information from Al Omrane's website https://www.alomrane.gov.ma/index.php/Notre-reseau/Al-omrane-casablanca-settat/Produits/Projets. For the displacement of the medina extension, see Berry-Chikhaoui 2010, 2012.
17 We collected the training data manually but provided additional reference sites for the year 2019 from Open Street Map (OSM) data. The validation procedure utilised 300 manually collected points for each urban and non-urban class in GEE, with an additional 300 random points generated and determined in QGIS. For the most recent 2019 satellite image, we used another validation dataset from OSM data due to their matching temporal properties. For more details on the technique, see Belgiu/Drăguţ 2016.
18 Rabinow 1989. For a more detailed history of colonial Casablanca beyond the scope of this chapter, see Adam 1968, Cohen/Eleb 2002, and Wright 1991.
19 Chouiki 1997, 85.
20 Rabinow 1989, Rabinow 1992, Cohen/Eleb 2002.
21 «In the early years [of the French protectorate], investors drove land prices skyward but built relatively little. Areas in which building and habitation did take place often had extremely elevated densities (...).» Rabinow 1989, 38.
22 AUC 2008.
23 Escher et al. 2018, Spotorno 2019.
24 Berry-Chikhaoui 2012, 111.
25 Rabinow 1989, 36.
26 Benlahcen Tlemçani/Missamou 2000, 114, Naciri 1980, 36.

27 Rachik 2002, 10.
28 Berry-Chikhaoui 2012, 111; Berry-Chikhaoui 2010, 223.
29 Rabinow 1989, 37.
30 Zaki 2006, 307; Rabinow 1989, 38.
31 Zaki 2005, 82–83; Rachik 2002, 49–55.
32 Zaki 2006, 307–308; Rachik 2002, 11.
33 See Zaki 2010. As Rachik (2002, 49–55) argues, the restructuring of scattered *bidonvilles* was a common policy of colonial authorities during the 1930s.
34 Sieburg 1938.
35 Cattedra 2006.
36 Rabinow 1989, 38.
37 Rabinow 1989, 41–42, Rachik 2002, 20.
38 Rachik 2002, 20.
39 Rachik 2002, 47–48.
40 Rachik 2002, 11.
41 Beier/Strava 2020, 12.
42 Rachik 2002, 56.
43 Rachik 2002, 64, own translation.
44 Rachik 2002, 31–33.
45 Chaouni 2011.
46 Following the modernist ideas of the Congrès Internationaux d'Architecture Moderne (CIAM), former Corbusian associates were the architects of Casablanca's colonial public housing such as the *Nid d'Abeilles* building in Hay Mohammadi. See Mumford 1992, 409 and Cohen/Eleb 2002.
47 Rabinow 1992, Strava 2017.
48 Chaouni 2011.
49 Rachik 2002, Strava 2017, 332.
50 Beier 2019a, 184; Beier 2020b, 1835. In this research, the first author of this chapter used mixed methods including surveys, qualitative interviews, and document analysis to compare the life of people living in Casablanca's *bidonville* Er-Rhamna with the life of people resettled from Karyan Central to Nouvelle Lahraouiyine. The aim of this research was to understand the impact of displacement and relocation on the resettled *bidonville* dwellers.
51 Beier 2019a, 116–117.
52 Arrif 1999, Beier 2020a, Bénit-Gbaffou/Oldfield 2014, Zaki 2005.
53 Zemni/Bogaert 2011, 409.
54 Abu-Lughod 1980, 233–234.
55 Benlahcen Tlemçani/Missamou 2000, 112.
56 Chouiki 1997, 94; Zaki 2006.
57 Rachik 2002, 94ff; Zaki 2006.
58 For a more detailed discussion of the complex infrastructure development in *bidonvilles*, see Zaki 2010 and Navez-Bouchanine 2012.
59 Beier 2019a, 87–89; Beier/Strava 2020, 6.
60 Turner 1968, Turner 1977.
61 Seddon 1984.
62 Benlahcen Tlemçani/Missamou 2000, 115.
63 Beier 2021.
64 Zaki 2005, 87.
65 Rachik 2002, 158.
66 Le Tellier/Guérin 2009, 662; Navez-Bouchanine 2003, 64.
67 Le Tellier/Guérin 2009, Navez-Bouchanine 2003.
68 Zaki 2005, 47.
69 Zemni/Bogaert 2011, 409.
70 King Mohammed VI in a speech of October 2002, quoted in MHPV 2013, 68.
71 Bogaert 2011, 721; Zemni/Bogaert 2011, 409.
72 Le Tellier 2009b, 198.
73 Zaki 2013, 45.
74 Zaki 2013.
75 Beier 2021.
76 Political rhetoric about the pro-poor effects of resettlement has been strongly contested by both conceptual and empirical research (see Bartoli 2011; Beier 2019a; Harroud 2019; Zaki 2013). The same holds true for related political claims that resettlement should promote social mixing of different communities (see Chinig 2020).
77 As Beier 2019a has shown in the context of a larger study on the resettlement of residents from Karyan Central, even if people are looking forward to resettlement, they are likely to suffer from diverse adverse effects of displacement and relocation – including disruptions to social life, isolation, and boredom, as well as a loss of net income. According to United Nations' standards, resettlement should only be applied if in-situ upgrading is not possible.
78 Although the VSB programme made participation a compulsory element of every project, in practice it was mainly used as a tool to make people accept resettlement and to avoid larger eruptions of protests (see Bogaert 2013 and Toutain 2011).
79 El Kahlaoui 2023, Portelli/Lees 2018.
80 Since a regional administrative restructuring in 2015, Greater Casablanca has been part of the new region Casablanca-Settat.
81 Chambre des Représentants 2013, AUC 2008.
82 AUC 2008, Florin/Semmoud 2010, Rousseau/Harroud 2019.
83 Aljem 2016, Barthel 2010, Cattedra 2001.
84 Berry-Chikhaoui 2010.
85 Barthel 2010, Barthel/Planel 2010, Aljem/Strava 2020.
86 Bogaert 2018.
87 Amarouche/Bogaert 2019, Aljem/Strava 2020, Barthel 2010, Barthel/Planel 2010, Beier 2019b, Wippel 2021.
88 Berry-Chikhaoui 2010, Berry-Chikhaoui 2012.
89 Bogaert 2018, 2–3.
90 Zemni/Bogaert 2011, 409.
91 Al Omrane is a financially autonomous real estate company that replaced former public housing agencies but continues to be closely supervised by government institutions as well as the royal palace. Together with Idmaj Sakane, which the Ministry of Interior created especially for Casablanca, both agencies are in charge of the construction of low-income housing, mainly on freely mobilised public land. Because of their political significance, they can act like oligopolistic private companies

that seek profit maximisation without being much affected by market competition (see Barthel/Zaki 2011 and Bogaert 2011, 722).

92 Rousseau/Harroud 2019, 345.

93 Le Tellier 2009a.

94 Rousseau/Harroud 2019, 347.

95 Al Omrane 2012, 4.

96 In most cases, the costs of 20,000 Dirham (approximately € 1,850) per household were paid by the third-party investors, who also financed the construction of the house. Consequently, the dropout rate of people unable to afford the resettlement costs was very low (see Zaki 2013). There is no reliable information about where these people have moved.

97 Beier 2021.

98 Own calculations based on the data from HCP 2014.

99 The term «sealed surface area» refers to the part of the province covered by artificial constructions such as buildings, pavements, and roads.

100 Given the relatively comparable resolution of the two satellite pictures on which the calculations are based, we have concentrated on the comparison of the 2004 and 2014 data. Using the 2019 data, coming from a satellite picture with significantly increased resolution, would have produced a significant bias (see map 2).

101 Florin/Semmoud 2010, Navez-Bouchanine/Dansereau 2002, 20.

102 Beier 2020b.

Abu-Lughod 1980
J. L. Abu-Lughod: Rabat: Urban Apartheid in Morocco (Princeton, NJ 1980).

Adam 1968
A. Adam: Casablanca: Essaie sur la transformation de la société marocaine au contact de l'Occident (Paris 1968).

Al Omrane 2012
Al Omrane: Opération de résorption du bidonville «Carrières Centrales», Casablanca, 2009–2012. Une expérience pilote de recasement, d'accès aux services de et d'inclusion urbaine (La Newsletter d'Al Omrane) 2012, https://www.auc.ma/docs/124112008133350.pdf (26 October 2020).

Aljem 2016
S. Aljem: Politique des Grands Projets et Gouvernance Urbaine à Casablanca. Dissertation (Rabat 2016).

Aljem/Strava 2020
S. Aljem / C. Strava: Casablanca's Megaprojects: Neoliberal Urban Planning and Socio-Spatial Transformations. TRIALOG – A Journal for Planning and Building in a Global Context 135, 2020, 12–19.

Amarouche/Bogaert 2019
M. Amarouche / K. Bogaert: Reshaping Space and Time in Morocco: The Agencification of Urban Government and its Effects in the Bouregreg Valley (Rabat/Salé). Middle East – Topics & Arguments 12, 2019, 44–54.

Arrif 1999
A. Arrif: Les compétences citadins à l'épreuve de l'exclusion: L'exemple du bidonvilles de Ben M'Sik à Casablanca (Maroc), in: P. Signoles / G. El Kadi / R. Sidi Boumedine (eds.): L'Urbain dans le monde arabe. Politiques, instruments et acteurs (Paris 1999) 297–317.

AUC 2008
Agence Urbaine de Casablanca: Schéma Directeur d'Aménagement Urbain du Grand Casablanca (SDAU) 2008, https://www.auc.ma/docs/124112008133350.pdf (1 December 2020).

Barthel 2010
P.-A. Barthel: Casablanca-Marina: un nouvel urbanisme marocain des grands projets. Autrepart 55, 2010, 71–88.

Barthel/Planel 2010
P.-A. Barthel / S. Planel: Tanger-Med and Casa-Marina, Prestige Projects in Morocco: New Capitalist Frameworks and Local Context. Built Environment 36, no. 2, 2010, 176–191.

Barthel/Zaki 2011
P.-A. Barthel / L. Zaki: Les holdings d'aménagement, nouvelle vitrines techniques de l'action urbaine au Maroc. Les cas d'Al Omrane et de la CDG Développement, in: L. Zaki (ed.) : L'action urbaine au Maghreb. Enjeux professionnels et politiques (Paris 2011) 205–225.

Bartoli 2011
S. Bartoli: « Eliminer les bidonvilles = éliminer la pauvreté », ou les charmes pervers d'une fausse évidence. L'Economie politique 49, no. 1, 2011, 44–60.

Beier 2019a
R. Beier: From the City to the Desert: Analysing Shantytown Resettlement in Casablanca, Morocco, from Residents' Perspectives. UA Ruhr Studies on Development and Global Governance, vol. 72 (Berlin 2019).

Beier 2019b
R. Beier: Worlding Cities in the Middle East and North Africa: Arguments for a Conceptual Turn. Middle East – Topics & Arguments 12, 2019, 28–32.

Beier 2020a
R. Beier: Ganz gewöhnliche Viertel: Stigma und Realitäten in Casablancas Slum Er-Rhamna. sub\urban 8, no. 3, 2020, 73–96, https://doi.org/10.36900/suburban.v8i3.592.

Beier 2020b
R. Beier: The world-class city comes by tramway: Reframing

Casablanca's urban peripheries through public transport. Urban Studies 57, no. 9, 2020, 1827–1844, https://doi.org/10.1177/0042098019853475.

Beier 2021
R. Beier: From Visible Informality to Splintered Informalities: Reflections on the Production of ‹Formality› in a Moroccan Housing Programme. International Journal of Urban and Regional Research 45, no. 6, 2021, 930–947, https://doi.org/10.1111/1468-2427.13001.

Beier/Strava 2020
R. Beier / C. Strava: Losing or Gaining Home? Experiences of Resettlement from Casablanca's Slums, in: A. Storey / M. Sheehan / J. Bodoh-Creed (eds.): The Everyday Life of Urban Inequality: Ethnographic Case Studies of Global Cities (Lanham 2020) 3–22.

Belgiu/Drăguţ 2016
M. Belgiu / L. Drăguţ: Random forest in remote sensing. A review of applications and future directions. ISPRS Journal of Photogrammetry and Remote Sensing 114, 2016, 24–31.

Bénit-Gbaffou/Oldfield 2014
C. Bénit-Gbaffou / S. Oldfield: Claiming ‹Rights› in the African City: Popular Mobilization and the Politics of Informality, in: S. Parnell / S. Oldfield (edS.): The Routledge Handbook on Cities of the Global South (Abingdon, New York 2014) 281–295.

Benlahcen Tlemçani/Missamou 2000
M. Benlahcen Tlemçani / R. Missamou: Habitat clandestin et insalubre au Maroc: vers une stratégie d'intervention plurielle. Les Annales de la Recherche Urbaine 86, 2000, 111–118.

Berry-Chikhaoui 2010
I. Berry-Chikhaoui: Major Urban Projects and the People Affected: The Case of Casablanca's Avenue Royale. Built Environment 36, no. 2, 2010, 216–229.

Berry-Chikhaoui 2012
I. Berry-Chikhaoui: Les habitants face à la rénovation urbaine. Négociations, ajustements et résistances: L'exemple de l'Avenue royale à Casablanca, in: F. Navez-Bouchanine / A. Deboulet (eds.): Effets sociaux des politiques urbaines. L'entre-deux des politiques institutionnelles et des dynamiques sociales: Algérie, Maroc, Liban, Mauritanie (Paris 2012) 109–163.

Bogaert 2011
K. Bogaert: The Problem of Slums: Shifting Methods of Neoliberal Urban Government in Morocco. Development and Change 42, no. 3, 2011, 709–731.

Bogaert 2013
K. Bogaert: Cities Without Slums in Morocco? New Modalities of Urban Government and the Bidonville as a Neoliberal Assemblage, in: T.R. Samara / S. He / G. Chen (eds.): Locating Right to the City in the Global South (Abingdon 2013) 41–59.

Bogaert 2018
K. Bogaert: Globalized Authoritarianism. Megaprojects, Slums, and Class Relations in Urban Morocco. Globalization and community, vol. 27 (Minneapolis 2018).

Cattedra 2001
R. Cattedra: La mosquée et la cité : la reconversion symbolique du projet urbain à Casablanca (Maroc). Doctoral thesis (Université François Rabelais de Tours 2001).

Cattedra 2006
R. Cattedra: Bidonville: paradigme et réalité refoulée de la ville du XXe siècle, in: J.-C. Depaule (ed.): Les mots de la stigmatisation urbaine. Collection Les mots de la ville, vol. 4 (Paris 2006) 123–163.

Chambre des Représentants 2013
Chambre des Représentants: Texte intégrale du discours de SM le Roi Mohammed VI à l'ouverture de la première session de la troisième année législative de la 9ème législature - 11/10/2013. http://www.chambredesrepresentants.ma/fr/discours-royaux/texte-integrale-du-discours-de-sm-le-roi-mohammed-vi-louverture-de-la-premiere (21 July 2017).

Chaouni 2011
A. Chaouni: Depoliticizing Group GAMMA: Contesting modernism in Morocco, in: D. Lu (ed.): Third world modernism. Architecture, development and identity (New York 2011) 57–84.

Chinig 2020
S. Chinig: Strategies of Social Mixing and Social Distance in a New Neighbourhood: The Case of Lotissement Said Hajji in Salé, Morocco. TRIALOG 135, 2020, 34–41.

Chouiki 1997
M. Chouiki: La ségrégation sociospatiale à Casablanca. L'Homme et la société 125, 1997, 85–105.

Cohen/Eleb 2002
J.-L. Cohen / M. Eleb: Casablanca. Colonial Myths and Architectural Ventures (New York 2002).

El Kahlaoui 2023
S. El Kahlaoui: Claiming their right to possess: the Guich Oudaya tribe's resistance to land grabbing. The Journal of North African Studies 28, no. 1, 2023, 36–56.

Ennahid 2022
S. Ennahid: Searching for Rome: French colonial archaeology and urban planning in Morocco, in S. Greaves / A. Wallace-Hadrill (ed.): Rome and the Colonial City: Rethinking the Grid (Oxford 2022) 353–365.

Escher et al. 2018
A. Escher / S. Petermann / G. Arnold: Das neue Marrakech. Eine Materialisierung des Mythos von Tausendundeiner Nacht? Geographische Rundschau, no. 7/8, 2018, 52–57.

Florin/Semmoud 2010
B. Florin / N. Semmoud: Mobilités résidentielles et territorialisations dans les villes du Maghreb. Espace populations sociétés, no. 2/3, 2010, 365–377.

H24info 2018
Casablanca: Près de 400 ménages bénéficient d'une opération de relogement à Hay Hassani [Casablanca: Nearly 400 households benefit from rehousing in Hay Hassani]. H24info, 9 July 2018, https://www.h24info.ma/maroc/casablanca-pres-de-400-menages-beneficient-dune-operation-de-relogement-a-hay-hassani/ (28 January 2025).

Harroud 2019
T. Harroud: D'une marginalite à l'autre. Droit à la ville et pratiques de réadaptation des bidonvillois dans les nouvelles marges urbaines de Rabat. Annales de géographie 2019, no. 5, 14–37.

HCP 2014
Haut-Commisariat au Plan – Direction Régionale du Grand Casablanca: Recensement Général de la Population et de l'Habitat 2014. http://www.hcp.ma/reg-casablanca/attachment/673642 (24 July 2017).

Larousse 1971
Éditions Larousse (ed.): La Grande Encyclopédie Larousse – 1971 à 1976 (Paris 1971).

L'Economiste 2014
Casablanca/Habitat insalubre L'échéance encore reportée à 2018 [Casablanca/Slum housing Deadline extended again to 2018]. L'Economiste, 28 April 2014, https://redac.leconomiste.com/article/940861-casablancahabitat-insalubrel-echeance-encore-reportee-2018 (28 January 2025).

L'Economiste 2015
Casablanca-Médiouna: Grosse opération de recasement [Casablanca-Médiouna: Large-scale resettlement operation]. L'Economiste, 24 March 2015, https://www.leconomiste.com/article/968983-casablanca-mediounagrosse-operation-de-recasement (28 January 2025).

Le Tellier 2009a
J. Le Tellier: Les deux volets de la lutte contre l'habitat insalubre au Maroc: la prévention et la resorption, in: J. Le Tellier / A. Iraki (ed.): Habitat social au Maghreb et au Sénégal. Gouvernance urbaine et participation en questions (Paris 2009) 101–108.

Le Tellier 2009b
J. Le Tellier: Programme Villes Sans Bidonvilles et ingénierie sociale urbaine au Maroc, in: J. Le Tellier / A. Iraki (ed.): Habitat social au Maghreb et au Sénégal. Gouvernance urbaine et participation en questions (Paris 2009) 193–212.

Le Tellier / Guérin 2009
J. Le Tellier / I. Guérin: «Participation», accompagnement social et microcrédit logement pour la résorption des bidonvilles au Maroc. Revue d'Économie Régionale & Urbaine, no. 4, 2009, 657–682.

Médias24 2018
Casablanca: après El Ouasti, trois bidonvilles à Ain Sebaâ seront démolis, le conseil de la ville craint des protestations [Casablanca: after El Ouasti, three slums in Ain Sebaâ will be demolished, the city council fears protests]. Médias24, 28 September 2018, https://medias24.com/2018/09/28/casablanca-apres-el-ouasti-trois-bidonvilles-a-ain-sebaa-seront-demolis-le-conseil-de-la-ville-craint-des-protestations/ (28 January 2025).

MHPV 2013
Ministère de l'Habitat, de l'Urbanisme et de la Politique de la Ville: Discours et Interviews de Sa Majesté le Roi Mohammed VI. Habitat, Urbanisme et Politique de la Ville, January 2013. https://aua.ma/wp-content/uploads/2018/02/Royaume-du-Maroc.pdf (11 April 2020).

Mumford 1992
E. Mumford: CIAM Urbanism after the Athens Charter. Planning Perspectives 7, no. 4, 1992, 391–417.

Naciri 1980
M. Naciri: Les formes d'habitat «sous-intégrées». Éssai méthodologique. Hérodote 19, 1980, 13–70.

Navez-Bouchanine 2003
F. Navez-Bouchanine: Les chemins tortueux de l'expérience démocratique marocaine à travers les bidonvilles. Espaces et sociétés, no. 112, 2003, 59–82.

Navez-Bouchanine 2012
F. Navez-Bouchanine: Les nouvelles voies de la négociation dans les politiques de résorption des bidonvilles au Maroc. Entre recasement et accompagnement social, in: F. Navez-Bouchanine / A. Deboulet (eds.): Effets sociaux des politiques urbaines: L'entre-deux des politiques institutionnelles et des dynamiques sociales (Paris 2012) 166–218.

Navez-Bouchanine / Dansereau 2002
F. Navez-Bouchanine / F. Dansereau: Les stratégies résidentielles dans la ville fragmentée. Le cas de la ville marocaine, in: F. Dansereau / F. Navez-Bouchanine (eds.): Gestion du développement urbain et stratégies résidentielles des habitants (Paris 2002) 19–65.

Portelli / Lees 2018
S. Portelli / L. Lees: Eviction and Displacement from the Neighbourhood of Douar Wasti in Casablanca, Morocco. https://www.ijurr.org/news/eviction-and-displacement-from-the-neighbourhood-of-douar-wasti-in-casablanca-morocco/ (26 November 2020).

Rabinow 1989
P. Rabinow: Governing Morocco: Modernity and Difference. International Journal of Urban and Regional Research 13, no. 1, 1989, 32–46.

Rabinow 1992
P. Rabinow: France in Morocco: Technocosmopolitanism and Middling Modernism. Assemblage 17, 1992, 52–57.

Rachik 2002
A. Rachik: Casablanca. L'urbanisme de l'urgence (Casablanca 2002).

Rousseau / Harroud 2019
M. Rousseau / T. Harroud: Satellite Cities Turned to Ghost Towns? On the Contradictions of Morocco's Spatial Policy. International Planning Studies 24, no. 3–4, 2019, 341–352.

Seddon 1984
D. Seddon: Winter of Discontent: Economic Crisis in Tunisia and Morocco. MERIP Reports 127, 1984, 7–16.

Sieburg 1938
F. Sieburg: Le role économique de Casablanca vu par un écrivain allemand. Bulletin Economique du Maroc 5, no. 21, 1938, 205–207.

Spotorno 2019
M. Spotorno: Gentrification and European Entrepreneurship in Marrakesh, in: M. Paradiso (ed.): Mediterranean Mobilities: Europe's Changing Relationships (Cham 2019) 167–176.

Strava 2017
C. Strava: At Home on the Margins. Care Giving and the ‹Un-homely› among Casablanca's Working Poor. City & Society 29, no. 2, 2017, 329–348.

Toutain 2011
O. Toutain: Retour sur l'expérience d'accompagnement social des projets de résorption de l'habitat insalubre au Maroc, in:

L. Zaki (ed.): L'action urbaine au Maghreb: Enjeux professionnels et politiques (Paris 2011) 169–182.

Turner 1968
J.F.C. Turner: Housing Priorities, Settlement Patterns, and Urban Development in Modernizing Countries. Journal of the American Institute of Planners 34, no. 6, 1968, 354–363.

Turner 1977
J.F.C. Turner: Housing by People: Towards Autonomy in Building Environments (New York 1977).

Wippel 2021
S. Wippel: Tangier's Current Re-Confgurations from a Multi-Scale Spatial Perspective: Emerging Transregional Ties and Local Repercussions, in: R. Ouaissa / F. Pannewick / A. Strohmaier (eds.): Re-Configurations. Contextualising transformation processes and lasting (Wiesbaden 2021) 83–104.

Wright 1991
G. Wright: The Politics of Design in French Colonial Urbanism (Chicago 1991).

Zaki 2005
L. Zaki: Pratiques politiques au bidonville, Casablanca (2000–2005). Dissertation (Paris 2005).

Zaki 2006
L. Zaki: L'action publique au bidonville: L'État entre gestion par le manque, «éradication» des kariens et accompagnement social des habitants. L'Année du Maghreb 2, 2005/06, 303–320.

Zaki 2010
L. Zaki: L'électrification temporaire des bidonvilles casablancais. Aspects et limites d'une transformation. Politique africaine no. 120, 2010, 45–66.

Zaki 2013
L. Zaki: Montée en puissance des mobilisations dans les bidonvilles et transformation de l'action publique au Maroc: de l'ouverture des années 1990 au printemps arabe, in: P.-A. Barthel / S. Jaglin (eds.): Quartiers informels d'un monde arabe en transition. Réflexions et perspectives pour l'action urbaine. Conférences & Séminaires, vol. 7 (Paris 2013) 37–52.

Zemni / Boagert 2011
S. Zemni / K. Bogaert: Urban Renewal and Social Development in Morocco in an Age of Neoliberal Government. Review of African Political Economy 38, no. 129, 2011, 403–417.

Image Sources

1 Roads & Overview map: © OpenStreetMap-Mitwirkende | Satellite basemap: © Copernicus data (2020) | Administrative boundaries: OCHA, HDX; License: Other; No changes were made | Bathymetry: GEBCO Compilation Group (2020) GEBCO 2020 Grid.

2–4, 7, 8 Photos by Raffael Beier.

5 2006 OrbView-3 image collected by GeoEye, provided by Nasa through EarthExplorer; 2021 PlanetScope from Planet Team (2018). Planet Application Program Interface: In Space for Life on Earth. San Francisco, CA. https://api.planet.com.

6 Urban footprint 1994 & 2004 (derived from): Landsat-5 image courtesy of the U.S. Geological Survey | Urban footprint 2014 (derived from): Landsat-8 image courtesy of the U.S. Geological Survey | Urban footprint 2019 (derived from): © Copernicus data (2020) | Administrative boundaries: OCHA, HDX; License: Other; No changes were made | Terrestrial basemap: NASA, SRTM | Bathymetry: GEBCO Compilation Group (2020) GEBCO 2020 Grid.

Urbanising the Desert
The Case of Nouakchott

Zuzanna Krzyżanowska, Chloe Loader, Elizabeth Ryall

Most cities exclude nature, but in Nouakchott the large sand seas that lie around the town also enter it [...] The winds, coming fiercely across the desert, pick up sand and dust and bring them into town. It is part of life, on office floors, in each mouthful of rice, between the pages of books, under your fingernails and in your ears and eyes.[1]

Peter Hudson, 1990

Introducing Nouakchott

Nouakchott is the capital city of Mauritania in northwestern Africa (fig. 1). Formerly no more than an insignificant fishing village (*ksar,* see key terms in table 1), Nouakchott was designated the capital city of the newly established Islamic Republic of Mauritania three years before the region gained independence from French colonial rule in 1960. The new capital has faced challenges, including a lack of drinking water, scarce resources, salty soil, floods, and the encroaching desert. Yet it is still an incredibly dynamic place. As the meeting point of the Arab and African worlds, straddling the Atlantic Ocean and the Sahara Desert, the city has experienced explosive urban growth. The result is a sprawling, culturally diverse city with a distinctive morphology.

Mauritania, and in turn Nouakchott, has a hot, dry, and windy climate with a heavy exposure to the effects of desertification. The geography and climate of the country, dominated by the Sahara Desert, mean that resources are scarce. Although there is an abundance of raw materials such as iron ore, gold, and copper, most finished goods are produced elsewhere due to the lack of infrastructure for manufacturing. Produce has to be imported due to recurrent cycles of drought.[2] The long distances of transport routes increase prices, reduce product freshness, and affect the stability of supply chains. Low population density across the region results in weak links between cities, further aggravating these problems.[3]

To understand the significance of the fast-paced urbanisation of Nouakchott, it is important to understand the nomadic roots of much of Mauritania's population, particularly those from the north. Pre-independence, around 70% of the population living in the region of modern-day Mauritania were nomads. They would traverse the Sahara Desert, following caravan routes but

1 Location of Nouakchott.

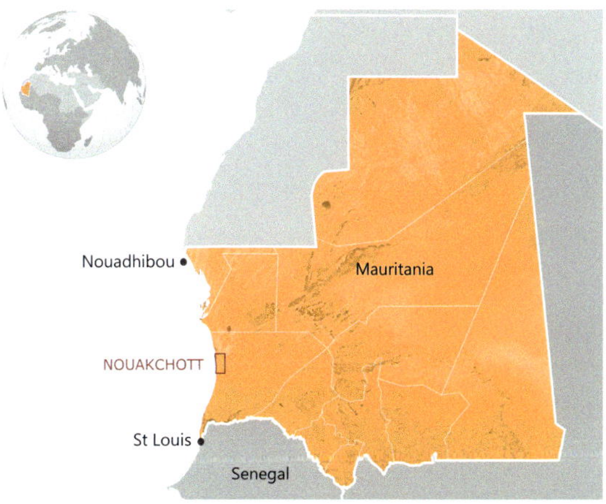

Arab Berbers	ethnic group, also known as Bidhan or (White) Moors, of nomadic origins from the north of the country. Also spelt Bidān, Beidan, Baydan, or Beydan.
Black Africans	ethnic group made up of Pular, Tukulor, Fulani, Soninke, and Wolof tribes, historically pastoral with settled communities, inhabiting the south and east of Mauritania.
Haratine	ethnic group, also known as the Black Moors. The Haratine are ethnically Black Africans, but as former slaves of the White Moors, they are culturally and linguistically closer to the Arab Berber group.
Informal settlements	settlements where people assert land rights not registered in their names, or government land, or legally owned by others.
ksar	«market town» or «small fortified town», often referring to Berber fortified villages. Not to be confused with the Nouakchott municipality district of Ksar.
kebbe	informal settlements largely characterised by tent structures and barracks. Translated from Hassaniya, the word means «spontaneous», «unplanned», or «thrown away».
gazra	a «squat» – the illegal occupation of public or private land, with the hope of achieving ownership, often characterised by an empty plot surrounded by a breeze-block wall.

Table 1 Key terms.

adapting to the changing weather and seasons, or in search of grazing land for livestock.[4] Sometimes they would choose to settle in villages or *ksars* temporarily, depending on the season. Mobility was key in utilising the scarce, temporary, and scattered resources available. As such, the concept of exclusivity in land ownership and its use, though well suited to settled agrarian societies (which is the basis of Western understanding), was not applicable in this situation.[5] The nomadic philosophy may be defined as «permission to use a common resource intermittently».[6] In this framework, no one person has the exclusive right to the use or occupation of land, as this is not critical to its effective use. Nomadic tribes would graze their livestock based on season, rainfall, and climate, utilising shared water stations, with tradition regulating who can use which resource at what time. As no one exclusively owned any particular resource, such as water stations, any of the nomadic tribes could use them intermittently.[7] However, Mauritania's modern administrative system is based on the French colonial system, which included the concept of exclusive land ownership. The process of urbanisation meant a direct confrontation between the two systems, the implications of which are still visible in the urban fabric of Nouakchott today.

Today, the population of Mauritania and Nouakchott comprises three major ethnic groups, who battle over the country's national identity: the Arab Berbers of nomadic origin – the dominant group in Mauritania's politics and economy; the Black Africans – historically settled tribes from the south of the country; and the Haratine – former slaves of the Arab Berbers (see table 1). Both the Black Africans and the Haratine continue to be economically and politically marginalised. The decision to locate the capital city in Nouakchott, midway between regions inhabited by the three ethnic groups, was intended to demonstrate political and social neutrality. This choice was also influenced by Nouakchott's proximity to the ocean and by its climate, which is slightly milder than that of other areas of the country.

The new capital was designed and constructed predominantly as an administrative centre, intended to house only a small number of residents. However, the Great Sahelian droughts of the 1970s and 1980s, and the resulting loss of livelihood, drove the widespread rural–urban migration of nomads and pastoralists from across the country into the new capital.[8] In addition, cultural and political factors, such as compulsory schooling, forced the nomadic population to become sedentary, encouraging the move towards urbanisation.[9]

This rapid influx of population resulted in a culturally diverse city, with many denizens of the city not accustomed to urban life. Unhindered by physical barriers, the city has continued to expand into the surrounding desert to this day. Despite growing to be one of the largest cities in the Sahel region,[10] Nouakchott has a remarkably low population density: only 5,000 persons per km^2 (or 50 persons per hectare).[11]

Nouakchott was built to create a sense of identity and unity for a new nation. Decades after its initial designation as a capital city, the forces that formed Nouakchott still manifest in the present-day city – both in the social experience of its inhabitants and its physical morphology. This chapter explores the relationships between the city's people, the environment, and the spaces they have made within it, all the while in the midst of one of the planet's most inhospitable environments.

2 Diagrammatic illustration of a traditional *ksar*.

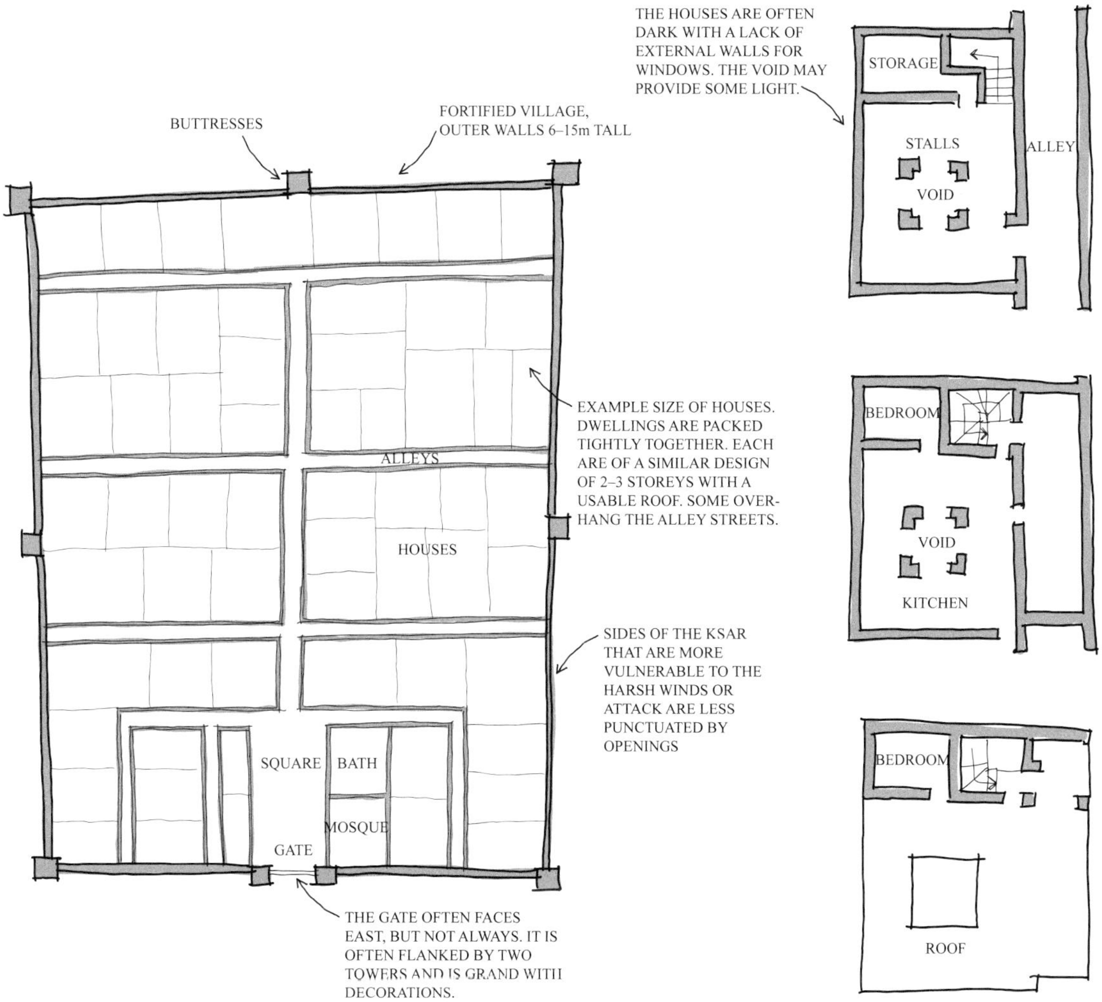

Pre-Independence and the Origins of the City

Little is known about pre-colonial Nouakchott. Before colonial rule and subsequent independence, the area now known as Mauritania was a mostly rural tribal region, rather than a defined and governed country. Mauritania has an oral tradition, and as such much of its pre-colonisation history remains unwritten. From its founding in the 17th century until it was chosen as the capital in 1958, Nouakchott was a small, fortified fishing village (*ksar*). While little evidence exists of its exact morphology, it was thought to be small and sparsely populated,[12] home to some 500 people.[13] The *ksar* of Nouakchott was almost entirely destroyed in 1950 by a severe flood of the Senegal River.[14] Although the settlement was partially reconstructed, many structures were probably made from adobe or were not permanent and have not survived to the present day, but the area in which the original *ksar* was located remains as a district called Ksar (see F in fig. 6 later).

Ksars exemplify typical pre-colonial villages in this area of west Africa, and are a product of the nomadic lifestyle of the region. They would be constructed of materials found in the vicinity, such as dry stone in mountainous regions and desert, or adobe in the southern and coastal regions.[15] Most *ksars* were located in relatively inaccessible regions and did not undergo significant development under French colonial rule. They were generally formed of family dwellings facing multiple streets or alleys within a larger rectangular structure (as shown in fig. 2) and encouraged a sense of community and tribal security from danger.[16] This was especially clear in the *ksars* deeper in the desert, which grew up along caravan trade routes. These settlements tended to be occupied only seasonally and used for storage the rest of the time. As such, they had to be easily surveyable by the few members of the nomadic community who would stay behind to ensure the security of the contents of houses when occupying households resumed their nomadic lifestyle with the herd.

Post-Independence: The New Capital

French colonial influence in the area that is now Mauritania began in 1900, and in 1920 the region was established as part of the larger colony of French West Africa. The colonial period was relatively short, as faced with widespread international opposition to colonial holdings after World War II, France began the process of returning autonomy to the region in 1946.[17]

As Mauritania began preparing for independence in the late 1950s, it had no capital city of its own, having been administered from St Louis in Senegal until this point. The new capital would aspire to be a spatial assertion of nationalism and shared identity – similar to other capitals built in newly independent countries in the 1960s–1980s. This goal was especially pertinent in the context of Mauritania, a country made up of multiple disparate tribes and ethnicities, and a contributing factor for the choice of Nouakchott given the perceived cultural and political neutrality of the location. However, the proposals for the city also had to address the constraints of rapid construction and economic efficiency, limited by scarce resources.

Multiple master plans were drafted for the city. A grid-system plan was proposed in April 1957 by Hirsch (a French national who was Director of Public Works in Mauritania), following the characteristic form of segregated colonial towns (fig. 3) with the primary arterial road running east to west, passing by a mosque and a hospital that delineated two sectors. To the north was the administrative district, with the presidential palace, embassies, and other administrative buildings; and to the south the working-class neighbourhood, with a large outdoor market. This plan provided for a population of 8,000.[18] Another plan, proposed by Cerutti Maori in May 1957 (French architect of the General Government of French West Africa), also established clear divisions in the city, the indigenous working class separated from the ruling class by a road running east to west (fig. 4). A later plan,

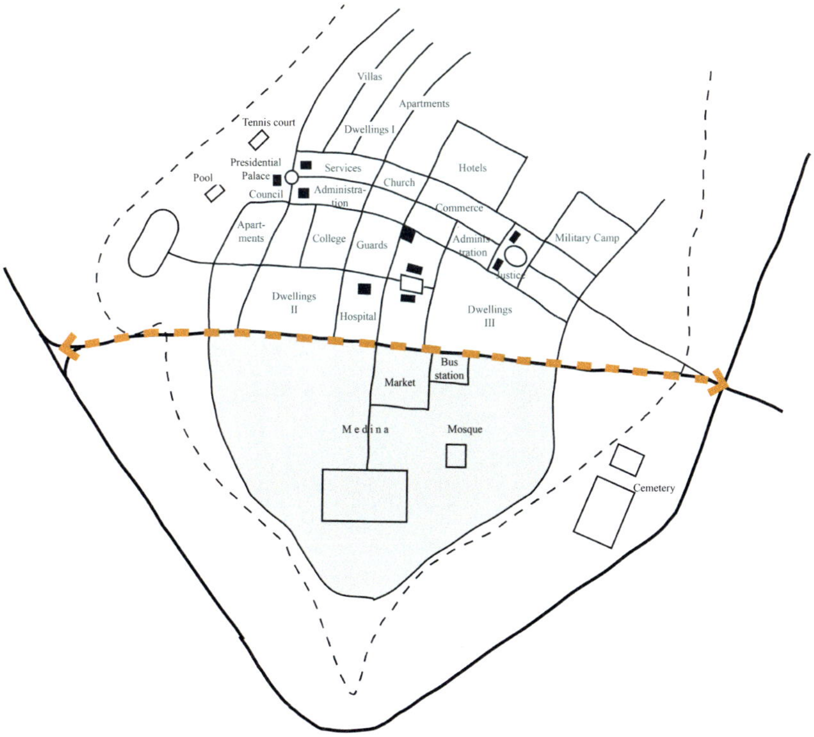

3 1957 Master Plan by Hirsch.

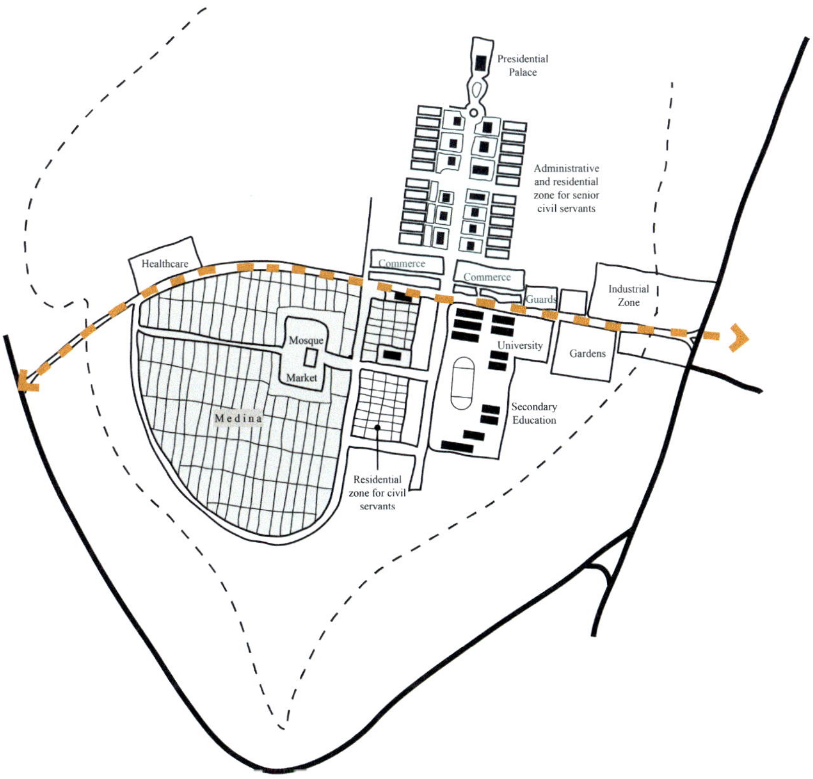

4 1957 Master Plan by Cerutti Maori.

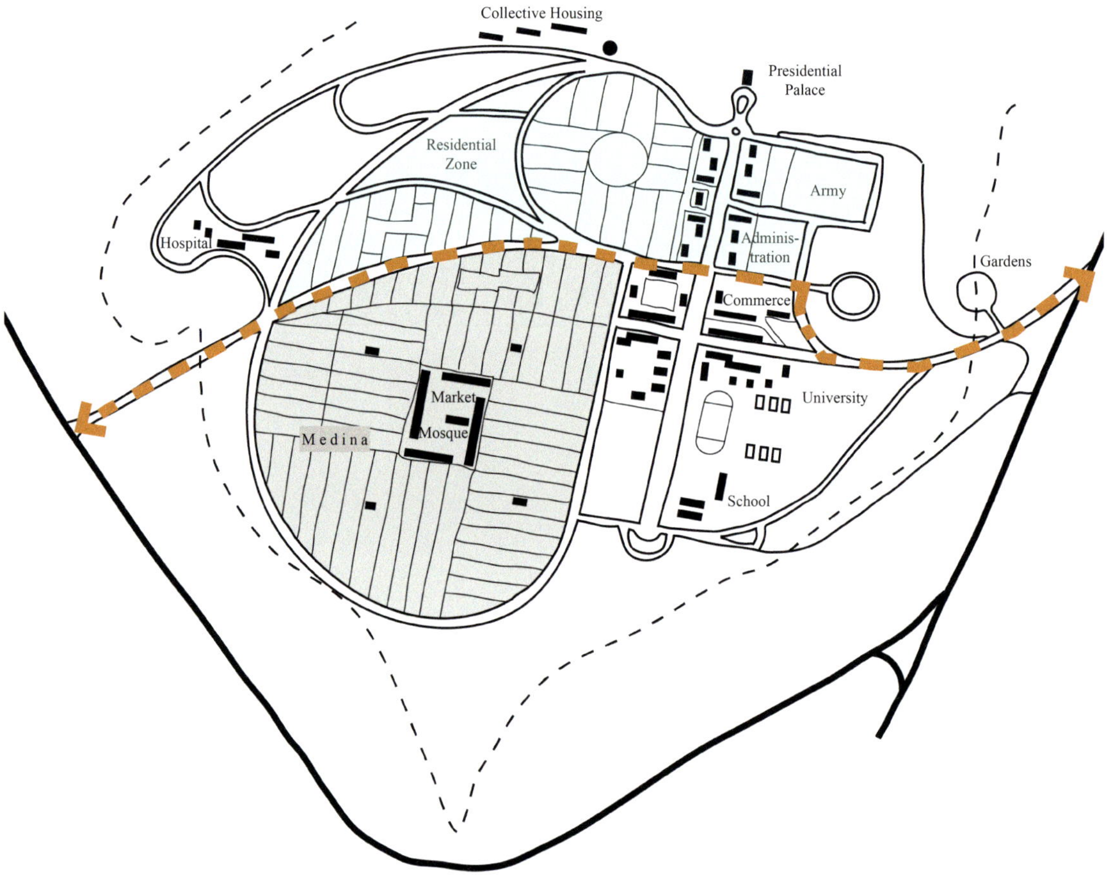

5 1957 Master Plan by Lainville.

submitted by Lainville (an architect working in the Directorate of Urban Planning and Public Works in Dakar) in the summer of 1957, was adopted in 1958. It was similar to Cerutti's plan, following the principles of a typical colonial city, again encouraging social segregation with the separation of administration and the upper class from working-class neighbourhoods (fig. 5).[19]

The new city needed to be built on high ground to reduce the likelihood of flooding and other environmental challenges. The only high point in the area was a dune identified in topographical surveys in 1957, which was 2 km west of the original village (see fig. 6 later).[20] Construction began in 1958 as the region readied itself for independence from France, and the base of the city was finished by the time of independence in November 1960.[21] At this time, 70 % of Mauritania's population was still nomadic. It was expected that this would continue and the role of Nouakchott would be predominantly administrative, not the significant population centre it has become.[22]

Rapid Expansion

In the 1970s Nouakchott began to experience an influx of internally displaced persons as a direct result of the Great Sahelian Droughts that began in 1968.[23] While this region of Africa has a pattern of rainfall cycles and associated desertification processes, the droughts of 1968–1988 were «exacerbated by overpopulation and poor land management»,[24] including deforestation which contributed to the advancement of the desert. The droughts caused agricultural output to fall drastically, impacting the livelihoods of people relying on agriculture and livestock herding.[25] Nomads and pastoralists who lost their livelihoods looked to the capital city for a means of rebuilding their lives, contradicting the original assumptions about Nouakchott being only an administrative centre.

These people began to occupy the peripheries of Nouakchott as they arrived, establishing informal settlements (see table 1). The most significant growth happened between 1970 and 1974, when the population increased by 325%.[26] This rapid rural–urban migration led to a period of over-urbanisation and growth of unplanned settlements, putting a strain on the limited services the city possessed. Access to drinking water and sanitary facilities was not universal even in the formal developments, and most certainly did not reach the sprawling peripheries. Many of those newly settling in Nouakchott were from agricultural backgrounds and did not possess suitable skills or trades which they could apply in the city. High unemployment and a sense of dislocation ensued.[27]

At this point in the city's growth, incoming migrants tended to settle with tribal relations already living in the city, maintaining the micro-social structures from their pre-urban life. However, this pattern also facilitated the continuation of slavery. Although officially abolished in 1903, domestic slavery was exempt from legal abolition since it was seen as being equivalent to servitude.[28] Consequently, Haratines (former slaves) often lived with and laboured for their former masters in exchange for shelter and food.[29]

Between the mid-1970s and the 1990s, more migrants arrived, independently of pre-settled relatives. Unauthorised camps were set up along the roads they arrived on – predominantly the main tarmac roads, the road to Rosso to the south, the «Road of Hope» to the east, and the Atar Road to the north (fig. 6). This expansion has transformed the resulting crossroads into community centres. Sometimes these settlements broke away from the existing urban fabric and became their own entities. This distinct pattern of settlement, divided along ethnic lines (discussed later in this chapter), is now permanently etched into the character of the city's periphery.[30] This division manifests itself in the distinct urban typologies seen along the transport arteries, in the clothes worn in the neighbourhoods, the presence or absence of various animals, and most distinctly in the wares sold at the local markets.

In response to the swelling of the city and ensuing disorder since the first big wave of rural migrants, a second urban plan was adopted in 1970, the SMUH (Secretariat des Missions d'Urbanisme) plan, which designated specific residential areas, amenities, and industrial zones. The plan predicted the presence of 100,000 inhabitants in the city by 1980 and aimed to provide structure for the city's growth. This urban plan designated four areas: the Capital (the administrative and business centre), the Ksar (the site of the pre-1958 village), the Wharf (the industrial port area), and the Plage des Pêcheurs (the fishermen's beach).[31] The aim was to bring order to the high rate of growth of the city; however, like its previous iteration the plan did not fully anticipate the extent of Nouackott's continued expansion.

In 1972, in a departure from pre-planned development by the administration of the adopted master plan, two new districts were created.[32] These were followed in 1974 by the creation of 8,700 new plots to the north and south, and 16,000 additional plots over the following decade – becoming the districts Teyarett, Sebkha, and El Mina. At the same time, the high-end residential neighbourhood of Tevragh Zeïna was developed, providing some 2,500 additional plots (fig. 6). In 1989 the new primarily residential districts of Arafat, Riyad, and Dar Naim were created.[33] Much of this new development happened in areas vulnerable to

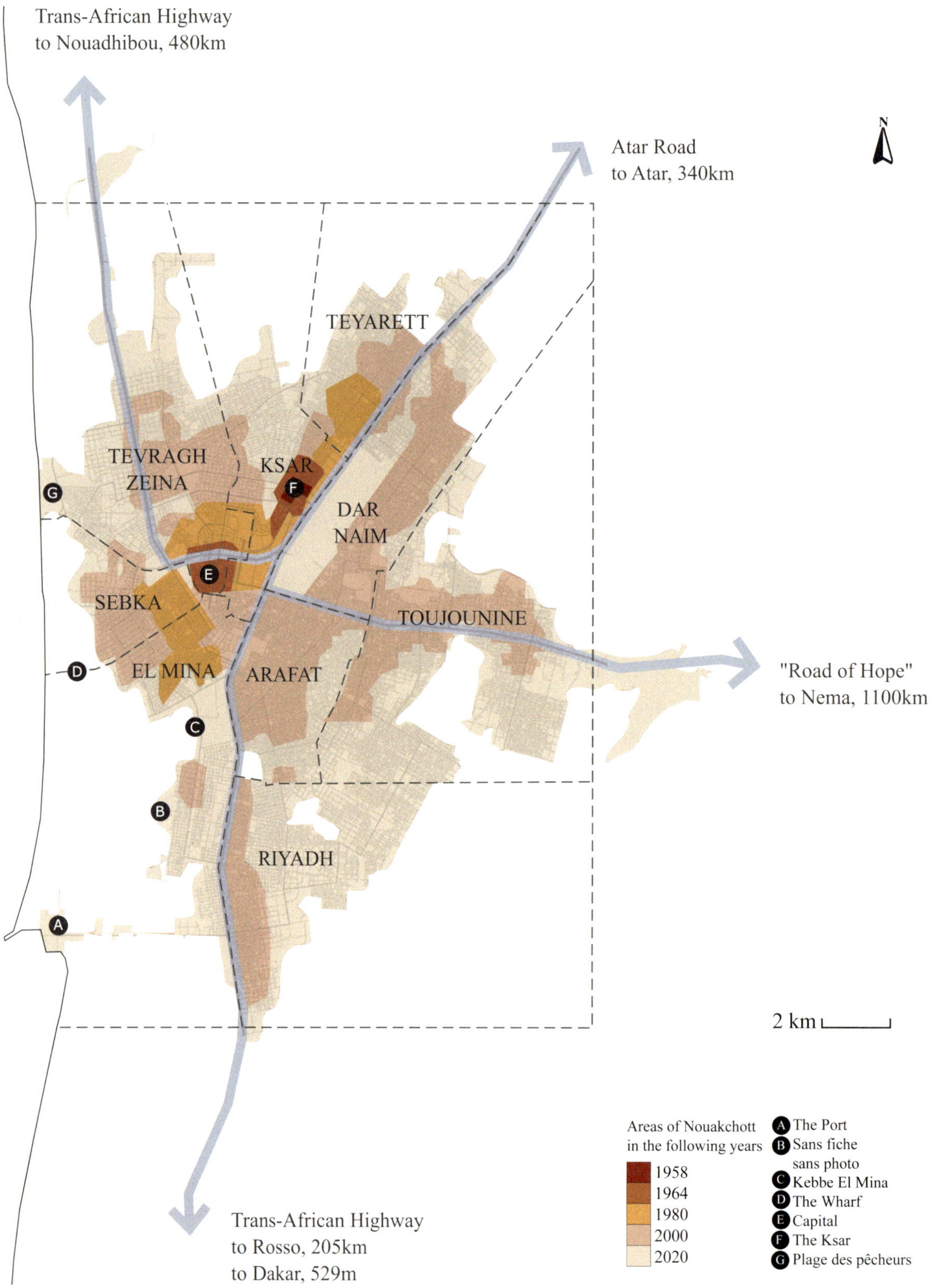

6 Growth of Nouakchott from independence to present day.

threats of flooding and the encroaching desert, placing inhabitants at significant risk. It also outpaced the government's ability to provide services such as running water, sewage, and electricity.

Growth in Spite of Environmental Challenges

The location of the city exposes it to significant environmental risks. Although its climate is relatively mild in the context of Mauritania due to the coastal location, Nouakchott is trapped between the rising sea and the encroaching desert. Fig. 7 shows that significant areas of the city are under threat of regular flooding and that sand incursion severely limits the areas safe for construction and inhabitation. Meanwhile, north-easterly winds drive sand dunes into the city from the Sahara Desert, threatening the population with the encroaching desert and limiting potential areas of growth.

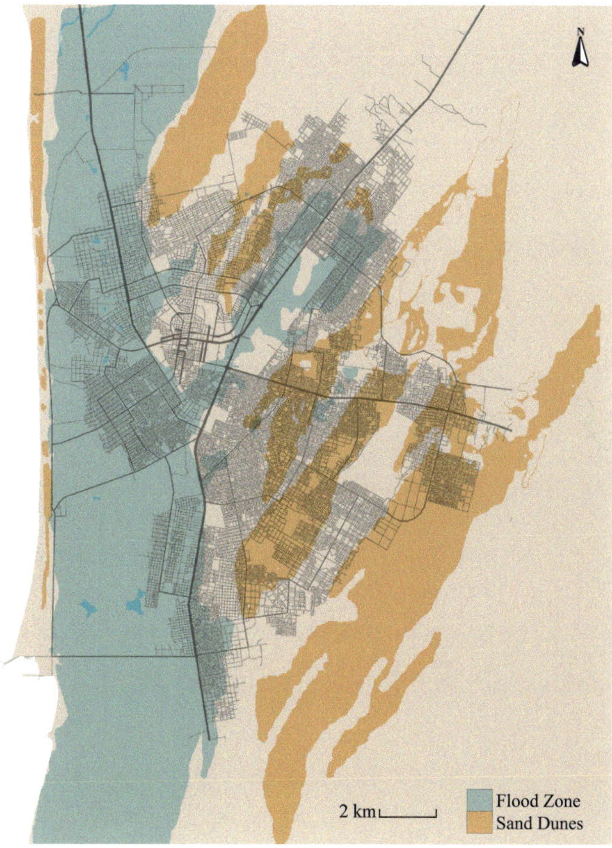

7 The city in its environment.

Flooding in Nouakchott has two main causes: rainfall and rising sea levels. From the west, rising sea levels threaten to submerge the city. Exacerbated by breaches in the coastal dunes, which have been dug up for sand to make concrete, storm surges also pose a growing threat. Since the entirety of Nouakchott is either at or below sea level, research predicts that by 2030 79% of the city's surface area could be underwater.[34] Heavy rainfall in the wet season is unable to drain away as Nouakchott lies at and below sea level and has limited drainage infrastructure, leading to widespread flooding in many areas of the inner city (see fig. 7), including wealthy districts such as Tevragh Zeïna. Although it is one of the neighbourhoods with the most well-established services and built environment, Tevragh Zeïna suffers greatly from flooding and stagnant ground water, which poses threats to health throughout the flood-prone areas of the city.[35] In response to these conditions, many buildings in these areas are constructed on a deep plinth as a means to keep the flood water out. Over time the floor levels are incrementally raised to bring the ground floor level higher than the flooding (fig. 8)[36] – this is enabled by the predominantly single-storey typology of buildings throughout the city, but is not sustainable as a long-term solution.

To compound the challenges caused by flooding, the high salinity of the water table causes corrosion and degradation of the urban environment from the bottom up. This process is especially visible in Sebkha and El Mina. The sea winds drive salt into the city, exacerbating the corrosion of materials and buildings above ground. There are several options available to protect buildings, including special concrete mixes and damp-proof courses, but these solutions are not cheap, and require skilled labour. One protective method developed by residents is to cover the west facing elevations with tiles. However, tiles are not locally made and

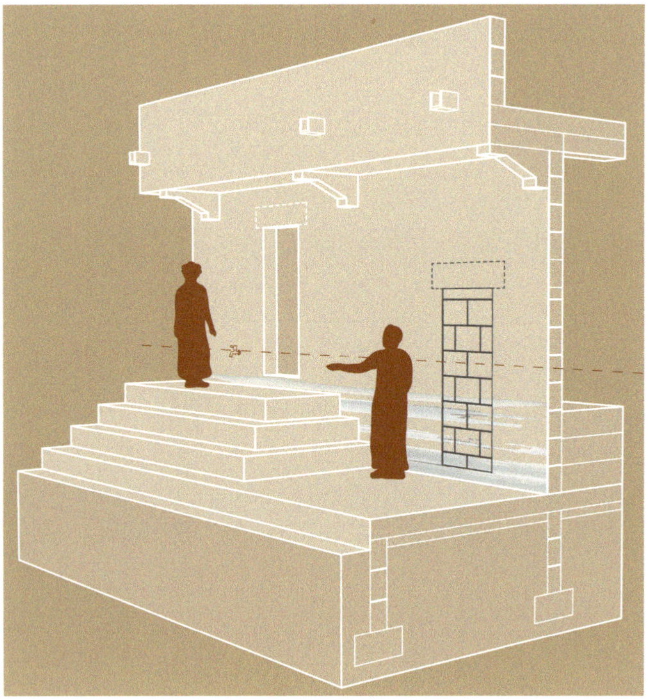

8 Diagram showing the incremental adaptation of houses in response to floods.

need to be imported, making them a luxury only the wealthy can afford.

The desert poses another set of problems. From the north-east, strong seasonal winds drive sand and encroaching dunes from the Sahara desert into the city. Much of the uncontrolled growth of the city has occurred on the eastern fringes of the city, where settlements are most exposed and face a relentless battle against moving dunes.[37] The shifting landscape is difficult to urbanise and maintain, with the abrasive sand pummelling roads and buildings as many as 160 days a year. While many ancient *ksars* in the desert were built with tall surrounding walls encompassing smaller walled complexes, divided by narrow winding streets (see fig. 2), the sparse low-rise build-up of the neighbourhoods in Nouakchott provides little protection from the sand or sun (as illustrated in fig. 9). The safety and durability of the informal settlements being built on the sand dunes around the city are even more precarious, and while more

9 Diagram showing the incremental adaptation of houses in response to floods.

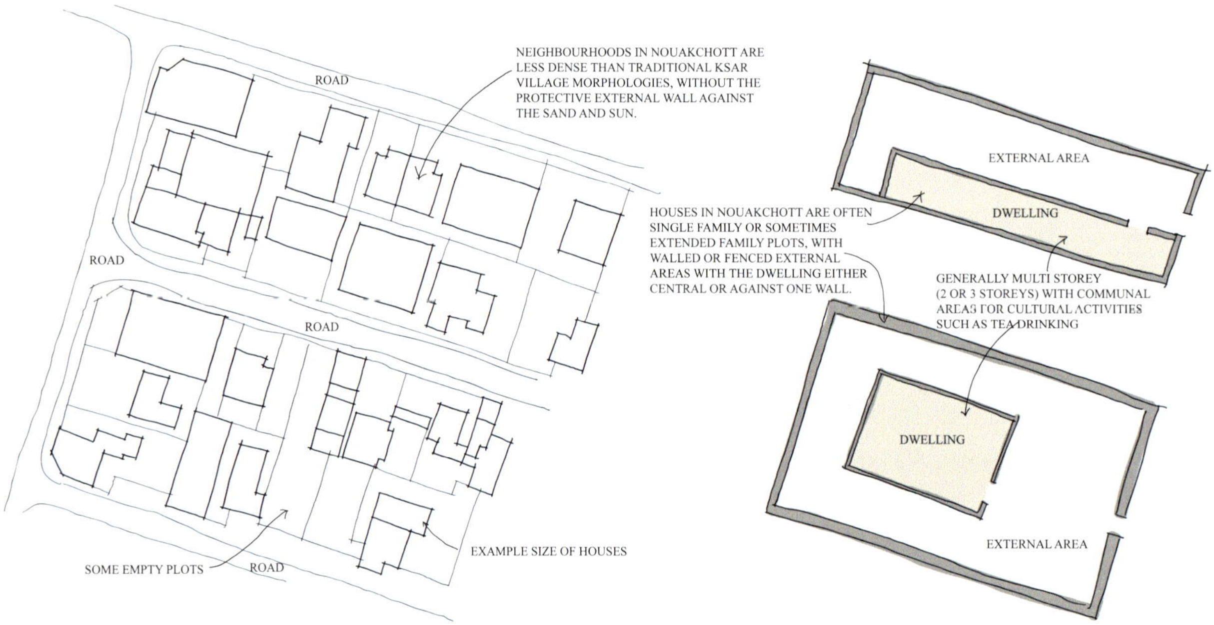

densely built, their temporary nature and the scarcity of building resources makes them vulnerable.

Unlike the pre-colonial *ksars*, there is an overall lack of traditional earthen and stone architecture in the modern settlements. Nouakchott is a concrete city; heavily influenced by Western use of the material. The city's urban growth is therefore highly dependent on importing concrete.[38] Across the formal areas of the city, buildings are typically constructed using concrete breeze blocks, which are occasionally rendered with a cement-based render. This type of construction offers little thermal regulation or protection from the heat. Moreover, due to lack of enforced building standards and scarcity of resources, the aggregate in the concrete is often replaced with seashells from the local shore, compromising the material's strength and structural integrity.[39] The reliance on concrete also puts pressure on the local systems as its production requires potable water, a scarce resource in Nouakchott, which might otherwise be used for drinking. Despite the strong potential and abundance of more traditional materials in Nouakchott such as raw earth, the mistaken perception that these materials are «poor» and «weak», together with a lack of training and incentives for their use, prevents Nouakchott's urban communities from adapting these materials for modern-day use.[40] Concrete blocks are used because they are easy and quick to build with, and familiar to the local labour force. Concrete therefore persists as the predominant building material despite clear limitations and poor suitability to the environmental conditions, and concrete has become the defining feature of Nouakchott's urban landscape.

Informality

Widespread informality is the result of this rapid expansion of the city, which the local authorities have been unable to keep pace with and regulate. People arriving in Nouakchott would build shelters wherever they could, irrespective of provision for amenities. Over the years, distinct types of informal settlements have emerged, some of which are unique to Mauritania, such as *kebbe* and *gazra* on a micro scale. Informal settlements generally consist of non-permanent structures such as shacks and tents. The chapter later describes how these distinct formations of informality shape the urban fabric of the city as a whole on the macro level.

Kebbe refers to a type of unplanned informal settlement characterised by tent structures and barracks.[41] The term, translated from Hassaniya, means «throw away» (see table 1), and entered popular circulation among the residents of Nouakchott after a slum clearance action by the authorities in 1971, when the residents were «thrown out».[42] *Kebbe* are clearly distinguishable in aerial photographs by their huddled structures in organic clusters (fig. 10). They often occupy land belonging to private individuals, and as such their inhabitants face a significant risk of eviction. The materials used to create *kebbe* shelters reflect the precarious nature of their situation – canvas, tarpaulin, and corrugated steel are easy to dismantle and relocate to a different plot. Many materials are re-appropriated for use in the built environment, such as car tyres for marking land boundaries and pallet wood (from freight ships) for shack walls. Areas of *kebbe* are evident across the city, both on the periphery and closer to the centre of the city, particularly in areas where there are opportunities for employment. With only 8.3 % of Mauritanians employed with a formal contract, those seeking jobs often find informal employment in wealthier neighbourhoods in domestic roles.[43] *Kebbe* can take the form of smaller shelters inserted into odd empty lots of land, or form entire districts. A prominent example of the latter type is the *kebbe* of El Mina (see fig. 6), just to the west of the city centre, which has grown to house around 50,000 people, mostly of Haratine background.

Gazra, a second distinct type of informal settlement, refers to a «squat» – the illegal occupation of public land with the hope of achieving

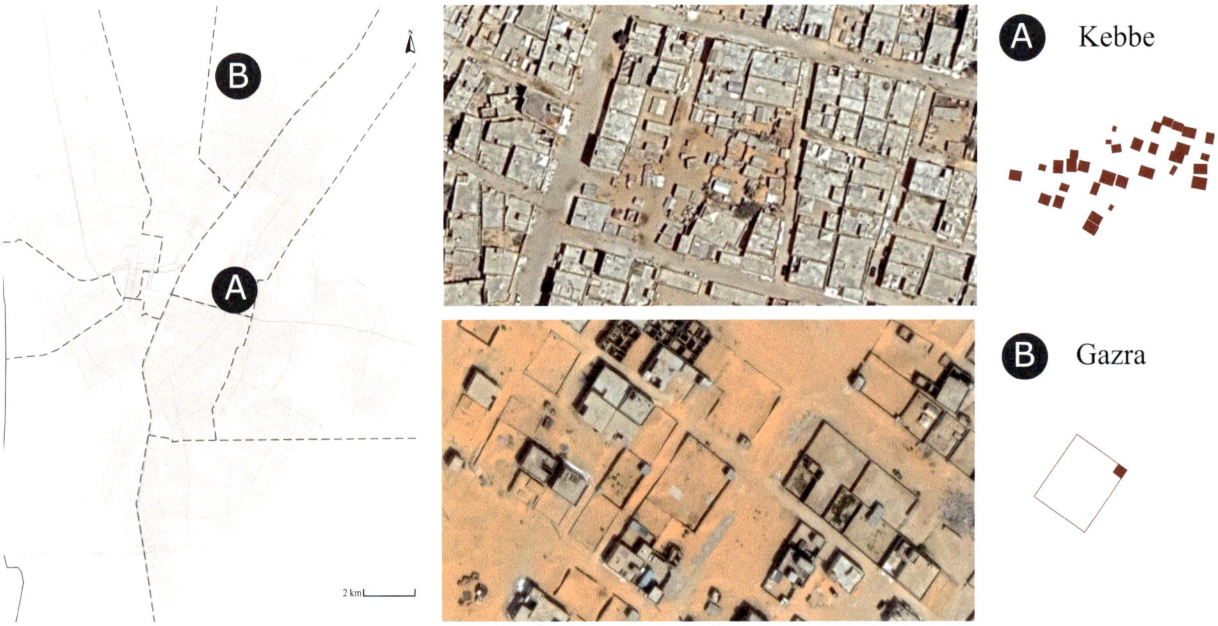

10 Diagram illustrating *kebbe* and *gazra*.

ownership, often on the periphery of the city (see table 1). This term also emerged from the residents of the city. These settlements are distinguishable in aerial photographs (as seen in fig. 10) by an empty plot of land demarcated with a breeze-block wall, containing a small structure generally also made of breeze block. The use of breeze block here serves a dual purpose. It is a more solid material, aiming to indicate permanence, while also being quick and easy to assemble, allowing rapid construction, often overnight, to lay claim to the land. A significant example is the *gazra* located in the district of Arafat, which at one point housed a third of the district's population.

Land tenure can be gained on *gazra* sites through a government scheme designed to promote formal structures as replacements for shacks;[44] however, this system has been abused by the speculative purchase of additional land to make a profit. Land speculation in this context is the utilisation of *gazra* sites to gain legal ownership before selling the blocks on for a profit.[45] The Mauritanian government issued over 200,000 plots to new residents between 1974 and 1988, but many of these were then sold for profit.[46]

Many of the new neighbourhoods resulting from informal settlement were never officially named as part of the policy to curb their growth. However, unofficial names made it into wider circulation, often reflecting the fraught relationships between policy-makers and the inhabitants of these informal settlements.[47] The driving force behind eradicating slums has come from top-down policies, incentives, and urban programmes aiming to reduce poverty administered by organisations such as the World Bank and the International Monetary Fund. In Nouakchott there have been a number of *déguerpissements* (a term used in French-speaking Africa to describe forced resettlements) and subsequent demolition of slums.[48] The Urban Development Program was developed in 2001, funded by the World Bank, aiming to improve the living conditions of people living in precarious neighbourhoods in Nouakchott and Nouadhibou.[49] This improvement was meant to be achieved by subdividing the neighbourhood, then registering the residents so that they could obtain an official plot of land in the neighbourhood, with cash to cover travel costs, access to a social housing programme, and the option to take out a microloan to fund the building of one bedroom. However, there was not enough space to resettle all of the residents, resulting in a dispute over who would stay and who would move. Leaders were chosen to decide who would get the plots in El-Mina, while the remaining households were resettled in an underdeveloped area – the so-called neighbourhood of «Sans fiche sans photo» («the people without files or photos»), where hundreds of households were forcibly resettled from the *kebbe* of El-Mina after they did not qualify for rehousing. An alternative name that emerged for «Sans fiche sans photo» was «Tarhil» («the displaced»), showing the dissonance between the official discourse of «resettlement» and the feelings of the individuals who defined themselves as «displaced».[50]

A key difference between the inhabitants of *kebbe* and *gazra* is their socio-economic status. While kebbe represents a genuine materialisation of poverty, gazra can also be inhabited by residents with greater financial means, who see their squatting as a way to increase their wealth. However, for those in genuine need of shelter, both forms are inherently precarious. Informal settlement growth reflects the resilience and agency of the communities, particularly those of urban migrants who have moved to the city in search of employment and an increased standard of living, but instead are faced with an inhospitable environment, cultural challenges, and inadequate housing.

In addition to *kebbe* and *gazra*, Nouakchott is host to further housing typologies. The third type of informality in the city is developed informality, where the perishable building materials used to create the early 1970s informalities have been replaced with more permanent ones over time while keeping the organic formation of the settlements – resulting in the «old slums» discussed later in this chapter. The fourth type is temporary informality, which as the name suggests, refers to the perishable shacks and tents widely dispersed throughout the city – referred to in the following section of the chapter as «recent slums». While these processes are common in slums and informal settlements globally, the rate at which these types of settlements have developed in Mauritania sets them apart and they have been uniquely influenced by the nomadic lifestyle traditionally practised by many Mauritanians, as is evident in the materials used and the arrangement of dwellings. Beyond these typologies, another mode of informality has emerged, which refers to a behaviour rather than an urban form – the practice of «*tcheb-tchib*», which is a process of creative improvisation to counter the state's technologies of governance, performed by both the poor and wealthy as means of increasing capital. The wealthy employ others to occupy an empty parcel of land situated in an area designated for redevelopment. The aim is for the authorities in charge of the survey preceding the redevelopment to register that the land is occupied. In that case, the people occupying the land will be given the title to the plot in exchange for a symbolic financial amount. If the plot is situated on land designated as public space or for utilities according to the urban master plan, the occupants will be allocated a plot, free of charge, in another area. The new «landowners» can then sell that land for a considerable profit – which goes to the employer. To be successful, these practices require knowledge of urban development processes and socio-political networks.[51] As a result, the greatest benefits of any land allocation schemes are enjoyed by the wealthiest in society, while the poorest remain stuck in precarious conditions.

When discussing issues related to various forms of informal settlements and land speculation, it is important to keep in mind the cultural relationship nomadic people have with land. With

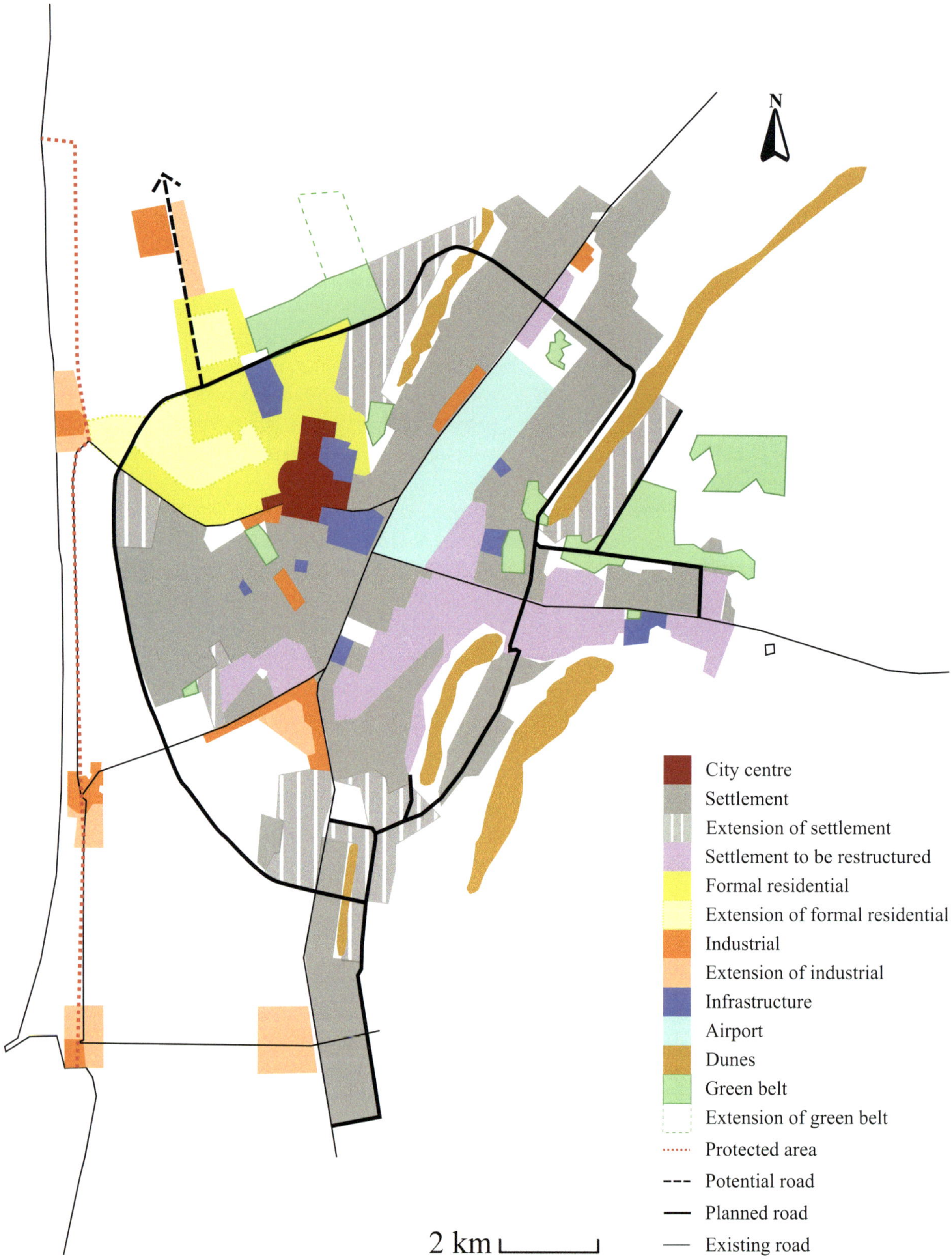

11 Diagram of the SDAU 2003.

many Mauritanians leaving the nomadic lifestyle only two generations ago, their relationship with permanence and the concept of exclusive land ownership differs from those of settled communities.[52] This value system clashes with Western-based concepts of exclusive land ownership, on which the urban plans for Nouakchott were formed and which contribute to the forced resettlements. Many of the residents of Nouakchott have come from nomadic cultures with very different approaches to land ownership. As they settled in the city, they had to adapt not only to an urban lifestyle, but more specifically to the Western concept of exclusive land ownership.

Formalisation of Urban Expansion

As the city continued to grow, more attempts were made to contain and formalise the irregular expansion through the introduction of a third urban masterplan. The 1983 master plan, designed by BCEOM, a French engineering company, aimed to tackle the chaotic urban environment and curb the practice of land speculation. It proposed further development of residential and public buildings to the north of the city, and designated the sand dunes east of the city, where much of the informal settlement was happening, as green spaces. However, the expansion of the city failed to follow the plan, and informal growth continued to happen to the east where some 5,000 plots were regularised by the administration, further undermining the efforts of the BCEOM plan to curb expansion in the area.

In 2003 the SDAU (Schéma Directeur d'Aménagement Urbain) masterplan (fig. 11) was introduced, designed by the Swiss bureau Urbaplan, with support from the World Bank. This plan projected the future of the city up to 2020. As with the previous plans, it aimed to contain the urban sprawl and to densify existing neighbourhoods. It introduced the idea of a ring road around the city, which was to provide a physical barrier to outward growth. Unlike the previous plans, the SDAU plan was not based on zones (industrial, residential, green spaces), and it was the first plan to consider the city's specific environmental conditions. Yet again, however, new development did not always follow the principles established in the plan. While it was legally binding for the administration, it was not so for private owners who could build outside of the restrictions of the masterplan – due to severe lack of provision, many residents did not rely on the municipal infrastructure anyway. Moreover, the SDAU plan was not accompanied by a law to punish abuses of the planned land distribution.[53] Consequently, there were attempts to revise and update the plan in 2013, but these efforts were eventually abandoned.

The current plan governing the development of Nouakchott has been developed by the Japan International Cooperation Agency (JICA): it is a revision of the 2003 SDAU plan up to 2018, with a projection to 2040. Fig. 12 shows a prediction of how urban sprawl might continue in the city if the plan is not enacted – continued spread along the main arteries and in the highly flood-prone zone near the port. Fig. 13 shows the growth of the city as anticipated by the SDAU 2018, which aims to concentrate the new growth to the north and south-east, containing the city and increasing density instead. It is interesting to note that all of the urban plans up to this date have been developed by foreign institutions. This perhaps explains why their models have been unsuccessful – as they are based on the Western idea of what a city is and should be, rather than a response to the city's specific cultural context.

The cycles of rapid growth and attempted formalisation, as well as other factors discussed earlier such as the continued waves of migrations and the different socio-economic conditions of the inhabitants, have resulted in a highly diversified urban landscape with specific features. The following paragraphs describe the range of spatial typologies within the city, with more dense areas in the city centre and less dense areas on the

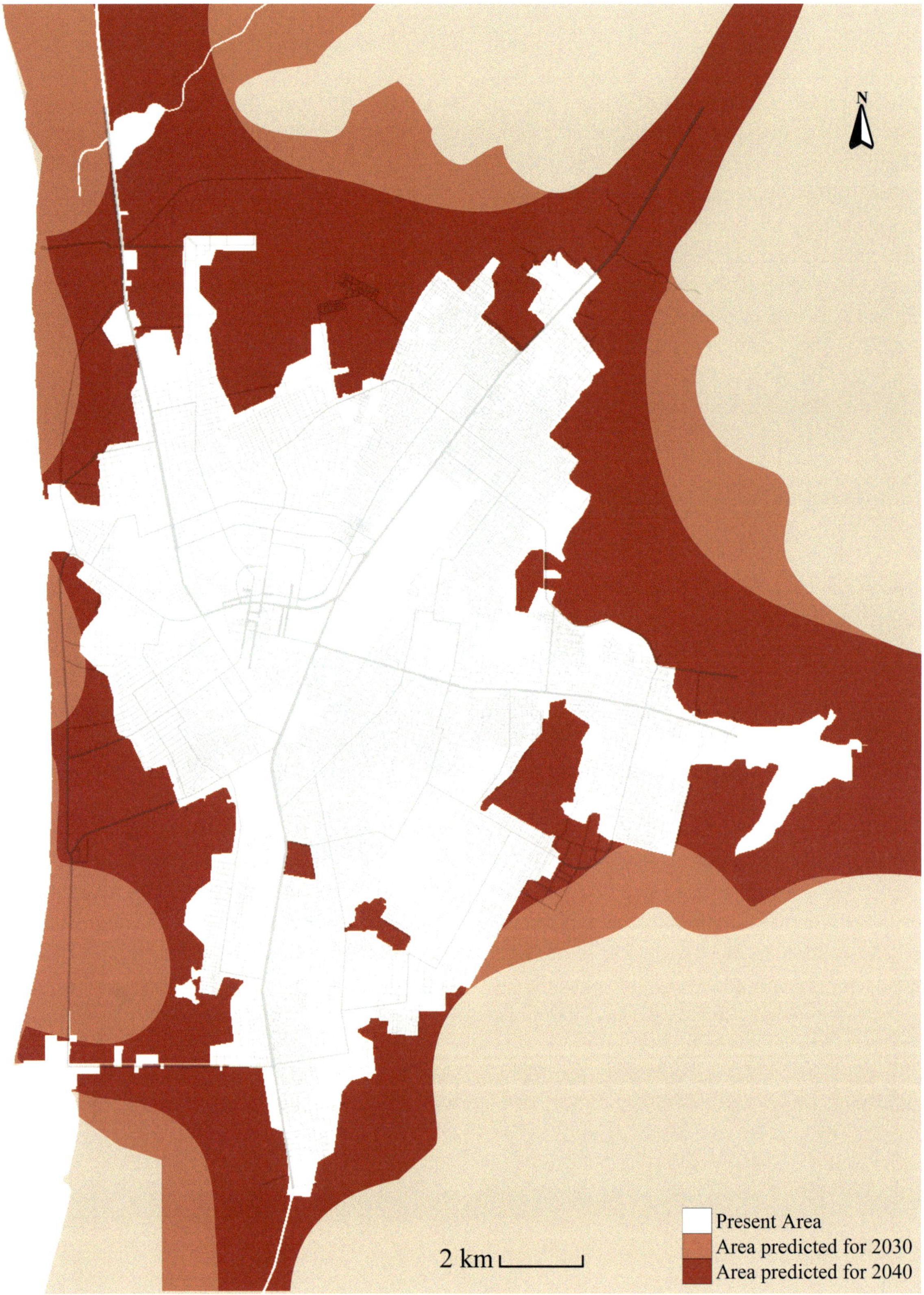

12 Predicted sprawl of the city if the SDAU 2018 masterplan is not implemented.

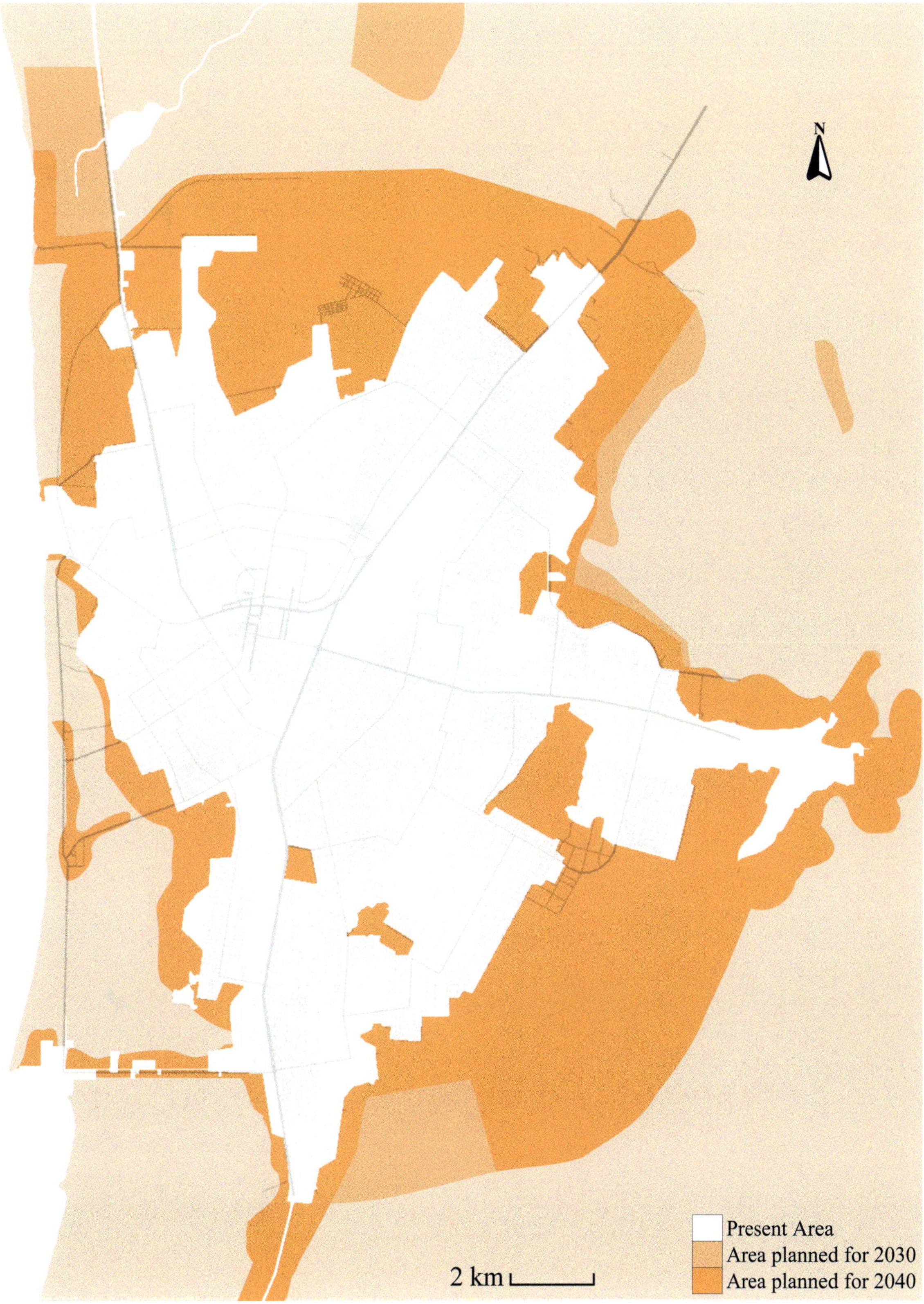

13 Desired growth of the city under the SDAU 2018 masterplan.

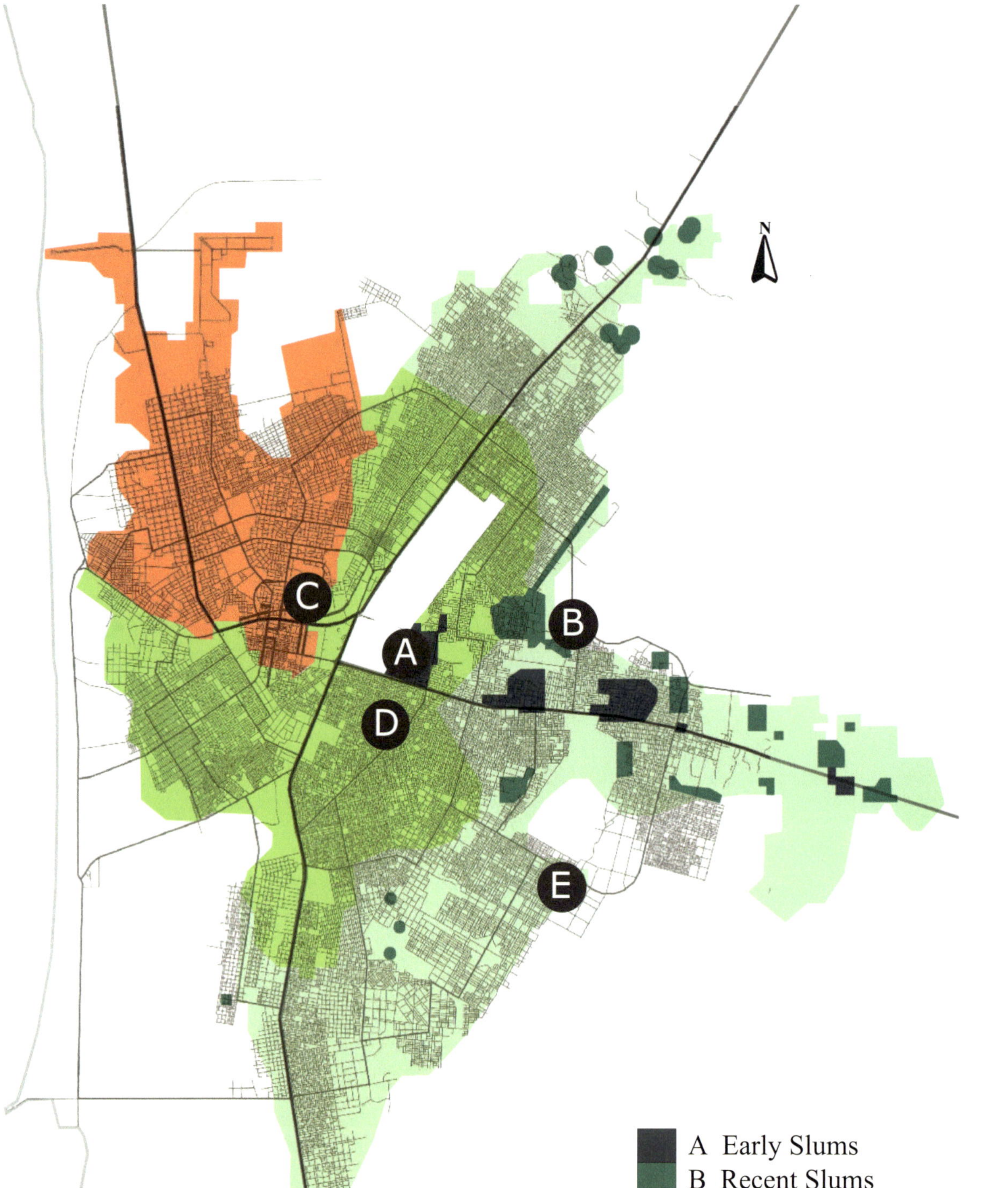

14 Urban typologies of Nouakchott.

periphery. While this is a common morphology of many cities, in Nouakchott it is partially driven by the planned structure of the city centre, in contrast to the informal structure of the periphery.

Early slums

These are early/original slums from the first period of rapid expansion during droughts of the 1970s and 80s (figs. 14 and 15). They consist of residential areas that were formerly slums and have developed over time, yet have kept their organic morphology typical of informal settlements, without being demolished and redeveloped or planned. In some cases the government granted ownership of land based on what people had built already rather than formal division of plots. The ownership of land is still being resolved by the state and people who have settled there. These older slums have a semi-formal status today as they are built of older materials, such as concrete and tiles, than those used in the newer slums.

Recent slums

These are areas of recent and current unplanned growth on the periphery of the city, which have formed in the past decade (figs. 14 and 16). These areas are characterised by the use of informal materials, precarious construction such as shacks built from pallets and tents made from canvas, and no formal ownership of land among residents.

15 Early slums (location A).

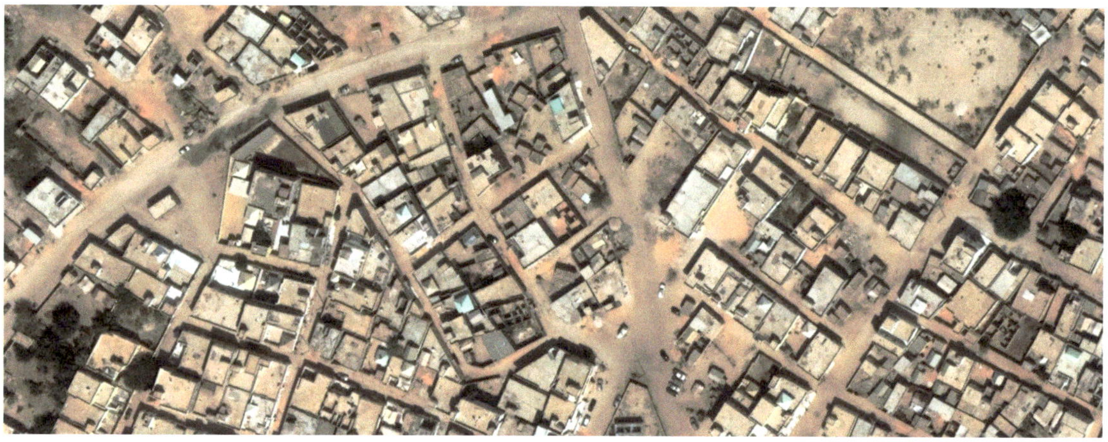

16 Recent slums (location B).

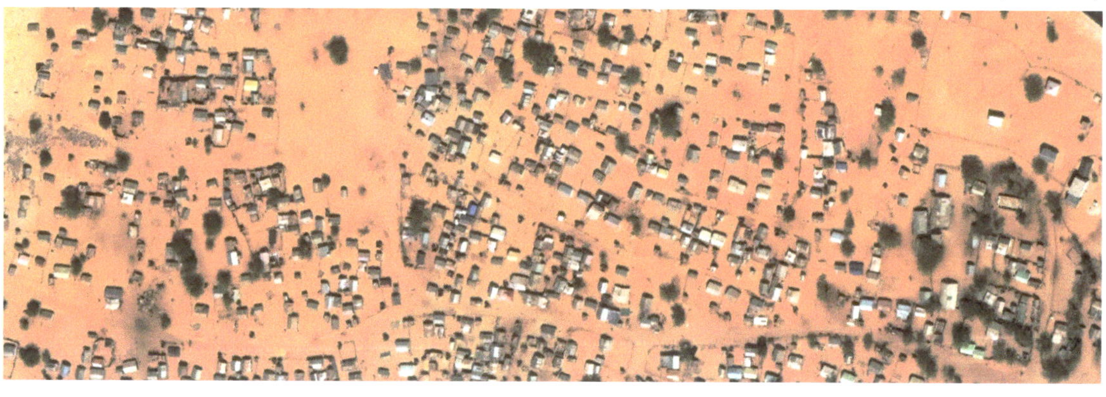

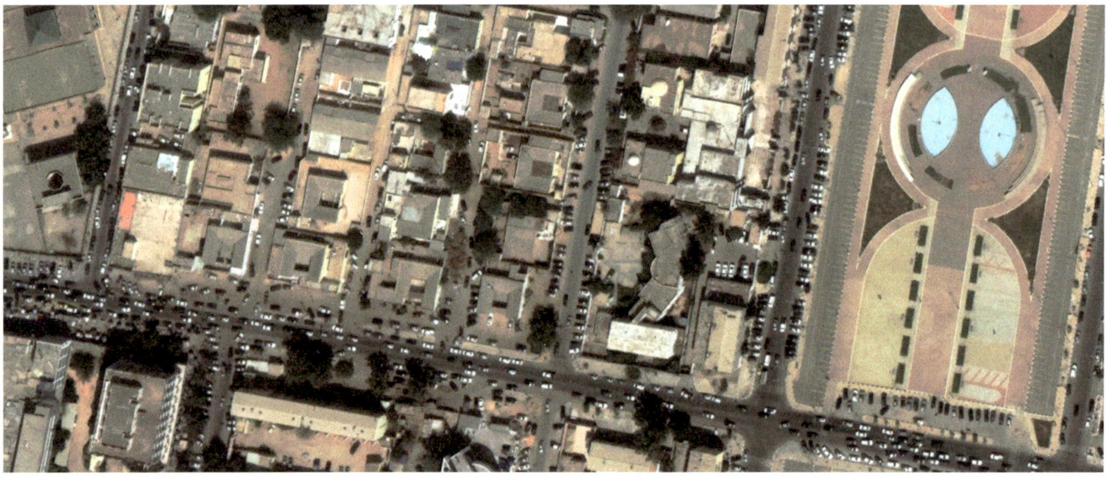

17 Hard standing (location C).

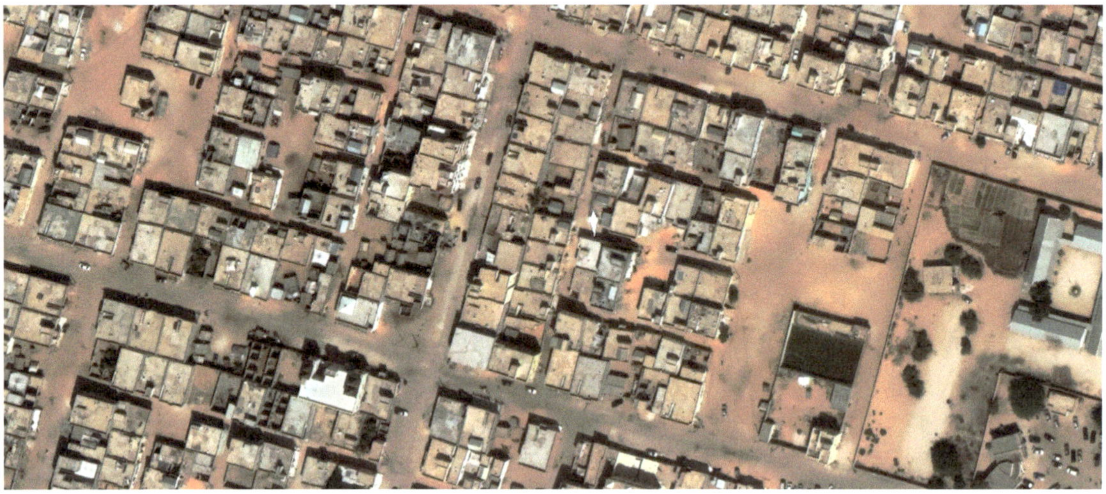

18 Medium standing (location D).

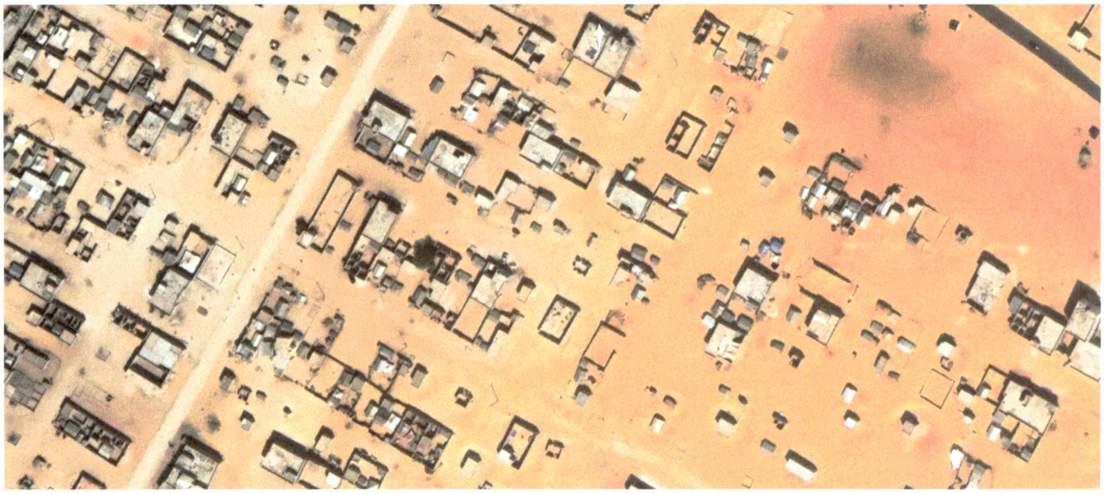

19 Low standing (location E).

Hard standing
These are some of the oldest formal parts of the planned city, based on early urban masterplans, and with access to infrastructure and services (figs. 14 and 17). Plots in these areas are often for larger-scale buildings, with a focus on commercial and public uses. Most roads use tarmac.

Medium standing
These are residential suburbs that grew out of the original working class-neighbourhoods and characterised by some access to services (figs. 14 and 18). The main arteries are made of tarmac, but the majority of roads are not. These areas are mostly comprised of permanent buildings, with occasional infill areas of *kebbe*.

Low standing
These areas are located on the periphery and precarious edge of the city, with emerging signs of new development and infrastructure (figs. 14 and 19). There are clear indicators of *tcheb-tchib* tactics and *gazra* in the form of large plots of land contained within rough walls, with incomplete structures inside.

Housing Schemes

In addition to the urban plans that attempted to tackle the extent of urban sprawl, several social housing programmes also operated in the city. These programmes were developed to address the lack of affordable housing and precarious housing in informal settlements, but they have faced criticism and challenges. The ADAUA developed one such project as early as 1977, composed of 128 model affordable homes and using, instead of the already ubiquitous breeze blocks, some of the few locally available building materials, such as sun-dried bricks made from the earth on site, gypsum from a source close to Nouakchott, and lime fired from locally collected seashells.[54] Imported cement was limited to foundations and floor finishes. However, the project achieved mixed results, with families reluctant to pay the officially set fees for land and provision of drainage. The ADAUA ran into conflict with the local administration, in the face of which international donors withdrew their support and the scheme was not developed further.

The SOCOGIM (Property Construction Management Company of Mauritania) was established in 1974 and tasked with finding solutions to the living situations of the working class and the provision of public housing. Instead, it built 1,200 villas (targeted at the wealthier population) in connection with agreements in place with banks. This outcome shows that while schemes can be intended for or marketed as social housing projects, they may have other incentives.[55] Another social housing project was the «Twize» programme (2002–2008), which was based on the concept of spatial agency through financial assistance. Micro-loans and self-build initiatives aimed to regularise and encourage the building of permanent formal structures in place of the informal structures. The project was criticised, however, as it required disadvantaged communities to actively participate in the building of their new homes.[56] The few social housing projects that were actually built were mostly aimed at civil servants, rather than targeting specifically identified vulnerable people. These social housing projects also often broke up community networks created in the informal settlements, demonstrating a physical expression of the government's anxiety about citizen organisations.[57] As a result, construction of social housing is severely insufficient for the needs of the city's population.[58]

Social Impacts of Urbanisation

Nouakchott is often referred to as «the capital of nomads». The implications of the term «nomads» in this context means Bidhan (also known as White Moors or Berber), the light-skinned tribes from the north of the country (see table 1). However, this designation is misleading, as Nouakchott (and Mauritania as a whole) is not just the home of the Bidhan, but also of the Halpulaar, Peuls, Soninké, and Wolof peoples, commonly grouped together under the term Black Africans. Unlike the nomadic Bidhan, Black Africans were historically pastoral, settled communities, inhabiting the south and east of Mauritania. There is also a third group, the Haratine, who are ethnically Black Africans. However, as former slaves of the Berber, they are culturally and linguistically closer to the northern Arab culture than those of the Black Africans.

Ethnic identity remains a significant factor in Mauritania, overlaid with social hierarchy. The Bidhan hold most social authority and political power, and the associated wealth. The emphasis placed on Arab culture in the country is a political one, tending to marginalise the non-Arab populations, who do not see themselves reflected in the official national image. This problem exacerbate resentment between the different ethnic groups. One significant event, the repercussions of which are still felt, occurred in 1989 when the government forcefully expelled tens of thousands of Black Africans to Senegal and Mali. Many have since returned, but many of these returnees have struggled to secure access to full citizenship and to recover their lost land. Census data does not record ethnicity, making detailed information difficult to obtain.[59]

These divisions are now reflected in the way the city is inhabited. The wealthier class is predominantly Bidhan, and as such, they tend to live in the wealthier northern districts, such as Tevragh-Zeïna (see fig. 6). The Haratine tend to live in the slums to the south of the city. The Black Africans tend to occupy the peri-central neighbourhoods, such as Sebkha, which often lack infrastructure provisions such as tarmac roads, electricity, and water supply. This division also reflects the pattern of settlement, in which populations originating from the northern, southern, and eastern regions of Mauritania are more likely to settle in the corresponding regions of the city,[60] a continuation of the rural-to-urban settlement of Nouakchott along the four main arteries of the city that occurred between the mid-1970s and the 1990s.

This distinction between the rich and poor areas of the city, which was established by the first urban master plans and accentuated by the subsequent plans, continues to be evident in the contemporary urban landscape. It is visible in the difference between the size of the plots of land or houses, the colours dominating the streetscape, and in the presence of tarmac on roads in wealthier neighbourhoods but not on poorer ones. It is also often expressed in the toponyms throughout the city. The streets in the wealthy administrative north continue to be named after prestigious figures from world history, and shop fronts tend to have signs in French or Arabic, the two official languages of the country. In the southern working-class neighbourhoods, street names tend to come from the local history of the region, and are more likely to have signs in the dialects of the various Black African tribes.[61] Then there are also the unofficial names of neighbourhoods, such as Sans fiche sans photo, mentioned earlier, which are a direct expression by their residents. These are all further indications of social-cultural divisions in the city. Nouakchott has become fragmented, a mosaic of desperate neighbourhoods on the outskirts of the city, inhabited by the various ethnic groups which make up the nation.

As we have seen, the rapid process of urbanisation in Nouakchott has been, to an extent, shaped by existing social relations and structures. However, these social relations and structures have also altered over the decades, adapting to the changing realities and conditions. Significant areas where these changes can be observed are the status of the Haratine, and the role of women in society.

The urban margins became a space where the Haratine could redefine their relationships with their former masters. As mentioned earlier in this chapter, the process of abolishing slavery in Mauritania is still ongoing. Although slavery was outlawed by the French in 1903, then abolished by Mauritania in 1981, criminalised in 2007 and again in 2015, these declarations were of little effect as the legal system was complicit with the Bidhan, the ruling social class and slave-owners. According to a 2010 UN report, although in a different form, slavery «de facto continues to exist» and permeates the nation's culture, politics, and social structures.[62] In the city, although still trapped in subservient positions, Haratine started becoming wage-workers following the abolition of slavery, occupying land independently (albeit precariously), and having the opportunity to form social networks outside of the household of their masters. These developments have resulted in a national anti-slavery movement.

The move away from reliance on slaves, and the decrease in wealth among a significant number of former slave-owners, placed new demands on women and men. Migrants who lost their livelihoods in the droughts were compelled by economic necessity to find new ways of living. With men spending more time away from the home working, and their incomes affected by the absence of slaves to work for them and the fact that they were no longer able to rely on their herds for income, women also began to join the informal workforce. The development of urban vegetable markets around the city in the 1970s and 1980s, which became dominated by women, had a significant impact on traditional expectations of gender roles.[63]

Public space in Nouakchott is highly gendered – it is very rare to see women in the streets, unless in the vicinity of markets.[64] Their presence is very much linked to the activities of buying or selling. Markets have become important spaces for women to exercise their economic autonomy, as well as providing places for socialising and entertainment. On a wider scale, although there have been improvements made in women's rights through the implementation of legal frameworks, such as the ability to work outside the marital home and to access higher education, there is still a strong gender divide and a patriarchal view of the family unit in Mauritania.[65] As in other places, there is a disparity between women's freedoms depending on their families' wealth and social status. There remains a notable lack of representation of women in professional roles and graduating from higher education, with the investment in education mainly going to boys.[66]

The global community continues to be concerned about other aspects of the experience of women in Mauritania, such as the practice of *leblouh* (force-feeding girls to improve their marriage prospects), female genital mutilation, child labour, modern slavery, and human trafficking.[67] With slavery passed through the maternal line, women and girls are especially at risk of human trafficking. While this is less evident in the city than in the countryside, it is still observable as many national aspects impact people across urban and rural areas.[68]

Mauritania is a conservative Muslim country that implements religious restrictions, including the prohibition of alcohol – the only country in Africa with a total ban on alcohol.[69] With very few spaces for cultural and sporting events, the mosque is the social hub of the city and at the centre of the community. The limited number of restaurants and cafes means that social gatherings, meetings, and visiting friends almost always occur over tea and within the privacy of one's home – sometimes spilling out into the streets, such as during weddings or other celebrations. On these occasions, public space temporarily becomes the extension of private space. The activity in the streets is dictated by the sun and shade and heat. The mornings are the busiest time of day, and the coolest, with a noticeable lull at midday, only for activity to pick up again in the evening, as the winds change and the sea breeze can be felt. Those wealthy enough to own a car, do not walk, even if only a short distance is involved.[70]

Identity of the Modern Capital

Six decades on from its establishment as a capital city of a new nation, Nouakchott continues to grapple with its identity – a struggle shared by many post-colonial new cities. From an administrative centre, the city has grown into a significant cultural, political, and population centre. As such, it has become significant in the formation of the «official» national identity of Mauritania. In a country whose population is formed of communities of different origins, with different traditions, languages, social norms, and relationships with space and the land, this formation of a national identity is a challenge not to be underestimated. Moreover, as a country at the meeting point of the Arab and African worlds, being seen as belonging to the former is a contested political issue.[71] The vision for the capital as a unifying space was undermined over the decades of post-independence by a series of government linguistic and cultural policies clearly aimed at Arabisation, and favouring the Bidhan community.[72] As the financial elite, this community owns much of the urban fabric and land in Nouakchott, consequently having a disproportionate influence over the image of the city.[73] The government often looks to the Gulf Emirates as the aspirational example of a modern Arab state, with a specific architectural and urban model expressing its socio-cultural context. This tendency is reflected in the urban landscape of the city, featuring Saudi-styled mosques and neo-Arab palaces within the central areas of the city, while the Black Africans are relegated to the peripheries of the city.[74] Many of the new upmarket Gulf-inspired developments spurn traditional local building methods and materials, employing materials such as glass and steel that are difficult and expensive to import to Mauritania. Their resulting association with modernity and progress contributes to the socio-cultural rejection of materials and building methods that could be more suitable for the local conditions.

These aspirations of emulating the Gulf states were further fuelled by the discovery of oil supplies off the coast of Mauritania in 2001. The discovery led to hopes that Mauritania would become a new oil emirate.[75] However, since extraction began in 2006, the promised wealth has failed to materialise. Daily extraction has been far below the estimates, and the oil was found to be of low quality, which means it had to be sold at reduced prices. Eventually, production ceased in 2017, and the decommissioning of the oil field began in 2019.

Nonetheless, luxurious new villa projects were constructed around the city, their development made easier by government land-ownership programmes, allowing easy clearance of informal settlements. As urban space became a source of considerable enrichment, the wealthy Nouakkchotti's place in society became measured not by heads of cattle owned, but by the number of plots of land and the opulence of villas.[76] However, the size of the local elite and expatriate communities is insufficient to cover the capital expenditure on these projects, and the majority of the city's inhabitants remain impoverished and in need of adequate housing and infrastructure.[77] This raises the question of to whom does the city belong, and whose needs are met by these projects.

In 2022 gas reserves were found off the coast of the Mauritania and Senegal border, which could produce up to $4.6 billion per year.[78] This development has once again fuelled the «Gulf Dream». The government plans to open a dedicated school for vocational training for mining, oil, and gas, which would be situated in Nouakchott[79] and could be a catalyst for significant change in the city over the coming years. It cannot go without noting, however, that the gas and oil industry that so many hopes are pinned on to bring prosperity into the city is the very thing which can lead to the city's obliteration due to the environmental impacts that these industries have on a local and global scale. As sea levels rise, propelled by climate change, studies show that low-lying, flood-prone

Nouakchott is at risk of being submerged by the sea.[80] More encouragingly, the city is also increasing engagement with renewable energy sources – in this aspect, Nouakchott is well positioned to take advantage of solar and wind power.

Conclusion

Nouakchott is the capital of a nation defined by the colonial powers at the time of its creation, defying geographical and ethnic logic. The nation's political and cultural difficulties have resulted in dictatorial rule and military coups, ethnic tensions, and a poor economy.[81] The problems that Mauritania faces directly affect the residents of Nouakchott, a city designed by outsiders to resolve ethnic and cultural tensions while a nation of rural and nomadic roots tries to adapt to urban living and a centralised government. As well as marking a shift in the concept of the nation to the population, the development of the city has also changed ideas about gender roles, «class», and slavery. The urbanising society of Nouakchott is reinterpreting traditional relations and structures.

The Nouakchott of today, after more than 60 years of growth and development, continues to suffer from socio-spatial segregation imposed by the north–south divide established at its inception – the wealthy and prosperous districts in the north, and the working-class, poorly serviced areas and informal settlements to the south. It is somewhat ironic that this traditional planning model, typically used to separate the colonisers and the indigenous population, was the foundation of the capital being built to bring the independent nation together.

As Nouakchott started to be designed and built, many previously colonised African nations were trying to adopt urban growth policies from France,[82] but these policies were not suited to the social and environmental problems being faced, such as urban sprawl and high levels of rural-to-urban migration. Planning models that are appropriate in Western towns and cities do not always resolve local planning issues.[83] The various urban plans introduced over the years retrospectively approved developments already made, rather than successfully framing and planning the development of the city. As such, the present form of the city has largely been formed in a bottom-up way, by the actions of urban actors (such as land speculation). However, this form of bottom-up activity did not come from an empowered and engaged civic society, but from the shortcomings of the state.

The environmental challenges have strongly influenced the morphology of the city, trapped between the sea and the desert, while battling threats of encroaching dunes, sand blown on the wind, and flooding from the rising sea level and the rainy season. These challenges have influenced not only the overall design and implementation of the city, but also contributed to the complex discourse on the necessity of material suitability while meeting the cultural needs of a developing and modernising city.

As the city grew in terms of population and physical size, informal settlements were established, primarily on the periphery. The sprawling development of the city has led to substandard infrastructure, precarious housing, and urban sprawl with low population density. Furthermore, the process of urbanisation meant a direct confrontation between the two systems and understanding of land ownership, which has contributed to practices like *tech-tchib* and the formation of *gazra*, *kebbe*, and temporary and developed informality. These practices are enabled by complex and unique socio-political networks in Nouakchott, with a social ability to adapt, particularly in informal settlements.

The city has grown from an administrative formality to a cosmopolitan Saharan city. It is a city in flux, where luxury villa developments stand alongside informal settlements lacking basic provisions, where satellite dishes are appearing in unelectrified neighbourhoods, where the tents of the nomads are fitted with solar panels so residents can charge their smartphones. Much of the city's heritage is intangible, yet glimpses of it can be seen in its urban form.

Nouakchott is a complex city composed of many social, economic, and environmental layers, despite being a relatively new planned city. As the city evolves and the residents reinterpret their nomadic ancestry, Nouakchott has an opportunity to redefine what it means to be a modern city by building on the cultural heritage of residents from different backgrounds. Today, Nouakchott is a city with a complex society and a redefined heritage.

With few historic buildings, the heritage of Nouakchott is instead brought to life through the relationships between its people, the environment, and the spaces they form. The residents of Nouakchott represent a myriad of ethnic groups, with strong ties to areas of origin – tensions between various groups are evident in the formation and occupation of the city. This neo-urban society is having to contend with profound changes in identity, and not least with a dramatic shift in understanding of land ownership. Land speculation is a fundamental component of urbanisation in Nouakchott, with the distinct forms of *kebbe*, *gazra*, and temporary and developed informality presenting a unique relationship between settlers, land, and landscape. This chapter demonstrates that behind the apparent chaos and informality dominating Nouakchott, there is an underlying organisation and ways of functioning understood by residents of the city.

1 Hudson 1990, 20.
2 WFP 2022.
3 World Bank Group 2020, 56.
4 Amara et al. 1990.
5 Wabnitz 2009, 194.
6 Wabnitz 2009, 194.
7 Wabnitz 2009, 194.
8 Vium 2016, 6.
9 Koita 1994, 101.
10 The semi-arid region of Africa between the Sahara Desert to the north and tropical savannas to the south. The countries of the region are Burkina Faso, Mali, Mauritania, Niger, and Chad.
11 World Bank Group 2020, 56.
12 Pazzanita 2008, 369.
13 Chenal/Kaufmann 2008, 166.
14 Taine-Cheikh 2007, 44.
15 Taine-Cheikh 2007, 40.
16 Taine-Cheikh 2007, 40.
17 Pazzanita 2008, 55.
18 Chenal/Kaufmann 2008, 169.
19 Chenal/Kaufmann 2008, 169.
20 Chenal/Kaufmann 2008, 167.
21 Pazzanita 2008, 369.
22 McDougall 2021, 165.
23 Pazzanita 2008, 168.
24 Pazzanita 2008, 168.
25 Pazzanita 2008, 370.
26 Pitte 1977.
27 Pazzanita 2008, 370.
28 McDougall 2021, 64.
29 McDougall 2021, 185.
30 D'Hont 1989, 78.
31 Chenal/Kaufmann 2008, 169.
32 Chenal/Kaufmann 2008, 166.
33 Taine-Cheikh 2007, 45.
34 World Bank 2010.
35 World Bank 2010.
36 Duval Smith 2016.
37 JICA 2018, 32; Les Ateliers 2014, 22.
38 Hardy 2017, 18.
39 García et al. 2009, 8.
40 Hardy 2017, 48.
41 McDougall 2015, 251.
42 Tanguy 2014.
43 ILO 2020.
44 JICA 2018, 100.
45 JICA 2018, 100.
46 Chenal/Kaufmann 2008, 172.
47 Taine-Cheikh 1998, 78–80.
48 Choplin 2014, 4–5.
49 Choplin 2009, 205.
50 Choplin 2014, 4–5.
51 Vium 2016, 345.
52 Wabnitz 2009, 194.
53 Choplin 2009, 207.

54 Association pour le Développement d'une Architecture et d'un Urbanisme Africains or Association for the Development of Traditional African Urbanism and Architecture. The organisation aims to promote indigenous African architecture and to train local inhabitants in the required building skills.
55 Biehler et al. 2015, 1–4.
56 Biehler et al. 2015, 5.
57 Biehler et al. 2015, 6.
58 Choplin 2009, 252.
59 As part of the research for the updated masterplan, JICA conducted social surveys in 2016; however the sample size was limited to 1,000 households.
60 JICA 2018, 15.
61 Taine-Cheikh 1998, 79.
62 Shahinian 2010.
63 McDougall 2021, 173.
64 Chenal 2014, 223–251.
65 World Trade Press 2010; OECD 2020.
66 Ballet et al. 2019, 97.
67 Cetorelli et al. 2020, 51–69; OECD 2020; Stewart 2018.
68 World Bank 2021.
69 Ferreira-Borges et al. 2015, 472.
70 Chenal 2014, 243.
71 Choplin 2010, 147.
72 Ciavolella 2014, 23.
73 Choplin 2009, 252.
74 Choplin/Ciavolella 2017, 8.
75 Choplin 2010, 146.
76 Choplin 2009, 238.
77 Choplin/Franck 2010, 201.
78 Fernandez 2022.
79 OR Noir Africa 2023.
80 Niang 2014, 155; Senhoury et al. 2016, 436–442.
81 Pazzanita 2008, 13.
82 Peil/Sada 1984, 7.
83 Faludi 1973.

Amara et al. 1990
H. Amara / B. Founou-Tchuigoua / S. Amin: African Agriculture: The Critical Choices (London, New Jersey, Tokyo 1990), https://archive.unu.edu/unupress/unupbooks/uu28ae/uu28ae00.htm#Contents (12 December 2022).

Ballet et al. 2019
J. Ballet / A. Bhukuth / B. Hamzetta: The Exploitation of Talibé Children in Mauritania, in: J. Ballet / J. Bhukuth (eds.): Child Exploitation in the Global South (London 2019) 93–107.

Biehler et al. 2015
A. Biehler / A. Choplin / M. Morelle: Social housing in Africa: a model to be (re)invented? Metropolitics, 16 October 2015, https://metropolitics.org/IMG/pdf/met-biehler-choplin-morelle-en.pdf (30 October 2023).

Cetorelli et al. 2020
V. Cetorelli / B. Wilson / E. Batyra / E. Coast: Female Genital Mutilation/Cutting in Mali and Mauritania: Understanding Trends and Evaluating Policies, Studies in Family Planning 51, no. 1, 51–69, 2020, https://doi.org/10.1111/sifp.12112.

Chenal 2014
J. Chenal: The West African City: Urban Space and Models of Urban Planning (Lausanne 2014).

Chenal/Kaufmann 2008
J. Chenal / V. Kaufmann: City Profile: Nouakchott. Cities 25, no. 3, 2008, 163–175, https://doi.org/10.1016/j.cities.2007.12.001.

Choplin 2009
A. Choplin: Nouakchott, au carrefour de la Mauritanie et du Monde (Paris 2009).

Choplin 2010
A. Choplin: From the Chinguetti mosque to Dubai towers: ‹extraversion›, connections and neo-urban society in a globalized Mauritania. The Maghreb Review 35, no. 1, 2010, 146–163, https://doi.org/10.1353/tmr.2010.0029.

Choplin 2014
A. Choplin: Les « Sans fiche sans photo »: Déplacements forcés et (non) mobilisation citoyenne à Nouakchott (Mauritanie). L'Espace Politique 22, no. 1, 2014, [online 17 March 2014], https://doi.org/10.4000/espacepolitique.2926.

Choplin/Ciavolella 2017
A. Choplin / R. Ciavolella: Gramsci and the African Città Futura: Urban Subaltern Politics from the Margins of Nouakchott, Mauritania. Antipode 49, no. 2, 2017, 314–334, https://doi.org/10.1111/anti.12268.

Choplin/Franck 2010
A. Choplin / A. Franck: A Glimpse of Dubai in Khartoum and Nouakchott: Prestige Urban Projects on the Margins of the Arab World. Built Environment 36, no. 2, 2010, 192–205, https://doi.org/10.2148/benv.36.2.192.

Ciavolella 2014
R. Ciavolella: Representing the Nation Horizontally and Vertically: Identity Differences and Asymmetries of Power in Mauritania. Middle East Law and Governance 6, no. 3, 2014, 327–346, https://doi.org/10.1163/18763375-00603008.

Curtis 1983
J. R. W. Curtis: Type and Variation: Berber Collective Dwellings of the Northwestern Sahara. Muqarnas, 1, 1983, 181–209, https://doi.org/10.2307/1523077.

D'Hont 1989
O. D'Hont: La population des quartiers spontanés de Nouakchott ou « Kébé » (Mauritanie). Les Cahiers d'Outre-Mer 42, 165, 1989, 73–95, https://www.persee.fr/doc/caoum_0373-5834_1989_num_42_165_3291 (30 October 2023).

Duval Smith 2016
A. Duval Smith: ‹The best solution? Move the Mauritanian capital›: water on the rise in Nouakchott. The Guardian, 25 July 2016, https://www.theguardian.com/global-development/2016/jul/25/the-best-solution-move-the-mauritanian-capital-water-on-the-rise-in-nouakchott (31 October 2023).

Encyclopedia Britannica 2022
Encyclopedia Britannica: Mauritania Summary, [online, 2022], https://www.britannica.com/summary/Mauritania (20 July 2022).

Faludi 1973
A. Faludi: A Reader in Planning Theory (Oxford 1973).

Fernadez 2022
E. Fernadez: Mauritania boosts its industrial investments after finding new gas reserves off the country's coasts, [online, 2022], https://atalayar.com/en/content/mauritania-boosts-its-industrial-investments-after-finding-new-gas-reserves-countrys-coasts (20 January 2023).

Ferreira-Borges et al. 2015
C. Ferreira-Borges / M.B. Esser / S. Dias / T. Babor / C.D. H. Parry: Alcohol Control Policies in 46 African Countries: Opportunities for Improvement. Alcohol and Alcoholism 50, no. 4, 2015, 470–476, https://doi.org/10.1093/alcalc/agv036.

García et al. 2009
I. García / F. Puertas / I. Oteiza / F. Martín-Consuegra / E. Heras / J.J. Legarra: Tests on mortars and concrete made with seashells as aggregate: Case study in Mauritania, in: P. Walker et al. (eds.): 11th International Conference on Non-Conventional Materials and Technologies, NOCMAT 2009, 6–9 September 2009, Bath, UK, Conference proceedings, 8 pages, https://www.researchgate.net/profile/Fernando-Martin-Consuegra/publication/282808178_TESTS_ON_MORTARS_AND_CONCRETE_MADE_WITH_SEASHELLS_AS_AGGREGATE_CASE_STUDY_IN_MAURITANIA/links/561cd4eb08ae78721fa3250d/TESTS-ON-MORTARS-AND-CONCRETE-MADE-WITH-SEASHELLS-AS-AGGREGATE-CASE-STUDY-IN-MAURITANIA.pdf (30 October 2023).

Google Earth 2020
Google Earth: Nouakchott, Mauritania. 18.1501709, -15.94219808. 2D map, [online, 2020], https://earth.google.com/web/@18.1501709,-15.94219808,1.02861098a,342.30403148d,34.99999999y,0.00029918h,0t,0r/data=MikKJwolCiExR0s3bkRYS01XSUZfMG5FZ0Z0V3dNT0FPbU1oNzN2TXIgAToDCgEw (31 October 2023).

Google Earth 2021a
Google Earth: Nouakchott, Mauritania. 18.07929738, -15.94991606. 2D map, [online, 2021b], https://earth.google.com/web/@18.07929738,-15.94991606,0.90739575a,763.27473575d,35y,-5.96992748h,30.00343011t,359.99679933r/data=OgMKATA (23 August 2022).

Google Earth 2021b
Google Earth: Nouakchott, Mauritania. 18.08851261, -15.91785323. 2D map, [online, 2021b], https://earth.google.com/web/@18.08851261,-15.91785323,1.71746494a,1071.23035301d,30.0002959y,0h,0t,0r/data=MikKJwolCiExR0s3bkRYS01XSUZfMG5FZ0Z0V3dNT0FPbU1oNzN2TXIgAToDCgEw (23 August 2022).

Google Earth 2021c
Google Earth: Nouakchott, Mauritania. 18.08970295, -15.97268046. 2D map, [online, 2021c], https://earth.google.com/web/@18.08970295,-15.97268046,5.45356687a,512.78106917d,30.0002959y,0h,0t,0r/data=MikKJwolCiExR0s3bkRYS01XSUZfMG5FZ0Z0V3dNT0FPbU1oNzN2TXIgAToDCgEw (23 August 2022).

Google Earth 2021d
Google Earth: Nouakchott, Mauritania. 18.06361187, -15.95263113. 2D map, [online, 2021d], https://earth.google.com/web/@18.06361187,-15.95263113,545.23254366a,0d,35y,-5.9707h,30.0000t,-0.0080r/data=ChAqDggBEgoyMDIxLTExLTMw?utm_source=earth7&utm_campaign=vine&hl=en (23 August 2022).

Google Earth 2021e
Google Earth: Nouakchott, Mauritania. 18.03204956, -15.91247556. 2D map, [online, 2021e], https://earth.google.com/web/@18.03204956,-15.91247556,660.28571493a,0d,35y,-5.9583h,26.5351t,-0.0099r/data=OgMKATA (23 August 2022).

Google Earth 2022a
Google Earth: Nouakchott, Mauritania. 18.0671706, -15.9535609. 2D map, [online, 2022a], https://earth.google.com/web/@18.06717055,-15.9535609,5.67272189a,44201.57334789d,35y,0h,0t,0r/data=CkkaRxJBCiQweGU5NjUyNmMxNmVjZTliZDoweDI3MDAwNWJkNTNjMWUxZjkqGU5vdWFrY2hvdHQK2YbZiNin2YPYtNmI2LcYAiABMikKJwolCiExR0s3bkRYS01XSUZfMG5FZ0Z0V3dNT0FPbU1oNzN2TXIgAQ (23 August 2022).

Google Earth 2022b
Google Earth: Nouakchott, Mauritania. 18.04693677, -15.95442861. 2D map, [online, 2022b], https://earth.google.com/web/@18.04693677,-15.95442861,2.60511284a,395.21204744d,35y,-5.970394h,30.00177867t,359.99079962r/data=OgMKATA (31 October 2023).

GRET 2011
GRET: Atlas de Nouakchott: Infrastructures et services urbains. CUN, [online, 2011], https://www.gret.org/publication/atlas-de-nouakchott/ (31 October 2023).

Hardy 2017
M. Hardy: The Mauritanian building sector, challenges, orientations and potentials for reform. Organization Labor International, [online, 2017], https://www.ilo.org/africa/information-resources/publications/WCMS_558531/lang--fr/index.htm (22 August 2022).

Hudson 1990
P. Hudson: Travels in Mauritania (London 1990).

JICA 2018
Japan International Cooperation Agency (JICA): Nouakchott City Urban Master Plan Development Project in Islamic Republic of Mauritania – Final Report, [online, 2018], https://openjicareport.jica.go.jp/pdf/12324729.pdf (30 October 2023).

Jourde 2001
C. Jourde: Ethnicity, Democratization, and Political Dramas: Insights into Ethnic Politics in Mauritania. African Issues 29, no. 1, 2001, 26–30, https://doi.org/10.2307/1167106.

Keeton / Nijhuis 2019
R. Keeton / S. Nijhuis: Spatial challenges in contemporary African New Towns and potentials for alternative planning strategies. International Planning Studies 24, no. 3–4, 2019, 218–234, https://doi.org/10.1080/13563475.2019.1660625.

Know Your Country 2017
Know Your Country: Mauritania: Risk and Compliance, 2017, https://www.knowyourcountry.com/mauritania (20 July 2022).

Koita 1994
T. Koita: Migrations, pouvoirs locaux et enjeux sur l'espace urbain. Politique Africaine 55, 1994, 101–109.

Les Ateliers 2014
Les Ateliers: Nouakchott – L'Avenir pour defi: Adaptation et mutation d'une ville vulnerable, Atelier International de Maitrise d'Oeuvre Urbaine Nouakchott, [online, 2014], https://ateliers.org/en/workshops/127/ (22 August 2022).

McDougall 2015
E. A. McDougall: Hidden in Plain Sight: Haratine in Nouakchott's «Niche-Settlements». The International Journal of African Historical Studies 48, no. 2, 2015, 251–279.

McDougall 2021
E. A. McDougall: «But I Am Confident: God Will Not Leave Us This Way»: From Slavery to Post-Slavery in Nouakchott's Bidonvilles, Mauritania. Journal of African Diaspora Archeology and Heritage 10, no. 1–2, 2021, 161–190, https://doi.org/10.1080/21619441.2021.1878794.

Niang 2014
A. Niang: Resilience against climate change: Case of Nouakchott City. Geo-Eco-Trop 38, no. 1, 2014, 155–168, http://www.geoecotrop.be/uploads/publications/pub_381_14.pdf (31 October 2023).

OECD 2020
OECD: Social Institutions and Gender Index: Mauritania (2020).

OR Noir Africa 2023
OR Noir Africa: Mauritania to build an oil and gas school, [online, 2023], https://ornoirafrica.com/en/la-mauritanie-will-build-an-oil-and-gas-school/ (20 January 2023).

Pazzanita 2008
A. G. Pazzanita: Historical Dictionary of Mauritania, 3rd ed. (Lanham MD 2008).

Peil / Sada 1984
M. Peil / P. O. Sada: African Urban Society (Chichester 1984).

Pitte 1977
J. Pitte: Nouakchott, capitale de la Mauritanie (Paris 1977).

Senhoury et al. 2016
A. Senhoury / A. Niang / B. Diouf / Y. F. Thomas: Managing Flood Risks Using Nature-Based Solutions in Nouakchott, Mauritania, in: F. Renaud et al. (eds.): Ecosystem-Based Disaster Risk Reduction and Adaptation in Practice. Advances in Natural and Technological Hazards Research 42 (Cham 2016) 435–455, https://doi.org/10.1007/978-3-319-43633-3_19.

Shahinian 2010
G. Shahinian: Report of the Special Rapporteur on contemporary forms of slavery, including its causes and consequences, Human Rights Council, 16 August 2010, https://www.ilo.org/wcmsp5/groups/public/---ed_norm/---declaration/documents/newsitem/wcms_146482.pdf (7 February 2023).

Stewart 2018
P. H. Stewart: The Courage of Women in Mauritania, [online, 2018], https://www.hrw.org/news/2018/09/05/courage-women-mauritania (24 July 2022).

Taine-Cheikh 1998
C. Taine-Cheikh: Toponymie et Urbanisation, in: A. M. Frerot: Espaces et sociétés en Mauritanie actes du colloque de Tours, (Tours 1998).

Taine-Cheikh 2007
C. Taine-Cheikh: The (r)urbanization of Mauritania : Historical Context and Contemporary Developments, in: C. Miller / E. Al-Wer / D. Caubet (eds.): Arabic in the city: issues in dialect contact and language variation (Abingdon 2007) 35–54.

Tanguy 2014
P. Tanguy: Gazra et Kebba: deux désignations de l'habitat populaire «informel», [online, 2014], http://www.citego.org/bdf_fiche-document-785_fr.html (31 October 2023).

UN Habitat 2020
UN Habitat: Informal Settlements in the Arab Region. [online, February 2020], https://unhabitat.org/sites/default/files/2020/12/regional_is_report_final_dec_2020.pdf (3 March 2025).

Vium 2016
C. Vium: Enacting immanent potentialities: Tcheb-tchib strategies at the centre of the urban fringe in Nouakchott, Mauritania. Singapore Journal of Tropical Geography 37, no. 3, 2016, 343–362, https://doi.org/10.1111/sjtg.12158.

Wabnitz 2009
H. W. Wabnitz: Return to the Sources: Revival of Traditional Nomads' Rights to Common Property Resources in the Code Pastoral of the Islamic Republic of Mauritania. Natural Resources Journal 49, no. 1, 2009, 191–218, https://digitalrepository.unm.edu/nrj/vol49/iss1/6 (19 October 2024).

WFP 2022
World Food Programme: WFP Mauritania Country Brief, May 2022, https://docs.wfp.org/api/documents/WFP-0000140787/download/?_ga=2.27459198.315327757.1658669554-1263444240.1658669554&_gac=1.261559807.1658669731.Cj0KCQjw2_OWBhDqARIsAAUNTTFlq65x15xEuLuRdAeImwzrjXlwGwYuvcXXTSpR7Fcx1lurAdYXChMaAh4IEALw_wcB (24 July 2022).

World Bank 2010
World Bank: Climate Change In Mauritania: Taking Action Before It Is Too Late. 24 February 2010, https://www.worldbank.org/en/news/feature/2010/02/24/climate-change-in-mauritania-taking-action-before-it-is-too-late (5 January 2021).

World Bank 2021
World Bank: Mauritania Economic Update: Why is it Essential to Enable Women to Participate Fully in Economic Activity? 1 June 2021, https://www.worldbank.org/en/country/mauritania/publication/mauritania-economic-update-why-it-is-essential-to-enable-women-to-participate-fully-in-economic-activity (12 January 2023).

World Bank Group 2020
World Bank Group: Mauritania: Country Economic Memorandum: Accelerating Growth Through Diversification and Productive Cities (Washington 2020).

World Trade Press 2010
World Trade Press: Mauritania Society and Culture Complete Report: An All-Inclusive Profile Combining all of our Society and Culture Reports (Petaluma, CA 2010).

Image Sources

1 Google Earth 2022a.
2 Curtis 1983.
3–5 Pitte 1977.
6 JICA 2018.
7 GRET 2011.
8 Diagram based on description by local resident in Duval Smith 2016.
9 The authors 2023.
10 left Google Earth 2020.
10 right Google Earth 2022b.
11 Chenal / Kaufmann 2008.
12 JICA 2018, 67.
13 JICA 2018, 67.
14 JICA 2018, 72; Google Earth 2022a.
15 Google Earth 2021a.
16 Google Earth 2021b.
17 Google Earth 2021c.
18 Google Earth 2021d.
19 Google Earth 2021e.
Table 1 The authors, with information from Encyclopedia Brittanica 2022; UN Habitat 2020, 9; Taine-Cheikh 2007, 46; Jourde 2001; and McDougall 2015, 251.

Contributors

Omar Abolnaga is a PhD candidate at the Bartlett School of Architecture, University College London. He holds a BArch and an MSc in Architectural History and Theory from Cairo University's Faculty of Engineering. In 2018, Omar began his academic career as a full-time educator and researcher at Cairo University, transitioning to the Bartlett School of Architecture in 2021 to pursue his doctoral studies in the stream of Architectural and Urban History and Theory. His PhD is supported by a joint scholarship programme between Egypt's Ministry of Higher Education and the British Council. Omar's research interests span a wide range of topics, including informal urbanism, urban governance, traditional Islamic architecture, the histories of Cairo, and Arab film and pop culture. ORCID: 0009-0006-2062-4330.

Raffael Beier is part of the research group International Planning Studies (IPS) at the Department of Spatial Planning, TU Dortmund University, Germany. He has been working on urban displacement and migration, resettlement, housing, and urban inequality – mostly in North and Sub-Saharan Africa. In June 2023, he concluded a research project on non-occupancy and secondary residential mobility in state-led affordable housing programmes, funded by the German Research Foundation (DFG). Previously, he was working as the coordinator of the PhD programme in International Development Studies at the Institute of Development Research and Development Policy at Ruhr University Bochum. He was further associated with the Centre for Built Environment Studies at the University of the Witwatersrand, Johannesburg, South Africa. His most relevant publications include the co-edited volume *Urban Resettlements in the Global South* (Routledge, 2022). ORCID: 0000-0001-9772-2293.

Suna Çağaptay is an associate professor of archaeology at Muğla Sıtkı Koçman University, Turkey. Trained as an archaeologist and architectural historian, she works on Late Byzantine, Early Ottoman, Crusader, and principality-period architecture and city-making practices in the Eastern Mediterranean and the afterlives of the ancient cities. She received numerous fellowships, fieldwork, and research grants, including the Dumbarton Oaks, Aga Khan Islamic Art and Architecture at MIT, ANAMED, and Barakat Foundation at the University of Oxford. From 2017 to 2023, she was a research associate in *The Impact of the Ancient City*, an ERC-funded project based in the Faculty of Classics at the University of Cambridge. Her publications include *The First Ottoman Capital: Bursa* (IB Tauris, 2020). She also co-edited a volume with E. Key Fowden, E. Coghill-Zychowicz, and L. Blanke titled *Cities as Palimpsests? Responses to Antiquity in Eastern Mediterranean Urbanism* (Oxbow Books, 2022). Previously, she conducted an archaeological survey and cultural heritage project in Bursa, and more recently, she has been leading the excavations and public archaeology project at Anaia (Tr. Kadıkalesi) in Kuşadası, Aydın. ORCID: 0000-0002-4362-4134.

Mirhan Damir is a specialist in the inventory and transnational valuation of industrial heritage, with a particular focus on Egypt within the broader context of relations between the MENA region and the West. She has extensive experience in research, teaching, and academic coaching across both academic and governmental institutions in Egypt and internationally. Dr. Damir earned her PhD in Heritage Conservation and Building History from the Bauhaus-Universität Weimar in Germany. She currently serves as a Lecturer at the Faculty of Fine Arts, Alexandria University. From 2014 to 2024, she was actively involved in teaching within the international master's program Revitalization of Historic City Districts, jointly offered by Alexandria, Cairo, and BTU Cottbus-Senftenberg universities. She has also organised and led several international student workshops. Her recent research includes the MHFL Project (Modern Heritage to Future Legacy), funded by the Berlin University Alliance. Dr. Damir is a co-opted board member of TICCIH and co-leads its Communication Commission. Her scholarly contributions appear in peer-reviewed journals, conference proceedings, and the TICCIH Bulletin. ORCID: 0000-0002-8191-3949.

Torben Dedring holds a M. Sc. in Geomatics and a B. Sc. in Geography from Ruhr University Bochum, Germany. Since July 2021, he has been working as a research fellow and doctoral candidate in the Geomatics working group at Ruhr-University Bochum. In his work, he focuses on artificial intelligence for geospatial data processing, especially on generating synthetic remote sensing data. Additionally, he holds lectures on geoinformation systems, radar remote sensing, and artificial intelligence and their applications in geography. He has gained practical experience through internships at esteemed institutions, such as UN-SPIDER in Bonn (Germany) and GRID Arendal (Norway), enriching his expertise in geospatial technologies and environmental analysis. ORCID: 0000-0002-6818-0461.

Sami Ibrahim is an urban planner specialising in strategic urban planning, governance, and transnational urbanism, with a profound understanding of the urban development context of Gulf cities. Holding a PhD in urban planning from the Paris School of Urban Planning, University of Gustave Eiffel, he currently leads the strategy department at a premier urban planning consultancy in France, directing the development of urban strategy and policy projects globally. Previously, he served as an advisor to the Government of Dubai, UAE, overseeing the implementation of the city's urban development agenda and leading the formulation of the Dubai 2040 strategic urban plan. Alongside his professional roles, Sami engages in research, particularly focusing on the transfer of urban models, and contributes as a lecturer at his alma mater. ORCID: 0009-0000-1413-6986.

Zuzanna Krzyżanowska is a practising conservation architect and an associate lecturer at Oxford Brookes University, in the School of Architecture, where she earned her MArchD with a specialisation in International Architectural Regeneration and Development. Her research focuses on the relationship between identity, memory and the built heritage. She is a member of the Society for the Protection of Ancient Buildings. ORCID: 0009-0001-6944-5265.

Chloe Loader is an architect, based in the midlands. She specialised in development and emergency practice at Oxford Brookes for her MArchD, following a focus on humanitarian architecture and informal settlements in her BArch at the University of Lincoln. Chloe won the 2017 RIBA Norman Foster Travelling Scholarship for her proposal *Emerging Cities: Sustainable Development in the Global South.*

She has presented her research at Foster + Partners, the RIBA, the Norman Foster Foundation and a number of universities and architectural practices.

Farnaz Mohseni is an urban planner and heritage specialist with a passion for the visual and cultural dynamics of cities. She holds a bachelor's in urban planning and a master's in urban design from Shiraz University in Iran. She earned her PhD in Heritage Studies from Brandenburg University of Technology, Germany, where she focused on historic urban landscapes. Her expertise span across urban planning, urban and historic landscapes, and the visual aesthetics of urban spaces. With hands-on experience in urban development plans and visualisations in Germany, her work balances between analytical depth and artistic sensitivity. In addition to academia and professional practice, she is a skilled sketcher and painter. ORCID: 0000-0003-0765-8692.

Elizabeth Ryall is an architectural designer, based in Oxford, currently specialising in advanced manufacturing. She completed her MArchD at Oxford Brookes University, specialising in development and emergency practice. With a focus in building social capital through construction, participatory and process driven design, her thesis project titled *Unearthing resilience in Nouakchott* was nominated for the RIBA Silver Medal 2021 and won a RIBA South Award 2021.

Zeido Zeido is a researcher focused on the urban heritage of Europe and the MENA region. He is especially interested in heritage in the context of conflicts and urban development. Zeido received his doctoral degree for for his thesis on the heritage of Aleppo city at the Chair of Architectural Conservation at Brandenburg University of Technology Cottbus-Senftenberg (BTU), where he remains an associated researcher. His research was supported by the generous funding of the Gerda Henkel foundation. He was also awarded funding from both the DFG Research Training Group 1913 and from the Faculty of Architecture, Civil Engineering and Urban Planning at BTU to publish this edited volume. Zeido is a frequent guest lecturer and a practicing architect with a working experience in several countries including Germany, Turkey, Saudi Arabia, and Syria. ORCID: 0000-0002-3754-0452.